UNWELCOME MUSE
Chinese Literature in Shanghai and Peking 1937–1945

STUDIES OF THE EAST ASIAN INSTITUTE   COLUMBIA UNIVERSITY

UNWELCOME MUSE

*Chinese Literature in
Shanghai and Peking
1937–1945*

EDWARD M. GUNN, JR.

NEW YORK   COLUMBIA UNIVERSITY PRESS   1980

The Andrew W. Mellon Foundation, through a special grant, has assisted the Press in publishing this volume.

Columbia University Press
New York   Guildford, Surrey

Library of Congress Cataloging in Publication Data
Gunn, Edward M
Unwelcome Muse

(Studies of the East Asian Institute)
Includes bibliographical references and index.
1. Chinese literature—China—Shanghai—History
. and criticism.   2. Chinese literature—China
—Peking—History and criticism.   3. Chinese
literature—20th century—History and criticism.
I. Title.   II. Series: Columbia University.
East Asian Institute. Studies.
PL3032.S48G8   895.1'09'005   79-19754
ISBN 0-231-04730-4

THE EAST ASIAN INSTITUTE OF COLUMBIA UNIVERSITY

The East Asian Institute of Columbia University was established in 1949 to prepare graduate students for careers dealing with East Asia, and to aid research and publication on East Asia during the modern period. The faculty of the Institute are grateful to the Ford Foundation and the Rockefeller Foundation for their financial assistance.

The Studies of the East Asian Institute were inaugurated in 1962 to bring to a wider public the results of significant new research on modern and contemporary East Asia.

Contents

Preface

Amputation is an ugly word that
suitably describes the political and military situation of China from
1937 to 1945, when the Chinese nation, struggling to piece itself
together, was dismembered again by war. Yet during all this
upheaval, the portion taken by Japan, including the cultural centers
of Shanghai and Peking, sustained a cultural life that made a significant contribution to modern Chinese letters. The basic task of this
book is to offer an outline of the literary history of wartime Shanghai
and Peking, and its ultimate purpose is to focus critical attention on
the works of greatest literary merit. The form this study has taken is
heavily influenced by the contemporary state of scholarship on
modern Chinese literature and history. There is little attempt to
remind the reader of the major trends and events in literature amply
discussed elsewhere, to repeat in biographical detail introductions to
writers available in several well-known book-length surveys and
papers, or to speculate on related topics for which we currently lack
sufficient and reliable information. This study, then, is designed to
fill the gaps that existed at the time of publication, and to emphasize,
in terms of the war period and the larger context of modern Chinese
literature, the achievements deserving continued appreciation.

This study began with my work as a student at Georgetown
University and developed with the advice and encouragement of
Professor C. T. Hsia of Columbia University. Indeed, Professor
Hsia's *A History of Modern Chinese Fiction* provoked my initial
interest in the period. In addition, I am grateful to a number of

persons who contributed of their knowledge and resources to various aspects of my study: Chang Ai-ling, Chin Hsiung-pai, Fan Chung-yün, Hsü Yü (Hsü Hsü), Jao Yu-wei, Li Cho-ming, Liu I-ch'ang, Liu Tsun-jen, Klaus Mehnert, P'an Liu-tai, Robert Ruhlmann, Harold Shadick, Stephen Soong (Sung Ch'i), Takeda Taijun, Ting Wang, Ting Chia-shu, Wong Chun-tong (Huang Chün-tung), and Yao Hsin-nung (Yao K'o). I hope that a portion of their knowledge is not inaccurately reflected here.

During 1976–1977, research abroad was funded by a Fulbright-Hays grant. My work in Hong Kong was greatly facilitated by the Universities Service Center and its staff. Final work on the manuscript was aided by funds from the Cornell University China-Japan Program. To these programs and people, and to those at a dozen libraries and institutions who shared their resources and made this study possible, I am gratefully indebted.

EDWARD M. GUNN, JR.

UNWELCOME MUSE
Chinese Literature in Shanghai and Peking 1937–1945

STUDIES OF THE EAST ASIAN INSTITUTE   COLUMBIA UNIVERSITY

Introduction

This is a study of aspects of Chinese literature written in the areas under Japanese military occupation during the Sino-Japanese War of 1937–1945. It is concerned primarily not with the sociology of literature or the moral dilemmas of intellectuals, but rather with a critical appreciation aimed at fitting this literature into the mainstream of modern Chinese literary history and criticism.

The war period considered here began in the summer of 1937, when Chinese troops struck out against growing Japanese strength in the Shanghai and Peking regions. In the full-scale war that developed, the Japanese slowly and at great cost drove the main Chinese armies back from the coastal areas into the underdeveloped "great interior." They gained a solid reputation for brutality toward the Chinese population, first in the pillage of Nanking and then in a savage punitive campaign against Communist guerrilla incursions in North China. By 1940 the war had largely stagnated; with the exception of a final Japanese drive through South China in 1944, there were no decisive military operations. The Japanese held major coastal cities and the fertile Yangtze River region to feed their troops, while Chinese armies harassed them in the outlying countryside until they reoccupied Japanese-held territory following the Allied victory over Japan in the summer of 1945.

Even though it appears as a historically well-defined period, the Sino-Japanese War was an extension and intensification of decades of foreign domination and exploitation and the threat of more of the same. While Nationalists denounced Communists as pawns of Soviet Russian expansionism and Communists denounced Nationalists as compradores for Western powers, the Japanese military in the early thirties seized Northeast China and gradually extended their control over North China. All these issues and more had been prominent in the literature of China. When in 1937 the elite of China made their unprecedented stand against Japanese incursions by committing the nation to full-scale war, the patriotic literature that attended this decision was largely an extension of what had come before. All writers had come to be seen as directly or indirectly contributing to the aggravation or solution of these national issues, and with the start of war all writers were expected to provide a literature of patriotic resistance to Japanese aggression. This meant the exodus of the major literary establishments that had grown up in Peking and the Shanghai foreign concessions, as the former was occupied by the Japanese and the latter engulfed by the Japanese military in the summer and fall of 1937.

Of the large numbers of writers who scattered to areas beyond Japanese control, relatively few were attached to the armies or witnessed front-line fighting. They were primarily members of educational institutions or editors of publications that decided to move away from the zones of fighting and enemy occupation. The colony of Hong Kong, long a target of anti-imperialist writers and itself culturally moribund, burst into literary activity with the arrival of numerous well-known playwrights, poets, and authors, who addressed fellow refugees from occupied Peking and battle-torn Shanghai. Other groups of writers practiced their arts in Kweilin, Kunming, Chungking, Yenan, and until they fell to the Japanese, Canton and Hankow. Just as writers attached to universities and publications relocated with them, writers who were members of propaganda organizations were assigned locations. It is in part for this reason that a number of committed Communist writers remained in the Shanghai foreign concessions after the surrounding region had fallen to the Japanese.

It was a time of particular economic hardship for writers, and even those who were prominent did not find it easy to get by in the underdeveloped interior or overcrowded Hong Kong. The deterioration of social conditions in the interior as the war took its course only deepened the severity of the problem. This was a strong factor in discouraging some writers from leaving Japanese-occupied territory, particularly those who feared they would be unable to support their families without the firm offers of employment in the interior that were so hard to come by. Thus, a number of writers never left Peking or Shanghai, and a few even returned to these cities after going to the interior, to wait out the war under foreign authority as their colleagues for the most part did in the interior.

Another reason that writers remained in Japanese-occupied territory was the less tangible one of deeply felt ties to a given region or city and its life, regardless of whether it was temporarily under foreign control. The work of a number of writers, both leftist and otherwise, is deeply rooted in their sense of being part of a particular community or regional affiliation and their writing as a commitment to it. Thus, there were many reasons why certain writers stayed and others fled, but none were political. It would be difficult to demonstrate that any writers of creative literature remained in Japanese-occupied territory out of sympathy for Japanese militarism or hope for political favor under Japanese rule.

The literary enterprises that had flourished in Peking and Tientsin up to the eve of the war vanished in 1937. It was over a year before the few remaining writers and academics agreed to contribute anything to a new publication, and another year before some semblance of sustained literary activity began. This was largely the result of an influx of young writers, students, and intellectuals from Japanese-held Manchuria and Taiwan, who joined with the remaining local students. The situation in Shanghai was different, for the International Settlement and French Concession there, which had always attracted writers, remained for a long time under European control and only gradually succumbed to Japanese domination. In 1940 the French Concession accepted allegiance to Vichy France, thereby retaining a semblance of autonomy from the Japanese by cooperating with the policy of a German-Italian-Japanese Axis alliance. The International Settlement remained predominantly under British administration until it was seized by the Japanese military at the outbreak of the Pacific War on 8 December 1941. The Japanese

administered the settlement through its municipal council until it was
given to the Wang Ching-wei Nanking regime late in 1943. The
exodus of Chinese writers from the foreign concessions came in three
stages. It began in late 1937 with the fall of Greater Shanghai to the
Japanese, was followed by a trickle of departures in succeeding years
as Japanese influence limited the expression of patriotic sentiment,
and ended in December 1941, when a half-dozen writers and editors
quit the concessions upon their seizure by the Japanese military.

In the opening years of the war, the Japanese spent considerable
time and effort in locating and inducing or coercing local Chinese
talent to create literature and theatrical productions propagandizing
their cause. The first notable defection of Chinese writers from the
policy of resistance, when it finally came, arose not in occupied China
but in areas free of Japanese control, such as Hong Kong, where the
propaganda machine for the Wang Ching-wei peace movement was
organized in late 1939 and early 1940. These writers included a few
from the old Creation Society (Ch'uang-tsao she) and from the more
recent group centered around the magazine *Les Contemporains*
(*Hsien-tai*). After the fall of Hong Kong and the Shanghai International Settlement, a few writers until then associated with the Lin
Yü-t'ang publications also helped foster a benevolent image of the
Wang Ching-wei regime. Wang Ching-wei was an established
political leader of China in eclipse under his rival Chiang Kai-shek,
and thus had a measure of legitimacy the Japanese utterly lacked.
However, if in organizing a peace movement and a government in
Nanking under the Japanese Wang's aim was to ameliorate conditions for the Chinese under enemy occupation and win back some
national autonomy, the failure of his actions was apparent long
before the end of the war and from the start generated no popular
support. Thus, although he had a corps of writers at his disposal,
they were employed not to politicize creative literature, but to write
editorials, attend Sino-Japanese cultural functions, and provide occasional testimonials as the needs of a political façade and circumstance
demanded. It was for these activities, rather than any creative work,
that collaborationist writers later suffered assassination, imprisonment, and social ostracism.

The chapter on literature and political initiatives is designed to take up these and other related issues in the historical sequence of the war period. The general failure of the Japanese and the Chinese regimes they sponsored in North and Central China to develop a politicized literature is its theme. Indeed, the only significant Chinese works of pro-Japanese propaganda were some films produced under direct Japanese supervision, and these were relatively few given the total number of films produced under the occupation. The discussion of films in this book is limited primarily to this chapter, for the films themselves have not been available in recent years, and their interest seems mainly confined to their role in mass entertainment under Japanese supervision. A lengthy survey of the lackluster role of literature in propaganda programs might not seem to be warranted. Yet, given the natural curiosity and suspicion regarding the nature of literature under the occupation, it is important to attempt to demonstrate the limits of Japanese political influence and make clear that Chinese writers for the most part responded to the proscriptions of censors rather than the prescriptions of propagandists. Such a survey also serves as a chronological introduction to the history of literary activity under the occupation, allowing a more analytical discussion of various works in later chapters.

The alternatives to a literature sympathetic to Japanese policies was a literature of resistance, dissent, or disengagement. The existence of works advocating resistance or expressing dissent is discussed in the chapter on literature and political initiatives, but those of literary interest are discussed individually in later chapters, together with the works more aptly considered as "disengaged."

The fact that so many works might be placed in the "disengaged" category is natural considering government censorship and the departure of many writers with reputations as social activists. But works offering themes of dissent or resistance appeared throughout the occupation period; and if more did not, it was not simply a matter of the Japanese presence. The writers who went into the interior of China to serve the army and the people with resistance literature found that by 1941, that population too was wearying of patriotic war stories. The literature of disengagement—escapist works and themes unrelated to fighting the Japanese—were common not only to Shanghai and Peking, but to the interior as well. Indeed, the earliest and loudest calls for a literature that transcended the topical issue of the war of resistance were sounded in the interior, notably by the critic Liang Shih-ch'iu, who was dismayed with the superficial, stereotyped quality of much resistance writing. Although Liang had his supporters, he was denounced by a chorus of writers from Chungking to the Shanghai concessions who still maintained their autonomy from the Japanese. But by the outbreak of the Pacific War in late 1941, the public had largely decided in favor of works less directly concerned with the immediacies of a stagnating war. It was then that the Shanghai International Settlement fell to the Japanese. If the writers there were immediately affected by the Japanese presence, they were also in touch with literary developments in the interior and did not create a literature unique to their situation under enemy occupation.

There were, after all, important social continuities, as well as literary ones, between the Nationalist-held interior and the occupied zone. Aside from continuing, quiet economic intercourse and political arrangements between the two regions, in terms of daily life hard times fell on most people, including writers, and the black market was a feature of life across China in the quest for day to day survival. Equally a common feature of the mental landscape was the notion that these circumstances were temporary. If many expressions of loyalty in the interior were deemed a temporary necessity to drive out the Japanese, acceptance of the reality of Japanese authority under the occupation was seen as a temporary necessity to survive to VJ day. Just as there was no consensus among writers in the interior on the proper degree of commitment to any faction (beyond the ultimate commitment to a liberated China), there was little consensus in the occupied zones over how to accept the fact of Japanese-sponsored regimes. Therefore, the relative activity or passivity of a writer's "acceptance" must be determined in a case by case review.

In this connection, having drawn some lines of continuity between writers in the interior and under the occupation, it might be noted that, in contrast to many European countries under unpopular regimes, little in the way of "underground" literature in occupied

China has come to light. We might consider as underground literature any work whose content is subversive to established authority,
but basically, it is literature produced, published, and/or distributed
outside legally established channels. The famous *Edition Minuit* of
Paris under the Nazi occupation, for example, contained many works
unrelated to the topic of resistance, as well as fulfilling its role as an
anti-Nazi organ. Many of its contributors simply refused to be
associated with legally approved publications, regardless of whether
or not their writing was concerned with the war and enemy
authority. In occupied China, however, it would appear that if a
writer published his or her work, it was done in legally approved
ways. The result was that, while productions of some plays were
curtailed or modified and some magazines suspended, a number of
works passed by the censors clearly put the results of Japanese rule in
an unflattering light.

There is a contrast, then, between the social background and
literary milieu of an occupied France and an occupied China. Yet for
both societies the experience of occupation resulted in particularly
important literary achievements. The focus of this study is on
examining works for their place in the wider context of the history of
modern Chinese literature. The terms employed to organize the later
chapters on romanticism, traditionalism, and antiromanticism were
chosen in the light of research on other periods, as well as the occupation itself. They are not introduced as original terms with new
definitions. Placing a work in one of these categories does not imply
that the label provides the ultimate appraisal of the work, but that its
dominant qualities respond more to one term than another. It might
be argued that the terms chosen for this study also have a limit to
their usefulness on account of their broadness and lack of precision.
But to have approached the period as a whole by way of other
applicable critical terms, such as Mandarin Duck and Butterfly
School, regional literature, literature for the masses, and so on,
would have resulted in hair-splitting definitions that could only divert
attention from the individual work itself. Nor would a study
organized by genres or chronology have allowed integrated discussions of the many writers whose contributions spanned more than
one year and a single genre.

The first such chapter, on the decline of the May Fourth legacy of romanticism, might also have been called the decline of May Fourth literature. But the term "romantic" has been taken up by scholars within and without China and refers to important aspects of literature that dominated much of the achievement of the May Fourth period and that have also reoccurred in various forms since that time. The romanticism treated by Leo O. Lee's important study of early modern Chinese literature may be distinct from the "revolutionary romanticism" purveyed in China during the 1960s and 1970s, but they are related in important ways. Among the works considered in this book we can see the relation to the romantic ethos of May Fourth. The writers are concerned with attacks on social institutions of authority, wealth, class, the marriage system, and so on. Each writer finds an individual protagonist of some heroic stature who steps out of the moral and physical wreckage of society to proclaim an individual victory with deliberately broader social implications. In form these writers, if not iconoclastic, are consciously modern. There is little or no appeal to tradition in their use of the polemical essay, the diary, and autobiographical forms for fiction or the spoken drama.

Ironically, although the spoken drama was a self-consciously modern form, interest in combining it with traditional themes and stories and elements of traditional opera was well under way by 1937. A startling aspect of the war period, and particularly the occupation, was the growth of the spoken drama movement, as it was called. No less interesting is the degree to which the movement appealed to tradition. This is the topic of chapter three. Less spectacular but equally interesting is the topic of chapter four, the traditionalism apparent in the familiar essays of many writers who borrowed from the traditional esthetics and were concerned with continuities in Chinese culture. Indeed, both plays and essays were frequently exercises in cultural loyalty, attempts to continue the reevaluation of traditions begun during the May Fourth movement. But not always; within this traditionalism were examples in drama of Mandarin Duck and Butterfly literature as well as examples of affinities with regional literature in some essays.

The final and most original development in the literature of the occupation period is dealt with in the chapter on antiromanticism. Breaking away from the themes of individual self-assertion, the writers of antiromantic literature are more concerned with individual failures caused by self-deception. The psychological orientation of these works, in their unreforming vision of unheroic characters during the decay of wartime society, has some affinity with earlier works of modern Chinese literature and bears evidence of an appreciation of traditional literature as well, yet seems primarily an outgrowth of the British literature of disillusionment following World War I.

The diversity of the literature of the occupation period was one of its strengths. If it is a challenge to the schematizing mind of the literary historian, it also proved a challenge to Japanese propagandists. Although Japanese authorities suppressed Communist and resistance literature, they also sought to stimulate literary activity in the hope of turning it to their own use. But Japanese cultural workers never found a literary general around which to rally a movement, nor did they develop social controls to do more than proscribe frankly anti-Japanese works. As a result, a kind of literary anarchy flourished: output was primarily of works that, the Japanese admitted, ignored or reflected poorly on their rule, and of some that reached the point of satire and dissent. By the conclusion of the war there was far more to be said about what individual Chinese imaginations had created than what Japanese authority wanted from them.

CHAPTER ONE

Literature and Political Initiatives

"During the war, both the Japanese government and civilian writers were virtually unable to mount a program for the writers of China. In the war zone no one paid attention, for the assertions of the Japanese were utterly meaningless and absurd. Moreover, the effort on the part of the Japanese, while it did have a capital façade, was so meagre that it practically amounted to zero."[1]

This was the view of Takeda Taijun, an eminent Japanese writer who spent much of the war period in China. Takeda was a soldier, a member of the Sino-Japanese Cultural Association, and a scholar of Chinese literature. As a verdict on Japanese-sponsored literary programs, his view is not at variance with statements by historians on the overall lack of a coherent ideology or policy among Japanese militarists in China. Indeed, one can still read the efforts of propagandists for the Japanese in China laboring late into the war to formulate a "central ideology."

Despite this lack of coherent policies and ideology, Japanese and puppet government propagandists did seek in various ways to use literature as an instrument of politics. Authorities supplemented these initiatives with censorship, arbitrary arrest and confinement, and in a few cases, torture and execution. Although a record of the activities of governments administering the occupied zone is not itself an explanation for the literature of the occupation, political activities did play a role. This chapter will examine the extent of that role and its overall influence on literature in China during the war period.

Literature and the New Order:
1937–1941

As the main force of the Chinese armies fell back into the interior, large numbers of writers and intellectuals moved with them to propagandize the war effort, and debates on all aspects of war propaganda were numerous. Drama, as a prime instrument of mass propaganda, became a particular focus of concern. Several writers emphasized the use of regional forms to appeal to the population of the interior, and one writer added a special note of urgency by commenting that while Chinese writers were in the throes of uncertainty as to how to address the masses, the Japanese were already taking initiatives. He cited reports that in the Shen-kan-ning region, a Japanese-sponsored troupe was touring with a regional-style adaptation of *Ta yü sha chia* (*The Fisherman's Revenge*) called *Sung-hua chiang* (Sungari River).[2]

Indeed, the Japanese were not slow to recognize the popularity of Chinese theater and its role in society. Pacification teams (*sempu ban*) followed up the advances of Japanese forces, organizing theatrical troupes for propaganda purposes with personnel selected from local companies. As one Japanese officer related:

> There was a small theater, the Hsin-shih-ch'ang, on Chungshan Road in Hankow. Immediately after the fall of the city, the empty interior of this theater became home for thousands of refugees. They were, however, for the most part addicted to opium. One day we went out to recruit coolies at this theater, and we found out that mixed in with these refugees were dozens of performers who had formerly worked in the theater. . . . We decided to mobilize this group as the Pacification Troupe, and laid plans for the stabilization of post-combat sentiment, at the same time propagandizing ideology to oppose the Communists, defeat Chiang Kai-shek, and build the New Order in East Asia.[3]

The Japanese coaxed the actors into performing a resistance play they had staged prior to the fall of the city, and studied the themes and techniques of resistance drama. Meanwhile, the actors were allowed to resume performances in the Hsin-shih-ch'ang Theater on their own in order to restore an audience and bring back other performers who had fled the neighborhood. From the troupe that emerged, the Japanese selected the best performers and prepared a show to take on tour through the countryside. When the performers balked, explaining that other Chinese had threatened them and made attempts on their lives, the Japanese closed down the theater. Left without a livelihood, the actors capitulated. The Japanese officer noted with satisfaction that the training regimen required of the actors rid them of their opium habit.

The play chosen was a regional version of the story of Liang Shan-po and Chu Ying-t'ai. The Japanese supervisor claimed that an exposé of the tyranny of the Communist army and anti-Communist ideology were woven into the play. Unfortunately, the script of this unusual achievement is not available. The Japanese allowed for considerable variations in style, depending on location. The troupe organized in Nanking for example, performed modern spoken dramas:

> The hit play of the Far East Troupe is a piece dealing with the submission of bandits entitled "A Bright Future Lies Before Us (Kuang-ming tsai wo-men ti mien-ch'ien)." Currently the play is "Patriotism and Self-Defense (Ai-kuo hu-chi)," which . . . deals with the relationship between families, some of whose members join in a guerrilla unit which blows up the Nanking-Shanghai rail line.[4]

Allegorical drama was also attempted in a play published by the Great People's Society (Ta min hui) called *The World Attains Peace*. Aimed at generating racist sentiment, it portrays several brothers of the Huang (Yellow) family, who represent the KMT (the Nationalists) and the CCP (the Communists), debauching themselves with characters who represent England, France, the United States, and the USSR. The brothers quarrel over redeeming their debts by selling their sister, who represents China, to the foreign characters. Hua Te-lin (China's virtuous neighbor, Japan) arrives to rescue the girl and marry her with the aid of another brother, Wang Ching-wei.[5]

Traditional themes such as family virtues and filial piety were also used. "Hsin-hun chih ch'ien" (Before the Wedding) portrays young people defying their parent's arrangements for marriage and facing, as a result, a future with no values or material support.[6] In "Fu tzu chih chien" (Between Father and Son) an aging peasant sits cursing the Communist Party for turning his son into a fugitive. His son finally appears and cries woefully: "I am no longer your child. . . . I have been sacrificed to the tyranny of the Communist Party. Forgive me! I just want to be your servant." The father is eager to forgive his son, but the young man's older brother continues to rebuke him. Only after considerable arguing is the younger brother successful in convincing his older brother of the sincerity of his repentance: "I want to walk on that bright and glorious road of the New Order. . . . East Asia is the East Asia of East Asians."[7]

Besides touring cities and hamlets, the propaganda theater companies were also sent to entertain at mass rallies and official celebrations, and to take their message to schools, POW camps, and workers at construction sites. Despite these programs, propaganda theater amounted to only a portion of the theatrical activity in China, and the Japanese never made thoroughgoing efforts to bring all theater under their direction. In the fall of 1937, following a summer of strict curfews and blanket censorship, the classical theater companies of Peking were permitted to resume public performances. These troupes were kept under close surveillance, encouraged to perform martial dramas, and summoned to mass rallies on occasion. However, there was apparently little attempt to politicize the content of the Peking Opera, and plays with overt political messages were left to troupes specifically formed for that purpose.[8] In the Shanghai concessions, the offerings of independent drama companies were reviewed by censors, and in late 1943 a company was compelled, after much procrastination, to perform in Nanking to celebrate the return of the foreign concessions to the Wang Ching-wei regime by the Japanese. However, the play produced for the occasion was a revival of a popular adaptation of Pa Chin's *Chia* (Family), and not a work tailored to affirm pro-Japanese policies. Few well-known playwrights produced propaganda works for the Japanese-sponsored programs. Available sources offer only the name of Ch'en Ta-pei as head of the Nanking-based Far East Troupe (Yüan-tung chü-t'uan). Ch'en was a well-known writer of the early modern dramas known as *wen-ming hsi* (civilized drama), and in the thirties had a reputation as a writer of comedies.[9]

The literary pages of officially supported newspapers provided another platform for propaganda dissemination that included the publication of play scripts. With the outbreak of full hostilities in China, the Japanese government had begun requiring publications in Japan to carry items on the China Incident, and writers were recruited to develop patriotic literature. These policies began to be reflected in certain Chinese newspapers in 1938. In Peking a hack writer named Keng Hsiao-ti (Keng Yü-hsi) became editor of the literary supplement of the *Hsin min pao* (New People's Herald), the daily organ of the Hsin min hui (New People's Society), a puppet party organized along fascist lines. The events of 1937 had been the departure of most writers from Peking and the suspension of literary publications. Keng urged young people to take advantage of the vacuum left by the departed writers to create a "new people's literature," which should reflect a new era of peace and strength for China.[10] Such a literature should not be oriented to social classes and cliques; it should strive to preserve the "superbness" of China's indigenous literature and develop its excellent qualities. This meant attention to the compressed style of Chinese letters, and avoiding imitations of Western syntax, diction, and discursiveness.[11]

Keng himself wrote a few political pieces, including a play scenario, *Ti? Yu?* (Friend? Foe?), which portrays a Japanese soldier winning the confidence of the Chinese as he treats the wounds of a guerrilla fighter left behind by his comrades.[12] However, he spent virtually all his creative energies writing titillating novels in serial form on the sexual mores of university students and faculty. He himself seems to have been little concerned with superbness of style, let alone ideological depth. According to one commentator: "His novels were written from day to day, always taking the news from the day before and inserting it into his fiction on the following day. Although it was fresh and novel, still it was assembled at random, without any prepared conclusion."[13] It should also be noted that Keng is credited with a satiric novel on the political and social conditions in Peking during 1943.[14]

Keng's counterparts in central China were no more coherent or influential. In the *Hsin shen pao* (New Shanghai Report), a Shanghai daily controlled by the Japanese army, one contributor outlined "The Mission Which Literature Should Undertake":

> Heretofore the attitude of most people towards literature has been to regard it as an item for relaxation. This sort of traditional notion is now gradually being eliminated. . . . True literary works must reflect the special characteristics of a race and an age.[15]

Here the author offers the new literature as a countercurrent to rather than a revival of tradition. Nor does he urge a return to an indigenous style, as Keng does, to win credibility for the new literature. On the other hand, the themes of racial pride and the new age of East Asia are emphasized, just as they were by commentators in North China. The regimes, however, being separate by Japanese design, the literatures proposed went under different names: "new people's literature" in the north, and "peace literature" in the south. One advocate of "peace literature" wrote that it was a portrayal of the needless sufferings of the people for the Nationalist and Communist resistance effort and was an expression of the people's hopes for peace. He illustrated this theme in several pieces that argue the futility of dying for a government which does not care for the welfare of its people.[16]

The view of the KMT and CCP as infected with the decadence of the West and the very call to oppose the inroads of Western culture continued to focus attention on Western literature. In a sense, this relieved writers of the burden of defining carefully what the elements of the new Chinese literature should be. The most extensive discussion of a new literature to appear in *Hsin shen pao* argued that Chinese had lost respect for their own culture in favor of the West and had westernized their language. These were hardly new arguments. Moreover, the bulk of the article outlined the lessons the West had to offer, referring to the examples of ethnic literary movements and to the concept among European thinkers of the West as a single entity. This notion, he argued, should be turned against them as Asians looked to the "collective strength of the East."[17] Obviously, the realities of political alliances precluded any broad development of this theme. Moreover, even the *Hsin shen pao* ran appreciative articles introducing European writers. The quantity of politicized literature, on the other hand, remained but a fraction of the offerings appearing in literary supplements.

Propagandists, in addition to attempts to foster ideology in the popular columns of newspaper supplements, also sought to make a platform out of literary periodicals appealing to the cultural elite. The initial issue of the first literary magazine published in Peking after its occupation by the Japanese carried the following disclaimer by its editor, Fang Chi-sheng, known in Peking literary circles as an experienced editor and scholar of Japanese literature:

At first I had no intention of managing a magazine at this time. No, when Mr. Lu Yü-ping [Lu Li] first raised this topic, I politely declined. Early last month Mr. Lu again visited me with the proprietor of the Tung-fang Bookstore, and repeatedly talked about the current silence in northern literary circles and the lack of periodical reading matter among the intellectual class. He explained that the motive for having the bookstore publish a periodical was purely to respond to the needs of the times, and that this could offer to the middle and upper classes some sustenance for the spirit, there being absolutely no other intentions. It was with such loftiness of purpose and interests, with such fullness of sentiment, that I thereupon agreed to give serious consideration to the matter, under certain conditions, among them, not to discuss the political situation, to reserve all rights in editorial matters, and to share responsibilities with Mr. Lu.[18]

Fang Chi-sheng then carefully explained that the name he had given the magazine, *Shuo feng* (Northern Wind), signified only its northern location geographically and the time of its first publication, October of 1938, the season of northwesterly winds. Fang solicited contributions from several members of the remaining literary community in Peking: Chou Tso-jen, Ch'ien Tao-sun, Shen Ch'i-wu, Chang Shou-lin, Ch'en Mien, and others.[19] Indeed, the early issues were of the "pure literature" variety. By the eighth issue, however, Fang Chi-sheng's name was dropped from the editorial credits, to be replaced with the name Lu Li (Lu Yü-ping), and then the anonymous Northern Wind Society. The original contributors began to disappear, and in the tenth issue inserts were included with such slogans as these:

Opposing communism is everyone's responsibility.

East Asians arise to establish together a New East Asia.

When China and Japan truly collaborate, then there can be co-existence and co-prosperity.

Opposing England is a crucial step toward China's emancipation.

By the eleventh issue, the "pure literature" items were reduced to a quarter of the contents to make room for articles discussing the political situation and political theory.

In September 1939, at the time that *Northern Wind* was completing its transformation into a propaganda platform, a new literary magazine called *Chung-kuo wen-i* (Chinese Arts and Letters) appeared. This monthly magazine was one of eight subsidiary publications of *Wu-te pao* (Martial Herald), a newspaper whose title amply indicated its pro-Japanese position. The syndicate was managed by one Kameya Riichi, and *Chinese Arts and Letters* itself was staffed by a group of young men of no previous literary reputation. Contributions were obtained from the original contributors to *Northern Wind,* and the format was expanded to bring in works in all genres by young, unknown writers, as well as translations and articles on foreign and domestic arts and entertainment. However, this time the intention was not simply to create an accepted platform to be coopted by propaganda, but to foster a new literature itself embodying propaganda themes. The opening issue of the magazine stated that editorial policy should be responsive to the demands of readers.[20] In January 1940, the magazine published "Chien-she hsin wen-i ti ke-chieh hung-lun" (A General Discussion from All Quarters on the Founding of a New Literature), with the opinions of ranking educators and editors of other publications. If the various statements can be fairly summarized, they included these themes: the abandonment of the May Fourth literary lions who had spread confusion and dominated culture as "literary warlords"; the adoption of a strong ethical stand based on Confucian values; and concern for the lives of the masses to free them from their spiritual torment.[21] But such prescriptions were neither systematically proposed nor imposed on writers. Moreover, nothing in such statements necessarily furthered the image or goals of Japan. Concern for the masses is a piece of casuistry that any politically inspired literary movement would advocate. Repudiation of the writers of the May Fourth movement and advocacy of Confucianism were the practice among the powerful right wing of the KMT in the interior, not to mention the denunciation of all but a few May Fourth writers by the Communists that began with Mao's Yenan talks.[22]

The initiatives of theoretical articles on literature were augmented by the formation of literary associations. Japan's increasingly expansive effort to organize and mobilize her own writers in support of the war effort, however, was only feebly reflected in China. In January 1941 more than 120 writers met in the Peking YMCA to inaugurate the North China Literary Association. Chou Tso-jen was named chairman in his absence, while the staff of *Chinese Arts and Letters* took over actual organizational affairs and published a supplement on the association for several months until funds ran out.[23] The organization naturally afforded opportunities to indoctrinate writers and increase surveillance on them, but had little impact on literary publications.

Similar efforts were made in central China. In December 1939 the existing puppet government associated its propaganda with the rising "peace movement" under Wang Ching-wei and organized the Chinese Literary Association (Chung-kuo wen-i hsieh-hui) in Nanking, denouncing feudalism, white imperialism, and Communism, while championing an optimistic literature for peace, the establishment of a New East Asia and, later, Three People's Principles. None of the association's two dozen staff members had any previous literary reputation or was prominent in later cultural programs. The Society for Literary Research (I-wen yen-chiu she), headed by Chou Fo-hai, was little more than a front for the collection of funds for the peace movement. In mid-1940 Lin Po-sheng, Wang Ching-wei's minister of propaganda, could talk of a literary renaissance and the restoration of Confucian values, but could not elucidate Wang's own views on Confucianism. Lin believed Wang was a follower of Wang Yang-ming's school of thought.[24]

Many writers who joined the peace movement were in fact not employed as creative writers. Mu Shih-ying, a young writer whose short stories in various styles had attracted much favorable comment prior to the war, joined the peace movement in Hong Kong and was sent to Shanghai for a brief and fatal career as editor of a peace movement newspaper there, *Kuo-min hsin-wen* (National News). Liu Na-ou, a friend of Mu's with experience in film work, was also assassinated after joining a Japanese-controlled film company. Perhaps the best-known writer to join the peace movement, Chang Tzu-p'ing, remained in good health. Known for over a decade as a novelist specializing in the portrayal of triangular love affairs, Chang produced little creative work during the war. He held a variety of educational and advisory positions, including chairmanship of the committee for cultural enterprises of the peace movement, which produced a flood of reading matter.[25] In Nanking, the monthly journal *T'ung sheng* (Accord), edited by one Hsia Sun-t'ung, aimed at refined, conservative tastes. It featured poems in the classical style by prominent peace movement figures such as Wang Ching-wei, Chiang K'ang-hu, and Liang Hung-chih, together with articles on classical poetry and belles-lettres. A series of pro-peace movement magazines were published for more popular tastes: *Yüan-tung yüeh-k'an* (Far Eastern Monthly), *Hsin Shih-chi* (New Century), *Keng Sheng* (Revival), and so on.

The most substantial moves to organize writers were initiated by the Japanese. The first was the founding of the Sino-Japanese Cultural Association (Chung-jih wen-hua hsieh-hui) in July 1940, "to bring about the merger of the cultures of China and Japan" and establish a basis for friendship between the two nations.[26] The association was to sponsor lectures on literature and scholarship, colloquia, translation projects, mutual academic research projects, book and art exhibits, and concerts and dramas. It did do these things, though on a scale that has left but scant impress in the available records of the times. Beginning at the same time, a number of literary associations were formed in Nanking, Soochow, Canton, and Wuhan.

A second initiative by the Japanese was the establishment of the China Film Company (Chung-hua tien-ying kung-szu) in 1938 in Shanghai. Liu Na-ou, who had directed several films prior to the war, became managing director. He was joined by a handful of other directors, including Huang T'ien-shih and Hsing Shao-mei, formerly of China United Film Company, an independent studio in the International Settlement. The former studios of the Star Motion Picture Company (Ming-hsing tien-ying kung-szu) on the outskirts of Shanghai were occupied after extensive damage sustained during the fighting in 1937 was repaired. Handsome bonuses and salaries were offered to lure actors out of the foreign concessions, though with little success at first.[27] In July 1939 studios in north China and Shanghai were merged under the China Film Corporation, Ltd. (Chung-hua tien-ying ku-fen yu-hsien kung-szu), with headquarters in Nanking. There is, however, little secondary material, let alone the films themselves, from which to judge the content of productions prior to the Pacific War.

Resistance Literature in the Shanghai Concessions:
1937–1941

A chief impairment to Japanese-sponsored cultural activities was the continued publication of hostile writers within the foreign concessions of Shanghai. A major source of such irritation was the newspapers in the Shanghai International Settlement. With the withdrawal of Chinese forces from the Shanghai region, the municipal council of the International Settlement forbade newspapers to print inflammatory articles, including the use of the word "enemy" to refer to Japan. Violators were threatened with suspension.[28] Editors took to the practice of *x*ing out specific words that might be considered beyond the limits of censorship rules, but still passing articles and works reflecting anti-Japanese sentiment. In fact, a perusal of samples of these newspapers indicates that they frequently flouted censorship strictures. Japanese and peace movement agents responded by assassinating editors and bombing newspaper offices. Resistance agents responded in kind. Newspapers would be suspended for weeks at a time, only to resume publication with continued anti-Japanese literature. The newspaper war reached a peak of intensity in the summer of 1939. In one raid by peace movement agents on a block housing several blacklisted newspaper and news agency offices, the casualties ran to five killed and twelve wounded. Following this, settlement officials had the block flanked with concrete machine gun emplacements and patrolled by armored cars.[29]

Editors of literary columns were not exempt from violence. One such victim was Chu Hsing-kung, editor of *Yeh kuang* (Night Radiance), the literary supplement of *Ta mei wan-pao* (Great American Evening Herald). Leftist writers greeted with cynical skepticism his being blacklisted by the Wang Ching-wei regime as a Communist. When Chu received a threatening letter warning him to refrain from allowing anti-peace movement articles in his supplement, he replied openly in his column:

There are many causes of death: poverty, suffering, accident, poisoning. But the most glorious death is to be murdered by the puppets, for then the victim becomes a martyr. . . . I shall neither submit nor beg for mercy. For what I do follows the dictates of my conscience. Alive I am only an insignificant person, but dead I shall become a heroic ghost.[30]

Chu was soon shot to death on his way home from work. His fellow editors and writers in fact paid scanty public attention to his passing in their newspapers. Finally, when over a week of strained silence has passed, the editor of the literary column of *Wen hui pao* (Consolidated Report) expressed his indignation that Chu's death had been ignored and wrote an elegy. The martyr, he commented, may have had little to offer as a writer, but he had stature as a patriot.[31]

By contrast, Japanese and peace movement publications were filled with expressions of sympathy and appreciation for Mu Shih-ying, the editor of *Kuo-min hsin-wen,* shot to death while riding a rickshaw on 28 June 1939. Although Mu had not anticipated his death with a final statement, his friend Kao Ming published a number of patriotic sentiments voiced by Mu shortly before his death.[32] Although only a few issues of the newspapers published in the settlement prior to the Pacific War are presently available, one gauge of the gradual decline in their patriotic fervor may be found in the still extant essays of the *tsa-wen* writers in the literary supplements. These essays, written to taunt the Japanese and their collaborators and sustain the will to resist, had their heyday from 1936, when they came into vogue following Lu Hsün's death, until 1939–1940, when their tone and approach began to withdraw from direct attack on immediate issues. Most *tsa-wen* writers stopped altogether by late 1939. A few continued, but the field narrowed considerably as newspapers submitted to political pressures, were bought out by agents for the peace movement, or went out of business for purely financial reasons.[33] When, following the Japanese occupation of the International Settlement on 8 December 1941, the remaining independent newspapers changed hands, the entire staffs of these papers were retained save for the ranking editors.

Another activity that attracted the attention of authorities was the publication of *Lu Hsun ch'uan chi* (Collected Works of Lu Hsün). This was the work of a secret organization, the Recovery Society (Fu She), which took its name from the late Ming literati movement. Cheng Chen-to recounts that the society had twenty dues-paying members who raised the capital for publication of the collected works. The members of the editorial committee were all active in literary circles, although Cheng stressed that membership in the society embraced all social classes.[34] The chief editor, Wang Jen-shu (Pa Jen), was editor of literary supplements in newspapers, a critic of Lu Hsün, and a *tsa-wen* writer himself. Hsü Kuang-p'ing (Ching Sung), the chief compiler, was editing *Fu-nü pan-yüeh k'an* (Women's Fortnightly). Cheng Chen-to himself was teaching at Chinan University and collaborating with Wang Jen-shu and K'ung Ling-ching, Mao Tun's brother-in-law, in compiling *Ta shih-tai wen-i ts'ung-shu* (Great Age Literary Anthology), a set of volumes chiefly devoted to essays by local resistance writers and translations from Soviet literature and criticism.

The society was probably also responsible for the publication of *Das Kapital* (*Tzu-pen lun*) and *Selected Works of Lenin* (*Lieh-ning hsüan-chi*).[35] Cheng states that, "though the enemy exhausted every means to apprehend its leaders, yet they were never able to discover who, after all, were the leaders of the Recovery Society."[36] When the settlement fell, a number of its members were arrested and tortured. Cheng testifies to the cruel treatment given Lu Hsün's widow, Hsü Kuang-p'ing, when she was confined, although his attributing her white hair to the stress of her experience must be regarded as a fiction by conventional medical knowledge.[37] Wang Jen-shu escaped before being caught. Cheng was allowed to live out the occupation in seclusion after declining an invitation to edit a magazine.[38] The chief casualty of the authorities' thirst to liquidate the leftist literary establishment was Lu Li. He had remained in Shanghai to manage Pa Chin's Cultural Life Publishing Company (Wen-hua sheng-huo ch'u-pan she) after Pa Chin's departure for the interior in 1940. The circumstances of his death, however, are obscure. It appears that he was not arrested immediately after the Japanese occupied the settlement, but remained for some time at the publishing office instead of going into hiding. Eventually he was taken away for questioning and died in confinement.[39] In sum, the initial ferocity of the authorities had its effect, and organized underground literary activities ceased.

There were few magazines expressly devoted to resistance literature even prior to the Pacific War. Pa Chin relocated *Na-han*

(Outcry) and *Feng-huo* (Beacon) following the retreat of Chinese forces in late 1937. Thereafter, the chief venture among resistance writers was *Lu Hsün feng* (Lu Hsün Current), a small magazine devoted primarily to *tsa-wen* essays and lasting only from January to September 1939. A dozen other publications appeared only to close after a few issues, often only one. Less antagonizing were *Yü-chou feng i-k'an* (Cosmic Wind II) and *Hsi-feng fu-k'an* (West Wind Supplement), offshoots of two well-established Lin Yü-t'ang publications, begun as outlets for writers in the International Settlement. In October 1940 *Hsiao-shuo yüeh-pao* (Fiction Monthly) appeared, followed shortly by a general interest magazine, *Wan-hsiang* (Phenomena), which offered a range of all genres in writing and proved successful commercial ventures while avoiding political stands. Despite individual cases of antagonistic expression, these publications were not wholesale cause for offense to the authorities.

The theater and cinema of the settlement were clearly allies of the resistance, though they too were in large part circumscribed by censorship and primarily produced costume dramas that often featured patriotic scenes, along with adaptations of Western works. Japanese-sponsored programs made little attempt to coerce theater or film workers, while voluntary recruitment into puppet-controlled productions lagged until the fall of the settlement. Modern spoken drama (*hua-chü*), on the other hand, grew in popularity from semi-professional standing to a viable commercial enterprise, and although companies relied frequently on the works of writers in the interior, it was works by local writers that brought unprecedented success to Shanghai theater, a success which continued to grow with the outbreak of the Pacific War and the embargo on American films.

Literature for a Greater East Asia: 1941–1945

The Japanese were to pay considerably more attention to the film industry with the outbreak of the Pacific War. At the time the settlement fell, the major release by an independent producer was *Family,* adapted from Pa Chin's novel and directed by Chang Shan-k'un of the New China Motion Picture Company (Hsin-hua tien-ying kung-szu). As the Japanese laid plans for yet another consolidation of film companies under the name China United Film Company (Chung-hua lien-ho tien-ying kung-szu), Chang Shan-k'un accepted a position as managing director, and continued to work on adapting Pa Chin's novels with productions of Ch'un (Spring) and Ch'iu (Autumn). Chang also became the principal recruiter for China United, or Hua Ying, as the company was generally called, offering not only handsome salaries but a sense of purpose as well. The playwright Yao K'o commented on Chang's methods to enlist personnel for film work under Hua Ying:

> To be fair to many of those who joined Hua Ying, I must point out that they swallowed Chang's bait not because they were willing collaborators, but because Chang was a very persuasive man. One of my protégés told me that he signed up with Hua Ying because he was convinced that Chang was *not* a traitor. "He reasoned with me," he said, "and pointed out that he accepted the offer of managing director of Hua Ying because otherwise a willing running dog would have been appointed to run the entire film industry. There are hundreds of players, he added, who are willing and ready to do anything to please the Japs and puppets, if you don't want to sign up with Hua Ying. Then he put the question to me: what's your choice, to save the industry from complete Japanese-puppet domination or to let a bunch of heartless hams sing praise to the Greater East Asia Co-Prosperity theme on the screen all over the occupied areas? So, I signed up."[40]

The capture of the International Settlement brought another exodus of writers: the Communist playwrights Ch'ien Hsing-ts'un (A Ying) and Yü Ling, the left-wing literary critic Wang Jen-shu and his opponent in literary debates, Hsü Hsü, playwright, novelist, and editor of several magazines with Lin Yü-t'ang, and the two Huangs, Huang Chia-yin and Huang Chia-te, editors of Hsi feng (West Wind) and its subsidiary publications. Schools were temporarily shut, magazines suspended publication, a production of Ts'ao Yü's Shui pien (Metamorphosis) closed, and theaters temporarily went dark. For the first few months of 1942, the Shanghai literary scene was virtually silenced.

Despite the importance the Japanese placed on motion pictures as a prime vehicle for propaganda, film productions were not greeted by critics with any degree of reverence beyond that required by censors looking for political indiscretions. Chang Shan-k'un was himself the object of satire, albeit indirectly, in a play by Yao K'o entitled *Yin-hai ts'ang-sang* (Vicissitudes in the Film World). Although the irreverent responses of such critics never amounted to a concerted counterattack against the film industry, it is evident from the records of commentators that the Japanese-sponsored films showed an obvious lack of ideological coherence and, often enough, even relevance to the needs of political indoctrination. What is one to make of all the articles in journals and newspapers solemnly invoking the restoration of Confucianism while at the theaters were playing films such as *Ch'un Chiang i-hen* (Sorrows at Spring River) which, according to a film historian, "showed the Taiping Rebellion as supported by a wise Japanese antiforeign movement, and as betrayed by the British"?[41] What did the lavish eulogy of Lin Tse-hsü in *Toward Eternity* (*Wan-shih liu-fang,* literally, Fame to Last Ten Thousand Generations) have to offer as antiforeign sentiment that was not exploited by the Communists fifteen years later?

If the themes of some films were antiforeign, the life style portrayed in most movies was not. Despite all the talk in theoretical articles about indigenous style, the existing film reviews explicitly record the persistence of foreign elements. One critic judged *T'ang fu* (The Vamp) as "out-Hollywooding Hollywood."[42] In a more reflective and wittier passage, the writer Chang Ai-ling reviewed *The Call of Spring,* summing up the portrayal of the hero by the actor Liu Chen as follows:

> In the role of an actor, Liu has the opportunity to do bits as Romeo and as Armand of *La Dame aux Camelias.* In another play within the play, Liu makes a convincing old man, but an Occidental one who digs his thumbs into his waistcoat pockets à la Lionel Barrymore. The hero of the picture writes plays with the help of coffee, and the camera dwells with genuine delight on the glittering coffee-pot. When in distress, he gets drunk in a bar. When he falls into poverty, he works as a coolie in a park, his overcoat shabby but shapely like that of a smart foreign tramp; his life in the park seems a perpetual picnic with lots of time for brooding by the campfire.
>
> It is appalling to reflect that, in the imagination of young Chinese intellectuals nurtured on a quarter of a century of foreign films and fiction, there is so little room for anything really Chinese.[43]

This is said not of an adaptation of a Western work, but of an original piece. Straight adaptations of American films continued, such as *The Struggle for the Spring* from *The Great Lie, Cloud Over the Moon* from *Daytime Wife,* and *On with the Show (Ten Thousand Violets and One Thousand Red Blossoms)*, modeled on American extravaganzas such as *The Gold Diggers* or *The Big Broadcast. On with the Show* featured Li Li-hua doing a benefit performance to raise funds for an orphanage. She was joined by the Takarazuka Dancers from Tokyo, then on tour in China. Dressed in skimpy costumes with Mickey Mouse ears, they pranced about Li Li-hua, who was seated atop a huge birthday cake. Of this doubtful contribution to the "merger" of the cultures of China and Japan, Chang Ai-ling noted: "In Chinese eyes, the Takarazuka Dancers are expressive only of the splendor of youth, health and intelligent discipline." The whole film was "meant to 'feed the eyes with ice cream and seat the heart in a sofa'—to quote the phrase a Chinese critic applied once to these American extravaganzas."[44] Chang added that what the audience really enjoyed were "the practical jokes the hero and heroine play upon each other—Li Li-hua fries some bad eggs for her admirer and he sends her an empty cup of ice cream. Also well received are the Chinese Laurel and Hardy who mess about in the restaurant kitchen."[45]

Chang Ai-ling also pointed out other themes with which movies flirted. From one of her reviews we may judge that the theme of filial piety received no unified treatment in films, despite its use by propagandists. Summing up three films on the topic, Chang wrote:

> Whether the panacea of modern psychology offered by *Mother* would work any radical change in Chinese domestic ethics is another question. The important thing is the awakening of the Chinese mind to the obligations rather than the privileges of parenthood. The mother in *Mother* is fully conscious of her responsibilities; in the *Soul of Liberty,* she feels them only in relation to the family dead; in *Two Generations of Women* she shamelessly hoards up man-power [her son] in accordance with the proverb: "Rear a child to guard against old age; store up cereals to guard against a famine."[46]

Other themes of potential significance were fear and disapproval of big cities and advanced education. In *New Life* a father, who has refused a neighbor's request for funds to help put his son through primary school because he is intent on putting his own son through a big city university, finally learns of his son's decadent ways at college and founds a primary school in his village. Chang interpreted this as a "veiled disapproval of modern universities."[47] In another film, a struggling young artist falls in love with a fishergirl: "The fisher-girl apologizes to the art student that she is unworthy of his attentions, and he replies in great heat, 'I don't like educated women.'"[48] *New Life* was intended as a didactic piece, but the result, according to Chang, was reminiscent of the "literary movies" of the early and mid-thirties:

> Unlike its predecessors, *New Life* makes a courageous if rather messy attempt to grapple with the question, whither lies the path of the hero after his repentance. *New Life* is definite where earlier films give only a vague sense of New Year's resolutions. *New Life* presents the ideal modern young girl, played by Wan Tan-fung [Wang Tan-feng], who befriends the hero for mutual improvement of knowledge and refuses his love on the grounds that this is no time for romance. After graduation she teaches in school in the interior and becomes an extremely decorative dean with a big bow in her hair. Under her influence the hero joins a band of colonists on their way to some barren border-lands. Totally unpremeditated, his salvation suggests only the call of romantic distance and would seem to imply that in the immediate surroundings nothing can be done—which is rather impractical advice to the average able-bodied, well-intentioned young man.[49]

The Japanese did send large numbers of their own people to colonize Manchuria, and the Japanese army had for years extolled the virtues of peasant life over the decadence of big cities. However, the Japanese are not known to have fostered any "down to the countryside" movements among the Chinese urban residents. The movie remains an expression of common sentiment rather than the publicizing of a policy.

Several years before the Pacific War a leftist writer in Shanghai accused the newly formed China Film Company of conspiring: "one, to defame China; two, to extol the awesomeness and benevolence of the 'Imperial Army'; three, to publicize the serenity of the occupied territory; four, to incite lewdness."[50] As stated earlier, there is too little material on which to base a judgment of film work prior to the Pacific War. However, given the available material on the Pacific War years, some attempt can be made to discuss these statements. There seems no question but that certain films were designed to extol the Japanese army and portray the occupied zone as prosperous and stable. The first and fourth charges are more difficult to assess, but do open up two final aspects of wartime films that should be considered.

It would seem at first thought that the Japanese stood to gain little by any sweeping defamation of China, although they certainly argued that the KMT and CCP were the running dogs of foreign interests. Nevertheless, the film historian Jay Leyda has stated that one "propaganda line was to place Chinese in humiliating situations, even in relation to each other." He continues:

> The most lurid trial of this tactic was *Chu [Ch'iu] Hai-t'ang*. . . . The first part is based on a real incident in the 1920s, but one that the Chinese would never have filmed in this way. Chu Hai-t'ang is a famous and handsome actor of female roles in Peking Opera. He attracts the attention of a general who "makes advances" to him that are at first rejected. A beautiful heroine, fresh out of normal school, is introduced as a candidate for the general's third wife. To save her from such a fate Chu Hai-t'ang sacrifices himself to the general's clearly expressed wishes. The whole film puts unusual stress on sensuality and no one, least of all Chinese society, comes off with much dignity. . . . The film is guaranteed to disgust and discourage its audience.[51]

It is difficult to accept Leyda's account of this film. *Ch'iu Hai-t'ang* was originally a novel by one Ch'in Shou-ou, serialized in *Shen pao* (Shanghai Report) in 1941, prior to the newspaper's being seized by the Japanese navy. During 1942–1943 a trio of playwrights turned it into the most successful play of the war. While the play was being written, Ch'in released his novel to Ma-Hsü Wei-pang for a film adaptation on the condition of "absolute fidelity to the original work."[52] In 1944 Ch'in fled to Kweilin, still unoccupied by the Japanese. Complaining merely that the stage version had reduced his novel to a love story, he revised the script with a suitably patriotic emphasis. In all available versions of *Ch'iu Hai-t'ang* the hero meets the heroine after she has become the third concubine of the warlord who, when he discovers this illicit affair, ruins Ch'iu's career by disfiguring his face, not raping him. The film apparently followed this story line faithfully to capitalize on its popularity.[53] As to whether there may have been other films that deliberately put Chinese in humiliating situations, the significance of such an approach would depend entirely upon the implied or stated causes and solutions of the situation. Failing that, there would be little by which to judge a work as propaganda for one cause or another.

The second consideration is whether films were intended to incite lust, a charge of immorality of the kind perennially employed to discredit persons or activities, but one which, nevertheless, should not be totally ignored. There do not seem to be any records in which propagandists obligingly stated that they intended to promote lewdness. Chinese moviegoers were accustomed to representations of illicit relationships, and were certainly not disappointed during the war. Given the current materials available, there are two ways to consider the question: the degree of explicitness in portrayals of illicit sex, and the consequences of illicit behavior.

One reviewer recommended the daring of a film "dealing with a subject untouchable for Hollywood." The scene he describes as surpassing the inhibitions of American movies is recounted as follows:

> The heroine . . . has worked out an extraordinary solution for the problems of her life: while five rich and unpleasant gentlemen shower her with money and gifts for the privilege of taking her to the ballrooms of Shanghai, she in turn keeps half a dozen poor but attractive young men. This is revealed in a scene which Hollywood would never dare show: Miss Yang, after a night of dancing and drinking with her rich admirers, lies voluptuously in bed and pushes button number two (or number six as her fancy may strike her).[54]

That is the extent of the scene. It was not filmed by a Japanese-controlled company, but by the still independent Shanghai Hsin Hua Company in late 1941 and early 1942.[55] The same reviewer later recalled that no films produced during the war attempted more than this scene, which remained during the occupation the most daring footage for a general public that would not have readily tolerated greater explicitness.[56] This is not to say that filmmakers were not interested in titillating audiences—they clearly were—but that their techniques conformed to those of their predecessors before the war.

Two more films reviewed by Chang Ai-ling dealt with the issue of infidelity. She summed up one as follows:

> The wife who undergoes all manner of unpleasantness to safeguard the child of her husband's mistress is fundamentally Oriental in spirit because of our traditional emphasis on the importance of keeping up the family line. She is possessed by one idea—to get the baby born. She has considerable trouble stopping her husband's mistress from having an abortion. As to what to do with the child once it falls into her hands, she appears to have very vague ideas beyond watching it grow.[57]

Of the other film, she notes:

> Mei Nian [Niang] is hurried from situation to situation in the tragedy of the divorced wife familiar to us all: she stumbles in the rain, kisses her child across

the windowpane, and dies at length in the arms of her repentant husband. The film has all the tried-and-true elements of legitimate melodrama but is affected by incredibly poor lighting.[58]

From such reviews it is apparent that under Japanese control producers continued to offer films according to established tastes, and did little to promote radically different views about sexual relations.

Since the early efforts of 1938–1939, the Japanese had made little progress in developing the ideological content of other genres to suit the themes of propaganda, and literary societies were nearly moribund. Following the outbreak of the Pacific War, the existing writers' organizations in Japan were disbanded and replaced with the more comprehensive Japanese Literary Patriotic Association (Nihon bungaku hōkokukai) in May 1942.[59] At the same time, the theme of Greater East Asian literature (*daitōa bungaku*) was promulgated. Similar initiatives were made in occupied China. In Peking writers and editors met at the Peking Restaurant to form the North China Writers Association (Hua-pei tso-chia hsieh-hui). The organizers, Kameya Riichi, Chang T'ieh-sheng, Liu Lung-kuang, and one Huang Tao-ming ("the yellow way is bright"), called for a revival of the North China literary scene to stage a "literary renaissance" and establish a new ideological movement. They admitted that previous attempts to form a writers' association had been unsuccessful. Liu Lung-kuang, brought back from Osaka to manage the new organization, declared that the authorities had found a lack of "spirit" in recent writing; to stimulate writers, awards would be established and an effort made to promote respect for writers in society and raise their current low status.[60] In central China the response was somewhat different, with less pressure on writers to join organizations. The Wang Ching-wei regime was primarily represented by a group of writers who were acquaintances of long standing, including Chang Tzu-p'ing, Chou Ch'üan-p'ing, Chou Yü-ying, Kung Ch'ih-p'ing, and Ting Ting (Ting Chia-shu). These writers, together with others employed in the Nanking regime's propaganda ministry, organized associations and published a series of unsuccessful magazines. That this work was done with little enthusiasm as a required response to Japanese pressure is suggested by the fact that the chief organizer in this group, Ting Ting, was actually an intelligence agent from Chungking.[61]

The major initiative taken by the Japanese during the Pacific War years was the organization of the three sessions of the Greater East Asia Writers Congress (Daitōa bungakusha taikai; Ta-tung-ya wen-hsüeh-che ta-hui). This program was the brainchild of Kikuchi Kan and Kume Masao, who had previously been with the Japanese army in China and in 1942 became executive director of the Japanese Literary Patriotic Association. Since August of 1940 these two men had been working on the idea of a Sino-Japanese Writers Association, and with the start of the Pacific War had adapted their plan to include writers from Japanese-held territories throughout Asia.[62]

The initial list of Chinese writers to be invited included the best-known names in occupied China: Chou Tso-jen, Yü P'ing-po, Chang Tzu-p'ing, T'ao Ching-sun, Yeh Ling-feng, and Kao Ming.[63] In fact, none of these writers attended. When the first congress assembled in Tokyo in November 1942, there was an assortment of lesser-known and unknown writers. From North China there were the scholars and translators of Japanese literature Ch'ien Tao-sun, Chang Wo-chün, and Yu Ping-ch'i, together with Chou Tso-jen's protégé Shen Ch'i-wu, and the Japanese army propaganda advisor in North China, Kataoka Teppei.[64] From central China there were the writers for *Tso-chia* (The Writer)—Ting Ting (under the name Ting Yü-lin), Chou Yü-ying, and Kung Ch'ih-p'ing, with the Japanese advisor Kusano Shimpei—and the Shanghai writers Liu Yü-sheng, member of the staffs of the Sino-Japanese Cultural Association and the propaganda ministry; Chou Hua-jen, Wang Ching-wei's chief editorial writer for *Chung-hua jih-pao* (Central China Daily News); P'an Hsü-tsu (Yü Ch'ieh), a minor writer not in government service; and Hsü Hsi-ch'ing, another propagandist.

These writers were joined by three from Mongolia and seven from Manchuria (Manchoukuo), as well as delegates from the colonies of Taiwan and Korea, together with representatives from other Japanese-held territories. Advance publicity had proclaimed that the congress would "discuss ways and means of how literary circles of the four countries can offer cooperation toward the prosecution of the Greater East Asia War and the creation of literature and art characteristic of East Asia."[65] Naturally, the dominant culture represented was Japan's, and writers entering Japan were given various tours and demonstrations to impress upon them the traditions and strength of Japan. Any egalitarian spirit was dismissed by the policy of leaving all remarks in Japanese at the congress untranslated, while other languages were translated into Japanese. Although the Taiwanese and Korean delegates responded with praise for Japanese language and culture, the Chinese delegate Ch'ien Tao-sun responded with suggestive reserve:

> Unless we mutually shift our positions and try to find a common ground, in other words, unless we meet with a feeling that our countrymen should try to become your countrymen and your countrymen try to become our countrymen, and arrive at this spirit in viewing matters, will any true sympathy and, hence, empathy emerge? Temporarily it may seem a strong admonition against a sense of superiority. Yet, if we can come to hold true sympathy, I do not believe it will be an issue.[66]

The well-planned congress ignored such suggestions. Okumura Kiwao, vice-chief of the information bureau, opened the meeting with a call to "crush the evils of US and British civilization which have oppressed East Asia and [to] revive Asiatic culture." He further announced that the assembled delegates were not defenders of an old culture, but fighters for a new culture, and concluded by leading the audience in the cheers, "*banzai!*" and "Asia is one!"[67]

The Chinese response was cooperative but generally muted throughout several days of speechmaking. Ch'ien Tao-sun noted that "the traditional Chinese ideal of universal brotherhood has much in common with the Japanese ideal of *hakkō-ichiu.*" Western culture, he continued, like the Confucian inferior man, emphasized material gain, while the spirit of Asia was rooted in the righteous conduct of the superior man.[68] Liu Yü-sheng also emphasized Confucian thought:

> Merging the feelings of the people is the first step toward establishing the spirit of East Asia. All Asians should cherish Asia. Therefore, I and other writers should through our literary work create universal warmth and love. Love of one's country is the first step. Love for neighboring nations is the second step. An all-embracing love for Asia is the third step. To uphold the principles of morality and seek the principles of righteousness are the loftiest goals in Asian culture. It is literature which instills this thought and illuminates life. I hope, then, that in this task all Asian writers will strive together.[69]

The Chinese also joined in making proposals for continuing cultural programs. P'an Hsü-tsu proposed an institute for research into East Asian culture. Chou Yü-ying joined in calling for a congress every year, as did Ting Yü-lin in the proposal to present awards for Greater East Asian literature.[70] There were proposals to sponsor lectures and translation projects, to exchange writers, and to promote culture among youth. Finally, Kataoka Teppei urged cooperation with the New People's Society movement and the pacification campaign.[71]

A number of these resolutions were carried out to some extent, although little can be said for the degree or results of the efforts. Translations, of course, had been going on for some time in China. Hino Ashihei's *Tsuchi yo hei* (Earth and Soldiers) had been available in Chinese since 1939, and a number of other translations of wartime works followed. On the other hand, most translations were of Japanese works that long antedated the war, including classics such as *Ise monogatari,* which was out of favor with Japanese authorities. Chinese and Japanese writers had been traveling back and forth between the two countries, especially Chinese writers employed by the *Osaka mainichi shimbun* syndicate and Japanese writers sent to cover the war in China. Prior to the second Greater East Asia Writers Congress in Tokyo in August 1943, five writers from North China were sent on a brief tour of Japan.[72] Following this second congress, T'ao K'ang-te from Shanghai remained in Japan. He studied under Andō Hikōtaro of Waseda University until March of 1944, when he returned to Shanghai. His output as a writer during the war was very slight. Lectures had been and continued to be presented by the Sino-Japanese Cultural Association, whose most ambitious program was the National Cultural Representatives Congress (Ch'üan-kuo wen-hua tai-piao ta-hui) of March and April 1943, with Chou Tso-jen as the featured speaker. Of course, a great quantity of propaganda had been aimed at youth in China, and such programs went on. The East Asia Cultural Research Institute was never realized.

The effects of these programs on literature itself were meager. After the start of the Pacific War and extending through early 1943, there were occasional essays and editorials calling for a literature that offered portrayals of the war. A series of "award-winning" stories appeared showing positive support of the puppet regime in North China in the *Hsin-min pao pan-yueh k'an* (New People's Herald Fortnightly). These stories portrayed the conversion of Communist guerrillas and westernized intellectuals to the values of Confucianism, especially filial piety. Unrepentant Communist guerrillas were shown to be not only unfilial, but parasitical, callous, and brutal toward the common people. Their supposed atrocities are given special attention, including scorched earth tactics, rape, and beheading the elderly. The settings and plots frequently centered on a rural village and its struggles with guerrillas, and offered scenes of puppet government troops and village militia overcoming guerrillas in combat. Perhaps the saddest of these short stories is one in which the daughter of a policeman killed in action is convinced that his sacrifice was for the benefit of the nation.[73] It is interesting to note that these stories refer neither to the KMT nor to the Japanese, and that the themes are no different from those which appeared before the Pacific War. Curiously, the flags and slogans pictured in the illustrations of the Peking stories are those of the Wang Ching-wei regime, not of the North China Provisional Government. More important, such stories were a fraction of the total literary output of occupied China.

It may be helpful at this point to introduce some observations from various sources indicating the general lack of response among writers to Japanese-inspired initiatives. In the last year of the war, a survey of the literature published in China during 1944 appeared in the Shanghai general interest magazine *Wen yu* (Literary Companion), owned by the *Osaka mainichi shimbun*. In this introduction, the reviewer commented that writers and publishers continued, as in the past, to be motivated by profits and satisfying the tastes of the public:

> As a result, the majority of literary works have not managed to cast off the airs of "refinement," "nostalgia," and Western-style Mandarin Duck and Butterfly writing. Add to these the insufficiency of writers' experiences in life, and their deficiencies in common knowledge of the social sciences, and it amounts to observations and portrayals of current society which are superficial in the extreme.[74]

This wartime writer's disapproval of most literature under the occupation is matched in Joseph Schyns's *1500 Modern Chinese Novels and Plays* by a commentator's postwar dismissal of a collection of short stories. The commentator wrote:[57]

> The book was published under the Japanese occupation and is necessarily deprived of any serious subject. It contains nothing but sentimental stories without moral elevation. It reflects the temporary conditions in which it appeared.

Of the hundreds of novels and plays written and published under the occupation and reviewed in Schyns's compendium, itself a project begun under the occupation, this is the sole instance in which a reviewer noted that the book was even influenced by the occupation. And even in this unique instance, and whether or not the reader agrees with the reviewer's sweeping dismissal of occupation literature, there was nothing of ideological significance that struck him. Over two decades after the war, the editor of a microfilm compilation of the Peking *Shih pao* (Fact Herald) made the following notes on the contents of the paper under the occupation:

> Narcotics cases, kidnapping, theft and robbery, family problems, corruption in the various echelons of the government, and other social problems occupied most of the space of the newspaper. Even the literary section reflected the predominance of the negative element in society at that time.[76]

As testimony to the lack of response to Japanese cultural programs this statement is all the more relevant, for the editor of *Shih pao* during the war, Kuan I-hsien, was also the minister of propaganda for the North China Provisional Government. He was arrested and executed after the war.[77]

Japanese commentators also had little to say for the quality and content of the "literary renaissance" they proclaimed. In particular, they looked to *I-wen tsa-chih* (Arts and Letters Review), which began publication nominally under the direction of Chou Tso-jen, by far the most respected writer among the Japanese. (In fact, Chou wrote that he had nothing to do with editing the magazine, but had agreed to let the editor, Yu Ping-ch'i, use his name.)[78] A Japanese commentary on this magazine noted that the translations of the *Ise monogatari* and *Haiku* poetry did not reflect the severity of contemporary realities, while the original short stories were mediocre to poor: Wen Kuo-hsin's portrait of an opium-sodden warlord was written with true feeling, but little else; Mu Ya-p'ing's tale of simple-mindedness was uninteresting; Mei Niang's distraught heroine was a feminist statement overladden with eroticism; Kung Ming's description of an old man defeated in his attempt to cope with his son's death reveals a dispirited, troubled writer.[79]

A month after this criticism appeared, an even more acerbic review was published by Yoshikawa Kōjirō, the ranking Japanese scholar of Chinese literature, under the title "Ni-ka no bungakusha ni" (To the Writers of Japan and China). Yoshikawa introduced his article by asserting that the literature of Republican China had degenerated into a preoccupation with the ugliness of life and human fate to the exclusion of joy, beauty, and human aspirations. He cited Mao Tun's *Tzu-yeh* (Midnight) as a landmark work representing the trend to exposé literature bereft of any guidance for the human spirit and consumed with the need for social reform. By contrast, traditional fiction, such as *Shui-hu chuan* (Water Margin) and *Han shu wai-ch'i chuan* (The History of the Former Han: Accounts of Families Related to Emperors by Marriage), possessed a sublime quality that raised them up from mere portrayals of human ugliness.

In the contents of *Arts and Letters Review* Yoshikawa saw the inheritance of the dismal state of modern Chinese literature. Passing over Chou Tso-jen's essay on literary history and Ch'ien Tao-sun's translation of *Ise monogatari* with unenthusiastic politeness, Yoshikawa turned to the short stories and condemned them all as unintelligible or worse. Wen Kuo-hsin's opium-sodden warlord is rendered as an object for pity, with no moral stand or signs of hope. The confession of the heroine in Mei Niang's story is so utterly devoid of values in its portrayal of adultery and despair that it ranks among the most degenerate pieces Yoshikawa had ever encountered. In Mu Ya-p'ing's villainess, a woman who beats her maid to death, there is some feeling for the cruelty of the woman, but it is stereotyped, and the work degenerates into a bleak, nihilistic tale. Kung Ming's story depicts an old man who remains unperturbed over his wine upon hearing of his son's execution, and then remains equally impassive on hearing that his son has not been executed after all. Yoshikawa commented that whatever the lesson this is supposed to provide on how to cope with adversity, it is utterly devoid of human aspiration.

Yoshikawa wrote he was heartened to hear that fellow Japanese in the Greater East Asia Writers Congress, aware of the unfortunate state of Chinese literature, were attempting to do something to put it on a positive path. He urged that Japanese of critical acumen and expert in Chinese be employed to guide writers in China away from these dispiriting themes. Japanese, however, must be humble over their modern achievements, as Chinese must admit their old weaknesses and cease dwelling on past glories.

In the second issue of *Arts and Letters Review* Yoshikawa did find a story which, while ultimately unsatisfactory, offered some signs that a positive shift in Chinese literature might take place. The story was "Sen-lin ti chi-mo" (The Stillness of the Forest) by Yuan Hsi. Through the tale of a young man who, loathing the city, finds employment in a forest, Yuan Hsi, in a prolix style, introduces the theme of the sublimity of man in nature. Yoshikawa also cited it as revealing a perception of detail lacking in Republican literature. To Yoshikawa's dismay, however the theme of sublimity gives way to yet another tale of adultery that is seemingly unconnected with the earnestness of the first portion.

Yoshikawa wrote his criticism shortly after the second Greater East Asia Writers Congress in August 1943.[80] In view of his remarks, it is interesting to note that this was the congress at which the first award for Greater East Asian literature to be given to a Chinese was presented to Yuan Hsi for his novel *Pei-k'o* (Seashells), a work Yoshikawa pointed out he had not read when he wrote his article. One can only guess what Yoshikawa's reaction might have been had he read the novel, for it is not only without the sublimity he had glimpsed in "The Stillness of the Forest," but thoroughly within the genre of exposé fiction he had denounced. In fact, it was on this basis that the publishers of *Sheashells,* New People's Press, promoted it:

> In this novel, which had the honor of the first prize awarded for Greater East Asian Literature, Yuan Hsi has penned a description of the lives and loves of modern youth. With the underlying theme of the poison of Western liberal thought, he has produced a trenchant criticism of love as purveyed by individualism.[81]

In the novel, a young woman, Li Mei, married four months to a forty-two-year-old professor of education at a Peking university, discovers she is pregnant from a premarital affair with another man. Unable to obtain an abortion, she travels to a family residence in Tsingtao with her younger sister, Li Ying, in order to conceal the pregnancy from her husband. On the way they meet a young rake, Po-shu, and once in Tsingtao he introduces the sisters into a smart set and seduces Li Ying. Li Mei meanwhile ponders renouncing her feminist attitudes and giving up Christianity for Buddhism. She helps Li Ying break off with Po-shu once it is revealed that he is carrying on with several women. Li Ying returns to Peking, where she becomes hard and cynical, rebuffing page after page of admirers. Li Mei delivers a boy and also returns to Peking. There she is again pursued by her lover (who is arrested as a heroin smuggler), blackmailed by a physician, and finally stricken with tuberculosis. The novel ends as Li Mei is sent to a sanitorium.

Seashells does offer a crude satire of fashionable and irresponsible liberal individualism and romantic love, but chiefly through the deranged Po-shu. The novel is saturated with illicit sex, or attempts at it, as well as physical and mental illness. The lives of the characters are made to appear contaminated morally and intellectually, and there is just enough portrayal of intellectual contamination to give the book its excuse as a contribution to ideological warfare. But it is not much more than an excuse. The characters are all weak, confused, and degraded in some way, and all are touched with Western thought. But the novel is set in 1935, and it is the chief villain, Po-shu, who remarks sarcastically, "I find it really strange that so many people have turned into patriots this year."[82] Hence, there is not only nothing in the novel that makes it pro-Japanese, but there is evidence to interpret the work as a statement on how Western thought was distorted to the point that some Chinese were too weak to resist the Japanese. The novel can stand only on the ground that it submitted to debate the question of the role of Western thought among the Chinese, and that ground is shaky indeed. The theme is momentous, but the treatment is inarticulate.

Seashells received little critical attention in either Japan or China. The author in his own introduction to the novel made no mention of the political situation, only that he wished to describe the deterioration of young intellectuals mired in "confusion and distraction." A brief biography of Yuan Hsi in Schyns's *1500 Modern Chinese*

Novels and Plays describes him as a refugee from Manchuria, imprisoned for two years after he returned to the Northeast and joined the resistance there. Following his release he began writing for a Manchoukuo periodical, attempting to describe "the emotions of the people under Japanese rule."[83] He then moved to Peking, where he continued to write. Another biography appearing in Liu Hsin-huang's "K'ang-chan shih-tai luo-shui tso-chia shu-lun" (Survey of Writers Who Sold Out During the War of Resistance) fails to confirm his resistance activities, but cites his association with Japanese in Peking.[84] Neither biography can trace his whereabouts after the first few months following the end of the war, though Liu notes he was not pursued by the law.

The second Greater East Asia Writers Congress was the last major show of interest in developing an ideological literature. Approximately the same number of Chinese delegates attended, and although there were several who had not attended the first congress, they were drawn from the same circles.[85] A series of discussion groups were held, but only the topics were revealed publicly: cooperative efforts in filmmaking, intensification of the modern drama movement, a history of Greater East Asian literature, a joint publication, permanent exchange of writers, and so forth.[86] The atmosphere remained dominated by expressions of Japanese cultural superiority, and several Japanese made abrasive comments to the Chinese delegates. Fujita Tokutaro "made a blistering attack on any Chinese writer who dared pronounce the characters for his name in some other fashion than *fujita*."[87] Kataoka Teppei attacked Chou Tso-jen (in absentia) as a "reactionary" writer. Hostility and fanaticism were brought to their extremes in the remarks of a Japanese journalist back from the front line in the Pacific:

> I cannot be satisifed with merely [the slogan] annihilation of English and American culture. Even if a thousand volumes of the collected works of Shakespeare rained from the sky, it would be no problem, but even a single bomb would be a different matter. . . . I am prepared to throw away my pen and pick up the sword. . . . On the occasion of this congress for decisive battle, the literary spirit ought to undergo a great conversion.[88]

No conversion was forthcoming, however. In April 1944 the Information Bureau was reorganized and Kume Masao was replaced, ending the principal force behind the Greater East Asia Writers Congress. Nevertheless, a third session had already been scheduled to be held in Nanking, so the Japanese felt committed. The Chinese dutifully organized to play host, but a spokesman for the North China Writers Association noted that they had made little progress in developing literary programs, were unclear as to what the nature of Greater East Asian literature should be, and added that "many people have a skeptical attitude toward the Greater East Asia Writers Congress."[89] The Chinese writers had every reason to be skeptical. The two works by Chinese given awards for Greater East Asian literature at the third congress were *Hsieh (Crab)* by Mei Niang (Sun Chia-jui) and two pieces by P'an Hsü-tsu (Yü Ch'ieh), an essay titled called "Jih-pen Yin-hsiang Chi" (Impressions of Japan) and *Yu Ch'ieh tuan-p'ien hsiao-shuo chi* (Collected Short Stories of Yü Ch'ieh).

Mei Niang, it will be recalled, had been criticized by Yoshikawa Kōjirō for a story he regarded as degenerate. Mei Niang, a native of Manchuria, wrote several volumes of short stories during the war, most of them before the Pacific War when she was employed by the *Osaka mainichi shimbun* in Japan. In 1941 she married Liu Lung-kuang, who edited several literary periodicals and newspaper supplements [90] and in 1942 became director of the North China Writers Association and editor of its publications. Mei Niang's stories show more sentiment than eroticism, and a tendency to portray women as the dupes of callous men or the soul mates of harmless ones. *Crab*, written in early 1941 and published later that year,[91] concerns the fortunes of an extended family household in the Japanese-controlled state of Manchoukuo in Northeast China. The Sun family has risen to prominence through former contacts with Russian traders and now seeks to maintain itself by securing civil service appointments under the patronage of the Japanese. The adult members of the family are mostly given to venality and incompetence, arousing the contempt of Sun Ling, the young daughter of the deceased family patriarch. Her primary act of dissent is her refusal to burn the Russian books her father gave her and which the family now fears will bring accusations that they are Communists. Ling's overwhelming frustration is that the Japanese occupation has blocked her hopes of going south to

Peking to study engineering. She has been left with an inferior education, including a particularly tiresome course in Japanese cooking. At
the close of the novelette, Ling decides to run away. Oddly, this final
scene portrays her inspired by the sight of the setting sun, implying
the promise of a new tomorrow. Since Japanese propagandists made
much of their symbol of a rising sun, Mei Niang's choice of a setting
sun to symbolize hope shows at least a marked indifference or
insensitivity to, if not actual rejection of, Japanese propaganda themes
and symbols.

The same may be said of the rest of the novelette, in which the
portraits of Ling's relatives as civil servants are most unflattering and
the glimpses of Japanese less than impressive. If there is a ray of
hope, a note of moral triumph, it is the property of the heroine in
lonely defiance of stagnation and corruption, not of a new social or
political system. The novel, then, has no discernible propaganda
value for Japanese policies, and there is little more to recommend it
as literature. There are scattered instances of good imagery, vivid dialogue, and moments of satire. But the story is rambling and sketchy,
and the heroine too shadowy a character to sustain unity or provide
particular depth. It is probable that the work was chosen for an
award because Mei Niang was the wife of Liu Lung-kuang and had
also translated some of Kume Masao's fiction.

Yü Ch'ieh's essay "Impressions of Japan" is a bland account of his
trip to the second Greater East Asia Writers Congress in Tokyo,
with no references to the proceedings of the conference itself or to
Greater East Asian literature. Instead, the author describes the tour
the Japanese gave him in an endless series of vapid superficialities
and references to Japanese hospitality. There are the tea ceremony,
the Imperial Hotel, Shinto shrines, Kabuki, the Ginza, Nara, Uji,
Kyoto, and a half-dozen other side trips and experiences. The author
takes particular delight in describing a waitress who spoke Chinese in
his native Anhwei dialect, in quoting from English-language guide
books, and in noting that Kikuchi Kan explained a Kabuki performance to him by writing notes in English. Finally, the guide on the
tour bus in Kyoto spoke only Japanese, so he did not understand a
word of what she said.

The short stories in *Collected Short Stories of Yü Ch'ieh* all relate to minor experiments with life by ordinary residents of Shanghai. In one story Mr. Li gives up his nightly glass of wine, and in another Mr. Chao gives up cigar smoking. In each case the men's families react with amused skepticism and heartily approve Mr. Li's decision to resume his nightly glass of wine and Mr. Chao's return to cigar smoking. Other stories are bland accounts of young love. One pathetic pair passively submit to the end of their innocent relationship when a fortune teller convinces the girl's mother to find a different suitor for her daughter. In another a young schoolteacher tries to retain two men as drinking partners, but finds it impossible to allay their unfounded mutual jealousy. Another couple is brought together through a common interest in photography. In Yü Ch'ieh's stories there are no violent issues, no social creeds, no illicit affairs, no risqué behavior. There is simply mild hedonism and a comic tone in a very simple style.

Yü Ch'ieh was one of the better established of the various minor writers in wartime Shanghai. Like many other writers, he had abandoned another profession, in his case law, to take up writing, and since the early thirties had supported himself as a middle school teacher and editor for book companies. During the war he contributed freely to numerous magazines, and although not employed by the Nanking regime, was closely acquainted with a number of writers who were. The selection of his works for the award was probably a deliberate show of superficial cooperation with Japanese programs, based on his willing association with members of the Nanking regime's propaganda circles.[92]

In November 1944, as Yü Ch'ieh and Mei Niang received their awards in Nanking, Wang Ching-wei's death in a bomb shelter in Japan was announced. Japanese forces in China were still on the offensive, but the Japanese homeland was coming under attack and the vision of a Greater East Asia now seemed doomed. Although the closing year of the war marked a final desperate drive to mobilize writers in Japan, the departure of the Japanese delegates from the November congress in Nanking brought to a close efforts to indoctrinate writers in China.

With the end of Japanese initiatives, the Nanking regime did nothing to continue what the Japanese had begun. The Nanking regime had never developed its own prescriptive programs for literature, though many of its members involved themselves in literary activities in one way or another. Although in the late 1930s Nanking agents used terrorism to crush resistance propaganda, once this was accomplished the government relied on censors to prevent any recurrence of openly seditious writing and attempted to turn a liberal face to independent literary circles. A mark of this overall policy, or lack of one, is the behavior of T'ang Liang-li, who was notorious for his involvement in the terrorist attacks on journalists in Shanghai. As a recruiter for propaganda writers he was reputedly courteous, never resorting to coercion or attempting to punish writers who refused his offers. Hence, during the Pacific War a number of periodicals that were clearly part of an organized response to Japanese-sponsored programs appeared, such as *Tso-chia* (The Writer), *I-pan* (In Common), and *Ta-ya-chou chu-i yü tung-ya lien-meng* (Greater Asianism and the East Asian League).[93] On the other hand, these magazines were overwhelmed, both in number and circulation, by literary periodicals that ignored propaganda, such as *Wan-hsiang* (Phenomena), *Ch'un-ch'iu* (Spring and Autumn), *Wen-i ch'un-ch'iu* (Arts and Letters Spring and Autumn), *Ta-chung* (Masses), and *Tz'u-lo-lan* (Violet). While these magazines included occasional contributions from writers for government-sponsored publications, such works were not politicized, and the publishers and editors were not associated with either the Nanking regime or Japanese organizations.

In between the magazines supported by official programs and those of independent origin were a number of periodicals published as the private ventures of members of the Nanking regime or persons associated with them. The various newspapers owned by the Japanese or the Nanking regime represented a number of cliques and became platforms for continuous mutual bickering. This was much less true of the literary periodicals that emerged following the outbreak of the Pacific War. Although it may be argued cynically that the politicians and civil servants, chiefly educators, who published or contributed to these magazines wrote to vindicate themselves as individuals as well as to find release from official life, there is little in the magazines' content which speaks in behalf of the regime and its programs. On the contrary, considerable disillusionment is evident, as will be discussed in greater detail in later chapters.

The first new magazine to appear, in March 1942, was *Ku chin* (Past and Present), a monthly devoted to nonfiction prose. The owner, Chu Hsing-chai (Chu P'u), formerly an editor for *Tung-fang tsa-chih* (Eastern Miscellany) and a vice-minister for communications in the Nanking regime, announced he was seeking some diversion from the current scene and hired the former editors of *Cosmic Wind II*, T'ao K'ang-te and Chou Li-an, to put the magazine together. It contained a number of contributions by leading members of the Nanking regime, including memoirs by Wang Ching-wei, Chou Fo-hai, and Ch'en Kung-po. Other writers and historians contributed familiar essays and antiquarian studies, and some later began their own periodicals. In 1943 *Feng-yü t'an* (Wind and Rain Chats) appeared, offering fiction and familiar essays under the editorship of T'ao K'ang-te and Liu Yü-sheng as part of their Pacific Bookstore (T'ai-p'ing Shu-chü), which also published a number of single-volume collections of essays and short fiction. The most successful of their contributors was Su Ch'ing (Feng Ho-i), a woman writer whose novel, *Chieh-hun shih-nien* (Ten Years of Marriage), was serialized in *Wind and Rain Chats* and attracted wide readership. She then became editor of *T'ien ti* (Heaven and Earth), a fortnightly largely modeled on *Past and Present* and reputedly backed by Ch'en Kung-po.[94] The success of *Heaven and Earth* begat *Hsiao t'ien ti* (Little Heaven and Earth), edited by Pan Kung (Chou Pan-hou), whose familiar essays and discussions of Western literature regularly appeared in the above magazines.

Larger in format and commercially more successful than any of these and similar periodicals was *Tsa-chih* (Miscellany), begun by Yuan Shu in 1938 as an organ of the Japanese-sponsored Asia Development and National Reconstruction movement (Hsing-ya Chien-kuo Yun-tung). Originally devoted to current events, by 1942 it was converted into a literary magazine, virtually devoid of politics and current events except for extensive reviews and gossip columns on literary activities in the interior. Yuan Shu and a co-editor, Lu Feng (Liu Mu-ch'ing), were reportedly Communist agents, and Yuan later served as a specialist on Japanese affairs in the foreign ministry of the People's Republic of China.[95]

The lack of attention to ideology became a source of embarrassment to the propaganda ministry, and the refusal of these magazines to accept articles from the ministry became a source of friction with the minister, Lin Po-sheng. When the journalist Chin Hsiung-pai applied for a license to publish his periodical *Hai pao* (Poster) which he intended as a respite from the political content of the two semi-official newspapers he edited for Chou Fo-hai, Lin Po-sheng was reluctant to grant permission. Lin suggested that there were enough such magazines on the market and agreed only after Chin used Chou Fo-hai's name to back his request.[96] An article by Su Ch'ing shows that smaller magazines, no matter what their connections, felt threatened by the government's paper-rationing policies, while publications with wealthier backing were allowed to circumvent the system by using the black market.[97] Another sign of displeasure from the propaganda ministry appears in an announcement in the magazine *Chung-lun* (Mass Forum) calling for "serious essays" to upgrade the quality of the magazines and to "establish a bright future for our nation."[98] However, publishing circles in Shanghai continued their uncooperative course. Even the newspapers showed no response, as one reviewer noted: "In the literary supplements of these important newspapers there is a common failing: works dealing with current events have been scarce, while as for essays of a militant, incisive nature, they are simply nonexistent."[99]

Satire of aspects of the regime did appear occasionally and received varied treatment from the authorities. P'ing Chin-ya began the general interest magazine *Phenomena* in July 1941, and after 1942 it became the best-selling periodical in Shanghai, with a circulation of 30,000 copies per month.[100] P'ing also experimented with satire in a subsidiary publication, *Wan-hsiang shih-jih k'an* (Phenomena Ten-Day Supplement) during 1942. Under the name Ch'iu Weng he managed to publish at least two caustic essays before the magazine was suspended and he was jailed for a month.[101] Nevertheless, he resumed writing and the name Ch'iu Weng appeared in a number of magazines. Chin Hsiung-pai records that in his contributions to

Chin's *Hai pao*, P'ing Chin-ya ridiculed every prominent figure in Shanghai, including Chin himself.[102] The first issue of the Japanese-owned *Literary Companion* reputedly contained an essay that resulted in its temporary suspension. The author took the well-known phrase "To starve to death is nothing; to surrender is grave," and reversed it in a satire of the Nanking regime to read: "To surrender is nothing; to starve to death is grave."[103] Whether or not this one was intended also to allude to serious food shortages in Shanghai, other quips dwelled on that issue more pointedly. In *Heaven and Earth* one writer styled himself The Book Eater (Ch'ih Shu-jen) and called for edible editions of published works. The works he recommended for publication in edible editions included *Mein Kampf*, the *Shen pao* (organ of the Japanese navy in Shanghai), and the "Ning-po maid's" *Ten Years of Marriage*, an unflattering reference to Su Ch'ing, the editor of *Heaven and Earth*, and her best-selling novel.[104] Chin Hsiung-pai recounted that in *Hai pao* proofreaders let slip a phrase reading "the bogus Manchoukuo puppet emperor Pu-i." Fearing the consequences, Chin enlisted the aid of Chou Fo-hai, who immediately arranged a dinner party:

> That evening there were few guests, but besides myself, the host and hostess, all were Japanese officers, among them the chief of police and the chief of the information bureau. During the party Chou appeared absorbed in casual conversation. Eventually, in an offhand manner, he brought up his friendship with me and added something about *Hai pao's* "special style." Naturally, while he had not uttered the least request for a favor, the Japanese understood the real reason they had been invited that evening. Unable to refuse Chou under the circumstances, they passed over the matter lightly, and we got through the issue peacefully.[105]

Although none of these examples of a common phenomenon are of literary importance in themselves, they do indicate the degree of latitude allowed publishers. Another show of independence in several magazines, such as *Phenomena* and *Spring and Autumn*, was the publishing of a quantity of short works by writers in the interior, from Chang Hen-shui to Pa Chin, Lao She, and Tsang K'o-chia. Finally, by the last year of the war, the Soviet consulate in Shanghai subsidized a monthly magazine called *Liu i* (Six Arts), which publicized the virtues of Stalin, Stalinism, and the bravery of resistance fighters against the Nazis.* Interspersed between the propaganda items were essays and fiction by writers hardly known for their appreciation of Stalinism, such as Stephen Soong (P'ang Kuan-ch'ing), Ting Ti, Chou Leng-ch'ieh, and Kikuchi Kan. This tactic of juxtaposing propaganda with works unrelated to the aims of propaganda was similar to that employed in the Japanese-sponsored literary magazines.[106]

As to serious, direct dissent with Japanese policies, the major effort was undertaken by Chou Tso-jen. Because of Chou's importance as a literary figure and his influence on other essayists, his work is given individual attention in a later chapter. When one looks for "underground" literary work during the Pacific War years, the only substantial pieces are the autobiographical polemics of Tsou T'ao-fen (Tsou En-jun) in *Huan-nan yü-sheng chi* (Final Years of Adversity). As head of Life Publishing Company (Sheng-huo Shu-tien), Tsou was an important figure in literary circles. Life's monthly publication at the time of the war, *Wen-i chen-ti* (Literary Front), was edited by Mao Tun, the leading communist writer outside Yenan, and Life published such authors as Kuo Mo-jo, Shen Ts'ung-wen, and Li Chien-wu. Tsou had left Shanghai in 1937 and remained in Hong Kong until its fall in 1942. From then on he was on the run, hunted by both Nationalists and Japanese, and finally appeared in Shanghai in early 1943 with a malignant brain tumor.

While underground workers arranged a false identity card and shifted him from one hospital to another, he worked on *Final Years of Adversity*. It is a tract detailing the incidents that necessitated his flight, his views on progressive culture, and the contributions made by Life Publishing Company. All was designed to support his deathbed request to be admitted to the Communist Party. It is interesting to note that Tsou wastes little time on the Japanese or the puppet regimes. Although Chou Tso-jen, in a conspicuous position in the North China Provisional Government, felt compelled to voice his dissent, for Tsou T'ao-fen and presumably his colleagues, the Japanese were no longer as vital an issue as the reactionary nature of

* *Six Arts* was by no means the only instrument of Soviet propaganda under the Japanese occupation. In addition to films, the Soviets published a news-oriented weekly magazine titled *The Epoch (Shih-tai)*.

the KMT. Tsou finally died in July 1944. The news of his death, however, was announced through sources in Chungking, and his presence in Shanghai was never discovered by the Japanese.[107]

The momentum built up by the modern drama movement in Shanghai was only temporarily broken by the occupation of the International Settlement, and by the summer of 1942 it was on its way to an unprecedented commercial boom. According to the playwright Ku Chung-i, censors could be bribed, and a number of plays alluding to the theme of resistance continued to be staged under new names.[108] Yao K'o's costume drama on the theme of treason, *Yuan-yang chien* (Twin Swords), was allowed to run for a month before censors telephoned to advise that the play be closed down. The most successful of the restaged productions was Wu Tsu-kuang's *Cheng-ch'i ko* (Song of Righteousness), revived in 1943 as *Wen T'ien-hsiang* without the name of the author, who was then in Chungking.[109]

The Nanking regime and its Japanese advisors attempted to get the acting companies to perform at official celebrations by threatening to disband the companies if they refused. The artists procrastinated for months at a time, with neither side wishing to force the issue. A showdown finally came in 1943, when the Japanese with great fanfare turned over the administration of the International Settlement to the Nanking regime. Given a nonnegotiable demand to perform in celebration of this event, members of the Shanghai Art Theater (Shanghai I-shu Chü-t'uan: SAT) traveled to Nanking and restaged an adaptation of Pa Chin's *Family*.[110] There were other ways in which the drama circle felt threatened, as is reflected in an anecdote by Yao K'o:

> What we really feared was not undisguised political persecution but the pup-
> pet bureaucrats' occasional manifestation of good will, which was far more dif-
> ficult to resist. For instance, the deputy chief of the secret police (No. 76 Yü
> Yuan Rd.), P'an Han-hsing, once came to the Paris Theater to see *Sport with
> the World* (*Yu-hsi jen-chien,* a sort of Congrevian comedy written by the
> talented Yang Chiang, wife of Ch'ien Chung-shu, and directed by me). P'an
> happened to like the performance so much that he extended a whimsical invita-
> tion to the entire K'u-kan Players to a banquet at his residence. It was such a
> bolt from the blue that we were at a loss what to do. If we should decline his
> invitation, he would doubtless regard it as a slap in the face and that would lead
> inevitably to unthinkable consequences. But for a group of the staunchest
> resistance theater workers to wine and dine at P'an's house—that was

absolutely out of the question. There seemed no way to wriggle ourselves out of this predicament. The only person who might be able to get us off the hook was Fei Mu, the director of the Shanghai I-shu Chü-t'uan [SAT] at the Carlton Theater. He was a born diplomat with a flair for squaring the circle. So I went to him for help. To make a long story short, he called on P'an and, believe it or not, actually succeeded in coaxing him to withdraw the invitation.[111]

In sum, the records indicate that while commercial theater in Shanghai was not given over to revivals of resistance dramas, the authorities, despite interference, were not concerned with prescribing the content of drama or its style.

Conclusions

A number of key issues, or potential issues, pertain to Japanese cultural policies and the literature that emerged during the occupation. These include language and style, cultural identity, attitudes and values to be expressed, and the notion of a literary renaissance.

The Japanese never showed signs of imposing on China the policies of "linguistic colonization" they had developed in Korea and Taiwan. There seems to have been little effort to train Chinese writers in Japanese, and many Japanese cultural workers seem to have shown little interest in learning Chinese. The Japanese did crush the Hsin-wen-tzu movement as a Communist activity. But there was no attempt to impose a standard dialect, to encourage the use of *wen-yen* over *pai-hua,* or vice versa. There is nothing in the language and style of occupation literature that suggests Japanese influence.

The Japanese were far more active in encouraging the notion of a common cultural identity between China and Japan and asserting that it had been disrupted by Western influence. The basis for such an appeal lay in Confucianism and common anti-Western sentiments. Occupation literature shows very little cultural identification with the Japanese. The essays that do discuss Japanese culture invariably contrast it with Chinese customs and attitudes, even in those cases where the writer urges China to take Japan as a model—for example, for discipline and courtesy in public situations. Neither can it be said that interest in Japanese culture displaced attention to

Western literature and culture. As to Confucianism, despite a deluge of propaganda on the subject, the most widely published writer to have declared himself a Confucian was Chou Tso-jen, and he spent much of his time dissenting from the kind of Confucianism purveyed by Japanese militarists. Aside from this fact, it must be noted that resistance literature drew heavily on Chinese traditions, and the KMT Provisional National Congress in April 1938 called for the elevation of Chinese traditional studies as well as modern scientific education. Hence, an appeal to traditions could never of itself be regarded as a basis for interpreting a work as serving Japanese policies. In the same vein, anti-Western sentiment was but a step away from antiforeign sentiment in general, and the Japanese appeal to despise the Americans and the British while accepting the Germans, the Italians, the French, and the Japanese themselves was artificial in the extreme. The point is that the invocation of themes already indigenous to China before the occupation were very rarely at the service of a notion of cultural affinity with Japan.

Japanese cultural workers showed considerable concern over the need for writers to express attitudes and values in a positive way, but the Japanese themselves did not formulate this concern in any coherent way. There was Yoshikawa's concern for sublimity, and Kataoka Teppei's arrogant confidence. There were strident editorials calling for war literature, and appeals by organizers to Chinese writers to show some "spirit." But the failure of functionaries to inject writers with a sense of joy, confidence, and militant mission is evident not only from a perusal of the contents of the literature, but from explicit statements by Japanese critics themselves.

If Japanese initiatives can be summarized in any ultimately coherent fashion, it would be to say that their activities were attempts to insert their goals into and exploit indigenous literary trends as they perceived them. But they had no inside track and relatively few cultural workers. Their primary mission was to revive literary activity in order to exploit it by converting it into propaganda. The activity was restored, but never seriously exploited. Hence they followed whatever was available and popular, from regional drama to American-style films. If local newspapers carried resistance literature, they would introduce "peace literature." If youth was a key to a popular literature, then there would be "new, progressive" writers to replace the "old, reactionary" writers of earlier decades. One propagandist saw the advent of the "literary renaissance" in the familiar essay, while another theorized it would come in a new wave of indigenous romanticism to replace the earlier, artificial romanticism borrowed from the West.[112] There were constant attempts to proclaim a program or a movement, and a few pieces to exemplify the slogan. But if the Japanese had not the means to impose official programs on many Japanese writers, they certainly did not have them for a thoroughgoing program in China.

When one turns to Japanese sources, there is in addition an evident lack of interest in and attention to literature in occupied China. Yoshikawa published the most substantial piece of criticism in Japan, and yet he was a scholar of traditional literature and paid little attention to contemporary events in China. Scholars of modern literature, such as Takeda Taijun and Takeuchi Yoshimi of the Chinese Literature Research Society (Chūgoku Bungaku Kenkyukai), has little sympathy for propaganda programs, let alone the entire war effort, and devoted their energies to well-known writers in the interior. Militant army propagandists such as Katatoka Teppei, a *tenkō* writer converted from communism to fascism, could hardly have been satisfied with the bourgeois makeup and uncertain sympathies of Chinese writers. The indifference of much of the Japanese literary establishment was summed up in the remarks of Uchiyama Kanzō that he was disappointed because there were no prestigious writers from China at the Greater East Asia Writers Congress.[113]

In the conception and execution of Japanese initiatives, it is difficult to see any inspiration for a literary renaissance. During the war, several Chinese writers made comments refuting the notion that anything like a renaissance existed. Yet, given a perspective they did not have then, one cannot but wonder whether they were not being too deliberately harsh in their appraisals.

Chou Tso-jen, in an essay titled "Wen-i fu-hsing chih meng" (The Dream of a Literary Renaissance), noted that the word for renaissance was imported from Japan and refers to the European Renaissance, which was not simply a literary phenomenon but a broad cultural movement, one that could hardly be hoped for in China under the circumstances, though it was certainly to be wished. In his most pointed remark, Chou states that although the Greek and Roman cultures which inspired the European Renaissance were long dead, the current influences in China "are backed by a flag." He cites the persistence in China of the old civil service mentality and the eight-legged essay style as further obstacles, and wonders whether there was not a need for the influence of more than just one foreign culture at a single point in history if a renaissance were to be effected.[114] But in dissenting from propaganda claims, Chou deliberately does not take into account the value of his own writing during the war, a period that was both prolific and in some ways dynamic for his work. Nor does he take into account his own endorsement of two experimenters with the familiar essay, Chi Kuo-an and Wen Tsai-tao, at a time when he saw only difficulties for the essayist and potential for drama and fiction.[115]

No Chinese writer during the war was more skeptical of and satirical about Chou Tso-jen than T'ang T'ao, the Shang-hai essayist. In 1943 T'ang wrote a caustic comment on the literary circle associated with Chu P'u's magazine, *Past and Present*. T'ang recalled Shen Ts'ung-wen's disgust with the Shanghai literary scene a decade before, when Shen had described Shanghai literature as the merger of "literary wits" and "commercial auctioneers." T'ang T'ao reflected that this was no longer adequate to describe the situation as of 1943. Businessmen, T'ang wrote, no longer engaged in auctioneering, but hoarded government-rationed goods, waiting for an opportunity to sell at inflated prices. As for the so-called Shanghai literary set, it was no more than a witless, nonliterary mahjong-and-opera clique (a reference to the contributors to *Past and Present*). So the Shanghai scene was really no more than "a cross-breed of spiders and centipedes."[116] Yet T'ang T'ao himself wrote and published under the occupation. One of the magazines he contributed to was *Phenomena,* edited by his close friend K'o Ling (Kao Chi-lin), who was also active as a playwright. Several of his scripts were staged during the war, one of them an adaptation of Gorky's *The Lower Depths* under the title *Yeh tien* (The Night Inn). Written in collaboration with Shih T'o (Wang Ch'ang-chien), another regular contributor to *Phenomena,* the play was published in that magazine in 1944 and went on to a production at the end of the war which received accolades from leftist writers returning from the interior.

A third commentator, equally removed from Chou Tso-jen and T'ang T'ao, was Hu Lan-ch'eng, a propagandist for the Nanking regime who in the last years of the war left government service for private ventures in publishing and journalism and wrote a number of essays on contemporary literature. One of his articles, "Luan-shih wen-t-an" (Wartime Literature) reflects his flair for lively criticism:

> Since the start of the war the writers in Shanghai have been under pressure. When asked why they don't write, they either say they are hindered by the environment, X X X X X X X X X X X X X X X X X X X X X X X X X X X X X X X X X X X X X X X X Or they say that works can only be produced when one can think clearly. The present being as it is X X X, they can only lay down the pen. The expressions on their faces are truly bitter and strained.
>
> They are like common, mediocre artists. When such an artist portrays the seasons, he inevitably uses the plum blossom, orchid, bamboo, or chrysanthemum as his subjects. Good works, however, need not be politically pointed. The statement that circumstances in Shanghai are not good is valid. Yet, neither Chungking nor Yenan has produced really good works, although there have been some fine-sounding titles, such as *Steppes of the Korchin Banner.*[117] Otherwise, they have resorted to reprinting translations of Turgenev's fiction. In Turgenev's fiction there are no wars of resistance, no peasant uprisings, nothing more than love stories; and yet, they contain things which are much more thought-provoking than the likes of *Steppes of the Korchin Banner.*
>
> As for the statement that there cannot be literature in a time of upheaval and confusion, this is a mere pretext. In any kind of disturbed environment individuals may stumble and fall, but mankind does not, and thus it is able to continue on into future generations. However, in such difficult circumstances, there is depravity and a loss of tranquillity. This depravity is not manifested in unruliness, but is manifested rather in quickly yielding to disruption. Therefore, those who equate art with tranquillity do not produce anything. Those who equate art with flag waving and shouting also do not produce anything.
>
> Now the writers for *Les Contemporains* magazine have fallen silent, and the reportage literature of leftist writers is without an audience. Poverty and lack of leisure time are reasons. X X X is also a reason. But these are not the chief reasons. Currently there is only a renewed flood of the shallow love stories of the Mandarin Duck and Butterfly school. Yet the style has changed, and the quality of even this has dropped as people no longer have patience for the sentimental, and all that is left over is frank passion. The *Lun-yü* magazine clique has gone overseas to entertain Americans [Lin Yü-t'ang and Hsü Yü]. Naturally, some of them are still in Shanghai or the interior. But the stately gowns of these ridiculous gentlemen have been stripped off, and they have become the butt of ridicule in the mosquito press. Just so, their productivity has fallen off. The times want simplicity. It is an evanescent thing.[118]

Hu's remarks are quoted at length because they capture so well the atmosphere of stagnation that marked much literary activity after the productivity of the thirties and the fate of so many of the cliques and trends of the previous decade. And yet, he has exaggerated for effect, and his eye for large movements failed to account for the wartime theater boom and overlooked such individual writers as Ch'ien Chung-shu, who did not publish until after the war, and Chang Ai-ling, for whose work Hu had unbounded admiration and whom he took as his wife.

His remarks have an odd echo of others made by his polar opposite in Yenan, Chou Yang, who stated in 1941:

> In Yenan some friends interested in creative writing have felt that they cannot write anything any more. But the life we have here is a new, meaningful life, and creation here is free. Then why the cessation of creative activity, why is so little written?[119]

Yenan, one might well argue, was not so sterile as Chou portrayed it. Hu made no pretense that creation in occupied China was free. Despite the lack of freedom, there was no lack of creativity. Nowhere in China was the time right for a literary renaissance, for the challenges to writers everywhere were new and threatening. In occupied China the literary generals had left, and near-anarchy reigned on the literary field as writers sought to embody the tastes of the times and struggled for autonomy.

The coming of war dealt a blow to the Peking literary scene from which it never recovered. For the most part, writers continued in a rather uninspired fashion the literary trends of previous years. Although without depth of characterization, Ma Li's *T'ai-p'ing yuan* (Prayer for Peace) is perhaps most representative of the continued work in regional literature (*ti-fang wen-hsüeh*) presided over by Shen Ts'ung-wen prior to the war, and offers some well-observed details of peasant life, portraying peasants quarreling at each others' expense while remaining subservient to corrupt officials.[120] Orientations to Western literature continued as well, but with little achievement. The French-educated playwright and director Ch'en Mien squandered his wit on adaptations of minor European plays and buried his potential in an opium habit.[121] The most notable literary work in Peking was undertaken by Chou Tso-jen and Wu Hsing-hua. Chou was influential throughout occupied China, while Wu brought the only substantial developments to Chinese poetry among occupation writers. By contrast, Shanghai, if not the site of a literary renaissance, was the center of literary activity and developments under the occupation, as well as the major publishing center.

CHAPTER TWO

The Decline of May Fourth Romanticism

In the early decades of the twentieth century, and particularly in the twenties, a new literature developed that was sometimes realistic in form, but infused by a sense of romanticism on the part of the authors, expressed in their ideals and their bohemian behavior. There was a heightened concern with the self, whether in celebration of its prowess or dwelling on its sensibilities. There was, against the bulk of traditional thought, a new belief in the self and an insistence that the liberation of the individual and the fulfillment of emotions were paramount considerations in the reformation of Chinese society. The potential of the self was idealized and its needs were affirmed.

Later in the twenties and during the thirties, developments in politics added a new dimension and new directions to this romantic literature of the May Fourth Period. As one critic has noted of this time: "Subjective emotionalism takes a leftward turn, and the role of the writer in relation to society undergoes agonizing reappraisal. Now young women are in suicidal despair because revolutionary experiences can be as disillusioning as love."[1] This shift is in some ways typified in the observation about Ting Ling's work that "her early feminist semi-autobiographical stories, with their overtones of Bohemia and anarchism, expressed the evolving consciousness of a young woman reaching for a liberated life style. Then revolution appears as the vaguely romantic alternative to sexual love."[2]

This new "vaguely romantic" affirmation of revolution appeared in various works for which the critic Leo O. Lee has used the term "leftism." Lee, more than anyone else, has developed a critical appreciation of romantic writing in modern China and analyzed its decline.[3] Much of what he found romantic in early twentieth-century Chinese literature has its roots in topics generally associated with Western romanticism. What in Western romanticism was deemed a fascination for "strangeness in beauty," for the bizarre, is seen among Chinese writers as a penchant for *étrangerié,* for the employment of foreign words, and strikingly Bohemian gestures and behavior usually learned from the West. The glorification of the commonplace, which Western romantics had often coupled with the cult of strangeness to upset the literary world, developed among Chinese writers as a strong tendency to idealization and the liberal use of abstractions to enhance their interpretation of rather mundane experience and their precarious place in Chinese society. Further, the free play of feelings and their preeminent place in literature emphasized by romantics compares with the emotionalism of modern Chinese romantic writers, some of whom vowed to commit themselves to "a life of emotions." To be sure, sentimentality is readily available in traditional literature; but the modern romantics were, after all, committed to their explorations of love and revolution as forces for social change, and it is this dynamic quality in their emotionalism that Lee has seen as novel. Above all, the romantic writer was concerned, in the radical individualism he wanted for his life and his work, with the image of the person of extraordinary sensitivity. He might be an iconoclastic hero in the tradition of Prometheus, or one abandoned to passions in the mold of Dionysus, or even a passive, sentimental young Werther, too sensitive for the vulgar world.

When the decline in romantic writing came, there was still a carryover into the new literature of leftism. The emotionalism, the idealization and abstractions, flowed into newer currents, and if the hero was to be more the Promethean type, conflicts of love and duty still complicated his life. Thus, the composite of elements that made for a romantic literature were breaking up to be reformed. By wartime, the decline in romantic writing that meets the criteria discussed above is so sharp that it is more valuable to discuss certain works in relation to romanticism, rather then to argue for a definition of them as absolutely romantic in themselves.

Essayists in the Style of Lu Hsün

The writers moving to the interior may have felt for a time committed to a tide of unified resistance against the Japanese. But those committed to resistance in Shanghai felt they were spokesmen against a rising tide of appeasement and compromise with the enemy that only added to the spectrum of sins, from venality to complacency, which had always characterized Shanghai in the eyes of writers. The foreign concessions became known as "orphan island" and "fool's paradise." Pa Chin, living as a recluse in the French Concession, called Shanghai "the Chinese Rome," and finally left for the interior in 1940.[4]

Writers more committed to Shanghai were hired by foreign-owned newspapers in 1936–1937 to write *tsa-wen,* topical and polemical essays in the style of Lu Hsün, both to continue a fashion Lu Hsün had made popular and to answer a need for patriotic writing. Of the seven principal writers to take up this form, only two, T'ang T'ao and Chou Mu-chai, were practiced hands. Of the others, K'ung Ling-ching and K'o Ling had been writing essays in other styles; Chou Li-an, as a follower of Lin Yü-t'ang, had been championing the Ming and Ch'ing essayists; and Wen Tsai-tao was silently immersing himself in Six Dynasties writers.[5] Finally, Wang Jen-shu (Pa Jen) had been primarily concerned with writing fiction, and by his own account wrote his first *tsa-wen* on the occasion of Maxim Gorki's death in 1936. This was followed by a good offer to write steadily for a newspaper, an offer Pa Jen took. He went on to write the major study of Lu Hsün's essays at the time, *Lun Lu Hsün ti tsa-wen* (1940) (On Lu Hsün's *Tsa-wen*).[6]

Basically, interest in the *tsa-wen,* or *tsa-kan,* was not inherently inimical to artistic values or insightful expression. While generally limited to from one thousand to fifteen hundred characters, it provided a prose model through which writers could attempt to discipline their art. Most of the Shanghai writers proved unequal to the task, and the form frequently degenerated into nothing more than straight cultural reportage with a rhetorical flourish, little subtlety, and much moralizing. Moreover, these writers were clearly given, far more than Lu Hsün, to positive, eulogistic statements. Although these were to serve the cause of "progressive culture," there was never a discussion of its form or elements, but rather allusions to its existence in philosophical works, the essays of Lu Hsün, or in the future. It is in this positive aspect of *tsa-wen* writing that the imprint of romanticism leaves its mark, as will be seen.

Prior to the war, agents under the KMT journalist P'an Kung-chan had attempted to disrupt the trend to *tsa-wen* writing. After the retreat of Chinese forces, pressure against the *tsa-wen* writers came not only from authorities, but from Communist critics as well. Ch'ien Hsing-ts'un had for a decade been a critic of Lu Hsün. Now, while admitting that Lu Hsün's essays had served a purpose in the past, he called on writers to transcend this past. Arguing the policy of the United Front, Ch'ien especially criticized the *tsa-wen* writers for their continued satire of other Chinese who were also resisting the Japanese, and for imitating rather than being creative.[7] Ch'ien's arguments were by no means decisive. The fact that most of the *tsa-wen* writers were from eastern Chekiang perhaps aided their temporary sense of solidarity, and together they put out two collections of their *tsa-wen, Pien ku chi* (Border Drums, 1938) and *Heng mei chi* (Angry Eyebrows, 1939) and collaborated on a monthly magazine, *Lu Hsün feng* (The Lu Hsün Current), together with Hsü Kuang-p'ing and others. It was a slim publication that lasted only from January to September 1939. But pressure from the authorities forced the writers to tone down their work, so much so that publishers became discouraged or frightened. In June 1941 K'o Ling complained that although Chungking had forbidden reference to Lu Hsün as a "revolutionary fighter," the Shanghai *Cheng-yen pao* (Truth Herald) forbade the use of Lu Hsün's name altogether in its literary supplement (*Ts'ao yuan*), which K'o Ling edited for a time.[8] Despite a brief revival in late 1941, the *tsa-wen* movement had spent itself by 1940.[9]

Artistically, the *tsa-wen* writers had but mediocre success. Pa Jen himself had been concerned with the caliber of the *tsa-wen* as an art form, and in 1940 he admitted that the efforts of *The Lu Hsün Current* group "had not raised the substance of the *tsa-wen*," concluding that "on the whole, it rather seems that the potency of the *tsa-wen* has indeed been killed off."[10] The attitudes of the various writers toward the question of artistic value were different, and sometimes left them in the position of defending the "eight-legged resistance writing (*k'ang-chan pa-ku*)." This term was never strictly defined, but it was widely used to deride and to complain about the commanding position of writings devoted to slogans and pro-war rhetoric at the expense of any other consideration. It was a formula for writing like the eight-legged essay in the Ch'ing Dynasty. Chou Li-an, for example, devoted several essays to this topic, arguing that even if writing on the war had become cliché-ridden, as long as the artist's standpoint was grounded in the idea of resistance, it was meritorious, unsullied work.[11]

Thus, the writers of *tsa-wen* spent much ink defending Lu Hsün's style, the need for satire, and the need for repeating worn themes; castigating Liang Shih-ch'iu; and pondering the actions of Chou Tso-jen. There was also plenty of attention paid to the cultural scene in Shanghai: women's liberation, exploitation, philistinism (*shih-k'uei chu-i*), collaboration with the enemy, and the absurdities of enemy propaganda. Many of Lu Hsün's techniques were incorporated: short play scripts, commentaries on traditional theater to express "progressive" ideas, literary allusions, ironic observations, cool dissection and passionate invective, the slow build and the quick kill. But these techniques, which could be imitated, were too often vitiated by a clumsiness and a lack of subtlety.

Two of the most successful *tsa-wen* writers were K'o Ling and T'ang T'ao. K'o Ling's work is often saved by sheer animation and occasional concrete vividness. A fair example of this, and of his infatuation with rhetoric, occurs in a description of an episode with a rickshaw puller K'o Ling had hired:

> Suddenly I had a charitable thought, and I felt exhausted for him.
> "Pull a bit slower," I said, drumming the footboard with my foot.

"What?" He turned his head, gave me a glare, and then pulled as fast as
ever. I thought he hadn't heard me clearly, and with a surge of
compassion, said, "You can pull slowly." "What?" Unexpectedly he
stopped suddenly, gave the rickshaw a kick, and demanded fiercely, "This
isn't fast enough?"

I knew he had misunderstood me, and it was a misunderstanding I had
no way of explaining. So I said nothing more, but just let him pull faster.
. . . "This isn't fast enough?"—The angry eyes and slanted eyebrows
indeed were an expression that he hadn't forgotten his place.[12]

At this point K'o Ling plunges into an impassioned explanation, lest
the reader be left to his own devices to ponder with amusement the
embarrassment of the young intellectual following in Lu Hsün's foot-
steps:

Slaves don't look for mercy from their masters. The oppressed never
want mercy from their oppressors, no matter whether consciously or
unconsciously. For these truly are invisible cangues and shackles. Between
me and the enemy there is only the difference of victory and defeat. There
is nothing to be said of kindness and malice. This is the true principle of
all those who struggle for freedom and liberation!

The themes and terms the *tsa-wen* writers chose almost inevitably
overlapped. K'o Ling in July 1939 wrote "Wu-sheng ti Shanghai,"
(Silent Shanghai), an obvious allusion to Lu Hsün's "Wu-sheng ti
Chung-kuo" (Silent China). K'o Ling's essay, however, describes the
silence that dominates a battlefield during a lull in the fighting. Now,
like the droning of flies and mosquitoes, the hawkers for peace spread
their shameless slanders and lascivious lies. But they are not the
sounds of men, and silence does not betoken defeat: "In the dark
night, the sounds of the city subside, and all is quiet. Yet, indeed, this
is in preparation for the activity of the day."[13] Similarly, T'ang T'ao
in July 1938 had written "Hai shih ch'ien-hsien" (Still the Front
Line) to reinforce the notion of resistance even after the departure of
Chinese forces the year before. But T'ang characteristically shows off
his erudition: his allusion is to the legend of Cadmus founding the
city of Thebes with warriors sprung from seeded dragon's teeth. Just
so, T'ang claimed, Shanghai is in a period of being sown with
dragon's teeth, and from them a new city will arise.[12]

If such rhetoric sounds forced, T'ang was capable of better writing.
One of his more elaborate manipulations of allusions is the essay

"Ch'ou" (December 1940) (Clown). He notes the arrival in Shang-hai of the "Kings of Clowns," Yeh Sheng-chang, and recalls how much talent is needed by clowns and singers, mimers and acrobats, in plays in which they take leading roles. Moving from a leisurely dis-cussion of this topic, T'ang takes up current events in the news-papers, from which he can see that collaborators, like clowns, covertly accept their master's wishes, but only to a certain point. They appear in person to accept their "feed," but do not always really listen to orders; they put a mask of sincerity and propriety over their buffoonery. These are the clown's special characteristics, since clowns must convince people that clowns are heroes and men of ability. But their marvelous talent lies in covering the traces of their antics. The agreement announced in the newspapers of the Nanking regime to recognize the "autonomy" of Manchoukuo reminds one of the Gogol character who lost his nose. That fellow put a hand-kerchief to his face and pretended to have a cold to conceal what he had lost. The political clowns of China have not caught cold; althought their voices are muffled, their words are clear. They have instead daubed on a little more white powder to cover up the place where their noses ought to be.[15]

T'ang's essays are rarely very penetrating as social commentary or perceptive as literary criticism, but in works like "Clown" there is a delicious meandering as he constructs his analogies and builds to his clever portrait of the Nanking regime. T'ang's wit could be quite crude. In "Liang chung lien-p'u" (Two Types of Masks), an image Lu Hsün enjoyed as well, T'ang described two types of writers for puppet government publications. The concoctions of one group, which claimed to be writing "pure literature," actually had a dash of the "aroma of politics." As for the other group, which promoted the tradition of literature as the "decorative vase" to serve the utilitarian purposes of government, T'ang remarked that they had converted the vase into a chamberpot.[16]

Though one of the most adroit essayists of the period, T'ang's work sometimes suffered from an affliction common to other writers who enjoyed stringing together allusions and quotations: the source material reads far better than the text into which it is introduced. For example, none of T'ang's own works match the caustic pithiness of a *shih* poem he borrowed to satirize Chou Tso-jen. The poem had been written by the Ch'ing dynasty scholar-playwright Chiang T'iao-sheng to ridicule Ch'en Mei-kung, who sought official appointment through the pretense of being a sage recluse. To T'ang T'ao, Chou Tso-jen's vow to live as a recluse under enemy occupation was only a prelude to his accepting a post in the puppet government in Peking. Chiang T'iao-sheng's poem reads:

> Strutting in mountain and grove with his grand airs,
> A petty connoisseur with pretensions to refinement,
> He disdains the quick path to the capital.
> A recluse boasting for all he's worth,
> He pads his work with learned allusions.
> A fly hums above the steam from the cooking cauldrons of the elite.
> It flies as if it were a stork among the clouds,
> Flitting in and out of the prime minister's mansion.[17]

Behind this acerbity was an impatient idealism and an almost religious attitude toward writing *tsa-wen*. Lu Hsün, seen as a brave, lonely, and outspoken fighter, provided T'ang not only with a model for his art, but also with a way of life. In the essay "Ts'ung tsa-wen te-tao i-chiao" (The Legacy of Tsa-wen), T'ang stressed the need to lead "a serious life" for composing *tsa-wen*, for "if you stand in the water, you can't criticize the mud." He continued:

> Lu Hsün fought tenaciously and wrestled against the spirit of falsehood, and this he accomplished by altogether unsullied conduct. Throughout his life there was nothing he did that he could not tell, nothing that he would hide. With a clear sense of right and wrong, he loved and hated intensely, laughing and cursing openly and candidly. Even though those ghouls emerging from the old society never stopped hoping to drag him into the mud . . . yet he pressed on, fixed rigidly, and they could not bend a hair on his body! "Trample down the barbed wire!" "Stride forward over the slain!" . . . Such spirit, expressed in his *tsa-wen*, is firm, pungent, released, and unbound. The casting of his imagery, the timeliness of his examples, the care with which he created his sentences, the perceptiveness with which he chose his words, all these have determined more or less the artistic quality of his writing, expressed his political stand through artistic form; and at the same time, they show how the ultimate entrance of this style through the great gate of the garden of literature has been chiefly due to Lu Hsün.[18]

Nowhere else does T'ang more clearly indicate the fundamentally romantic vision he cherished: Lu Hsün, the superior man, the hero of unconventional ideals, passionately committed to freeing the spirit of men from classical shackles, and creating a new literary form to embody his purpose. T'ang's *tsa-wen* also show the same bent on the relatively few occasions when he discusses other literary influences. In fact, he was indifferent to classical satire such as *Gulliver's Travels.*[19] It is the Marxist vision of *Don Quixote,* the man of justice who "risked himself for the masses," that inspired him.[20] It was not Columbus's bumbling explorations, but the assassination of Caesar in Shakespeare's drama that touched his soul.[21]

Unlike his colleagues, T'ang T'ao continued to write satiric *tsa-wen* throughout the war. But not all his essays display the aggressiveness of the *tsa-wen* artist. During the early years of the war, he suffered a severe personal crisis when two of his three young children and his wife died after prolonged illness. He described these events vividly in a tortured essay, "Wo yao t'ao-pi" ("I Want to Escape"), published in the March 1940 issue of *Cosmic Wind II.*[22] In the essay, he blames himself for neglecting his family for the idea that "society comes first." He eulogizes the self-sacrifice of his wife and her encouragement, displayed throughout the trying period of the battle of Shanghai, and their resettlement beyond the immediate reach of Japanese authorities. In recounting the details of the irreversible course of his wife's tuberculosis, he reveals just that sense of helplessness and vulnerability which finds no place in his polemical *tsa-wen.* Moreover, he shows an eye for detail in this work that is virtually absent in his other essays, including a vivid passage on his wife's last moments of massive hemorrhaging and his vain pleading with a physician to shorten the agony of his child in the last stages of tubercular meningitis. But, withal, T'ang T'ao nowhere showed the introspection of a Lu Hsün, and it may well be that these experiences reconfirmed his commitment as a gadfly of the Shanghai cultural scene.

The major part of T'ang's efforts after the occupation of the foreign concessions went into exploring a more lyric mode of essay. Several such pieces were published in the magazine *Wan-hsiang* (Phenomena) under the pen name Jo Ssu, and later collected in the postwar volume *Lo fan chi* (Furled Sail). In large part they appear derived from Lu Hsün's prose-poems in *Yeh ts'ao* (Wild Grass). But the differences can be easily stated. T'ang T'ao's settings and characters are exotic, mythic, even surreal, but he does not give them a framework, such as Lu Hsün's dream frame. T'ang's diction as well as some of his figurative language is more elaborate than Lu Hsün's. Finally, he is invariably committed to a clear, unambiguous statement of hope, optimism, or faith, some sense of the sublime that Lu Hsün does not hold out in the disturbing *Wild Grass* pieces. For example, one may compare two autumn meditations, Lu Hsün's "The Blighted Leaf" and T'ang T'ao's "From Spring into Autumn." Lu Hsün's piece is inspired by the discovery of a dried maple leaf pressed against the pages of a book of poems from the Yuan dynasty. The essay is very brief; Lu Hsün has a sensation of time passing so quickly that he cannot retain even any memory or appreciation of the past as it rushes on from season to season, carrying him into old age before he is aware of it. The discovery of the leaf embodies Lu Hsün's experience of discovering his relationship with time and nature, and the essay develops the related sensation of powerful motion beneath apparent stillness and limpidity. T'ang T'ao's essay presents a fairyland where flower petals fall continuously the whole year through, a bittersweet setting that evokes in the mind of the writer quotations from Goethe, Byron, and Juan Chi. Introducing the contrast of autumn, T'ang seems to be alluding both to his advancing years and his deceased wife. Finally, in a sunset scene, his child picks a flower; the narrator, meditating on his advanced age, inadvertently says. "You've plucked a spring." From his slip of the tongue the narrator takes heart. Although both writers were preoccupied with youth, T'ang is more determined to assert unambiguously its positive influence.

His essays offer fragmented fantasies with a jumble of statements. They are a deliberate abandonment of the rational framework and order of the *tsa-wen,* constructed primarily on contrast and conflict of oppressive solitude, darkness, lassitude, and cynical nihilism with strength of purpose, youth, light, and "dynamism." In each work the writer argues the triumph of the latter qualities, but it is his extended portrait of the nightmarish experience of the former that dominates the essays nonetheless.

"She" (Abandonment) recounts the trials of Prometheus, chained to a mountain and forced to undergo the temptations of fairy women, the reasoning of Hermes, and the torments of Zeus's dog, all in a vain attempt to force him to recant his having given fire to man. Although this is the most direct allusion to romantic motifs, all the essays convey the same urge to break out from an emotionally stultifying predicament and reassert moral absolutes and emotional dynamism. Whereas Lu Hsün's essays invariably stop short of any romantic resolution, in T'ang T'ao's the need to express a positive affirmation of life emerges in just those heroic, absolute terms that define the promethean strain of romanticism. These prose-poems do not add significantly to T'ang's stature as an essayist. On the other hand, Prometheus bound is probably as apt an image as any to describe the psyche of progressive writers under the Japanese occupation.

T'ang's output as an essayist during the Pacific War years was not large, and he continued to support himself as a post office employee. K'o Ling was much more active as an editor and playwright. Before 1942, he edited the literary supplements of *Wen-hui pao* and *Cheng-yen pao* and the short-lived magazine *Min-tsu hu-sheng* (Nation's Outcry). From 1943 to 1945 he edited *Phenomena* and, having written advertising copy for the Star Motion Picture Company prior to the war, began writing and reviewing scripts for K'u Kan Players. Most of his plays, such as *P'iao* from *Gone With the Wind* and *Ta-ti hui-ch'un* (The Return of Spring), met with little critical or commercial success, but his collaboration with Shih T'o on *Yeh tien* (The Night Inn), based on Gorky's *The Lower Depths,* was well received, although the primary burden of reinterpreting the play fell on Shih T'o, who wrote the last two acts. After the war T'ang T'ao and K'o Ling together edited *Chou pao,* a weekly magazine on current affairs, and thereafter continued their careers in The People's Republic.

Lu Hsün's image, it must be said, was not ignored during the Pacific War years. After the fall of the International Settlement, several appreciations of him appeared in the *Chung-hua jih-pao* (Central China Daily News), the official newspaper of the Wang Ching-wei regime. While Mao Tse-tung claimed him as a cultural hero, the Japanese commissioned Dazai Osamu to write an account of Lu Hsün's student days in Japan. Nor was T'ang T'ao alone in his attempts to experiment with the prose-poems of Lu Hsün. Another writer familiar to Shanghai readers, T'an Cheng-pi, wrote a series of essays (or prose-poems) titled "Ni Yeh-ts'ao" (In Imitation of *Wild Grass*).

T'an Cheng-pi, like Lu Hsün, was preoccupied with youth; like T'ang T'ao, he felt committed to the positive affirmation of ideals. His "Lo yeh" (Fallen Leaves) provides a convenient point of comparison with Lu Hsün's "Blighted Leaf" and T'ang T'ao's "From Spring into Autumn." T'an wrote that after three days of depressing rain, he took to the park with his child like a bird released from its cage. As the boy examined the wet leaves, which no artist could match, he grew sad over their evanescence. When he told the boy of his feelings, of the leaves as reminders of the beauty of life that inevitably decayed, the boy responded: "You always tell us to move forward, move forward, move forward bravely. Don't look back! So why do you then insist on looking back?"[23] The boy argued that the leaves, in sacrificing their own beauty and making way for new life, had their own glory. T'an concluded that he was still depressed, but only because his son's mentality had outstripped his own: "I want to be a child myself!" T'an Cheng-pi thus exposes his sentimentality and repeats the themes of transience and the reliance on children to stave off the dread that Lu Hsün and T'ang T'ao had expressed.

T'an reserved special sentiment for a young woman who had comforted him. As he explained in one essay, his seventh and most recent child died when only a few weeks old because of his wife's malnutrition, the general shortage of food, and his continued absence from home at various jobs. He complained of fistulas, melancholia, neurotic symptoms of fatigue, heart palpitations, and failing eyesight. He was depressed that he was just a "superfluous man" rearing children who would also just suffer through life. However, a young woman who was one of his students introduced him to an acupuncturist and herself proffered such care and sympathy that T'an's faith in life was restored.[24] Some of T'an's subsequent prose-poems seem designed as eulogies of this young woman. "K'u yang" (Withered Willow), for instance, tells of a decaying tree succumbing to the elements, saved by "Angel." Angel rejuvenates the tree, which weeps to hear rumors that Angel has fallen in love with him and wants only, then, to return to being a rotting tree. But Angel steadfastly refutes the ugly rumors, restoring the tree, proving her platonic purity, and returning to heaven.[25] In another prose-poem, "I-ko yung-shih" (A Brave Warrior), T'an recounts that he found a true heroine: "She wore a crownless crown, an armorless armor, wielding a weaponless weapon." T'an has her confront and vanquish the challenges of various skeptics who think to end her image of purity. Having proved her purity, she then confounds the accusation that she is simply cold and passionless by reaching into her chest and producing her heart, which bursts aflame: "The flame burned even more into each person's heart, inciting the flame in each person's heart, and the blood spread through each person's soul."[26]

Besides such personal affirmations, T'an wrote parables and allegories on topical issues. He took a progressive stand against authoritarianism, and for the value of the sciences and Western literature. Unfortunately, these pieces all resort to the same simplistic style and thought, reducing the already oversimplified contrasts in Lu Hsün's prose-poems to naive didacticism. In the letters addressed to his son that accompany the prose-poems, T'an reveals that they are exercises to help restore his morale and recover his mental health. For that reason, they may be appreciated. Unfortunately, as literature they are disappointing, especially for a man who contributed several studies of literary history and appreciation that are of value.

A number of writers seem prone to revealing trying episodes in their lives, always, like T'an Cheng-pi and T'ang T'ao, admitting to a flaw or weakness, but one that is mitigated somehow in a final justification of the course their lives have taken. One was the essayist and novelist Su Ch'ing, who rose to considerable popularity during the Pacific War years in Shanghai.

Su Ch'ing (Feng Ho-i)

Su Ch'ing began writing under her own name, Feng Ho-i, for *Lun-yü* magazine in 1935 and subsequently became a regular contributor to Lin Yü-t'ang publications. Following the Japanese occupation of the International Settlement, she continued to publish her familiar essays in the magazines begun by other former writers for Lin Yü-t'ang publications. By 1943 she was successful enough to begin editing a fortnightly, *Heaven and Earth*. Her two most representative works are "T'ao" (Swelling Wave), an autobiographical essay, and *Chieh-hun shih-nien* (Ten Years of Marriage), a quasi-autobiographical novel. The novel and the essay were both fuel to the fires of the women's movement, and each portrays a lonely but morally triumphant defiance of convention. Although there is nothing in this introduction to distinguish these works from those previously written by other women, there are important differences. It is only necessary to recall the work of Lin Yü-t'ang's earlier protégé, Hsieh Ping-ying, author of *I-ko nü-ping ti tzu-chuan* (Autobiography of a Woman Soldier) to see that in the presentation of the heroines and the development of themes, the contrasts between Hsieh Ping-ying and Su Ch'ing are as important as what they have in common.

Hsieh Ping-ying first attracted widespread attention and the encouragement of Lin Yü-t'ang in the late twenties with her autobiographical account of her radical, romantic youth, expanded and republished early in the Sino-Japanese War as the *Autobiography of a Woman Soldier*. The book deals with a tomboy who begins her revolt by threatening to starve herself to death when her mother tries to bind her feet, and then goes on to missionary school, where she writes anti-imperialist essays, becomes an atheist and activist, and develops ambitions to become a great writer. She volunteers to join the Nationalist Army during the Northern Expedition, serves in the infantry, and finally goes into hiding during the purge of the left wing. Returning home, she is confined by her parents to her room until she submits to an arranged marriage. Contemptuous of her husband's submissiveness toward the older generation, she runs away to a series of adventures among radicals in various cities.

Su Ch'ing's essay "Swelling Wave" also shows her to have been an active student, by no means untouched by the social upheavals into which Hsieh Ping-ying plunged. Nevertheless, "Swelling Wave" presents, through character and circumstance, a vision of life less romantically inclined than that of the older Hsieh Ping-ying. Hsieh was nearing maturity when the Northern Expedition got underway, and the radical movement was at its height. Su Ch'ing, on the other hand, recounts that she was still but twelve *sui* "on the eve of the storm." At that time coeducation was undreamed of, and Su Ch'ing also had to be advised by the principal of the school not to display too much curiosity about an older girl expelled for joining the KMT. When the KMT did arrive, the girls showed their rebelliousness by cutting their hair in bobs. But when the school was converted into a coeducational institution, Su Ch'ing's guardian, her grandfather, despite his sympathy with many progressive ideas, balked at the new slogans of free love and Communist controversy and kept Su Ch'ing from returning. Soon a purge of Communists took place, an event that touched Su Ch'ing's life only as a series of rumors concerning martyred teachers and venal officials.

When the school was once again converted to an all-girls institution, Su Ch'ing returned, plunging into KMT activities as a student speaker at local rallies and briefly attracting the advances of an older KMT officer. Moreover, when the girls insisted on joining in a local Double-Ten Day rally, they were pinched and leered at by rowdies in the streets and forced to retire from the demonstration. Su Ch'ing lost little of her taste for activism, but gained a new skepticism with it, admitting that "this society has really been unable to modernize and develop."[27] Such feelings inspired a deep sense of loyalty on the part of Su Ch'ing and her friends toward a young teacher of history who defied school policy by lecturing on current, controversial events, and who, it was discovered, was putting his lover through college to the neglect of treatment for his bleeding ulcer. As his condition worsened, the faculty ignored him and prohibited the students from doing anything for him. The teacher succumbed finally, and Su Ch'ing then led a student attack on the hypocrisy and callousness of the faculty, for which she was expelled.

The style of "Swelling Wave" is relatively simple and straightforward, and its contents are given at some length to show that, despite similar feelings for the shortcomings of society and a good deal of impetuosity in confronting them, the two women's resolutions were considerably different. Su Ch'ing's essay ends on a minor key of reflection and skepticism: the social movements and upheavals, the "swelling wave" has washed her up on a dry shore and departed, leaving her still not yet mature and yet stripped of that road to maturity taken by Hsieh Ping-Ying's generation.

Su Ch'ing's *Ten Years of Marriage* was first published serially in the monthly magazine *Feng-yü t'an* (Wind and Rain Chats) during 1943 and subsequently went through twelve printings in book form by 1945, as well as several thereafter, making it the most popular novel to appear at that time. It portrays a set of circumstances leading to divorce, but the story supports the theme that women in such circumstances need not fear divorce as a last resort. Su Ch'ing was herself a divorcée, and her novel was widely regarded as an autobiography. This is not surprising, for the book is also an outgrowth of previous essays,[28] yet the heroine of the novel, named Su, is not to be equated altogether with Su Ch'ing herself. Rather, she is a character designed primarily to portray the naiveté and longings of an ordinary girl in regard to sex and love, and endowed with an initial passiveness that is gradually overcome. Su Ch'ing denied criticism that she was attempting a sensational autobiography or was an advocate of divorce.

Both Hsieh Ping-ying's autobiography and Su Ch'ing's novel portray the protagonist reluctantly riding in a bridal sedan chair to her traditionally arranged wedding. Each writer uses this scene to convey the protagonist's contempt for her mother's archaic views and the oppressiveness of the traditional system of marriage. Hsieh Ping-ying's account reads:

> Inside the chair I lifted my veil and took out the little mirror that hung on a chain around my neck to take a look at myself, the clown of the show. It was really ridiculous. Embroidered shoes had taken the place of the straw sandals I wore as a soldier. My hand instead of holding a gun now wore a golden ring and bracelets. Two ancient coins weighing over a pound hung on my chest—they said these old coins would drive evil spirits away. They were so heavy that I was forced to bend my neck forward.[29]

Su Ch'ing's passage reads:

> Riding the bride's flower sedan chair was a virgin's privilege. Only if the bride was a virgin could she ride this sedan chair. . . . If, on her way to the wedding ceremony, a girl only pretended to be a virgin, it was said that the chair spirit would bring on a calamity. When the chair stopped, such a young woman's breath would be fatally cut off. Naturally, mother believed I was a virgin and therefore stoutly insisted that I ride in the flower sedan chair. . . . Inside the chair it was almost pitch black and

quite depressing. The warmer stove under my feet gradually got so hot I thought I would suffocate, and during the trip I muttered not a few unmaidenly curses at this injustice.[30]

Despite the similarities, these passages also suggest differences in the contexts from which they are drawn. The heroine of Su Ch'ing's novel goes on to endure a long series of disappointments and indignities before deciding that the survival of herself and her children demands a divorce from her husband. Thus, the novel is not a monument to radical individualism or idealism at any price. By contrast, Hsieh Ping-ying's rejection of her marriage from the start leads her on to further adventures as a teacher, underground fugitive, worker, and student in the leftist circles of Shanghai, another marriage and divorce in Peiping, a trip to Japan, and a return to China to claim a child by her second marriage left in the care of her mother-in-law. With the outbreak of war, Hsieh joins the army as a medic and war correspondent. In this reckless series of adventures, Hsieh glories in romantic gestures, Westernized ideals, and an egocentric iconoclasm to an extent hardly approached in the struggles of the heroine of *Ten Years of Marriage*.

As a narrator, Su is often ready to laugh at herself. She recalls herself as a plain schoolgirl at the age of fifteen *sui* when she was overtaken by an infatuation for the heroic character of Chao Yun in a play based on *The Romance of the Three Kingdoms:*

> He was my hero! Mine! Mine! Mine! . . . I needed a young, handsome, ardent man to embrace in my sleep night after night. No need to say much; our hearts would be one, matched spirit with spirit, flesh to flesh, forever fused in an embrace.
> But, in fact, I slept alone in a lonely dormitory room and faced an empty bed from head to foot. It was no easy process to go to sleep while bugs crawled up through the bed, up onto my pillow, and stole kisses on my neck and ears. Mine! All . . . mine? (pp. 22–23)

Such schoolgirlish scenes provide the prelude to her disillusioning marriage, the tiresome crassness of the wedding ceremonies and the perfunctory attentions of her groom, who prefers the company of an attractive young widow and shortly departs for Shanghai to study law. She seeks some romantic fulfillment at the university she attends, but discovers only that she is pregnant by her husband and is forced to return to the home of her parents-in-law. They are demonstrably disappointed when she gives birth to a girl, and she, kept from nursing her own child herself, seeks escape from the stifling, Neo-Confucian atmosphere of the household by teaching in the local school system. However, the family soon decides to curtail her independence and packs her off to Shanghai to join her husband.

Su has long since admitted to herself that: "I didn't really love him, but I didn't want him to fall in love with someone else" (p. 59). Yet, she is unable to submit passively to the role her husband expects her to play:

> I didn't know whether all men were like this in general or just my husband. He seemed very unhappy that I, like a dignified scholar, should bring newspapers and books home and read them myself. He wanted me to have the disposition of a lazy child, to want only to play, or, putting on airs as "the mistress of the house," to oversee the servants as they went about cleaning, shopping, and cooking; and, moreover, be his secretary, proofread his work, and so on. (p. 101)

Still, she tries to produce a son, again delivering a daughter, just as the Japanese attack Shanghai. To escape the fighting, she returns to the home of her parents-in-law. For a time, life is reduced to a struggle for physical survival, and she contracts tuberculosis while a nurse hired by the family neglects her newborn third child, also a girl, who dies. Here, essentially, comes the turning point in the novel. Su turns her paramount concern toward her children and her bitterness toward her husband and his family, who have only used her "as a tool for continuing the family line by producing a male" (p. 60).

Returning to her husband in Shanghai, she begins to acquire an independent income by writing familiar essays for magazines, a career that sees her and her children through the crisis of 8 December 1941, after which her husband loses his job and leaves home for a degenerate life. Su tries one more ploy to restore the family situation. Finally giving birth to a boy, her fourth child, she invites her father-in-law to Shanghai to see him, hoping this will restore her husband to a responsible role. However, the old man proves too ill to make the trip, and Su's husband dashes home to attend him instead. Su writes a letter to the grandfather revealing his son's profligacy and neglect. The patriarch dies in a fit of apoplexy on reading the letter, and Su's husband returns to accuse her and his mistress of being responsible for his father's death. Su and her husband divorce. Su soon learns from a woman physician that the course of her tuberculosis can be reversed. Thus a happy ending is arranged; Su is in an expansive, forgiving mood, though she regrets most the damage done to her children and feels that continuing the marriage would have been a viable alternative.

In view of the critical reaction to her novel, Su Ch'ing felt compelled to publish a postscript stressing that she was not freely advocating divorce and had presented a situation *in extremis*. She notes that the two most common motivations for divorce were wife-beating and the withholding of allowances from wives, both of which are portrayed in the novel, yet neither of which, she thought, should necessarily lead to divorce when children's futures were at stake. Judged as art, the novel is mediocre. There is little imagery that is memorable; some incidents are too melodramatically contrived; the characters, apart from the heroine, are flat; and the moral deck is so stacked that there is little sympathy left for anyone besides the mother and her children. Su Ch'ing is an accomplished writer in the style of unaffected sincerity, but that sincerity is limited in its insight and scope, and the novel is consequently limited as a literary achievement. Even given all this, the novel is not to be dismissed altogether. It certainly has some documentary interest as a composite account of failed marriages of the time and as a conscientious treatment of the issues involved. Indeed, it is potentially even more radical as an indictment of the social situation than that of Hsieh Ping-ying, whose persona had no patience with social conventions from the beginning. The heroine Su, however, is deliberately portrayed as a conventional young woman, so that her break with conformity cannot be laid simply to eccentricity. Further, Su is an ordinary woman with hardly more than a middle-school education, so that her ability to find employment and independence is an achievement addressed to other ordinary women who fear divorce, rather than to women of heroic ambitions. Finally, the novel suggests that it is the heroine's very willingness to submit to pressures, just as she agreed to ride in the flower sedan chair, which contributes to the destructiveness of the situation. For in the end Su bears a son only when it is plain that this could do nothing to restore the viability of her marriage, the validity of traditional demands, or a society crumbling under the strain of war.

Su Ch'ing freely acknowledged that her literary achievements were limited.[31] However, criticism of her work hardly stopped at that point. Like a number of writers in the *Past and Present* magazine circle, she published remarks complimentary to a member of the Nanking regime, in her case Ch'en Kung-po, and her magazine contained a number of contributions by its civil servants.[32] These associations reinforced rumors that not only was *Heaven and Earth* backed by Ch'en Kung-po, but that Su Ch'ing was his mistress as well (her self-acknowledged plain looks notwithstanding). After the war, she continued to write, and leftist columnists branded her a literary prostitute who had deliberately peddled pornography (referring to *Ten Years of Marriage*) as an associate of the puppet regime.

> As for pornographic reading matter, in the past year it has been selling more briskly than ever, such as the work of the two so-called woman writers, Su Ch'ing and X X X [Chang Ai-ling]. They were indeed able to attract attention throughout Shanghai under the total support of the peace writers. But, in fact, there is but one talent within their work, the allurements of sex.[33]

By that time Su Ch'ing had, predictably, embarked on another novel, *Hsü chieh-hun shih-nien* (Sequel to Ten Years of Marriage), describing the hazardous course of the divorcée. In it she included an essay intended to rebut the accusations against her personally, and denied being Ch'en's mistress:

> I wrote purely out of financial necessity, and however much I was urged on by my friends, I knew it was out of kindness toward me, to help me find a way to resolve the problem of having enough to eat. Although at the time I changed my name from Feng Ho-i, which I had previously used, to Su Ch'ing, this was not out of fear that I would be discovered and punished by underground workers, since at that time I really was unaware that such an organization existed. . . . I regarded my selling articles as a temporary way of life and looked forward soon to having steady employment and a steady income to take care of myself and my children. The more articles I wrote, the more appeared in print. The name Su Ch'ing gradually became well-known, but the steady employment I had looked for was nowhere to be found. . . .
> At that time I had no thought of going to the interior, as I had not a single friend there I could rely on. But, just as I did not join in conscious

resistance, I likewise never wrote anything in praise of Greater East Asia. . . . I thought that the question I faced was not whether or not I should write, but whether what I wrote was in any way damaging to the nation.[34]

The name Su Ch'ing vanished by 1949, while the tactics used to criticize her have appeared again and again as conventions of Chinese public accusations.

Shih T'o (Wang Ch'ang-chien)

Both T'ang T'ao's dogged attempt to affirm some romantic interpretation and Su Ch'ing's rejection of romantic resolutions are embodied in the work of Shih T'o, whose artistic endeavors outstripped theirs and evinced a more complex attitude toward romantic values. Shih T'o was a major writer of the occupation period, whether judged by the quantity of his work, his commercial success, his artistic achievement, or his literary experimentation. Although Shih T'o denied membership in any school or clique of writers,[35] he had emerged under the pen name Lu Fen in the thirties as part of a trend toward regional literature in the Peking area presided over by Shen Ts'ung-wen.

Li Chien-wu, in a prewar evaluation of Shih T'o's sketches, placed him in a line of literature whose devotion to observation of the rural scene could be traced from *Lao Ts'an yu chi* (The Travels of Lao Ts'an) to the stories of Shen Ts'ung-wen. But he contrasted Shih T'o's work with Shen's as well, asserting that in Shen's fictional world the wounds of experience had been healed over to form a comforting vision, whereas Shih T'o presented his experiences as still alive, with a somber, reproachful point of view. Li characterized Shih T'o's style at some length as quite individual. Shih T'o's vocabulary is rich with slang and dialect, immature yet, but promising and full of life. Short sentences of varied texture that deliver a satiric bite are favored. Sometimes they degenerate into coarse, superficial epithets, such as simply calling a villain a dog. On the other hand, there are well-constructed contrasts of the beauty and coolness of nature with the ugly, heated animation of human affairs, as in a description of a beautiful sunset concluded by directing attention to children "taking a walk" under rough, fully laden baskets.[36] By 1936, Shih T'o's reputation as a leading writer of regional literature was firmly established.

During the war, Shih T'o worked to expand his scope as a writer, turning to various genres, modes, and settings. Indeed, there seemed to be no predictability in the directions he took. Yet much of what Li Chien-wu observed may be seen in his later work. Two volumes of sketches provide continuity during this experimental period. They are *Shanghai shou-cha* (Shanghai Correspondence, written during 1939–1940, and *Kuo-yuan ch'eng chi* (Orchard Town), a collection of stories published individually from 1939 to 1944 and collected in book form in 1946.

Shanghai Correspondence appeared in 1941 as one of the last works under Shih T'o's original pen name, Lu Fen. According to his introduction, the sketches—on the vanity, selfishness, and horrors of life in Shanghai after the fighting there in 1937—were written in two batches to ward off drowsiness after lunch, and no complete work was intended or accomplished. Still, the stories contain some unity of theme and technique. The "letters" actually begin with the writer in the southern Chekiang countryside, living with "Mr. P" in a temple opposite a mountain. The mountain may actually be taken as a symbol of the ambivalence that underlies the letters as a whole. At first attracted to it, the two men finally agree it is, after all, bereft of those features that make landscape pleasurable; its attraction stems from the "immeasurable vitality" of its sharp ascent, a feature that begins to oppress them. When word finally reaches them of the Marco Polo Bridge Incident and the eruption of full-scale fighting, they start back to Shanghai, not wanting to be cut off from events. Lu Fen then renders an appreciation of their passage through mountains inhabited by simple peasants who are cut off from the world to which the two men are returning. As they draw nearer to Shanghai, making their way through decaying towns and past crowds of refugees, they are drawn into a world of ceaseless motion, of people attempting physically and emotionally to remove themselves from the oppressive reality and uncertainty of life. As with the mountain, the writer finds this human spectacle fascinating and repelling. His own account keeps shifting from one vignette to the next; finally he abandons sketches and introduces newspaper clippings before giving up his attempt to reorder this protean experience. The vain restlessness of his account is underscored by references to Mr. P who, going his own way, first stays with a detached literary scholar with whom he argues to no purpose, and then departs for the interior. The sketches close with word from Mr. P that he is still wandering through the interior and has finished writing two books. Repeated throughout much of the work is the motif that fate—perhaps like the mountain—originates and terminates beyond the individual's ken and mocks or oppresses human life.

Technically, the device of letters is never developed to warrant the term; they are addressed to no one and, topically, respond only to the writer himself. The epigrammatic lines giving the essence of his views are less than mature as sardonic wit. But there is a more disturbing failure in the author's vision. The people who comprise "the masses," for whom he expresses sympathy in their truly grim hour of need, are never individualized, but left to descriptions that merely generalize about them. In contrast, the bourgeoisie and petit bourgeoisie, on whom he lavishes varying degrees of contempt, are frequently sharply drawn individuals who explicitly or implicitly typify their kind. There are the men of the literary world: the detached, effete scholar Mr. Wei; the "writer" who has never written a line (Ma Shih-yü); and a former leftist writer who took employment smashing leftist bookshops and disrupting leftist theater productions, and now simultaneously edits a Trotskyite magazine, writes pro-Japanese propaganda, and holds a minor post in the puppet regime. There are the idle white collar employees of Chinese business firms ruined in the fighting; Mr. Ch'ien Ching-t'u working for a German business firm and concerned with withdrawing his bank deposits to purchase gold; and a family packing to leave Shanghai for Hong Kong, concerned only with their grotesque surfeit of bric-a-brac and coldly annoyed by callers desperate to sublet their flat.

There is some relief in a tale in which "the war has turned sorrow into joy and brought the scattered back together"—in this case, a political prisoner released on account of the United Front policy and reunited with his wife. But the generally dismal gallery is capped by a portrayal of a girl whose torso is grotesquely deformed, but who sits on a park lawn enumerating her wishes for high-heeled shoes, bracelets, and expensive perfume.

The stories in *Orchard Town* complement those in *Shanghai Correspondence* by describing life in a small town as opposed to a major metropolis. The dates of composition overlap and then follow up the Shanghai sketches, revealing the persistence of the same fundamental interpretation of life in China throughout the war. The stories portray the decay and stagnation of life in a small town just prior to the war, in particular through attention to its relationship to the outside world. If there is no sign of protest in these sketches, they reinforce the portrait of a level of consciousness that appalls and defeats the minds of those who have left the town and return, to find their vision of a benign existence soured. The narrator in "Shuo-shu jen" (The Storyteller) relates the frustration of his hope to hear again the cherished stories of the local storyteller who has died of tuberculosis. Without family, he has been left to die alone and is given a perfunctory burial. As might be expected, the speaker has a special sympathy with the dead man wholly unshared by the indifferent villagers. "Storyteller: a liar by special permission from the world at large" is the narrator's definition, a unique and untraditional one, yet one the narrator says is a title he would gladly take for himself. At the grave he pursues his sentimental elegy with an *ubi sunt* theme, wondering where now are the richly conceived worlds the storyteller created from an ordinary and bitter life. In deliberately choosing a list of fanciful names from the deceased storyteller's repertoire, the narrator emphasizes how unique and special was his world, now gone without a successor.

Meng Chi-ch'ing in "Meng An-ch'ing ti t'ang hsiung-ti" (Meng An-ch'ing's Cousin) is the son of a generous, personable squire and a moody, violent mother. Meng Chi-ch'ing takes after his father; he leaves for college in Peking, where be becomes outgoing and popular. But when his father dies, Chi-ch'ing's brothers prove so voracious in their greedy division of the inheritance at Chi-ch'ing's expense that he begins to let go his hold on life. Refusing to return home, he curtails his social life and buries himself in library work, commenting that a family is like a fire and a man like a potato: anyone dipped in would surely have his head roasted to a crisp. Refusing requests from his brothers to relinquish the property left him, he goes to seed as an alcoholic opera buff and dies prematurely. His brothers then squabble over the division of his property until, funds for legal suits exhausted and fearing loss of property to each other, the brothers tear down the buildings on the lots they have taken possession of, reducing them to ruins that children now use for playgrounds. Shih T'o's description is not a gratuitous exercise in sardonic wit. To all appearances thoroughly Westernized, and gifted with the character and personality to lead a dynamic and fulfilling life, Meng Chich'ing's consciousness is still thoroughly rooted in a debilitating past. For all his potential to deal with another life on its own terms, Chich'ing, while openly refusing to be drawn into the degrading spectacle of the fight over property, allows himself to be reduced by another strain of the same cynical self-destructiveness that motivates his brothers; he refuses to relinquish his property only because he knows it frustrates them.

This same inability to relinquish deeply felt but futile ties to the mentality of one's birthplace is played out in yet another tale, "I wen" (A Kiss). It opens with a scene set in the first year of the Republic in which a girl tending a fruit stall receives a kiss from a tinsmith's apprentice. The girl's widowed mother, fearing that her daughter's prospects—and consequently her own—will be compromised, promptly delivers her to a *yamen* secretary as his concubine. In due course they leave the town with the secretary as he follows the district magistrate to another post. When the daughter returns years later for a visit, she questions a rickshaw puller about her childhood acquaintances in the town. The result is a long catalog of the now dead and dying. It is only after prolonged discussion that she realizes the rickshaw puller is her childhood admirer. Ground down by a life of poverty, he has long ago forgotten that such a girl ever existed. At the last moment, before boarding the first train she can get out of town, she crams his hand full of banknotes and departs with a blushing smile. Only then does he guess her identity. Here, despite both their ties to a dying culture, time and fate have irrevocably broken the bond between these two. A similar story portrays a young man who once abandoned his fiancée in search of adventure, returning years later to find that he has been utterly forgotten by the town. Wisely deciding not to look up his old love, he faces the realization that "what waited for him were trains and rooms."[37]

These stories do not cover the entire collection, but are deliberately selected from those published from 1942 to 1944 to illustrate the persistence of Shih T'o's pessimism throughout the war period. As in *Shanghai Correspondence,* the ironies of fate, beyond the individual's reach, remain a theme. In "A Kiss" the narrator remarks: "Sometimes fate can play a joke on someone. Hu T'ou-yü had planned on learning to be a tinsmith, but as a result pulled a rickshaw."[38] The same ironic observations are expressed elsewhere. Meng An-ch'ing has left town to fulfill his dream of being a hunter, but "the result of his hunting was that he became a portrait and landscape painter."[39] C. T. Hsia has pointed out that these stories clearly and even deliberately hark back to Lu Hsün's accounts of the intellectual's return to his home region in the twenties, "to underscore the persistence of stagnation in a time of apparent change."[40] Indeed, the similarities are striking, but in recording the persistence of these conditions, there is even less expression of faith. Lu Hsün allows plum blossoms to persevere through the gloom of "Tsai chiu-lou shang" (In the Tavern) and concludes "Ku hsiang" (My Old Home) with reflections on the potential for improvement of the human lot, trying to make his mark as a social reformer. When Shih T'o refers to the children of the concubine of "A Kiss," writing "I hope they are fortunate as they grow up and don't follow their mother's example," he is closer to venting a frustration in the wake of a generation of reform.[41] Shih T'o does not attempt to prod the reader's consciousness by exposing the guilty ineffectuality of a persona, as Lu Hsün so often does in stories such as "My Old Home" and "Chu-fu" (Benediction). He does not ask the question of the intellectual's responsibility, but through narrative now sardonic, now sentimental, he raises disturbing questions about the relationship of anyone in China to any portion of that society. Just as the protean world of urban China shows a surface degeneracy, the conditions of small town life are revealed as no less pernicious to nourishing human society, as in story after story, reassuring notions of small-town China as stable, familiar, and restoring are demolished.

Zbigniew Slupski's study of Shih T'o's fiction has pointed out in it a continuing preoccupation with the theme of "an unknown and unknowable world," one that is consequently replete with surprises, in a style which represents a "departure from narrow literary realism."[42] Although Slupski's comments are derived in large part from study of works other than those presented here, they apply equally to collections such as *Shanghai Correspondence* and *Orchard Town*. And these considerations figure prominently in Shih T'o's novel *Ma Lan*, completed in early 1942. *Ma Lan* is set in the early thirties and abounds with allusions to social events and themes of the period. Yet, though it is thoroughly grounded in the milieu of that time, it is a psychological adventure as much as a topical commentary, and still very much concerned with the theme that, in Slupski's words, "there is more to life than we can see; life has no end, and we know practically nothing about it."[43]

Ma Lan may be considered as a romantic protest not only against social ills, but against deterministic and mechanistic thinking. Ma Lan, the young heroine of the title, is a wronged woman who takes her revenge on those who would use her and finally seems to transcend the cycle of abuse and revenge. Ma Lan first appears in K City, to which she has fled with a Communist schoolteacher, Ch'iao Shih-fu, after her merchant father, hungry for social advancement, pushed her toward a marriage with Cheng Ta-t'ung, a local warlord bordering on old age. But Ch'iao Shih-fu neglects her except to lecture her on Marxism, in the belief that she will channel her mounting frustration and discontentment into social activism, which he views as the only legitimate use of emotions. Ma Lan responds to these attempts to mold her into a revolutionary with cold fury, and falls in love with an art teacher, Li Po-t'ang. Failing to find fulfillment with Po-t'ang, however, she turns to another of Ch'iao Shih-fu's friends, the coarse Yang Ch'un, another Marxist who has hitherto disgusted Ma Lan by his appraisal of her as a sex object. She moves in with Yang Ch'un, only to abandon him and reappear at the side of the warlord, a cruel, self-willed potentate who imagines Ma Lan will comfort him in his old age. He takes her along on his hunting trips, teaching her to ride and shoot. But Ma Lan uses these skills to shoot his horse out from under him, breaking both his legs, and makes good her escape into the mountains. There she joins Mo Pu-tu, a shadowy figure who commands a band of rural guerrillas. Originally passive and inexperienced, Ma Lan has developed into a formidable harbinger of an unknown future for China, leaving in her wake the Marxist Ch'iao Shih-fu on the verge of a nervous breakdown; the abandoned, embittered Yang Ch'un no longer condescending; and the crippled, heartbroken warlord Cheng Ta-t'ung. But the novel is chiefly concerned with Ma Lan's relationship with Li Po-t'ang, and his fate is somewhat different. Having belatedly awakened to the realization of her love, Li Po-t'ang pursues Ma Lan into the mountains, only to have his advances gently rebuffed by her. He retires to K City, accepting his distance from her and pondering that he is "fortunate."

All this might read simply as an improbable fantasy were not the author equally concerned with experimenting with narrative technique and point of view in support of his exploration of character and theme. The reader is introduced by a "friend" of Li Po-t'ang to the contents of the novel, which consist of records kept by Po-t'ang and a diary kept by Ma Lan. These papers were simply given by Po-t'ang to his friend to do with as he wished; they are not intended as finished works for the general public, but are private ruminations and accounts that do not necessarily try to tie up all aspects of the action. Moreover, Po-t'ang at first appears to be the most reliable narrator. A young man of education and experience, he is handsome, self-possessed, and capable, and prides himself on his intellectual perspicacity and moral superiority. These qualities, however, soon prove to be emotional as well as practical defenses, not only against the treachery and deception of the world without, but for his flawed world within. He is too much tied to the past. Socially, he has served as a loyal aide to the warlord Cheng Ta-t'ung. In his personal life he has learned to disdain the superficialities of the young women of social standing he was raised to wed, and has maintained a deep emotional tie to his sister, whom their mother died giving birth to. But Cheng's political fortunes decline, and Po-t'ang accepts an offer to join the faculty of an art school in K City, where his circle of friends comes to include Ch'iao Shih-fu and Ma Lan. Po-t'ang's detachment over this course of events is shattered, however, at the death of his sister. This last vestige of love and link with a past gone, he is faced with an emotional crisis he little understands. Ma Lan comforts and restores him, and he becomes increasingly emotionally dependent on her. Yet he cannot bring himself to admit, even to himself, that he is passionately in love with her, and he is unable to see that she is not loved by his friend Ch'iao Shih-fu and has fallen in love with him.

The further truth of the matter is revealed to Po-t'ang only long after Ma Lan's marriage and her affair with Po-t'ang have failed and she has disappeared, leaving behind the diary that Po-t'ang reads. Ch'iao Shih-fu not only did not love Ma Lan, but held Po-t'ang in contempt. Po-t'ang's insistence on playing the role of friend and denying desire for Ma Lan were useless exercises in casuistry and hypocrisy that did nothing for Ma Lan's needs, even as she fulfilled Po-t'ang's. Her feelings of imprisonment have developed to the point of despair and nihilism. In a final appraisal of Po-t'ang, she emphasizes the centrality of love:

> As I see him, Po-t'ang forever remains a hero. His fundamental character is not what one could call either good or bad. Of course, I can't deny his chivalry and humaneness. But privately, I think his honesty is partly forced, and his inability to tolerate any evil is for the most part dictated by a sense of righteousness. His motivation is far from residing in love. As a consequence, although in every way he's far more fortunate than others, he has actually failed in everything.[44]

Ma Lan has already embarked on her desperate course when Po-t'ang reads this. But Po-t'ang, too, has been undergoing a change, for by that time he has emerged from prison for participating in demonstrations against the Japanese occupation of Manchuria, and so his progress has been steadily away from the sources of social order and convention—from aide to a warlord, to teacher, to convict. Now he abandons all social roles to search out Ma Lan, for she has left solid testimony of her love for him.

But just as he has finally abandoned all convention to restore their relationship, when he finally finds her, a fugitive in the mountains, she has adopted a new propriety as the companion of the guerrilla leader Mo Pu-tu, and she refuses his advances. Yet, it might be inferred, this is a new propriety based on her genuine relationship with

Mo Pu-tu, as distinct from the empty proprieties observed by Po-t'ang when she was married to Ch'iao Shih-fu. Moreover, Ma Lan rejects the diary Po-t'ang offers her as a testimony of her love for him, for it is a relic of the past. She leaves him with the thought that in the future she may be able to visit him in the city and ascends the mountain to the bandit stronghold, from which Po-t'ang is barred. He can only return to the city.

Ma Lan's final ascent into the mountain certainly suggests the theme that she has transcended the rational confines of Po-t'ang and his intellectual acquaintances. She has also transcended the past, the old and dessicated conventions, and the nihilistic defiance of them, to find a new life and a promise of a future. It is this transcendence that leaves Po-t'ang ultimately inspired, aware of life based on love and freed from the empty past.

That the exerience of love is central to both the social and the psychological themes in the novel is suggested by the character Mo Pu-tu, who makes few appearances, but always to argue against the mechanism and determinism of Ch'iao Shih-fu and his circle of Marxists, and also to advise Ch'iao Shih-fu not to use Ma Lan's need for love as a means to convert her to revolution, but respect her need for love in itself. Mo's arguments early on point the way to the themes; in the end, his presence just beyond the range of vision suggests the imagined but undefined new life that Ma Lan has found.

For Po-t'ang, Ma Lan becomes a symbol of regeneration, through her exerience of love, that lies beyond his ability to analyze, but that he can capture with images in his artistic sensibility. Still early in the novel, Po-t'ang describes walking home with Ma Lan:

> I walked with her up to the flat. Ch'iao Shih-fu was just then staring abstractedly out at the sky. We talked about his work. He claimed that recently he had sought an explication for a section of one of Marx's works. Then, with a light rustling sound, like a flash of brilliant light, Ma Lan emerged from her room. She was wearing a bright yellow knitted jacket and a black tie. Around her throat was a strip of pale blue silk. Below she wore a purplish rose skirt of fine linen. It was so elegant and lissome that it made one imagine it was not earth that touched her feet, that grime would not dare soil her body, and that every pleat of her skirt deserved praise. . . . She left behind the scent of new clothes, and in our mind's eye carried with her the brightness and color of human life. (pp. 74–75)

Toward the end of the novel, the prelude to Po-t'ang's final, unexpected interview with Ma Lan in the mountains is the transformation of the landscape from its recent devastation in civil war to its regeneration:

> Although all this is now long past, at that time the scene impressed me with its bright colors, and I have still been able to preserve it in my memory, vivid and clear, even today. When we started, the weather was oppressively hot. In the evening we took lodging at a Buddhist temple, and a heavy rain fell, washing away the dust from the hills, trees, and air. In the morning, not long after we had gotten under way, the sun rose joyfully, shining down everywhere across the fresh, tender green of the mountain grasses and trees. The sky was a pure, clear blue. Among the peaks high on the horizon, cumuli appeared in the deep blue, then gradually faded behind the crests. What was really unforgettable were the stone cottages on the mountain slopes that would appear without warning, everywhere showing off roofs finished with slabs of red and green. Both contrasting with and complementing the trees, these cottages added the final stroke to all the colors. And it was the most important and interesting touch of all. Because of this the canvas took on focus, bringing into a composed whole the surrounding scenery, so that the view was not an isolated array of scattered elements. (pp. 289–90)

Finally, Ma Lan's transcendence of the dry, formulated visions of the urban intellectuals is admitted in a conversation between Po-t'ang and his Marxist rival Yang Ch'un, which Po-t'ang recounts:

> Finally, when he had prepared himself, his face became drawn and expressionless, and as though fearful, he said slowly, "I hear you saw her last year. Did she have anything to say? Did she make any remarks about me?" Because I was still angry, I just said coldly, "This 'she' you speak of, is she 'yours' or 'ours'?"
> He was embarrassed by my dig. He gave an abashed smile and said, "Not ours and not yours, either. I'm talking about Ma Lan." (p. 281)

A good deal more could be said about the suggestiveness of many scenes and images, but they would still remain more suggestive than well-defined contributions to the overall pattern of the novel. A number of admirably written scenes, which give vivid impressions of the principal characters, still do not add up to a full, coherent account of the characters' development. Such an ambitious vision combined with such elusiveness does not make *Ma Lan* a convincing novel. It deserves special credit, however, for the bold individuality and sensitivity of its conception. Despite its social theme, *Ma Lan* is happily more than a "social document" of its time; it is a superior essay in individual imagination and hope. The tone of optimism on which it concludes is unusual in Shih T'o's work, and this degree of affirmation contributes to its being the most romantic. The vision of such a dynamic heroine, of the potential of the individual and the experience of love, seems to have waned in Shih T'o's work thereafter, though an incomplete novel written later may have also been intended to develop these themes.

Although Shih T'o moved away from such a romantic conception, the theme of the evils of urban society never left his works. His major experiment in fiction during the Pacific War years was neither surprisingly nor predictably a novel set in the late Ch'ing entitled *Huang-yeh* (Wilderness). It was serialized in the magazine *Phenomena* from August 1943 through June 1945, when the magazine ceased publication. At that point the novel had reached fifteen chapters and seems to have been left unfinished. Given its incompleteness, it is not possible to present a conclusive interpretation or evaluation. While *Wilderness* does not appear to add to Shih T'o's stature as a writer, it does offer evidence of his continued experimentation, as well as lines of continuity with other works. The narrator is obtrusively present, now as a traditional storyteller, now as a conscientious researcher, familiar with both town and countryside and intent on providing a faithful portrait of local customs and color, and of the language and psychology of his thoroughly Chinese characters.

Ku Erh-shun, outcast son of a ne'er-do-well peasant and leader of a small band of *hao-han* (brigands of a male chauvinist mentality), falls in love with the daughter of a widow, Chiao Chieh, a tomboy who has repelled the advances of so many village youths that she is now shunned and without marriage prospects. Ku Erh-shun's lieutenant and confidant Li Ssu-keng, true to his *hao-han* image, is skeptical of the nature and motives of women and worried about Chiao Chieh's influence on Ku Erh-shun. Chiao Chieh's mother is even more disturbed that her daughter is involved with a bandit. Ku Erh-shun and Chiao Chieh both wonder how he can escape the life of a bandit and settle into an idyllic vision of farming and housekeeping.

These threads of rural life are contrasted with the conniving world of the gentry, oriented to the town, for whom Ku Erh-shun's control of the countryside has become a scandal they use against each other in jockeying for political power. There are a number of well-handled scenes. The private and political corruption of the local elite is summed up in a satirically rendered interview between the leading local squire and a social climber (chapter 4). A rich spectrum of behavior is explored in the vacillation of Chiao Chieh between her loyalty to Ku Erh-shun and her devotion to the anxiety-ridden mother, obsessed with the thought of her own security. Similarly, the skeptical Li Ssu-keng is an effective foil for Ku Erh-shun. When it is apparent that Ku Erh-shun's intentions are honorable and filial, and that Chiao Chieh has no other prospects, her mother finally consents. Li Ssu keng also wavers, reflecting:

> Essentially his life as a kidnapper and brigand was a bit different from that of Ku Erh-shun. It was out of necessity that Erh-shun first mounted this "tiger's back," and later he became habituated to the practice, like a man living in an old house that may topple any day. He gets used to the predicament and takes lightly his foreseeable doom.[45]

Ssu-keng contrasts this motivation with his own, which arose from bitterness and a desire for vengeance after he was not allowed even half a day off from work to help his mother as she lay dying. Characteristically, he adopts a delightfully pedantic pose, earnestly citing operas to Erh-shun as cautionary tales against his involvement with Chiao Chieh. There is *Wu Han kuei han* (Wu Han Supports the House of Han), in which the hero Wu Han executes his beloved wife, the daughter of the usurper Wang Mang, in order not to vitiate his loyalty to the Han restoration. And there is *Mei-jen chi* (The Strategem of the Beautiful Woman), in which Liu Pei resists the attempts of Su Ch'üan to distract him from affairs of state through Su's sister's charms. But Ssu-keng's erudition falls on culturally barren soil. Erh-shun replies: "Liu Pei! Liu Pei!—No wonder everybody calls you old man muddle-mouth. Really serious things you never deal with. All you do is talk about Liu Pei! One of these days I'm going to shoot your Liu Pei!"[46] Ssu-keng thus gives in and faithfully carries out the plans for an expensive and gaudy wedding ceremony. The narrator comments on this pomp:

This all looked like madness, an act that "ruins families and destroys nations," but as the saying goes, "one should spend money where it is most needed." If it were otherwise, how would it seem that Erh-shun was getting married? Moreover, how else could it be made so clear what a good friend he was to Erh-shun?[47]

Chiao-chieh is thoroughly embarrassed by all this pomp and succeeds in having it dismantled. After the couple set up house together, they fall to quarreling, which distracts Erh-shun. He is caught in an ambush and carried off to the county magistrate. His Judas, a malcontent among the bandit gang, quickly goes into hiding in the town, where he discovers he has been deceived by a constable's false promises of reward and official employment. Indeed, as he retires into his temple hideout, the narrative describes a scene in which he is taken away to be executed with Erh-shun. As with so many scenes in older fiction, this one ends abruptly as Ku's betrayer awakes to find he has been dreaming. At this point the novel breaks off.

These selections, including the dream sequence, serve to show how rooted is the novel in the techniques and themes of traditional fiction. The central characters of the rural scene are *ta-fang* (outgoing, sincere, and spirited) as opposed to the caricatured villains whose stronghold is the county seat.[48] There are amused or satirical observations on both life styles by the narrator, the employment of suspense and foreshadowing, and long digressions to introduce characters or explain terms and names. Although such techniques deliberately recall traditional fiction, other motifs have no place in the traditions of *Shui-hu chuan,* and these, of course, have to do with the love theme. When Ku Erh-shun, and the Chiao Chieh, are stimulated by love, their thoughts are allowed to ramble in a series of disjointed images (chapters 3 and 10). Several times the landscape is used to reflect the moods and situation of the lovers as dynamic forces (chapters 7, 8, and 10), for the movements and contrast of elements in nature are emphasized. Hence, the lovers share in the life of nature in its capacity for renewal and transcendence of the confines of human society.

It may be said that *Wilderness* has points in common with *Ma Lan.* The hero in each case is a benevolent outlaw who rescues the heroine from a loveless life. In the town is villainy and sterility. In the countryside, beyond the reach of conventional society and authority, is space to pursue a dream of pastoral domesticity in harmony with a natural world. The centrality of the pastoral theme in Shih T'o's vision puts it at some remove from works of a romantic hue that emphasize *étrangerié* and maintains a continuity with his earlier work and that of other writers in regional literature. Further, it complements his pessimism over the future of China, a victim, not a beneficiary, of progress, and explains the grim vision present in his two major achievements during the Pacific War years. Both are plays, with an urban setting.

The first was *Ta-ma-hsi-t'uan* (The Big Circus), adapted from Leonid Andreyev's *He Who Gets Slapped*. The success of this play was followed by *The Night Inn*, based on Maxim Gorky's *The Lower Depths*. Both source plays are representative not only of modern Russian theater, but of Western drama as well, and both Andreyev and Gorky have been interpreted as romantic. Yet Shih T'o's task was to Sinify these works. In that process, in adapting them to his vision of China, he curtailed or eliminated the expressions of romanticism that appear in the sources.

The romantic elements in Andreyev's *He Who Gets Slapped* are primarily the property of HE himself, the solitary genius whose penetrating ideas and imagination have been vulgarly distorted for mass consumption; the plain but passionate lover whose bid to save the bareback rider Consuelo from contamination by cultured decadence and restore her to a transcendent, mythic vision is thwarted. In each case effacement is HE's fate, and he takes his vengeance by mocking the audience that laughs at him and poisoning Consuelo, along with himself, to deny her to a debauched baron. When the baron also commits suicide, the dying HE vows to carry the struggle beyond the grave. Mythic allusions raise the social polemic to a more universal notion of absolutes in contention. HE represents one of the chief factors in the discussion of Russian romanticism in late imperial Russia: the outcast, madman hero as the bearer of truth, "called upon to uncover the essential in the human soul."[49] But this expression of radical individualism, this conception of the hero of superior sensitivity, central to Russian romanticism and to Andreyev's work in particular, must have been found too alien or obscure for the Chinese stage. HE himself, in the Chinese version, is dispensed with.

The social polemic, however, remains in Shih T'o's play: impotence and subservience before wealth, misguided faith in the goodness of social myths that deliver innocence into corruption, blind rage and destructive revolt. But much of the rest is altered or eliminated. The story centers on the misfortunes of the young riding master in love with the bareback rider, who is to be sold by her father as a concubine. HE's role as counselor is given to Ta-tzu, a pathetic but wise and sympathetic old clown. HE's role as a lover is incorporated into Hsiao Ch'ung, the riding master, thus making him more assertive than Andreyev's proud, aloof Alfred Bezano. Hsiao Ch'ung's character, however, is not really a combination of his sources. Like a number of Shih T'o's characters, Hsiao Ch'ung is an orphan who was sold to the circus as an infant, a fact that weighs on his mind and figures in his passionate attachment to Ts'ui-pao, the bareback rider based on Andreyev's Consuelo, Sinified with a melon-seed face and twin pigtails. Hsiao Ch'ung complains to Ts'ui-pao:

> I'm a poor entertainer. Even now I don't know who my parents are. I can just remember being on a bridge; a man, sick, lying on the ground; a woman next to him crying. They were my parents. They had set me down there. I was so hungry I just bawled. But people went by paying no attention to us. Then an old fellow brought me a cake, and my sale to him was concluded. That old man was Manager Ma's father. Put yourself in my place, Ts'ui-pao. After all, you know you're from Shantung. But who knows where I was born, or where my parents are, alive or dead?[50]

While Andreyev's circus performers form a world apart from that of conventional culture and find fulfillment in their work, the circus in Shih T'o's version is dominated by a callous, venal manager, and the performers' attitude toward their work is quite different. This is the background for the following exchange between Hsiao Ch'ung and Ts'ui-pao, which is also central to the interpretation of Shih T'o's play in its divergence from its source:

TS'UI-PAO: So I always think: Never mind poverty and bitterness, just when can I plant my feet somewhere and not run around a wharf?
HSIAO CH'UNG: (*clapping his hands*): And I'm always thinking: If God would just give me a break and get me out of here. I've had enough of

selling an act in order to eat. (*Pressing his opportunity to bring up the topic, intimately*)Ts'ui-pao, you used to talk about your old home in Shantung, with the mountains, do you remember?

TS'UI-PAO: I remember. (*Recalling it her face brightens.*) Such huge mountains, with clouds above them. (*Only able to pass it off with a sigh.*) But that's so far away!

HSIAO CH'UNG: And then there was wheat—and peach blossoms. Do you remember?

TS'UI-PAO: I remember. I remember. The peach trees grew by the water. But Papa says I was just making that up.

HSIAO CH'UNG (*returning to reality*): Ts'ui-pao, just now when you were scolding me for beating the horse, do you know what I was thinking?

TS'UI-PAO (*looking at him questioningly*): What were you thinking?

HSIAO CH'UNG: I was thinking then: I want to carry you away to Shantung, back to your old home. I want to have you look at those great mountains, and the clouds atop the mountains, and the peach trees by the river.

TS'UI-PAO: How could you find it? Papa won't tell me the truth, and Shantung covers a lot of territory.

HSIAO CH'UNG: And then I felt it was just as though I were carrying you away from this man-eating place. And I thought, the faster the better, the farther the better, and completely forgot I was giving you a riding lesson.[51]

Again, in the last act, Hsiao Ch'ung urges Ts'ui-pao to recall her home in a vain effort to win her agreement to elope with him. Both passages are loosely adapted from Andreyev's play, when on two occasions HE urges Consuelo to view a mythic world that is her origin. Yet, whether on the literal or metaphysical plane, Shih T'o's version is at some remove from the vision of Andreyev, who has HE say:[52]

> Awake, goddess, and remember the time when, covered with snow-white sea foam, thou didst emerge from the sky-blue waters. Remember heaven, and the low eastern wind, and the whisper of the foam at thy marble feet. . . .

It seems apparent that Andreyev is alluding to a mythical world and a romantic conception that has no real counterpart in the vision of Hsiao Ch'ung. His imagination, on the contrary, sees a land of escape in an actual province. Again, this suggests that Shih T'o's romanticism is inseparable from a pastoral element and a feeling toward nature close to that found in traditional Chinese culture. The theme of revolt is carried out in actions, not in romantic polemics.

There are several other alterations of significance. In Shih T'o's *The Big Circus,* Andreyev's lion tamer, Zinida, a femme-fatale of both sympathetic and frightening character and less directly related to the plot than the theme of the play, is transformed into a ravenous Madame White Snake whose mischief and sexual misconduct have direct impact on the characters. Shih T'o has also chosen otherwise to restructure both the content and construction of several scenes, especially by allowing tension to develop and then be deflected, and by lively quarreling. Instead of the cultural elite, Shih T'o introduces a loquacious clown, Hui Hui, and his wife Peach, a chubby, assertive type who looks after a ten-year-old girl, Yin Niu-erh, while arguing with her husband with comic gusto. It is Yin Niu-erh who provides the link between comic and serious action. The affection and concern for her shown by the positive characters is contrasted with the meanness shown by several disreputable gentry types, including Ts'ui-pao's father. While the sympathetic characters are preoccupied with the problems of Ts'ui-pao and Hsiao Ch'ung, Yin Niu-erh runs away. She is obsessed with the notion of "going home" and slips away to the train station, only to be run over by a train before the adults can find her. This sentimental, "little girl lost" situation is a reflection on the plight of the young lovers themselves, for they also prove to be without the ability to escape.

A review of the original stage version of *The Big Circus* in the spring of 1943 outlined the conclusion of the play as follows:

> Meanwhile, the path of the young lovers is strewn with thorns: the girl's father decides to sell her as a concubine to a rich man's son. At a farewell party given in her honor, her lover asks her to drink with him a cup of poisoned wine. As the wine begins to take effect on them, he rushes from the room and sets a part of the circus on fire, in which he perishes. The tiger tamer rushes after him and they go up in flames together.[53]

This was the play as staged under the direction of Huang Tso-lin, one of the most successful directors in Shanghai during the war. However, when the script was finally published in book form shortly after the war, this spectacular conclusion was considerably muted.

The family of Huang Ta-shao-yeh, who is purchasing Ts'ui-pao as a concubine, has registered a complaint with the police that Ts'ui-pao and her father are swindling Huang. Ts'ui-pao and her father are taken off to jail, Ts'ui-pao at least somewhat relieved that her contract with Huang is broken. But Hsiao Ch'ung despairs and takes poison, dying offstage. The manager and his wife, the tiger tamer, are merely alluded to as being openly hostile toward each other now that her affair with Hsiao Ch'ung has been revealed in her hysteria over his death. Finally, Shih T'o allows the scene to focus on Hui Hui, Peach, and Ta-tzu, now unemployed and facing hopeless penury as they leave to shift for themselves. Like so much of Shih T'o's work, the play puts strong emphasis on the homelessness and rootlessness of its characters. Here they drift with the overpowering currents of exploitation, turn to self-destruction, or, as in the last scene, are left stranded, incapable of significant action and irrelevant to the social mechanism of exploitation.

Andreyev's play is "symbolic and romantic,"[54] but Shih T'o has turned it into a realistic play in which the romantic elements are only vestiges of even Shih T'o's pastoral vision. Instead of an intellectual choosing to rebel against corrupt conventions in the name of a transcendent vision, two young people are by birth trapped in a "man-eating" society, unable to escape to a vision of beauty and sublimity which they intuitively perceive as their hope.

The Night Inn more closely approximates the cast of its source, Gorky's *The Lower Depths,* and yet ultimately alters no less significantly the plot and characterization, and hence the entire interpretation of the work. This is all the more interesting in view of the introductory statements to the script written by Shih T'o. He notes that it is the characters and their situation which prompted the adaptation of *The Lower Depths.* Actually, when Huang Tso-lin, principal director for K'u-kan Players, approached him about writing the script, Huang said he wanted to stage the original but feared an adaptation would be necessary if it were to be favorably received by the public. Shih T'o at first declined, lacking self-confidence and standing very much in awe of the original and unwilling to tamper with it. But living conditions grew progressively worse under the occupation, and when his closest friend, K'o Ling, renewed the suggestion, he agreed to collaborate on an adaptation. K'o Ling wrote the first two acts; Shih T'o himself did the third and fourth.[55]

Gorky's play is set in a flophouse in provincial Russia in 1902. The grasping landlord Kostilyov alternately preaches to his tenants and spies on his wife, Vasilissa, who is intent on sleeping with Vaska Pepel, a young thief, and murdering her husband. The thief is in love with her younger sister, Natasha, who consequently suffers as the object of Vasilissa's sadistic rage. Anna, the wife of a locksmith, dying of tuberculosis, is comforted by a mild, religious old man, Luka. It is through Luka's rustic philosophizing that many of the other tenants are viewed, including Nastya, a prostitute, and several dropouts from society: Baron (Nastya's pimp), Actor, and Satin, a former intellectual. When the landlord is finally murdered, Vasilissa and Vaska Pepel are both taken away to jail, and Luka disappears. In the last act, Satin rises to dominate the remaining derelicts and finds his voice:

> When I'm drunk I like everything. He's praying [referring to Luka]? That's fine, let him pray. A man can believe or not believe. It's his own business. Man is free. Man—that's the truth. What is man? He's neither you nor I, nor them. No. He's you, me, the old man, Napoleon, Mohammed. All in one. (Traces with his fingers in the air the figure of a man) You understand? It's tremendous! In this is the beginning and the end of everything. Everything is in man and everything is for man! Only man exists. Man! It's magnificent! It sounds so noble! M-A-N! Let's drink to man![56]

Gorky has been called a "romantic-realist,"[57] and there is little doubt that Satin, an intellectual imprisoned for murdering a man who molested his sister, stands for the romantic assertions of the play against the mild pieties of Luka, the old wanderer who dispenses comforting lies. According to one Western critic:

> Gorky intended to contrast favorably the strong-minded murderer, who will stop at nothing to get his sweet revenge, with the elusive, soothing old man who tries to comfort every suffering person. . . . In the acted play Luka came out so creditably that Gorky later complained to Lunarcharsky that the actor, Moskvin, by taking Luka too seriously, had ennobled him out of all proportion to his merits.
> According to Gorky, Luka should have been a sly old fellow, who had become soft and pliable through having been knocked around a lot.[58]

The Chinese adapters, with more freedom than the Moscow Art Theater, were apparently not at all impressed with Satin, and virtually eliminated his part altogether. Indeed, he is the only character in the original play who has no defined counterpart in the Chinese adaptation. Luka, transformed into Ch'üan Lao-t'ou, a wandering peddler of medicinal herbs, becomes the principal character in *The Night Inn*, and the unqualified emissary of humaneness and hope, albeit unsuccessfully.

In Gorky's play, Luka is openly subject to the intellectual attacks of Baron as well as those implied in the views of Satin. However, in *The Night Inn* only one such assault is mounted, and that by the guilt-ridden cobbler Lai (Klesch) following the death of his wife, A-man (Anna), from tuberculosis. He fumes hysterically that Ch'üan is a "samaritan full of falsehoods, pouring honey over others' sores,"[59] and then disappears from the play altogether. But even this attack seems to reflect more on Lai himself in his private hell, rather than on Ch'üan Lao-tou, whose vision remains unchallenged by any other character. In fact, he is introduced as a man of uncanny perspicacity when, shortly after his arrival at the flophouse, as a total stranger he senses intuitively the evil domination of Sai Kuan-yin (Vasilissa). In this way he is quickly cast as the primary foil to the landlord's wife. His character is firmed up, and besides the comforting illusions of his white lies that he shares with Luka, he is given a moment of open defiance when the landlord, Wen T'ai-shih (Kostilyov), becomes too overbearing in ordering Ch'üan to vacate the premises. But there are more crucial alterations. In Gorky's play, Luka overhears Vasilissa propose to the thief Vaska Pepel that he murder her husband and take his place, which Vaska rejects absolutely. Thus, in the last act, when Luka could offer testimony to mitigate the charge against Vaska, he is instead made to vanish rather than stand up for "the truth." In *The Night Inn*, Ch'üan Lao-t'ou is not allowed to overhear Sai Kuan-yin's proposal to Yang Ch'i-lang (Vaska Pepel) to murder Wen T'ai-shih, and his role in the last act of the play is given a far more sympathetic interpretation. This requires attention to developments in the later stages of both plays.

In Act III of *The Lower Depths,* Vasilissa and Kostilyov catch and torture her younger sister for her relations with Vaska Pepel. In the uproar that ensues, Vasilissa murders Kostilyov, and her younger sister, in mental and physical anguish, blindly accuses both her and Vaska of the murder in front of the police, who take them both away. In *The Night Inn* the younger sister, Hsiao-mei (Natasha) is rendered so incoherent by her torturers that she clings semiconsciously to Yang Ch'i-lang, who ignores Ch'üan's urgings to escape before the police arrive. On the strength of Sai Kuan-yin's accusation alone, Yang is arrested, and his conviction is assured through bribery. Having taken the only constructive initiative at this crucial juncture, Ch'üan Lao-t'ou goes on in the fourth and final act to show the only active concern for the welfare of Hsiao-mei, who has run away following Yang's arrest. He braves cold winds and rain to find and care for her. While he is out, Hsiao-mei returns to the flophouse exhausted. There Sai Kuan-yin finds her and begins to stab her with a cobbler's awl. Hsiao-mei takes advantage of the return of some tenants from a drinking spree to make good her escape, but later, when Ch'üan returns soaked with rain and mud, he announces that Hsiao-mei has hanged herself outside. This, too, is at complete variance with Gorky's play, in which it is Actor's suicide that concludes the final act. This pathetic character has been abandoned by Luka and is deaf to the pronouncements of the visionary Satin.

A brief comparison of the roles of Actor in *The Lower Depths* and his counterpart, Hsi-tzu, in *The Night Inn* is also of value in interpreting the play as a whole. In each case, the actor is an alcoholic dropout who briefly takes heart from the encouragement of Luka or Ch'üan, and having fortified himself with more drink, gives a brief performance. Gorky's Actor recites the following:

> Good people! If the world cannot seem
> To find the path to holy truth
> Glory be to the madman, forsooth
> Who brings mankind to a golden dream.

> If tomorrow there were a dearth
> Of sunlight to illumine the planet's way
> Some madman's thoughts would show the way
> Tomorrow to light up the earth.[60]

In the immediate context of the verse, it appears that Actor is giving a eulogy to Luka. But when the play ends and Luka has proved an ephemeral, vain hope, Actor hangs himself, his verse now ironically suggesting the superiority of Satin's grandiose declarations. By contrast, Hsi-tzu, an unemployed *k'un-ch'ü* performer, sings a doleful aria from *Ch'ang-sheng tien* (The Palace of Eternal Youth) by Hung Shen:

> Our pennants fluttering in the setting sun,
> Cast long, weird shadows:
> Our horses doggedly plod on and on,
> Over the mountain path.
> The sky is dark with rain clouds,
> Monkeys bitterly wail,
> And the nightingale's song, so lonely and anguished,
> Is sad to hear.
> Few men have skirted this high mountain,
> And a cold wind blows the rain into our faces.[61]

The unrelieved gloom of this selection also serves its purpose in *The Night Inn,* for the play portrays not the transcendence of the mentality of a feeble old man, but the crushing defeat of the wise, humane, and constructive Ch'üan Lao-t'ou. This point is underscored by the invention of two exchanges between Ch'üan and the bullied streetwalker Lin Tai-yü (Nastya). At the close of the first act, Lin Tai-yü is in utter despair and cries out, "This hell, this ghoulish place, I really can't bear it!" Ch'üan replies with tough optimism, "Don't despair. Sooner or later hell will fall."[62] (At the end of the first act of *The Lower Depths,* by contrast, Luka says, "They've pounded me a lot. That's why I'm soft.") But at the close of the play, when Ch'üan has discovered Hsiao-mei's corpse, he collapses to the floor weeping, and it is Lin's turn to comfort him and repeat back to him his advice: "Did you fall, uncle? She's dead anyway, so don't cry. Crying's no use, is it?"[63]

With the elimination of Satin and the decision to sympathize with Ch'üan Lao-t'ou, the root of evil in *The Night Inn* is reduced, baldly, to money. Shih T'o points to Sai Kuan-yin as the vilest of all the characters, and calls on the reader to ask himself why this is so.[64] The answer, in immediate terms, is that her husband's obsession with wealth is inhuman and his sense of propriety is nothing but a cudgel of superstitions he uses to threaten people into submitting to exploitation. Hence, Sai's name, Kuan-yin, becomes a grim satire of the goddess of mercy, and she, in turn, becomes more ruthless and grasping than her husband, whose name, Wen T'ai-shih, is also an ironic reference to a hero of the novel *Feng-shen yen-i* (Canonization of the Gods). The other characters either go down to defeat before her, submit to servile collaboration, or remain in a state of paralysis. Ch'üan Lao-t'ou's nearly solitary efforts in the last act also seem to imply the need for collective action and collective strength, and this undoubtedly pleased the many leftists who have spoken favorably of *The Night Inn.* But, at the same time, Shih T'o does not seem at all optimistic about the possibilities of this, given his portrayal of the characters.

Finally, it is evident that romanticism has been completely abandoned in *The Night Inn,* since the authors have eliminated any expression comparable to that of Satin's in *The Lower Depths,* without offering an alternative strain of romantic vision. The play then becomes an exposé in keeping with the modern concern for social reform and offering the Chinese stage an unusual presentation of "dustbin realism." In his introduction to the play, Shih T'o again and again stresses the darkness, rot, and hopelessness of this lowest rung of society. It is just this aspect of the play that won praise from several critics. Hsü Kuang-p'ing (Ching Sung), So Fei, and Li Chien-wu all recommended the play as giving needed attention to the poor and oppressed. Pa Chin, most of all, praised its portrayal of social inequities and the playwrights' stripping off the "filthy clothes" of their characters to reveal their "naked hearts," finally abandoning any restraint to cry out:

> What good souls! They are not only of our race, they even surpass us. They understand love and understand hate. They can love and they can hate. Moreover, they understand how to sacrifice for this love. This is not a play. This is life: true, real life.[65]

No other play arising from the occupation received as much critical attention and praise from the literary left. *The Night Inn* was, in fact, originally published in *Phenomena* in 1944, but Huang Tso-lin delayed its production until immediately following the Japanese surrender, probably not so much in fear of puppet authority as out of a desire to impress writers returning from the interior with a fresh, trenchant drama with the impeccable name of Gorky as inspiration.

His offering did indeed command public praise from the likes of Pa Chin, Hsia Yen, Hsü Kuang-p'ing, Cheng Chen-to, and others with, one imagines, the implied approval of and harmonious sentiment with the Shanghai theater establishment.

In fact, *The Night Inn* is virtually a reworking of *The Big Circus,* which had already played successfully in 1942–1943. In both plays spurned older women (Kai San-hsing, Sai Kuan-yin) plot their revenge on their former young lovers (Hsiao Ch'ung, Yang Ch'i-lang) and their new loves (Ts'ui-pao, Hsiao-mei). These girls are passive types who respond to their admirers' urgings to run away with them but hesitate, unable to recognize the evil that will and does overtake them for their passiveness. The young men then fail to act decisively to free themselves or their lovers, and this leads to imprisonment (Ts'ui-pao, Yang Ch'i-lang) or suicide (Hsiao-mei, Hsiao Ch'ung). In each case they have been encouraged by well-intentioned and wise but ineffectual old men (Ta-tzu, Ch'üan Lao-t'ou). The last scene of each play focues on these old men in their moment of defeat. All characters in the play have suffered from the exploitation of a manager (Ma T'eng-chiao) or landlord (Wen T'ai-shih), who in turn is ruined: the former losing his circus, the latter losing his life. Both plays replace the scenes of intellectual polemic in their sources with other characters and scenes that are less demanding of the audience's intellect. Hui Hui and Peach in *The Big Circus* serve this function. The death of the little girl Yin Niu-erh in that play may be compared with the death of the tubercular A-man in *The Night Inn*: both call for sympathy and are ignored by the other characters.

Shih T'o's treatment of his sources has drained them of their symbolism, ambiguities, and ironies, replacing them with melodrama. The gestures of the characters are exaggerated beyond those of their sources. Although Shih T'o was undoubtedly drawn to Andreyev's cold sarcasm, he has allowed for scences of open hilarity in *The Big Circus,* and employed even greater sadistic violence in *The Night Inn* than Gorky did in *The Lower Depths.* While he failed to revive the intellectual force of the originals, the action substituted is at least carefully designed to support the main theme in a way that, if it is unduly melodramatic, was effective at the time. By all accounts Shih

T'o succeeded in the basic task of making the plays convincingly Chinese. In 1945 Cheng Chen-to offered his endorsement of this achievement in a manner that precisely reflects Shih T'o's dramatic techniques: "When I read *The Night Inn* adapted by Shih T'o and K'o Ling, I couldn't help pounding the table in admiration. It has been nearly a dozen years since such liveliness, drawn with mature skill and learning, and pungent dialogue have appeared on stage."[66]

Li Chien-wu

Shih T'o's romantic vision remained superficial, but it did provide the force for his satire of conventional society in its many ramifications and added depth to his pessimism. Indeed, the war and particularly the occupation made it difficult to exploit the romantic vein. In this regard, the work of Li Chien-wu shows a writer exploring aspects of the realist heritage, yet clearly still attached to romantic motifs. As a dramatist, Li's popularity in the thirties rested largely on *Che pu-kuo shih ch'un-t'ien* (This Is Only Spring), which employed the elements favored by a romantically inclined audience, including illicit love and fugitive revolutionaries. Yet Li insisted on maintaining a pose of objectivity concerning his success, and fairly ridiculed Pa Jen (Wang Jen-shu) when he praised the play: "Mr. Pa Jen rendered the greatest assistance in the production of this modest work. He stated, 'This is not a play, but life: no more, no less, it is human life. Is not life the highest level of art?' Mr Pa Jen tends to get intoxicated and talk in his sleep."[67] As a critic who championed Flaubert, Li Chien-wu was skeptical of realism and a defender of "beauty" and "poetic truth," albeit achieved through realistic detail.[68] Li's sympathy with romantic writers emerges clearly in critical essays such as his review of Hsiao Chün's *Pa-yüeh ti hsiang-ts'un* (Village in August). Li compares Hsiao Chün with a nineteenth-century French bohemian described by Balzac, and then contrasts them: "But thank heaven, thank earth, there is a fundamental difference between the two of them: Our bohemian does not live only for himself."[69] Similarly, Li contrasts Hsiao Chün's romanticsm with that of the English romantics: "Unlike those self-centered spirits from the first half of the nineteenth century, our writer harbors the enmity of a people and a nation."[70] Li goes on to sum up the spirit of the times in a like manner:

> We live in an age filled with the wrath of men and gods alike, where feeling overrides sense, and heatedness comes easier than coolness. Our sense of righteousness strengthens our feelings, which, however, has never promoted the tranquil state of mind necessary for artists. We do not want to forgive the enemy, nor point up the reasons for the triumphs of the enemy.[71]

Li's complaint that the detachment needed for creativity was nearly impossible to achieve was reflected in his dramatic work as well as in his criticism. Well aware of the rising trend of realism and romantic realism with the advent of the war, he did not altogether apply himself in that direction. In 1938 he joined the Shanghai Theater Arts Society (STAS) as a founding member, and the society revived his *This Is Only Spring* and staged his translation of Romain Rolland's neo-romantic play *Le jeu de l'amour et de la mort* (*Ai yü ssu ti po-tou*).[72] Thereafter he did collaborate on at least two history plays, *Ah Shih-na* and *Yuan Shih-k'ai*. Primarily he offered a series of adaptations from French "well-made" plays, chiefly by Sardou.[73] There was reason enough in 1939 to stage Romain Rolland's play. Rolland was popular, and the play satisfied in part the requirement made by the authorities in the French Concession that STAS perform French plays as part of their repertoire. Critics could graciously concede that the play's espousal of a progressive spirit was a contribution to resistance theater.[74] But the decision to use his name and talent during the forties to push Sardou's work met with as much indifference and hostility as success. His Sardou-inspired plays began appearing in December 1942, shortly after his production of a sentimental costume drama by Fang Chün-i (Wu T'ien) titled *Li-hen t'ien* (Realm of Transcendence), based on the tale of Liang Shan-po and Chu Ying-t'ai. The play failed drastically, and in his introduction to the published script Li remarked rather bitterly on the selfish competition of growing commercialization in the theater as a cause for the failure to mount an adequate production.[75] It is possible that, given his apparent cynicism toward the theater and his awareness that the authorities were keeping a close eye on him, Li deliberately turned to Sardou as the quintessence of a commercial drama, given over to suspense and escapism.

In adapting these plays, Li inevitably had to concern himself with their relevance to Chinese society, even at the most superficial level. His *Chin Hsiao-yü,* taken from *La Tosca,* is set in Peking under the control of a warlord in the twenties. Chin Hsiao-yü, a Peking Opera singer, is the wife of the warlord Sun Shou-hsiang. Hsiao-yü covertly frees her brother, a revolutionary held as a political prisoner by Sun, and hides him in the home of a friend, Fan Yung-li, an archeologist. Sun's agents torture Yung-li until Hsiao-yü, out of concern for him, confesses her brother's hiding place. The brother swallows poison to avoid capture, and Yung-li is thrown into prison to await execution. The police chief offers to free Yung-li if Hsiao-yü will submit to his advances. This she agrees to, but once Yung-li's release is arranged, Hsiao-yü finds an opportunity to stab the police chief and escape with Yung-li. All this might be easily taken as a tale of the Japanese occupation itself, but as art it is simply well-made drama, built on romantic sentiments and suspense mechanisms. One recalls in reading this play the actual shooting of the warlord Sun Ch'uan-fang by a young woman in revenge for Sun's execution of her father and the public sympathy for her when she was tried, wondering why Li would not use such material for a serious exploration of the themes he alludes to in so deliberately trite a fashion in *Chin Hsiao-yü.*

As for his adaptation of other French plays, they were even less attuned to any realities, and Li made no effort to argue that they had any significance. Instead, he offered the following explanation of the relationship between Sardou and his own times:

> His shortcomings show off his successes. Moreover, even if the passions of his characters and the romantic tones lacquer over the drabness of the bourgeoisie; even if we clearly realize that what is before us is merely a play and compare it with the utter gloom of the atmosphere we breathe, isn't that more than enough to endear it to us? Illusion may be forced into a semblance of reality: who, living under the present enlightened philosophy, would not agree?[76]

Li's earlier astuteness as a critic largely gave way to silence. Fortunately he occasionally rose above such disappointing statements as the above, which show a superficial delight in sentiment and device for their own sake. His decline as a dramatist during the wars years was partly redeemed by a romantic comedy, *Ch'ing-ch'un* (Youth). This play also betrays the same superficiality of vision that informs his work with Sardou, but as an original play, spiced with deft use of his native Peking dialect, lively characterization and action, and a well-made structure, it remains one of the better comedies of the war period.

Li's strong use of local color from the Peking region has made commentators compare it to a play he wrote a decade earlier, *Liang Yun-ta*. This play, however, was a tragedy, and Li's inspiration for *Youth* was probably Shih T'o's *The Big Circus*. Li had noted the importance of the romantic love in that play as a factor in its success. Moreover, there are important similarities between the two plays, primarily the repetition of the theme of an ardent young man attempting to persuade a maltreated, timid girl to escape with him from an oppressive environment, and the inclusion of a patronizing, older parent figure. What ultimately turns Li's play into a comedy is that the parent figure, in this case the young man's widowed mother, saves the day by rescuing the timid girl. Another important factor in comparing Li's play with Shih T'o's is the vivid dialogue and heated exchanges filled with the slang of the common man.

The action of the play, in five acts, runs from early summer 1908 to early summer 1909 in a North China village, a balmy, nostalgic setting, the stage dominated by a rustically dilapidated Kuan Ti temple which serves also as the village schoolhouse, symbolizing the decay of the Ch'ing dynasty. T'ien Hsi-erh is a mischievous youth filled with a hopeless love for one of the village headman's daughters, Hsiang-ts'ao. The mainstay of the play, Hsi-erh's mother (the widow T'ien), alternately scolds and beats her son for failing to make good, and, with righteous widowhood and indignant motherhood, rails hilariously at headman Yang, who is constantly trying to punish Hsi-erh for flirting with his daughter. Headman Yang attempts first to beat and then to hang Hsi-erh, but unable to circumvent widow T'ien's defense of her son, Yang precipitately marries his daughter to an eleven-year-old son of a neighboring gentry. This brings Hsi-erh to the point of despair and then determination in the fourth act. Searching out the equally miserable Hsiang-ts'ao, he recites his woes to her, and his determination and devotion: "For you I would kill, commit arson, steal, rob, stand trial, get my head chopped off. It wouldn't matter to me."[77] He identifies himself with the coming revolution, quoting an educated friend: "Ching *hsiang-kung* says the dynasty will soon change, and everything will change with it" (p. 236). He backs up his passionate assertions with action. Whereas in the first act he has not only allowed his mother to beat him, but even provided her with the stick, in the fourth act, when she interferes with his courtship of Hsiang-ts'ao, he threatens to beat her and locks her up in the Kuan Ti temple, along with other figures of authority, his schoolteacher and the *chü-jen* squire. "I've gone mad! Whoever gets in my way, I'll slaughter him!" he shouts (p. 235). Indeed, Li Chien-wu pushes the fun to its limits by the constant but inconsequential threat of violence. In the fifth act, Hsiang-ts'ao, having again failed to act, is caught by her father and ordered to commit suicide for her association with Hsi-erh. When Hsi-erh pleads for her life, his mother finally realizes how much her son's well-being depends upon Hsiang-ts'ao's survival. Unable to convince Yang to let Hsiang-ts'ao work for her as a maid, widow T'ien then begins to mother Hsiang-ts'ao and breaks down her resolve to obey her father. Unable to force the issue, Yang gives up in disgust, and the protagonists are left to live happily ever after.

It is Hsi-erh's rebelliousness and romantic love for Hsiang-ts'ao, his iconoclasm and sensitivity, that motivate the play, though it is his mother who resolves the action happily. Nonethless, the encroachments of modern civilization barely appear on stage, and even Hsi-erh's mentality is rooted in tradition, despite his flaunting himself as part of a reformist or revolutionary movement. He tells Hsiang-ts'ao of the bitter retreat he made to a city god temple after her marriage to the squire's son: "One by one I scrutinized the ten kings of hell. . . . It seemed they all had something to tell me. . . . It seemed they were telling me, 'This world is not you young people's, but that doesn't mean it's those older people's, either. Look you, it's ours . . . it's up to fate, not up to men!'" (p. 234). The underlying appeal of the play is just its portrait of a world where authority and traditions are collapsing, all for the better, all without odious consequences. Even widow T'ien is allowed to reflect, "These last years, since the

Long Hairs stirred up so much trouble, people must have changed, and it's hard to find a real gentleman anywhere anymore" (p. 224). The benevolent anarchism that flourishes in *Youth* is just the comic reverse of the paralyzing oppression that grips the world of Shih T'o's *The Big Circus* and *The Night Inn*.

So compelling was the nostalgic appeal of this play to some that one critic remarked: "This is that small bit of heaven and earth stored in everyone's bosom. When we've seen the play we can't help asking ourselves: And our beautiful youth? The happy and carefree companions of our youth?"[78] One important aspect of the play supporting this fantasy of the past is the sustained interest in and employment of various supporting characters. Notable among these is the wine-swilling, ghost-fearing Hung Pi-tzu (Red Nose), watchman for headman Yang's estate. Red Nose is frequently taken to task for his incompetence, and humiliatingly incriminated by the local urchins in the theft of peaches from the schoolmaster's orchard. He makes a fine storyteller for the children in one interlude, and this together with other incidental aspects of the play are reminiscent of traditional, popular performing literature. Finally, Hung Pi-tzu is given his moment of triumph in the adult world when the assorted figures of local renown locked inside the temple by Hsi-erh plead with Hung Pi-tzu to rescue them. It is a task he performs with delicious slowness.

Perhaps it is not too much to say of this play that in its comic way it represented a past which its audience could feel it had mastered against the present to which it was being subjected. In that sense, the play is tangential to one of the most significant trends in literature under the occupation, which was the exploration of tradition and a return to its resources for literary creativity.

CHAPTER THREE

The Resurgence of Tradition: Modern Drama

The war years saw the persistence of many works imitative of traditional forms. In the first year of the war, Huan-chu lou-chu's novel of supernatural knight-errantry, *Shu-shan chien-hsia chuan* (Swordsmen of the Hills of Shu), was published in book form after its serialization in a Tientsin newspaper to enthusiastic reception throughout China. During the war, swashbuckling tales continued to find a wide audience. A more sober attempt at *chang-hui* fiction was Chang Hung's historical roman-à-clef *Hsü nieh-hai hua* (Sequel to Flower on an Ocean of Sin), published in the Peking journal *Chung-ho* (Equilibrium and Harmony: The Sino-Japanese Monthly). Aside from fiction, there was continued practice of poetry in classical styles, notably in the Nanking periodical *T'ung-sheng* (Accord); the posthumous publication of Cheng Hsiao-hsü's verse in *Hai-tsang-lou shih* (Poems from Hai-tsang's Villa); and many essays in *wen-yen*. Classical theater remained very active despite the retirement of such figures as Mei Lan-fang. But for an occasional allusion or turn of phrase, in all this literature it might have seemed that the Ch'ing dynasty had never ended and no May Fourth movement had ever taken place.

The predominance of tradition in the literature of the occupation is not, however, measured solely by the output of works in pure traditional forms. What is more important to the study of modern literature is the influence tradition exercised over forms that from their inception were considered modern: the modern spoken drama (*hua-chü*), discussed in this chapter, and the vernacular familiar essay, which will be taken up in the following chapter. A number of noted dramatists and essayists under the occupation were aware of their inheritance of a progressive spirit in literature and vocal in their support of it, yet at the same time, for various reasons, reached an accommodation with tradition in form, subject matter, or theme. They did not collectively represent a movement or necessarily share any common ground in their personal and social lives, and their motives and methods were diverse. Indeed, the invocation of tradition as an influence is a theme of forbidding breadth. It could very well be used as an approach to a number of other authors, poets, and dramatists discussed elsewhere in different chapters.[1] Yet despite the diversity of styles and concerns in all genres, use of the resources of traditional forms was the dominant trend in drama and the essay, and it is most productive to concentrate on what a group of dramatists and essayists as successors to May Fourth did with what tradition offered them.

The Development of Commercial Theater

It was during the war that modern professional theater in Shanghai grew to proportions unprecedented in China. As commercial theater, it has never been matched since. A brief survey of the wartime history of this theater establishment reveals how much of its vitality was given over to examination of traditions both in styles and in themes.

Following the end of the fighting in December 1937, the departure of the remaining major playwrights from Shanghai left the theater in a lull for several months. After a few unpromising attempts to restore professional theater to the foreign concessions, seven playwrights organized what was soon known as the Shanghai Theatre Arts Society (Shanghai chü-i she), or STAS. Of these writers, only Li Chien-wu had a national reputation. Yü Ling, Ku Chung-i, and Wu Jen-chih were to become prominent figures during the war; Li Po-lung, Hsü Ch'ü, and Chang Chieh were to remain relatively obscure names. Through connections with the Sino-French Friendship Association (Chung-fa lien-i hui), they were able to obtain permission to stage plays on condition that they included French dramas. With this much foundation, they soon attracted most of the other playwrights then in the concessions, including A Ying (Ch'ien Hsing-ts'un), Ch'en Hsi-ho, Chu Tuan-chün, Hsü Hsin-chih, and Wu Yung-kang. In July 1938 they staged their first production, Ku Chung-i's *Jen chih ch'u* (Man at His Birth), adapted from the French drama *Topaze* by Marcel Pagnol. The choice was not fortuitous, as a previous translation of the play into Chinese had received a literary prize from the Sino-French Friendship Association, and the play was known to be an audience pleaser.[2] But for a year STAS remained on a semi-professional footing, with only one or two performances of each production on weekends, until by the summer of 1939 the company was able to summon the capital to rent a theater of its own. The first play to be given an extended run was Yü Ling's new drama *Yeh Shanghai* (Shanghai Night), a topical problem play on the theme of resistance whose performance was timed to coincide with the second anniversary of the Battle for Shanghai (13 August 1937). The play is certainly among Yü Ling's best efforts and was well received, but not so well as to meet production costs. The first commercial success followed in October 1939, with A Ying's *Ming-mo i-hen* (Sorrow for the Fall of the Ming) or *Pi hsüeh hua* (Jade Blood Flower), which ran for thirty-five performances to full houses and put STAS financially in the black.[3]

Until A Ying's success, there had been no appreciable difference in audience response to costume drama (*ku-chuang hsi-chü*) versus Western adaptations and plays in modern dress. But *Sorrow for the Fall of the Ming* signaled a potential for costume drama that was followed in 1940 by an increased number of historical plays. Until the last month of 1940, the principal successes at the box office were two costume dramas imported from the interior, Yang Han-sheng's *Li Hsiu-ch'eng chih ssu* (The Death of Li Hsiu-ch'eng) and Wu Tsu-kuang's *Cheng-ch'i ko* (Song of Righteousness). It must be said that not all costume dramas met with success, and much depended on the quality of the performance. This was the case with a work of modern scope, Wu T'ien's *Chia* (Family), adapted from the novel by Pa Chin and given a highly theatrical flourish by the director Hung Mo. *Family* opened in December at the Lafayette Garden Theater (La-fei hua-yuan) and ran to full houses for three months—the first play to break, let alone exceed by far, the record set by *Sorrow for the Fall of the Ming*. This production became the chief success of STAS and one of the four longest runs in Shanghai during the war.

The ability of STAS to cultivate a regular theater-going audience had long since begun to stimulate other groups, both amateur and professional. In 1939 a Sino-French Theater Society (Chung-fa chü-she) was organized, and late that year China's only prewar professional group of national reputation, the China Traveling Dramatic Company (Chung-kuo lü-hsing chü-t'uan), returned from an extended stay in Hong Kong, still under the management of T'ang Huai-ch'iu. But offerings by local writers were overshadowed by revivals of Ts'ao Yü's plays. In early 1941, a group of KMT operatives organized the Sky Breeze Theater Troupe (T'ien-feng chü-t'uan) and after a series of failures commissioned a rising young playwright, Yao K'o (Yao Hsin-nung), to write a play that might restore them to financial solvency. The result was *Ch'ing kung yuan* (Malice in the Ch'ing Court), translated by Jeremy Ingalls under the title *The Malice of Empire*. Directed by Fei Mu, the play opened in July at the Hsüan-kung Theater and ran well into October, making it the second of the four major commercial successes during the war.

The success of *Malice in the Ch'ing Court* produced by a relatively unknown organization perhaps brought to the fore internal dissensions within STAS. In August 1941 Yao K'o, Huang Tso-lin, Wu Jen-chih, and others formed the Shanghai Stage Society (Shanghai chih-yeh chü-t'uan) and occupied the Carlton Theater (K'a-erh-teng hsi-yuan) in late 1941. In December they were staging Ts'ao Yü's *Shui-pien* (Metamorphosis) when the Japanese entered the foreign concessions, and all theater groups voluntarily disbanded.

The disruption of the Japanese occupation of the concessions further fragmented the theater world. In February 1942 Fei Mu formed the Shanghai Arts Theater (Shanghai i-shu chü-t'uan), or SAT, from actors in the Sky Breeze company and various motion picture studios. With the exception of the mild success of Fei Mu's *Yang kuei-fei*, SAT limped through most of 1942 with little success. Other playwrights and theater workers were having no better luck. The former members of the Shanghai Stage Society merged again as the K'u-kan Players (K'u-kan chü-t'uan), and in early autumn 1942 agreed to joint productions with SAT. The K'u-kan–SAT merger produced two of the landmark works of the period, *Ta-ma-hsi-t'uan* (The Big Circus) by Shih T'o, and *Ch'iu Hai-t'ang* (Begonia) adapted from Ch'in Shou-ou's novel by Huang Tso-lin, Ku Chung-i, and Fei Mu. *The Big Circus* restored vitality to the stage with a forty-day run in October and November, as well as a revival the following year. *Ch'iu Hai-t'ang* broke all records, opening 24 December 1942 at the Carlton and running for 135 days to 9 May 1943. It has remained the most successful commercial stage production in modern China, with several revivals during and after the war.

Long before *Ch'iu Hai-t'ang* ended its run, new professional groups were formed and commercial theater was riding a wave of unprecedented popularity. By April 1943 there were six theaters offering modern "spoken drama" and seven theaters producing classical Chinese opera, predominantly Peking Opera with a revival of regional styles toward the end of the war. Moreover, theater managers offering modern drama were able to command prices of up to twenty yuan per ticket, against thirty yuan at classical opera theaters and five yuan at first-run motion picture houses.[4] By 1944 thirteen theaters were offering modern drama.[5] Against this portrait of commercialism it must be said that many of the theater workers refused higher commissions or salaries from the government-controlled film industry, nor did their income demands approach those of many classical opera performers. The profit motive was considered unfashionable, if necessary, in most theater circles.

As to the various successes of theater companies, no one group emerged as dominant. SAT, following *Ch'iu Hai-t'ang,* ran Ku Chung-i's *San ch'ien-chin* (Three Daughters, adapted from *King Lear*) for sixty-five days during May, June, and July, but then came under severe pressure from Nanking to participate in celebrations for the return of the foreign concessions to the Nanking government. After carrying out this unpleasant requirement by performing *Family,* Fei Mu disbanded his group in a cleansing ritual. It was reformed as New Arts Theater Troupe (Hsin i chü-t'uan), which staged his *Fu-sheng liu-chi* (Six Chapters from a Floating Life, adapted from the work by Shen San-pai), attracting audiences for over three months. Fei Mu could not duplicate the popularity of this production, however, and aside from the mild success of Li Chien-wu's *Ch'ing-ch'un* (Youth), little more of note emerged from Fei Mu's troupes.

Shanghai United Arts Theater (Shanghai lien-i chü-t'uan), formed from the disbanded STAS, picked up the first work by the rising woman writer Yang Chiang, *Ch'en-hsin ju-i* (As You Desire), as well as several mediocre pieces by Li Chien-wu. This group again disbanded and reformed as T'ung mao, performing another Yang Chiang play, *Lung chen ch'eng chia* (Swindle). K'u-kan, having broken off from SAT before its dissolution, picked up a third of Yang Chiang's plays, *Yu-hsi jen-chien* (Sport with the World), and concluded the war with the production of *The Night Inn* by Shih T'o and K'o Ling. Chou Chien-yun, an independent producer who had backed Butterfly Wu productions in the thirties, formed the Great Central Theater Arts Company (Ta-chung chü-i kung-szu), whose chief offering was Chang Ai-ling's *Ch'ing-ch'eng chih lien* (Love in a Fallen City), which ran well beyond a month. In 1943 a company at the Lyceum Theater (Lan-hsin ta hsi-yuan), the I-kuang chü-t'uan, restaged Wu Tsu-kuang's *Song of Righteousness,* dropping the name of the author, who was in Chungking, and changing the title to *Wen T'ien-hsiang,* the name of the hero. Despite its being considered a popular resistance play when it was first staged in 1940, its revival in 1943 proved even more popular, and *Wen T'ien-hsiang* went on to become the fourth of the most successful plays in occupied Shanghai. Ironically, by that time Wu Tsu-kuang himself had abandoned patriotic plays for the vapid comedies that were then in demand in Chungking, and it remained for a relatively unknown troupe in occupied Shanghai to continue the success of his best-known work.

There were also a number of notable flops during the Pacific War years, which indicated the unpredictability of audience tastes. At the Paris Theater (Pa-li ta hsi-yuan, the K'u-kan Players opened its own series of productions with K'o Ling's *P'iao* (Gone With the Wind), to no success, and followed it up hopefully with *Liang shang chün-tzu* (A Gentleman of the Beams), a minor masterpiece from Molnar's *Doctor Ur,* which did no better. The failure of an adaptation of a piece as popular in China as *Gone With the Wind* followed by that of a playwright and director who had demonstrated his ability to appeal to Shanghai audiences shook Huang's confidence in the potential of the audience. This, unfortunately, made him cautious and conservative in selecting scripts for production by the K'u-kan Players. Even more stunning were the miscalculations of T'ung-mao and Shanghai United Arts. The latter group attempted to capitalize on the popularity of *Ch'iu Hai-t'ang* by adapting Chang Hen-shui's recent novel *Man chiang hung* (Fire Over the Yangtze), employing the collective talents of Li Chien-wu, Wu Jen-chih, Li Chih-mo, and others to write and stage the production. It died quickly to the resounding indifference of the public and attack by the critics. T'ung-mao later invested its capital in a grand but stark production of *Family* as adapted by Ts'ao Yü. But even the names of Pa Chin and Ts'ao Yü could not pull the production past opening night. Performances of *T'ien Chieh-erh* (La Petite Chocolatiere), adapted from Paul Gavault's comedy by Wei Yü-ch'ien, proved the most reliable source of income for T'ung-mao.[6] Other companies such as the China Traveling Dramatic Company, kept to a more even but unspectacular course. On the second of two trips to Peking it fell afoul of authorities there, and the members were able to return to Shanghai only after a month in jail. They managed to survive the war chiefly on plays by Chou I-pai and a revival of *Malice in the Ch'ing Court.*

What emerges from this outline history of theater in wartime Shanghai is the predominance of plays that turned to tradition. Of the four major commercial successes, excluding *Family* by Wu T'ien, three were costume dramas with strong ties to traditional themes or materials: *Malice in the Ch'ing Court, Ch'iu Hai-t'ang,* and *Wen T'ien-hsiang.* It remains to examine the works of several representative writers in relation to the native tradition.

The Limits of Contemporary Realism: Yü Ling

With the departure of Chinese forces, the remaining playwrights in Shanghai still felt committed to resistance theater, and thought it an obligation to write or select plays for production that were in some way relevant to the war effort. While writers in Hong Kong or the interior were free to experiment with a variety of forms and vent their patriotism without restraint, the political situation in Shanghai limited, though by no means extinguished, this expression. The hostility of Japanese and puppet-government agents, combined with the censorship of concession authorities wary of allowing inflammatory literature, forced discretion and restraint upon playwrights and producers. The realistic portrayal of life in the foreign concessions itself carrying a patriotic theme was, hence, a challenge few writers attempted with any success.

Perhaps the most noteworthy efforts were those of Yü Ling (Yu Ching), a Communist playwright with considerable experience in agit-prop theater, who had been assigned to remain in Shanghai after the Chinese city fell in December 1937. Yü Ling was one of the founding members of STAS, which performed his *Hua chien lei* (Flowers Draw Tears) in February 1939 at the Carlton Theater. In this melodrama, Yü Ling does not even attempt to deal with the problem of life in the concessions following the Battle of Shanghai, but opens the action of the play prior to the outbreak of the war. The main plot is centered on Mi-mi, an orphaned Shanghai ballroom girl, who must refuse the advances of a poor but sincere student who cannot buy her out of a contract to become the concubine of a Hong Kong merchant. The student leaves to join the army and is succeeded by a young businessman who frees Mi-mi from her contract. But when complications arise that threaten his marriage to his boss's daughter, he attempts to lure Mi-mi into suicide. A girlfriend snatches a bottle of Lysol from Mi-mi's lips, exposes the young businessman, and takes Mi-mi off to join the army as a medic. On the battlefield Mi-mi finds courage and purpose as she tends the young student, now mortally wounded. This play has all the stereotyping and sentimentality, plus more than a few hints of class struggle, that one might expect from the typical Communist playwright trying to appeal to the masses in a popular form. An adaptation of a French film, *Club des Femmes,* titled *Nü-tzu kung-yü* (Women's Hostel), written for an all-women's amateur theater club and also performed by STAS in June 1939, further marked Yü Ling's themes as centered on young women, virtue, and patriotism.

This is no less true of his chief work during his stay in Shanghai, *Shanghai Night,* the first play to be given an extended run by STAS in August 1939. Yet in this play Yü Ling has managed to temper his portrayal into a problem play, no doubt deriving some lessons from Ibsen, particularly in the final act. The STAS program notes quoted the Bible to introduce the play: "Man does not live by bread alone." The notes went on as a manifesto of STAS:

> We engage in drama both for the sake of life [*sheng*] and livelihood [*huo*]. We engage in dramatic art for the sake of dramatic art. Naturally we cannot forget history, nor can we forget the age in which we find ourselves. Man has an "eternal life," yet he cannot "live" apart from "time" and "space." Thus, the so-called extended performance at this time and place cannot sustain our livelihood. Yet we seek "life"—life and livelihood in performing dramatic art. Man does not live by bread alone.[7]

The play on the word *shenghuo* to express the frustrated discontent and determined idealism of theater workers is taken from one of the crucial scenes in *Shanghai Night.* The play in general concerns the problems of refugees from the countryside in the concessions. One subplot deals with Yun-ku, a country girl, whose father is missing and whose mother is gravely ill. The landlord prepares to throw them out for not meeting the rent increase. Yun-ku turns for help to two neighbors, Feng Feng and Wu Chi, girls who have taken up taxi-dancing. Yun-ku does spend an evening selling herself as a dance partner, but when she returns home with medicine for her mother, purchased through her sinful activities, she finds her mother already dead. Despite the fact that Yun-ku is exonerated, since she has sacrificed herself on behalf of others, Yü Ling cannot help freeing her from this situation by having her mother die. This allows her to act on her bitterness and leave for the countryside, with the implication that she will join the guerrilla forces there.

The play touches on a number of pertinent problems, such as how to generate income without exploiting others, how to demonstrate sympathy for the resistance, the maintaining of optimism and faith in the resistance, and whether it is a time to begin a family or remain devoted to duty first (a traditional theme, brought up in the play through the phrase, "While the Hsiung-nü have not yet been vanquished, how can one raise a family?"). The main plot concerns the fortunes of the gentry family surnamed Mei who, fleeing from the countryside, are reduced to the verge of starvation by police barricades erected to keep refugees out of the overcrowded foreign concessions. When a resident, a young fellow-townsman named Ch'ien K'ai-chih, finally lets them slip through the barricade, they are chased by policemen and scatter, losing track of each other for two months. During that time K'ai-chih marries O-hui and supports her mother and their maid. Despite his initially honorable motives, K'ai-chih falls in with a plot by a friend to send O-hui's father back to the countryside. There, through connections with the Japanese, they plan to have the father made a local official and set up a silk business.

The father is found and returns to the countryside, not realizing the uses to which he is to be put. K'ai-chih's shady associate, however, is gunned down by underground workers for his association with the Japanese, and the father returns exhausted and furious at conditions in the countryside and the attempts to use him. Moreover, O-hui has seen K'ai-chih in the company of the ballroom girl Wu Chi, being used to entertain Japanese, and suspects K'ai-chih of infidelity. K'ai-chih is pitifully contrite, denying his infidelity and swearing to abandon all connections with collaborators. O-hui has nothing but contempt for K'ai-chih and adamantly insists he leave the household. The father, having doffed his *ch'ang-shan* as a symbolic act of rejuvenation and progressiveness, now urges O-hui to accept her husband's vow that he will start a new life. But O-hui shows no sign of backing down. However, as the curtain falls, K'ai-chih has gone upstairs to pack, while O-hui contemplates their situation, and room has been left for reconciliation. Yü Ling's restraint in this conclusion is worth noting, especially in comparison to the revised version of the play that appeared in the 1950s and 1960s. In these revisions the father extols the New Fourth Army, and the family unanimously shows K'ai-chih the door. In 1939 there was still some room for forgiving the contrite collaborator.

Yü Ling's problem play is essentially an extension of the questions raised in Mao Tun's novel *Tzu-yeh* (Midnight). For even though the war has flared up, the problem of how to live an honorable life that contributes to the sovereignty of China and the prosperity of its people when exploitive foreigners are in control remains. Short of joining the actual fighting, there is no clear-cut answer, and life remains a compromise in the hope of and faith in a liberation. But Yü Ling's sally into this much realism proved it to be a dead end. He had carried its possibilities as far as they could go, intellectually or legally, and the play still falls short of offering the kinds of heroism a patriotic movement calls for, and the spectacle that theater can provide. Moreover, Hsia Yen's "slice of life" plays on Shanghai were appearing as absorbing alternative approaches. Yü Ling's own answer was typical of his time. On the one hand, he wrote a patriotic costume drama, *Ta Ming ying-lieh chuan* (Heroes of the Ming Dynasty), and on the other, he turned again to adapting Western dramas, such as *Man ch'eng feng-yü* (A City Scandalized) from Galsworthy's *Show*, whose relevance to the war effort was at best indirect. Yü Ling's final answer was to leave Shanghai altogether for the interior before the Japanese took control of the foreign concessions. At that time he brought out a sequel to *Shanghai Night* called *Spring South of the River* (*Hsing-hua ch'un-yü chiang-nan*).[8]

The Rise of Costume Drama:
A Ying, Chou I-pai, Ku Chung-i

Adaptations of Western dramas, especially French plays in satisfaction of the requirements of the French authorities, offered relief from the themes of war and resistance, and were accepted with grace by most critics. But the demand for relevance to the war effort was acute in various circles, and even Wu T'ien's adaptation of *Family* came under attack. One Shanghai critic found himself constrained to say the following in defense of the production:

> Taking *Family* as an example, while it is not directly concerned with the endeavors of resistance and reconstruction, it portrays the dissolution and fall of the feudal extended family system, and reflects the struggle and opposition of a generation of youth toward the old society and the older generation. Therefore, at the same time, it teaches the audience that they must struggle against society and oppose the old conventions, arbitrariness, rites and superstitions. If we do not deny that these "archaic things" still seriously influence the progress of our society, and are at this moment particularly an obstacle to the development of advances in the war of resistance, then we have no reason to deny that the present performance of *Family* in Shanghai is of the utmost importance.[9]

But this was a time when the question of the survival of the nation took precedence over the question of its social progress, and playwrights found that they could allude to both issues through historical drama and transcend the complications of Shanghai and the United Front by donning the costumes of their ancestors. Moreover, they could make a living at it. The first concrete example of this was A Ying's *Sorrow for the Fall of the Ming*. And even as it was achieving success, Ou-yang Yü-ch'ien's play *Mu Lan ts'ung chün* (Mu Lan Joins the Army) was appearing as a film, providing added financial stimulus to dramatists.

The impetus for writing historical plays was strong and arose from a wide range of sources. A generation of modern dramatists had already experimented for two decades with historical materials for their settings and themes. From within the ranks of classical opera itself had come artists interested in accommodating the classical to the modern. Before the war, Mei Lan-fang and Ou-yang Yü-ch'ien had discussed adaptation projects with new writers such as Yao K'o and T'ien Han. In 1936, with war becoming inevitable, the Nationalist government launched an "indigenous culture" movement (*pen-wei wen-hua*) and published a list of heroes from Chinese history approved for artistic representation. Leftists and Communists too had their own interests in working with traditional resources to advance their movement for "mass literature" (*ta-chung wen-i*) with indigenous appeals to the broadest spectrum of Chinese society. With the advent of war, nearly every dramatist in China tried his hand at costume drama, stirring up an additional body of critical commentary on questions of both form and content in re-creating the past on stage.

As a Communist writer and critic, A Ying was undoubtedly responding to orthodox policy, just as his criticism of Lu Hsün and then Lu Hsün's imitators stemmed from his political associations. As A Ying or Wei Ju-hui, Ch'ien Hsing-ts'un wrote and published nearly a dozen plays between 1937 and 1942, by which time he fled Shanghai.[10] He had turned to writing plays just prior to the war, and most if not all of his plays are badly flawed. That the writer should have been committed to patriotic writing is more than justifiable, but one can only question his taste in which works as *T'ao-hua yuan*

(Peach Blossom Spring). A Ying's inspiration for this work derived from a translation in 1924 of Musakōji Saneatsu's *Tōkagen* (Peach Blossom Spring) by T'ien Han. A Ying objected to the "humane philosophy" and "antiviolence" of the Japanese author, and the play is turned into an unlikely propaganda vehicle. A young man and his beautiful mistress are forced to flee their utopian realm before invading hunters, who burn down the forest. When the forest has grown back, they return, now skilled in martial arts, to dance and sing that they will "guard our Peach Blossom Spring." That A Ying went to such lengths for militant literature borders on the absurd. On the other hand, the realistic potential of his play *Pu yeh ch'eng* (City of No Night) is smothered in tiresome expositions on the theme of class struggle. Even a sympathetic commentator, Ku Chung-i, could only remark that such works as *City of No Night* and *Orioles Flight* (*Ch'ün-ying luan-fei*) were "disappointing."[11]

A Ying had for a time before the war participated in the fashionable research into late Ming literature, especially the *Hsiao-p'in wen* essays popularized by Chou Tso-jen and Lin Yü-t'ang.[12] The advent of war had shifted attention in some circles to late Ming resistance against the Manchus (the Recovery Society or Fu-she was a reflection of this in Shanghai), and this interest provided A Ying with his central project, the creation of a cycle of four plays called the *Nan Ming shih-chü* (Southern Ming historical dramas). With copious notes from the research of his friend, the scholar-poet Liu Ya-tzu, A Ying brought forth heroes to compete with those of other playwrights. The first and most successful of the plays in the cycle was *Sorrow for the Fall of the Ming*, originally called *Jade Blood Flower*. It was soon made into a film under the title *Ko Nen-niang* by National United Film Company (Kuo-lien tien-ying kung-szu) and later restaged under that title.

The heroine of the play, Ko Nen-niang, is a beautiful misfit in the world of expensive Nanking prostitutes in the late Ming who practices fencing. As she explains, she was sold into prostitution by her uncle after she was orphaned. News arrives that Yang-chou has fallen to the Ch'ing forces, and that Ming officials in Nanking are preparing to hand over the city in hopes of preferment in the new regime. Nen-niang, a staunch loyalist, urges her young patron, Sun

K'o-hsien, to leave the city and join the resistance being organized under the prince of T'ang, vowing to follow him. But in the second act, set a year later in Fukien, we learn that Cheng Chih-lung has failed to mobilize his powerful forces in support of the prince of T'ang and is negotiating with Ch'ing agents. The remonstrances of his own family, including his son Cheng Ch'eng-kung, and Ko Nen-niang, acting as courier from the doomed prince of T'ang, have no effect on Cheng Chih-lung. Three years later, in act three, Nen-niang is reunited with Sun K'o-hsien in the hills of Chekiang, where she leads a band of women guerrillas. Refusing offers of amnesty from Ch'ing officials, the loyalists prepare to try to fight their way out of a Ch'ing encirclement. The effort having failed, the fourth act shows their conduct as prisoners. When Nen-niang and her confidante, Mei Niang, refuse the offers of the Ch'ing general Po-lo to make them concubines, he orders the execution of Sun K'o-hsien. When Po-lo attempts to fondle Mei Niang, a fight breaks out. Mei Niang lays hold of a knife and stabs one of Po-lo's puppet officials, and is then stabbed by Po-lo who, in turn, is attacked barehanded by Nen-niang. The guards drag Nen-niang off him, but she bites through her tongue in rage and spits blood into Po-lo's face. Sun exits to face his execution, laughing as a report arrives that a peasant army has invested Po-lo's position.

Hsia Yen's response to *Sorrow for the Fall of the Ming* was not favorable: "There is no way to associate the conclusion of historic tragedies with the actual events of a later time."[13] This charge, that the play was essentially irrelevant to the concerns of the modern age, was opposed by others. One critic wrote that since history is progressive the feudal past will not be repeated, but the writer can select events in history that contain points of similarity with the present and render those events as truthfully as possible, avoiding anachronisms. A Ying, he argued, had fulfilled these criteria for historic drama. Moreover, while the play is not intended as a portrait of the present, it is a reminder that the current struggle is the result of past events. In the third act, when the future destruction of the Ch'ing is implied by an actor, the audience is reminded of the Taiping Rebellion and Sun Yat-sen, and of its own place in the development of history.[14] Chou I-pai also wrote in defense of the content of the play by comparing it to its dramatic sources, a *ch'uan-ch'i* drama named *T'ieh kuan t'u* (Iron Crown Scroll), and a late Ch'ing *p'i-huang* adaptation, *Sorrow for the Fall of the Ming,* by two men later active in the Republican revolution. He stressed that the old plays had concentrated on the fate of the empire as the concern of the imperial household, to the exclusion of the theme that foreign domination concerned all the people. By contrast, A Ying's play portrays the "righteousness of the people" and the "ugliness of traitors," precisely what was lacking in the previous plays; it shows the masses, not simply an emperor or a few heroic figures.[15]

It is interesting to note in connection with this analysis of the play the spectrum of sentiments appealed to, for they incorporate both traditional and somewhat modernized statements. For example, when Cheng Ch'eng-kung urges his father to resist the Manchus, he twice raises the theme of family honor: "Father, we are both Ming officials. Alive we should be Ming officials. Dead, we should be ghosts of the Ming! If the Cheng family is to go down in history untarnished, then we must be scrupulous and serious in whatever we undertake."[16] When Ko Nen-niang joins in the debate, she adds another dimension:

KO NEN-NIANG: Think, my lord—the troops at the front have risked their lives, and now they're fighting with their backs against the wall—and all for what? The common people [*pai-hsing*] are offering up everything they have, helping us, and for what? It's for the common people everywhere! They've always held you in highest respect, so of course this will make them despair.

CHENG CHIH-LUNG: The common people don't understand affairs of state.

KO NEN-NIANG: What do you mean they don't understand? They understand more than we do. If they hadn't joined forces to help, not only would the prince of Lu have long ago been finished off, but you, my lord, would not be around today.[17]

Ko Nen-niang's implication that the common people were endowed with a national consciousness apart from that of the elite has a distinctly modern ring to it that suited the views of a leftist patriot during the United Front.

The characterization in the play was also examined by Chou I-pai in the light of classical theater, for the characters fit the stage types of tradition, such as Sun K'o-hsien as a *ching,* and Cheng Chih-lung and another collaborator, Ts'ai Ju-heng, as *ch'ou*. Such types, Chou stated, are quite alive at the present time among the heroes and traitors of China. But the characterization was not satisfactory to others sympathetic to the play as a whole. Hui T'ang could not help judging Ko Nen-niang's character as flat, while there were no real points of difference between the heroes Cheng Ch'eng-kung and Sun K'o-hsien, or the villains Cheng Chih-lung and Ts'ai Ju-heng.

The same critic also agreed that the structure of the play was quite loose, with each act virtually a play in itself. This is undeniable, for all that really matters in the play are speeches and gestures of loyalty and defiance. These are rather well done, though certainly not brilliantly, and the whole attitude toward the relationship of scenes to the play as a whole seems inherited from Ming and Ch'ing *ch'uan-ch'i*. So are many of the techniques in the play. There are scenes of singing and dancing to traditional tunes, comic relief, plot exposition, quotations from traditional sources, and even the use of *tao-pai*, stylized speech used in the spoken parts of classical opera. This last feature was strongly criticized by Li Chien-wu as an artificial form of expression that never had any currency in actual life and had no place on the modern stage as a representation of archaic speech.[18]

But *Sorrow for the Fall of the Ming* was probably too successful for A Ying to make much of the criticism to heart. After dashing off *Hai-kuo ying-hsiung* (Hero of an Island Nation), he continued to the third play of his series, *Yang O chuan* (The Story of Yang O), concerning another sword-wielding woman of the late Ming, this time an attendant of a consort to the Ming prince Chu Yu-lang. Yang O's husband dies in Burma, while she herself, in Kunming, tries to help organize resistance to the Ch'ing collaborator Wu San-kuei, and attempts to assassinate him. Yang O is given to strong fantasies, one an imagined reunion with her dead husband, and another a deathbed dream of skewering Wu San-kuei. Despite these turns in dramatic technique, *The Story of Yang O* is essentially a repetition of *Sorrow for the Fall of the Ming* in structure, character, and style. If anything, A Ying was even more intent on demonstrating his use of historical sources, and the script is full of footnotes testifying to the labors of scholarship. A Ying also testified to his concern with art. Liu Ya-tzu had pressed numerous notes and proposals for the play upon him, which A Ying studied, not without a touch of condescension: "What I couldn't altogether accept was that Mr. Ya-tzu occupied a historian's position, and hoped for a long narrative of historical facts, for in drama we must keep an eye on the dramatic nature of historical facts, and it is very difficult to render a thorough portrayal."[19] In truth, A Ying's work was questionable as history and half-baked as art. Nevertheless, *Sorrow for the Fall of the Ming* provides a respresentative model for a great many of the costume dramas being turned out in the early years of the war.

Two other Shanghai writers, Chou I-pai and Ku Chung-i, busied themselves with costume drama in 1940. Chou I-pai's *Pei-ti wang* (King of the North) contains four acts more or less related to each other concerning the fall of Shu to Wei at the end of the Three Kingdoms period. The play opens with the suicide of Li-shih, a patriotic woman mortified by her husband's craven surrender of his garrison to the Wei commander Teng Ai. The last three acts portray debates in the court of Sun Ch'üan over whether to aid Shu, and in the Shu court, where Liu Ch'an, emperor of Shu, vacillates pathetically. The whole play culminates in the suicide of his fifth son, Liu Ch'en, the king of the north, together with his wife and young daughter, all three committed to death before surrender. Another historical play by Chou, *Hua Mu-lan,* is more promising. Hua Mu-lan takes her sick father's place during a conscription to defend the Sui dynasty from T'u-p'o barbarians, and as a soldier successfully conceals her sex while foiling the plots of traitors and leading a small force to rout a vastly superior barbarian army. In the final act, Mu-lan is brought before the Sui emperor. Here one official demands she be punished for leading troops without a commission, but the emperor remains impressed at her decisive action after thirteen years of indecisive war, and offers his services in finding Mu-lan a wife. Mu-lan reveals her sex to the nonplussed court. While an official urges she be punished for fraud, the emperor invites her into his harem. Mu-lan refuses and asks only to go home. Finally out of patience with her, the emperor offers her the harem or decapitation. Mu-lan unhesitatingly chooses the latter, but as the ax is about to fall a messenger arrives with the report of another outbreak of fighting. A benevolent retainer urges that Mu-lan be commissioned to lead imperial forces in a campaign, and Mu-lan accepts, on condition that she be allowed to return home when the campaign is finished.

Obviously, Chou I-pai has stretched the tale of Mu-lan beyond all bounds of credibility; the characters are paper thin, and the play melodramatic. To its credit, however, it avoids sentimentality and self-pity, and contains a good deal of comedy and comic irony. Chou I-pai was to prove a much better playwright in coming years. Ku Chung-i's *Liang Hung-yü,* like the plays and films on Hua Mu-lan, was based on popular classical operas. Ku's version is filled with stilted rhetoric and more traitors foiled by another patriotic courtesan, Liang Hung-yü, who sings, dances, and insists that women owe loyal service to the Sung dynasty just the same as men. The service she has in mind is defeating the Chin invaders and exposing spies, which she accomplishes while becoming the wife of General Han Shih-chung. But Ku has imagined little for the general to say except speeches in praise of Hung-yü: "My wife really is wise and intelligent, daring and talented. Moreover, who doesn't believe that this fantastic person is the supreme beauty of the age. . . ."[20]

These plays, together with many by writers in the interior, took on frequent resemblances to each other. The central character is a young woman who is patriotic and assertive, outgoing, and generous. She has acquired masculine skills, but is endowed with feminine beauty as well. Much of the popularity of this stock character can be associated not only with traditional opera, but traditional fiction as well,[21] overlaid with the theme of women's liberation and the sheer titillation of comely women imitating men in dress and manner. She is supported by a leading man, or men, of good but less outstanding character, who are generally allowed to be no more than the woman's foil. Such protagonists are committed to defending a regime that is decadent though legitimate, in view of the threat of invasion without and subversion within. When the protagonists are defeated, it is laid to the corruption of the government, and especially traitors and spies collaborating with foreign invaders. The concern with capitulationists was apparently not only convenient as a device for personal confrontations on the stage, but throughout all the literature of the resistance was an obsession in itself. The *han-chien,* the traitor to the Han people, was a theme no writer could refrain from rendering; its features were again and again portrayed regardless of how abstract the foreign—the Japanese—invader remained. It was the traitor who was responsible for defeat, not the enemy's prowess. The family also occupied a prominent position in these works, frequently a conflict between nationalistic, idealistic youth and stubborn, cynical parents. A major character not involved in a family situation is invariably described as single and orphaned, another element frequent in wartime drama. The climax of the play is nearly always the martyrdom or near martyrdom of the protagonists in a gesture of defiance.

Unity and cohesiveness in plot structure are subordinate to the selection of scenes with the greatest dramatic potential, culled from historical manuscripts or theatrical sources. Characterization is intentionally reminiscent of the stereotypes of classical drama. Music and dance, as well as costumes and settings, and touches in the dialogue are all designed to play on audience appreciation of traditional theater. Much of the vernacular dialogue is given to plot exposition and wooden rhetoric. These factors, regardless of their timely success as entertainment and propaganda, vitiated the primary contributions the spoken drama in costume had to offer over its operatic predecessor—that is, the restoration of a sense of immediate reality and significance to the events of the past.

Developments in Costume Drama: From *Malice in the Ch'ing Court* to *Ch'iu Hai-t'ang*

Dissatisfaction over the costume drama was usually expressed in terms of the play's lack of strict fidelity to the details and facts of history. A Ying's reply, as noted above, was to argue for the need to select events suitable for dramatic purposes, even at the expense of absolute fidelity to history. Chou I-pai remarked that historical plays cannot be judged on the basis of whether their plots conform to historical records, and directed readers to the fact that historical plays have their own traditions; the significance of a play can be judged against that tradition.[22] None of these critical exercises was very conclusive.

Yao K'o (Yao Hsin-nung), in taking up the story of the Dowager Empress' conflicts with the Kuang-hsü Emperor and the Pearl Concubine (Lady Chen), inherited the wartime trends and critical concerns in historical drama. Yao's response to his play judged as history was more sophisticated. First, he challenged the historical records: "The facts and personages of history are absolutely not so simple as historians tell us. Given two historians with differing points of view or ideologies, their records and portrayals will certainly not be alike."[23] As to specific statements about the fidelity of his own play to history, he wrote:

> Some have said that the Kuang-hsü Emperor appears a bit too intelligent, and the Pearl Concubine a bit too wise and her personality too forceful. From the historian's point of view this statement is quite correct. But in my defense, in defense of *Malice in the Ch'ing Court,* [I say that] what I wrote is a historical play, and these two characters are not out of keeping with the nature of historical drama . . . Historical dramas, though they take their basis in historical fact, are not history.[24]

Yao, in fact, did not at the time elaborate on the nature of historical drama, but it is clear that he is arguing for the autonomy of the artist, that his work should be judged primarily on the substantiality of the world created within the play and on the significance of the theme it has drawn from its historical sources. Indeed, *Malice in the Ch'ing Court* shows an artist's concern with detail in settings, costumes, and manners that few other plays of the time showed, though a number of facts and events are employed or omitted in such a way that any historian would question the play as history. But the work does draw a theme of universal significance from its sources. and by comparison with its predecessors, conveys the reality of the past.

In conformity with historical dramas of the time, Yao has allowed the plot to sprawl over a considerable stretch of time, from 1887 when the emperor chooses his consort and concubines to 1900 when his favorite, Lady Chen, dies on the orders of Tz'u-hsi. Nevertheless, an impressive unity is maintained. The setting is limited to the Forbidden City, supporting the theme of the oppressiveness of Tz'u-hsi's rule, with its unyielding claustrophobia. The shifting of the settings within the confines of the palace marks the downfall and degradation of the Emperor and Lady Chen. The play remains closely focused throughout on the struggle between the three principals, rather than using one or all of them as the thread to link a set of disparate events. The dialogue explores virtually all the possibilities open to it without admitting anachronisms, *tao-pai,* or other devices to destroy its credibility. There are passages which, to another reader in another time, at least, sway too heavily to rhetoric or romantic sentiment, but they are never out of character. There are also moments when background and plot exposition are poorly integrated into the action of the play, but as often as not, exposition is skillfully combined with other elements of the work.

Although ritual court music is prescribed for certain scenes, the play does not rely on the traditional appeal of music and dance (scenes of Peking Opera could easily have been included but were not), and employs properties with symbolic value. A scene built around a camera serves to set off the conflict between Tz'u-hsi and Lady Chen. Lady Chen's interest and mastery of the camera implies her acceptance of foreign influence, and by association, her progressive spirit. As one of her maid's remarks, peering into the lens, "Everything really is upside down, really!"[25] To Tz'u-hsi, the camera represents only the threat of Lady Chen's unconventionality. The arrow of office that the Emperor entrusts to Yuan Shih-k'ai is tossed back at the Emeror's feet as a symbol of Yuan's betrayal and Tz'u-hsi's power, and also as a gesture of Tz'u-hsi's deliberately theatrical nature. The romantic sentiments and aspirations of the Emperor and his consort are embodied in a toy boat that Lady Chen carves in her captivity, and that is then burned by Tz'u-hsi for its subversive inscription. Later, the miniature oar she drops on the ground for the Emperor to find as a token of her loyalty is twisted into a sign of her disloyalty. The whole motif of a sculling boat on a treacherous river ends in the scene of Lady Chen's drowning in a stagnant palace well. The choice and employment of these properties is, as well, in the best of Chinese tradition, as seen in such masterpieces as the *T'ao-hua shan* (Peach Blossom Fan), where the symbolic significance of the fan undergoes a transformation while lending unity to the work. Similarly, the nightmare Lady Chen suffers in Act Two, Scene Three, while obviously reminiscent of the omens in

Julius Caesar, is interpreted in a thoroughly Chinese fashion. That these are all used to reinforce dramatic irony is abundantly clear, for a writer such as Yao K'o was not given to obscurities, but action and language that are immediate and apparent to a wide audience.[26] The climactic scene in which Lady Chen submits to death while the city is coming under a foreign artillery barrage is a moment of ultimate irony in the play, the interpretation of which is made explicit through the words of Lady Chen herself, as she addresses Tz'u-hsi:

> I am afraid the Empress Dowager will not have the triumph she hopes for. Two years ago the Empress Dowager took the powers of state into her own hands again and canceled the reforms. She thought that she had triumphed, but I told her then that she had failed—and now she sees my words fulfilled.[27]

The final scene is reminiscent, in the defiant martyrdom of the protagonist and the irony of the situation, of that in A Ying's *Sorrow for the Fall of the Ming.* But in *Malice in the Ch'ing Court* the theme is not the ultimate failure of foreign conquerors, but the ultimate failure of despotism "in all its guises."[28] Moreover, the play is concerned with the human failures despotism breeds. It is in characterization, as well as form and its embellishments, that *Malice in the Ch'ing Court* offers considerable advances over so many of the historical dramas then popular in China.

The central conflict is drawn along lines of classic family tensions: the maliciousness of a mother-in-law figure, Tz'u-hsi, toward a daughter-in-law figure, Lady Chen, over the loyalty of a son of less assertive personality, the Kuang-hsü Emperor. The conflict begins as personal, inner-court rivalry and feuding, and it essentially remains at this level for the Dowager Empress. The protagonists, on the other hand, come to see it as a question of national polity and survival, as well as personal power. The Dowager allows the Emperor certain reforms insofar as she sees that they enhance her position, and opposes reforms as they seem to threaten her hold. This toying with national policies renders her suitably evil, and quite uncomprehending of the rhetoric for progress hurled at her by Lady Chen.

The Dowager's personality is a true blend of cynicism and theatricality, as she tells the Emperor: "You and I are figures behind the screen in a shadow play."[29] Hence, the cruelty she unleashes is very much for show, but stems from genuine hatred and fear. This surfaces in a scene of near-hysteria when the Dowager confronts the Emperor with the failure of his coup:

> DOWAGER: So you sugar your malice with sweet words! (*She grinds her teeth and, in mounting fury, she grips the decree and reads from it.*) ". . . to enjoy the rest of life among the hills and waters of the Summer Palace." (*She screams the following words, full voice.*) Doesn't this mean you intend to drive me to my death—of despair?
>
> *The Empress Dowager's face, twitching and distorted, shows both wrath and genuine terror. She is trembling. It is clear that she is, in her own way, thoroughly shaken and miserable and, this time, not merely playing with anger for its effect.*)[30]

Moreover, she maintains a belief in her own sincerity and integrity, as she continues to berate the Emperor:

> I took you into the palace when you were five years old and I made you emperor. Now you are twenty-seven. I and only I gave you your prerogatives. I selected an empress for you. I even conceded to your authority in state affairs. Now in your ingratitude, you undertake reforms by following the advice of rebellious officials and ignoring the instructions of our ancestors. But even this is not enough. Now in my old age you want to destroy what life I have left. (*She speaks slowly and earnestly.*) Do you have any conscience at all?[31]

Having convinced herself of her position, Tz'u-hsi is ready to reassume posing for effect. In the final scene, in fact, it is her convincing performance before the Emperor that causes him to make the fatal mistake of doubting Lady Chen's resolve. Yao K'o, in presenting not only an ignorant, clever woman, but one who succeeds in convincing herself of the veracity of her own performances, has created one of the more memorable villains in modern Chinese theater.

The Emperor is politically a creation of Tz'u-hsi and personally a creation of Lady Chen, while living up to the expectations of neither of these women. The tentative assertiveness he shows in Act One, as opposed to his submissiveness and passivity in the prologue, is by implication partly the work of Lady Chen. That he has become actively involved in state affairs while yet struggling with his own maturity is rendered in an outburst of temper over the course of the Sino-Japanese War of 1894–1895:

Serves us right if we take a defeat. . . . Suppose the Japanese come here
and occupy the capital, wipe out the dynasty, kill us all. What of it? This
is the worst that can happen—and it might be the best for everyone.[32]

It is in the next scene that Lady Chen begins to redirect this anar-
chistic nihilism into an emotional idealism, following the course of his
conversation and guiding the emperor's mind to a commitment to
sweeping reforms instead of sweeping destruction. In the same scene
he experiments with asserting himself personally as well as politically
by disciplining an insubordinate eunuch. This still rather immature
behavior is transcended in his carefully reasoned decision to remain
in Peking after the failure of his reforms—the one time, in fact, he
comes to a decision that sways Lady Chen from her previous views.
But he is never free of his reliance on Lady Chen, and in the ensuing
months of confinement it is again necessary for her to keep him from
succumbing to despair. In the debate over how to handle the Boxer
uprising to their advantage, Lady Chen convinces him to stay in Peking rather than flee with Tz'u-hsi. When the dowager empress then
convinces him that Lady Chen has abandoned her pledge to stay and
is preparing to leave, the Emperor is rendered pathetically vulnera-
ble, and his own resolve breaks. Yao could not make the Emperor too
strong or too weak; he had to be someone who, in drawing his
strength from Lady Chen, is also dependent on her to the point of
weakness. He is made sympathetic through his sincere concern for
the nation, and his youthful exuberance and love of Lady Chen. Yao
never attempts to probe the full possibilities of his character, but does
endow him with enough depth to sustain his central role without
becoming merely a foil for Lady Chen, as is the case with the usual
historical dramas of the time.

That Lady Chen's role is to motivate and sustain the Emperor in
his bid for a reform is implied in the prologue scene, when the choice
of empress is made:

Patently terrified, the Emperor tenses his arms, thus partially
withdrawing the sceptre, which he holds with both hands. The Tatala
girl [Lady Chen], raising her head, looks at him directly and fondly.[33]

But the Emperor is guided by Tz'u-hsi to choose a girl from a rival
clan, the Yehonala, leaving Lady Chen and her sister, Lady Chin,

disappointed in the roles of concubines. In the first act, it is clear that the Emperor favors Lady Chen over the Empress, and that Lady Chen has not been reticent to make the most of this in planning for the future. That her motives stem from personal frustration is clear:

CHEN: People outside think we have such a fine life in here, happy as the Immortals. Nobody knows we're worse off than the poorest little housewives. And everyday, what are we doing? Bending our necks, docilely taking orders from those who won't give up one little inch of power. Instead they hate us. They hate us! This is not life at all. It's just misery![34]

That she plans to assert herself in tribal feuds through the Emperor, she also makes explicit to her sister:

Do you still imagine that the Yehonala crowd will remain in power here forever? Do you think that the Emperor is still a helpless child? There'll come a day when we will take over power here.[35]

The Emperor and his reform programs are thus part of a personal bid for freedom and autonomy, represented in Lady Chen's description of the boat people of Canton:

Husbands and wives, they live just on their boat, dry their clothes at the bow, cook their food in the stern. There's a small cabin in the middle where they sleep. It seemed to me they had no worries, that nothing could really bother them. They row east one day, west another, needing only a steering oar. To live like that is to be free.[36]

These fantasies, like the pastoral games of a Marie Antoinette or the curiosity of a Pao-yü toward the world outside Ta-kuan-yuan, are the means by which the Emperor and Lady Chen achieve intimacy and alliance. But it is in throwing themselves into the reforms that they develop as characters to the point that intimacy becomes selfless loyalty and fantasies of freedom become responsible commitments. It is in this context that Tz'u-hsi is graduated from a domestic tyrant to a national catastrophe. And it is through this theme, the fusion of loyalty to a person and a cause, that the positive side of the protagonists is meant fully to emerge.

The chief theme around which the action is built is the failure of trust, in contrast to the loyalty of the protagonists to each other. The primary acts of broken faith are by Yuan Shih-k'ai and Tz'u-hsi, both of whom are made to swear oaths that ironically predict their eventual unhappy ends. But it is the final scene which shows that the failure of trust is central not only to the plot, but to the theme as well. Lady Chen has sworn to remain behind with the Emperor in Peking to negotiate with foreign troops. Bent on avoiding this, Tz'u-hsi convinces the Emperor that Lady Chen has joined the courtiers fleeing the palace. While he dashes offstage to look for her, Lady Chen is brought out of concealment and ordered to throw herself down a well. Lady Chen takes herself to the well and throws herself in, an act that can only signify both defiance and submission. Before this, however, she cries out in despair: "Lies and lies! What I might have expected. But, (her voice is bitter), that the Emperor could let you trap him again, that he believes you, believes that I would break the promise we made."[37] Before jumping, she turns and calls out to the Emperor to come back, then dispatches herself without waiting. This bleak gesture upholds her pledge that she will not leave, but it carries the weight of other implications: despair that the Emperor has lost faith in her, spite in a gesture of personal triumph to demonstrate her courage in the face of the quavering Dowager Empress, and provocation to drive the Emperor to strengthen his resolve in opposing Tz'u-hsi. The final scene does unleash the capacities of the principal characters, and the theme of trust and betrayal runs to its ultimate psychological moment.

The primary goal of the play being to present patriotic ideals in a form Shanghai audiences would appreciate, Yao probably never intended any complexities that would appear distracting or obscure. His achievement lies in the superior craftsmanship he brought to a form of drama popular at the time, and in pointing to the potential of that form for serious character portrayal, thus restoring a sense of the reality of the past to the concerns of the present. Of course, the characters are seen through the filter of the intervening decades of May Fourth and the romantic period. But Yao's concerns lay primarily with the potential of aspects of traditional theater for adaptation to modern stage. As he has written:

> In my twenties and thirties, I used to be an Ibsenite as most of my contemporaries were. After my tour of Soviet Russia and Western Europe, my schooling at the Yale Drama School, and my extensive itinerary of theatergoing from

Moscow to New York, I began to have doubts about Western drama (I mean contemporary Western drama). To my mind, Western drama has gone too far intellectual and abstruse for its own audience, let alone Chinese theater-goers. . . . To such an audience, the way of life and its underlying thought reflected in the Western drama cannot but be completely alien. When I went to Yale in the spring of 1938 to study playwrighting, I was quite disappointed. All that Professor Eaton could teach me was dramatic technique I could have learned by myself merely by reading a few standard textbooks on the subject in a couple of weeks. In the last analysis, dramatic technique has always been invented by creative playwrights to suit their own purposes. . . . After my return to China in August 1940, I began to experiment with a new dramatic technique by means of wedding traditional Chinese form to Western craftsmanship. The first end-product was *The Malice of Empire* which, as you must have noticed, retained the episodic structure, and the subtitle for each act and scene, of the traditional Chinese drama, but was woven together more tightly and economically like a Western play.[38]

Actually, Yao had been interested in adapting traditional drama to the modern stage since 1936. Nevertheless, it had been one of several interests, and even by 1941, when he wrote *Malice in the Ch'ing Court,* he had no sure sense of direction in which to take his art. *Malice in the Ch'ing Court* was to be the start of a long series of experiments that were to find success a decade after the war in *Hsi Shih.* The remaining years of the war, however, did not bring him success as a writer equal to that of *Malice in the Ch'ing Court.* Those years were filled with other work, including teaching, managing, and directing, and the plays he turned out tend not to show the same thorough craftsmanship. They share in a common tendency to oblique commentary on topical issues built around themes of trust and betrayal, as in *Malice in the Ch'ing Court.*

In 1942, pressed to find and produce material to sustain actors who had followed him to attempt to establish a new company, Yao staged a hastily compiled adaptation from the *p'i-huang* opera *Pa-wang pieh chi* (The Leave of His Consort) titled *Ch'u pa-wang* (Overlord of Ch'u). The opera was a favorite with Mei Lan-fang and popular with audiences. Yao probably hoped for that response to support his adaptation, but without success. The action of the opera itself is abridged to a concentrated set of scenes, but Yao again opened up the structure to an episodic form spanning several years, this time without the numerous threads that carefully unite the action of *Malice in the Ch'ing Court.* Hsiang Yü's character is based on the sympathetic treatment given in the opera, and rather well developed to a point, as a man whose sensibility and vanity override his reason. Tired of his early campaigns, he wants a settlement with Liu Pang, which even his consort protests is unwise. Only when she conceives a son does he resolve to fight a war to end war:

> I don't want my children to suffer the pain of war, to witness all over again the horrors of bloodshed. Our generation has already been destroyed by war. Our eyes, our minds have become inured and numbed. We even think of war as something glorious, that killing is respectable.[39]

Hsiang Yü is aware of the weak points and treachery in his ranks, but is unable to face the truth about them, and unable to abandon or even bend his principles against the unimaginative but unprincipled Liu Pang. Hsiang Yü also acts out of vanity when he learns that his personal emissary to an enemy city was snubbed while one of his own advisors is well received. He thus dismisses his best and closest retainer. It is not Hsiang Yü's ambitions but those of his own retainers and kin that bring his downfall, for as collaborators with his rival Liu Pang, they are clearly Hsiang Yü's worst enemies. This is, naturally, brought to its culmination in the scene where Hsiang Yü and his consort, Yü Chi, listen to the songs of Ch'u, their home-land, sung by troops who have defected to Liu Pang and encircled him. There are moments of excellent irony, as when Hsiang Yü utters the historic phrase that if they cannot fight their way out of Liu Pang's encirclement, "It is that heaven has abandoned the Ch'u nation, not a flaw of strategy." He then turns to admit privately that he is not at all confident in the ability of the man appointed to cover his retreat. When Hsiang Yü faces his end, Yao's play is true to the opera. His refusal to make a final bid for escape is prompted by pride, a concern with "face":

> Heaven has forsaken me. Why should I ferry across? Moreover, I crossed the river to the west with eight thousand sons and brothers of the Chiangtung people, but now none of them is coming home with me. Even though their fathers and brothers may still recognize me as their king, out of pity, how can I look into their faces? Even if they will not say a word, how can I not be ashamed at heart?[40]

The production was altogether Yao's, and he reintroduced symbolic sets, perhaps for the first time, into a modern spoken drama.

Nevertheless, his actors balked at his attempts at innovation, such as masking their faces in classic fashion.

Another script based on traditional drama is *The Strategem of the Beautiful Woman*. Yao based his play on elements of the Yuan drama *Liang chün-shih ke-chiang tou-chih* (Two Generals Match Wits at the River) and the later *p'i-huang* play *Kan lu ssu* (Temple of Sweet Dew). The Yuan drama had focused on a struggle between Chu-ko Liang and Chou Yü, rivals during the Three Kingdoms wars, while offering some scenes of the psychological dilemma of Sun Shang-hsiang, the beautiful sister of Sun ch'üan, king of Wu, who is to lure and snare Liu Pei, king of Shu, in order to retrieve the territory of Ching-chou from Shu. The *p'i-huang* drama actually has Shang-hsiang marry Liu Pei, but pays no attention to her psychological makeup, and so loses all dramatic unity. It is the psychological dilemma of Shang-hsiang and her marriage to Liu Pei that attracted Yao as early as 1936. In that year Ou-yang Yü-ch'ien had discussed adaptations with Yao, and had gone ahead to publish an adaptation of *Ta-yü sha-chia* (The Fisherman's Revenge), but Yao had let his own project go until 1943. Yao apparently also saw the play as an oblique commentary on the necessity for the CCP and KMT to end civil strife and cooperate, and certainly an audience in those years would have inferred such a statement even if Yao had not intended it.

His major innovation in this work is the staging of five scenes before the proscenium curtain, a device that struck much of his audience as rather backward. Indeed, Yao was trying to save on electricity for lighting, which was being rationed during the war, but found himself in the position of having to explain that acting before the curtain had also been a common practice in Western drama.[41] Yao's real accomplishment in this piece is three acts of excellent comedy. Sun Ch'üan cuts a comic figure, henpecked by his wife, held in scorn by his mother, and getting entangled in his own intrigues, frantically improvising solutions to fill the loopholes in his scheme to hold Liu Pei under force or the charm of his sister in order to get the return of Ching-chou. Shang-hsiang and her mother share a mutual and exclusive devotion to each other. Shang-hsiang is a tomboy, ill-suited to the role of seducing Liu Pei. On the contrary, it is she who is finally swayed by Liu Pei's heroic determination to crush the threat the northern lord Ts'ao Ts'ao poses. But in agreeing to join him in escaping back to Shu to direct a campaign, Shang-hsiang violates the trust of her mother, who has been intent on keeping her daughter by her side. The amusement, then, gives way in the fourth act to a sobering scene in which Shang-hsiang is ostracized by her mother as the price of her decision.

But neither this nor Yao's other costume dramas were winning much popular success or bringing him any closer to hybrid forms. For several other plays he turned to more contemporary settings, although these too, in their way, testify to the strength of tradition. Among his adaptations of Western drama was *Ch'i ch'ung t'ien* (Seventh Heaven), the title in this case referring to a shanty atop an apartment building in the Shanghai concessions shared by a family fleeing the fighting of the Northern Expedition in 1927. The principal characters, as in the original *Seventh Heaven,* are a young girl and a truck driver who leaves her to fight in the war. Like many adaptations of Western drama at the time, the play follows its source closely, yet with major changes in the theme. The original play was religious and antiwar. Yao, on the other hand, chose the Northern Expedition as a worthy and just cause, and the play, in turning pro-war, suggests keeping faith with the resistance against the Japanese. Moreover, the religious significance of the original is eliminated, while the girl's final fantasy of her dead lover's return is retained. Thus, despite a thoroughly modern setting and theme carefully constructed around Shanghai in the twenties, the final scene has brought the play to a conclusion in no way at odds with a traditional *ch'uan-ch'i* tale. The girl, having developed over months of separation a fantasy of communicating with him, refuses to believe news from a returned friend that her lover is almost surely dead, having suffered a severe chest wound and capture. As the girl is left alone to pray, her lover's wraith appears in uniform, vacant-eyed and pale. He tells her:

> I almost died. But suddenly I thought of you. I know you pray for me everyday, watching for my return. I thought no matter what I could not die, I must return. Didn't I agree that I would definitely return? . . . You mustn't despair. Someday, I will see again. . . . At least I can see you, see our Seventh Heaven. Do you believe me. . . . We are forever inseparable:

Lo Ying, Chin Ko-erh, Seventh Heaven . . . Seventh Heaven. (*He collapses. She rests his head on her knee. Curtain.*)[42]

If *Seventh Heaven* was an attempt to appeal to audience taste of the time, Yao's one original play in a contemporary setting, *Yin-hai ts'ang-sang* (Vicissitudes in the Film World), touched on three topical issues within the Shanghai theater world itself. The play is set in Shanghai in the early thirties. Hsiao Han and Kao Shih-ch'i were once rivals in college for the hand of the pretty and talented Lin Ying, who chose the more dependent of the two, Hsiao Han, a writer who spurns commercialism and is unable to support his family beyond the subsistance level. To alleviate their plight, Kao Shih-ch'i, a director in a Shanghai film company, encourages Hsiao Han to write a movie script which he will direct. The script Hsiao Han writes is autobiographical. Lin Ying approaches Shih-ch'i to play the lead role in the film, and Shih-ch'i reluctantly agrees, although for Lin Ying it means violating her husband's sanction against her having anything to do with the movie industry. Hsiao Han soon finds out and concludes that they are having an affair. He disappears, taking their daughter with him. Several years later Lin Ying finds him, destitute and blind, making a living on the streets as a fortuneteller. Unable to feel anything but pain at their reunion, Hsaio Han swallows poison, leaving the daughter with Lin Ying and Shih-ch'i to start a new life away from the corruption of the movie world.

The play was originally designed as a satire of the movie magnate S. K. Chang, in charge of the Japanese-controlled motion picture company, who was attempting to buy up a number of theater workers for his films as well as establish a theater company under his direction. The movie industry is portrayed as a rather sordid, tawdry world, and the frustrated director, Kao Shih-ch'i, is made to condemn his producer: "For years now you have forced us to make so many stupid films that do nothing but drug the audience with sex. You've used your position to bully the employees and play around with the actresses. You've used the lowest tricks to destroy the family of my closest friends."[43] But the focus of the play is not on its attempt to decry S. K. Chang, but rather on the three misguided protagonists. Hsiao Han was based on the director and playwright Wu Jen-chih.

Wu earned a steady income by teaching school, and his wife walked out on him for a better life than teaching and theater could afford.[44] Wu Jen-chih himself wrote a preface to the play, taking it up as a rebuttal of Li Chien-wu's concurrent series of adaptations from Sardou. To Wu, Li Chien-wu's return to Sardou to present vapid, mechanical "well-made plays" was succumbing to the worst sort of commercialism. He pointed out that Ibsen had incorporated elements of the well-made melodramas into the more meaningful context of his problem plays.

Yao K'o, as an admirer of Ibsen, had also employed these devices, such as beginning the action in the middle of the plot. Unfortunately, problem plays were not having success on Shanghai stages, and to compete commercially Yao K'o could not develop his play in that genre. But the ingenuities in Yao's play stem not from the mechanics of plot, but from the psychological clash of the leading characters: Hsiao Han's pride and stubbornness, Lin Ying's headiness and vanity, Kao Shih-ch'i's friendship and strength.[45] In truth, despite Wu Jen-chih's well-taken defense of the play, both satire and problems are drowned in a soap opera conclusion strongly reminiscent of, and almost certainly influenced by, the popular play *Ch'iu Hai-t'ang.* As a writer of ability who had made a significant contribution to modern Chinese drama in *Malice in the Ch'ing Court,* Yao led a career during the Pacific War years that reflects the influence of certain important trends in Shanghai theater when a number of writers, involved as managers and directors of companies with an absolute need for commercial success, lost much ground as free agents and careful craftsmen.

Ch'iu Hai-t'ang (Begonia or Autumn Quince) both of itself and as representative of various aspects of wartime drama, exemplifies theater as a commercial art in wartime Shanghai. It was, in fact, the manager of the Carlton Theater who proposed and pushed for its production by the merged SAT and K'u-kan Players. In May 1943, the result was given the following comments by Chang Ai-ling, then employed as an English-language critic:

> Never before has the hardened city of Shanghai been moved so by a play as by *Autumn Quince,* a sentimental melodrama which has been running at the Carlton Theatre since December 1942. The majority of the audience attend the

performances so regularly that they learn the dialogues by heart and anticipate everything said, repeating aloud the more stirring speeches after the actors. Strong men weep copiously at the tragic downfall of a Peking Opera star, a female impersonator, who answers to the lyrical stage name of Autumn Quince. The success of the play has given rise to a host of imitators. At one time there were no less than six plays showing simultaneously in Shanghai which dealt with the private lives of Peking Opera stars and back-stage intrigues. . . . The color and atmosphere of Peking Opera strongly prevails in these plays, with here and there a brief interlude of actual Peking Opera. It astounds us to reflect that, although the new theatre of China has taken a firmly antagonistic stand against Peking Opera from its very inception, the first real triumph is a compromise—a humiliating fact.[46]

As we have seen, writers of costume dramas had already employed elements of traditional theater in their spoken dramas. But in such plays these borrowings from tradition seemed appropriate on account of their traditional settings. Ch'iu Hai-t'ang, on the other hand, was set in modern China and placed Peking Opera at the center of attention.

Ch'in Shou-ou's story of Ch'iu Hai-t'ang underwent several reincarnations as a novel, first serialized in Shen pao in 1941, a stage play, and a film. The main outline of the story remains the same, apparently, in all versions. The plot extends from the early 1920s to the late 1930s. Lo Hsiang-i, the graduate of a women's normal school forced by the reduced circumstances of her family to become the third concubine of a northern warlord, forms an illicit liaison with Ch'iu Hai-t'ang, a Tientsin performer of female roles in Peking Opera, who rues his profession and has taken an interest in progressive ideas. After an extended absence, the warlord, Yuan Pao-fan, returns to Tientsin and through a coldblooded orderly learns of the affair between Hsiang-i and Hai-t'ang. Yuan, who has lusted after both of them, slashes Hai-t'ang's face with a bayonet, intending to ruin his career by disfiguring him. Hai-t'ang, through a device inspired by a Peking Opera, manages to retain possession of the daughter, Mei-pao, Hsiang-i has borne him and leaves Tientsin to raise her in humble circumstances in the countryside. Some fifteen years later, when war breaks out, he moves with Mei-pao into the Shanghai International Settlement. Now beginning to cough blood from tuberculosis, he nevertheless plays the physically demanding role of military clown (wu-ch'ou) while Mei-pao, against his wishes, surreptitiously takes up singing Peking Opera songs in a restaurant.

Yuan Pao-fan has long since been killed in the Northern Expedition, and Hsiang-i has been looking in vain for Hai-t'ang, until she happens upon Mei-pao at the restaurant. She finds Mei-pao quite ignorant of her father's past renown or her mother's true identity. But how the recognition scene between mother and daughter and the resolution of the story work out varies from one revision to the next.

Ch'in Shou-ou himself listed the initial revisions. In the serialized version published in *Shen pao,* there is a recognition scene, followed by a quick rush to Hai-t'ang's living quarters, where mother and daughter find him already dead. Critics complained that Hsiang-i's behavior was too impetuous and the death too contrived to satisfy the requirements of realism. For a book edition of the novel, Ch'in rewrote the final scenes. Controlling her feelings, Hsiang-i does not immediately reveal her identity to her daughter, but arranges for a rendezvous with her the following day. Through this, Hai-t'ang, mortified by his own ugliness and downfall, learns that Mei-pao has seen Hsiang-i, and leaps from a building to his death to prevent his standing in the way of their future happiness. In writing a script thereafter Ch'in and others decided this was not suited practically or dramatically for the stage. Therefore, Hsiang-i is once again made to declare her identity in the restaurant and has Mei-pao take her, not to Hai-t'ang's living quarters, but to the theater at which he performs. When they arrive backstage, Hai-t'ang, upon seeing them, dashes on stage, performs strenuously, and collapses to die in the arms of Hsiang-i. The critics now complained that actors are bound by their cues and cannot simply leap on stage at will. Ch'in answered that, after all, "excitement" was more important then credibility, "and once the feelings of the audience have been seized, what is or is not reasonable is no longer so clear-cut."[47]

However, it was not Ch'in who was responsible for the script that was performed, for his original version was completely overhauled by three leading writers of the SAT and K'u-kan Players association: Fei Mu, Ku Chung-i, and Huang Tso-lin. It was they who worked out the plot for the stage presentation and added scenes of Peking Opera to make it a motif running through the play. At the time, Ch'in congratulated them on their ingenuity and craftsmanship. Later, in Kweilin, beyond the reach of the Japanese authorities, he expressed his consternation that they had cut out all the social significance in his story and made it purely a love story, albeit they had little choice under Japanese censorship.[48] To the three adapters, their success was a mixed blessing, so much so that Huang Tso-lin refused to allow the script to be published, and the original mimeographed scripts are not now available.[49]

Nevertheless, when Ch'in Shou-ou left Shanghai for the interior in 1944, he found such a demand for the play that he set it down from memory as the Shanghai playwrights had written it, adding a few lines to restore the social theme. This script was published in 1946 in Shanghai, and informants familiar with the original version have confirmed its overall fidelity to the original.[50] Even in this script, with its professed desire to be relevant to the theme of social progress, there is a pronounced ambiguity stemming from the degree to which it still relies on the appeal of Peking Opera and its customs. On the one hand, the progressive theme, denouncing feudal mores and social corruption, is embodied in the female impersonator Ch'iu Hai-t'ang, who wins the love of the educated concubine, Hsiang-i, by revealing his patriotism, his intellectual progressiveness, and his disgust with his lot in life. This theme is summed up in his death scene, in his dying words to Hsiang-i:

> The beauty of spirit, the beauty of character, Hsiang-i, it's not so at all.
> (With gravity) This is the beauty of blood and tears, of revenge and
> hatred. The rifles of warlords, the bayonets of running dogs, the whiplash
> of environment, the cruelty of society have created this bit of beauty.
> (Barely able to summon his breath, forcing one last cry) Hsiang-i,
> you . . . do you still recognize your . . . your Ch'iu . . . Hai . . . t'ang?[51]

Yet when Hsiang-i falls in love with Hai-t'ang, despite her own professed dissatisfaction with his career, she buys his records, listening with rapture to every falsetto note, and together they sing a favorite song from the Peking opera "Lo Ch'eng chiao kuan" (Lo Ch'eng Calls at the Gate). When Hai-t'ang is disfigured and reduced to anonymity as an acrobatic player, he still attempts to correct the faulty singing of a young actress who rebuffs his instructions as coming from a nonentity. Hence, when he dies revealing his former stage name, the stage directions close the play with the following:

> The stagehands and performers of the Red Stage Theater are all thoroughly
> shaken that this worm, an old and weak acrobat, his face covered with scars, is
> after all Ch'iu Hai-t'ang, once briefly famed as "the impersonator of young

women supreme in beauty and talent!'' Truly it is something they have never
guessed even in their dreams. They cannot but look at each other inquiringly,
whispering in low tones this great name, "Ch'iu Hai-t'ang?"[52]

The contempt for his profession that Hai-t'ang expresses cannot
but seem contrary to the enjoyment all the characters, including Hai-
t'ang, take in it and, moreover, to the script's own promotion of Hai-
t'ang's prestige and importance not as a progressive spirit, but as a
female impersonator. The play really draws its coherence from the
theme of a man whose worth and stature go unrecognized, not from a
clash of the progressive with the traditional. In the beginning of the
play, when Hai-t'ang is a successful performer, his lover discovers the
hidden patriotism and virility beneath the coy performance. When
Hai-t'ang later is reduced to being an ugly clown, his lover's arrival
reveals the fact that he was once a great female impersonator. At
least one Shanghai critic said he could not understand how a man
who professed such ardor for social progress would, instead, immerse
himself in an illicit affair.[53] Indeed, the lovers' daydreams seem little
concerned with social activism:

> CH'IU [HAI-T'ANG]:   Wouldn't it be great if we were just a couple of folks
> in the country, ignorant and illiterate. We'd live together in a little
> thatched cottage. During the day we'd work hard. I'd go to the fields,
> you'd cook the food, and when the work was done (as though reciting a
> poem) we'd go hand in hand into the mountains, wash our feet in a
> brook, listen to the birds sing among the trees, I gazing at you, you
> looking at me. Sometimes we'd look off into the distance, and watch a
> train pass through the forest. When it grew dark, I'd take you back
> home. . . .
>
> HSIANG [-I]:   And when we got home, I'd be sure to fix the best dishes
> for you. If you wanted *tien-hsin,* then I'd fix you the best *tien-hsin.*
> You know I can make steamed bread, steamed dumplings, *chiao-
> tzu.* . . . And I can make southern style *tien-hsin,* like lotus seed soup,
> and cakes, and. . . . [54]

Of course, the unhappy conclusion of the play is not native to traditional theater, but in sentiment and style, the appeal to tradition is
strong.

Ch'iu Hai-t'ang deserves attention not only as a work of such
popularity in China that it survived, with revisions, into the fities in
The People's Republic; it is also a veritable compendium of stage

conventions in wartime Shanghai theater. Large casts were the general rule, and *Ch'iu Hai-t'ang* employed some fifty-two performers, eight or nine with substantial roles. Minor characters are often made to chat with each other when there is a need for scene introduction and plot exposition. Plays were supposed to provide a full evening of entertainment (*Ch'iu Hai-t'ang* ran four hours, including intermissions), and the result was that scripts were often padded with unnecessary scenes and dialogue, such as the first scene in Act Four of *Ch'iu Hai-t'ang* in which country opera amateurs attempt to lure Mei-pao into a performing contract. Witty or touching lines are often achieved by apt quotation of classical sources or *ch'eng-yü* cliches. Actually, *Ch'iu Hai-t'ang* provides one of the most skillful applications of quotations in its sentimental framework. In the Prologue, Hai-t'ang is shown in a performance of *Su San ch'i-chieh* (Su San Goes into Exile), singing a well-known piece that is employed again at the end of the play to underscore his demise. As one critic has noted:

> It goes thus:
>
> Wine taken with a true friend—
>   a thousand cups are not enough;
> Conversation, when disagreeable—
>   half a sentence is too much.
>
> These words deeply touch Hai-t'ang, aged, disfigured, penniless, intensely lonely, when he sings them for an upstart actress who gets the beat wrong. To the audience, the situation is immensely enriched by the quotation.[55]

Even outside the realm of the costume drama on Peking Opera, allusions appear in the box set parlors of the contemporary middle class.[56] In general, the dialogue was written and delivered in *kuo-yü*, with some allowance for dialect, particularly in "character" roles.

Variations: Ku Chung-i, Fei Mu, Wu T'ien (Fang Chün-i), Chou I-pai

How prominent the concern with the theme of family life is in both the fantasies and conflicts of characters has been seen in several representative dramas. The domestic scene remained predominant in

the works of other writers, whether they turned to Western adaptations or costume dramas.

The men responsible for *Ch'iu Hai-t'ang* took separate and distinct careers following its run. Ch'in Shou-ou himself was a hack
writer who had chosen the characters for his name deliberately to be
confused with those of an established writer of love stories, Chou
Shou-chüan. Ch'in's career soon lapsed back into obscurity, and he
wrote little more creative during the war years. Huang Tso-lin and
Ku Chung-i both turned their attention to adapting Western drama.
These men were important figures in the Shanghai theater world, but
ultimately more as directors, teachers, and organizers than writers.
Huang's adaptation of Molnar's *Doctor Ur* as *a Gentleman of the
Beams* (i.e., burglar) did not fare well. However, his adaptation of
Barrie's *The Admirable Crichton* as *Huang tao ying-hsiung* (Hero of
a Deserted Island) was successful enough for three revivals during the
war, probably because it dealt with a family situation as much as it
conveyed an English notion of social equality. Huang did well to
limit his output. Ku Chung-i was more prolific and most often quite
mediocre, the dialogue of his plays being stiff and melodramatic. His
most ambitous and commercially successful piece was *Three
Daughters,* adapted from *King Lear.* To those raised in reverence of
Shakespeare's greatest achievement, Ku Chung-i's reworkings into
Chinese are a disaster. Ku abandoned Shakespeare for the bard's imitators and sources by letting Mei-chen (Cordelia) live on to render
filial devotion to Lear (Li Hsiang-tsun). Moreover, K'o-chen
(Goneril), as well as P'i Wang-t'eng (Edmund), are made to be quite
vocal in their contrition as they succumb to poison on stage. The
moors and castles of ancient Britain become the parlors and estates of
Republican China squires. Wit and imagery are stripped from the
dialogue. Interestingly, the first act follows the action of *King Lear*
much more closely than later acts. The action here centers on the *fen-
chia,* the division of family inheritance, and one is tempted to conclude, as above, that the success the play had was in large part
prompted by the theme of family life. The critical question with such
adaptations is not simply what has been stripped from the original,
but what has been introduced to compensate for the inevitable losses.
The answer, in this case as in so many others, is nothing, or next to

nothing of any significance. Despite the efforts of Ku Chung-i and Huang Tso-lin, as well as others, the most significant adaptations from Western plays remained those by Shih T'o.

Fei Mu, by contrast, invariably wrote plays based on traditional Chinese sources, and had considerably more success. Fei Mu has been credited with the authorship of at least four plays during the war years: *Mei-hua meng* (Dream of Plum Blossoms, 1941), *Yang Kuei-fei* (1942), *Six Chapters from a Floating Life* (1943), and *Hsiang Fei* (1943). All these plays did well, especially *Six Chapters from a Floating Life,* taken from two chapters of the autobiography of Shen Fu, with a run of over three months. Except possibly for *Dream of Plum Blossoms,* apparently a martial, patriotic play on the exploits of the Ch'ing general P'ang Yü-lin, critics have noted the lyrical quality dominant in his plays. This is attributed in large part to his extensive use of background music, composed by a collaborator, Huang I-chun. One critic also noted the lyricism of Fei Mu's dialogue (using the old term *t'ai-tz'u,* rather than *tui-pai* or *tui-hua*), and the unusual care and thoughtfulness given to gestures and movement. The effect, according to the critic, was as though Fei Mu were turning a stage play into a film.[57] Unfortunately, the scripts are apparently not available and, it is impossible to go beyond a few remarks by critics. Although Fei Mu's techniques were innovative on the *hua-chü* stage, his stories were all steeped in tradition, and the innovations themselves seem bent on restoring the full theatrical potential of the classical drama to the less colorful and unmusical modern stage.

Other writers turned to costume drama during the Pacific War years, with varying degrees of success. Following the production of *Family,* Wu T'ien changed his pen name to Fang Chün-i, and in 1942, living in reduced circumstances in the countryside, wrote *Li-hen t'ien* (Realm of Transcendence), taken from the regional *yueh-chü* script *Liang-Chu ai-shih* (The Sorrowful History of Liang Shan-po and Chu Ying-t'ai). The tale of the lovers Liang Shan-po and Chu Ying-t'ai is so well known that one would question what a *hua-chü* dramatist would bring to it. That the best student at a school for future civil servants in imperial China could for months at a time be ignorant that his roommate and constant companion was a girl, Chu

Ying-t'ai, might have been the basis for the greatest indictment of classical education ever penned. But Fang Chün-i was content to let Ying-t'ai follow in the line of assertive and transvestite women characters then popular in historical plays and wallow in sentimentalities of innocence laced with flowers, butterflies, embroidered slippers, and pastoral songs. There is a scene in Act Four in which Ying-t'ai attempts to discuss sex with Shan-po in concrete terms. Shan-po, however, still has no notion of the topic beyond *yin-yang* abstractions, and is prudently not allowed to be overcome with love sickness until after he discovers that Ying-t'ai is a girl. Li Chien-wu took personal charge of the production of *Realm of Transcendence,* training two girls to play the parts of Shan-po and Ying-t'ai (perhaps after the fashion of all-women Chekiang troupes). The failure of the play he blamed on the ruthlessness of rising commercialism in the theater, which left him without adequate resources to mount a good production.[58]

Fang Chün-i turned to contemporary life in Shanghai as the settings of his later plays. They are not without engaging scenes of comedy and satiric liveliness, but invariably succumb to sentimentality. Works that have modest potential as light satire or comedy are weighed down with the author's lack of restraint in summoning sympathy for her heroines and exposing the hypocrisies and vanities of the bourgeoisie.

Despite the mediocrity of his early costume dramas, Chou I-pai proved himself during the Pacific War years to be a writer of more ability that most dramatists of the day.[59] Chou wrote several plays with contemporary settings that did much to sustain the China Traveling Dramatic company before its demise at the end of the war. In these plays Chou shows much better control over his material, and writes better dialogue and fuller characterizations than is normally the case with writers such as Fang Chün-i and Ku Chung-i. On the other hand, there is noticeable padding in the scripts, albeit rather well done, to thicken the plots, and the plots dominate the plays. The plays are centered on the plights of young women in modern society, and if they have a relationship to traditional literature it is more by coincidence than design. In *Chin ssu ch'üeh* (Canary), a young women entertainer, desirous of leaving her profession to settle down with a husband of her choice, is caught in a dilemma, unable to buy her way out of her performance contract and unwilling to submit to being the "caged canary" of those patrons who can. The issue is basically no different than that found in traditional tales of prostitutes whose lovers are unable to buy them out of their brothels. But in this case, the woman's lover is already married and abandons her when she presses the issue of marriage. Similarly, the vain young girl in *Yang kuan san-tieh* (Three Variations on the Theme of Yang Pass) falls into a net of debts and unwanted suitor through her desire for success as a singer of classical opera. However, she is rescued by her brother and other youths in rebellion against the machinations of their elders.[60] Despite Chou's insistence in the introductions to his works on the social significance of these plays, one is primarily impressed by his competence as a craftsman of well-made plays. In 1944, Chou returned to historical drama. *Lien huan chi* (Strategem of Interlocking Rings) presented a melodrama built around the conflict among the Three Kingdoms figures Tung Cho and Lü Pu and the agent provocateur Tiao Ch'an. *T'ien-wai t'ien* (Beyond Heaven) followed, based on the Ch'ing Shun-Chih emperor's domestic life, discussed by contemporary critics as a full-fledged tragedy. In the absence of the scripts themselves, it is impossible to offer conclusive insights. Chou seemed to be following the trend for strong female leads by using material on Tiao Ch'an and Tung Fei, the Shun-chih emperor's consort. On the other hand, it is clear from contemporary criticism that these dramas were considerably more sophisticated than his propaganda costume plays early in the war.

It is most unfortunate that scripts by such important writers as Fei Mu and Chou I-pai do not appear to be available. But, with what little we know of these plays, together with the scripts that are available, several important points are evident. The war years in Shanghai presented an unprecedented boom in modern drama, and the dominant trend in that boom was the use of resources from traditional China. In these costume dramas women dominated the stage, and family relationships were most often the center of the action. Numerous experiments were attempted to synthesize a new style of drama, and although these were largely lost with the decline in theater activity following the war, a growing sophistication in the scripts and their productions, following the early years of propaganda plays deliberately designed for patriotic simplicity, was noted by critics and can be seen in the scripts themselves. Finally, despite the constraints of authorities, there was a continued effort to write costume dramas that were in some way relevant to the contemporary situation in China. This does not necessarily mean that they dealt with resistance themes or were blatantly topical. Rather, there was a desire to see the relevance of a play even when the script did not immediately seem to suggest any. Hence, even Fei Mu's *Six Chapters from a Floating Life* received the following comments from a contemporary critic:

> Why do I say that within the mentality of the modern Chinese intellectual lie buried the traces of this tragedy? Because Shen San-pai, the author of *Six Chapters from a Floating Life,* was a failure of the landowning class, and his lack of worldly ambitions happens to coincide with the experience of misfortune among a portion of today's intellectuals. Again, to compare the Shen San-pai on stage with the Shen San-pai who wrote the original *Six Chapters from a Floating Life,* there is a notable distinction. The former is melancholy. The latter, however, was a charming and graceful man of leisure. Thus, the Shen San-pai on stage is even more in keeping with present reality.[61]

Whether or not Fei Mu as attempting to draw a connection between the Ch'ing dynasty essayist and the contemporary intellectual, there was a group of writers in occupied China who were heavily engaged in a return to such materials as allusions and topics for their familiar essays. And, in their own individual ways, it is evident that they also, as members or successors of the May Fourth generation, wished to seek out the relevance of a portion of their cultural past to the present age.

CHAPTER FOUR

The Resurgence of Tradition:
The Familiar Essay

Chou Tso-jen

The chief essayist and the only leading literary figure up to that time to remain under the Japanese occupation was Chou Tso-jen. While Chou remained in Peking, he contributed to over a dozen different periodicals during the war, and after 1941 writers in Shanghai as well as Peking provided a school of followers.

Few writers in modern China have been vilified or mocked by such a broad range of their fellow writers as was Chou Tso-jen. Besides the official and semi-official condemnations of his actions during the war, Chou has appeared in an unflattering light in poems, essays, and fiction of the war period by writers including T'ang T'ao, Ai Ch'ing, Lao She, Hsü Kuang-p'ing, and Ch'ien Chung-shu.[1] Certainly much of his life during the war remains unrecorded or unverified, and Chou himself made little attempt to give a painstaking account of those years in his own memoirs. But it is possible to present a fuller record of his life than has thus far appeared, and against this outline, survey his essays of the war period.

In 1937, when the faculty and students of Peking University and other universities in the city began their southward trek to relocate in unoccupied territories, Chou announced his decision to remain. Subsequently he was given an official reason to remain in a telegram from Chiang Meng-lin and Hu Shih, appointing him and others who remained behind as custodians to take action to preserve university property. Chou's personal reasons for staying were given in a letter in which he stated that, as a grandfather, he had a household of ten relations in Peking plus relatives elsewhere in occupied China to look after, and had no way to move them, let alone assure their livelihood, except by staying in Peking to "live in bitterness."[2] It might be noted that one of his dependents was the estranged wife of Chou's younger brother, Chou Chien-jen, the woman being a sister of Tso-jen's wife. Chou Chien-jen remained in Shanghai throughout the war, doing editorial work for Commercial Press and research on eugenics, and was still writing encomia on Lu Hsün in the 1970s. Others have surmised that Chou had other reasons or hopes for remaining in Peking. Chou may have been pessimistic over the future of China and felt the war a hopeless waste.[3] On the other hand, he may have felt that with his background as a scholar of Japanese culture and prestige as a cultural figure, he could exert some influence on the Japanese to mitigate the condition of the Chinese under military occupation.[4] But no actual evidence has been offered for these views, and they remain conjectures. To all appearances, however, he did intend to live the life of a recluse as much as possible while supporting his family.[5] But this was not to be.

While the other professors assigned with Chou to protect university property either decided, after all, to flee south, or died, Chou remained alone. Fellow writers in unoccupied China sent him travel funds to leave Peking, and Chou irked them by replying that travel was not feasible, but that he would use the money to support his relations.[6] In May 1938 the *Osaka mainichi shimbun* printed a photograph of Chou and a report that he had attended a conference to restore Chinese culture (Keng-sheng chung-kuo wen-hua tso-t'an hui) in Peking. This aroused considerable attention in Shanghai and the interior, and Chou was queried by mail. He responded that the report was untrue, and that his only work at the time was research for his magnum opus on Greek mythology.[7] This, however, failed to stem doubts among Chinese writers, and the Wuhan Anti-Japanese Cultural Association (Wuhan wen-hua k'ang-jih hui) unanimously condemned him publicly, while the *Sao-tang jih-pao* (News Sweep Daily) in Hankow headlined the story "Chou Tso-jen shamelessly serves the enemy."[8] Out of concern for Chou's reputation and welfare, Hu Shih sent Chou a poem asking if he would leave occupied China, and Chou responded in September with a poem implying that he hoped someday to see Hu once again, but would remain to "live in bitterness."[9] In the fall of 1938 Chou released some essays written prior to the occupation but left unpublished to the new magazine *Shuo-feng* (Northern Wind) in Peking. In the meantime, his duties at Peking University brought him into contact with the Japanese military, although he apparently had made no commitment to cooperate with them at that time. However, on New Year's Day, 1939, gunmen entered his home, killing his rickshaw puller and slightly wounding Chou and one of his protégés, Shen Ch'i-wu. Chou believed that the would-be assassins had been acting on Japanese instructions.[10] Whether that was so or not has never been determined, but in any case, Chou regarded it as a warning that his lack of cooperation would not be tolerated by authorities, and it marked the beginning of his career under the occupation.

Chou accepted a position as librarian at Peking University, then as chairman of the literature department. From 1941 to April 1943 he held the office of minister of education in the North China Provisional Government. While declining many invitations at public functions, he did participate in some.[11] His name was used by several organizations with which he had little to do in reality, including the North China Literary Association and the magazine *I-wen tsa-chih* (Arts and Letters Review).[12] That he made announcements on behalf of the government was inevitable and irrefutable. One item bearing his name includes the following passages:

> What is important now is developing the central ideology of young students, as well as the intellectual class as a whole, to join together in the Greater East Asia War. What I have called the central ideology is the ideology of Greater East Asianism. Essentially, this thought has a history dating back some fifty or sixty years, flourishing at the end of the Ch'ing dynasty. . . . Later, through Sun Yat-sen's advocacy, this thought reached its ultimate expression as Greater Asianism. . . . Asia is one, and the wellsprings of its culture are one as well, mutually dependent upon each other as the lips are to the teeth, sharing joys

and sorrows, and absolutely inseparable. Therefore, to plant such thoughts cannot be reckoned as difficult. Now, the mission of the literati lies in carrying through this work, until the complete victory of the Greater East Asia War.[13]

In addition to these pressures, Chou was increasingly isolated during the war from his oldest and closest colleagues. Yü P'ing-po remained in Peking and taught at Peking University, but lived a rather secluded life and published only a few brief essays in *Arts and Letters Review* during 1943–1944. Feng Wen-ping (Fei Ming) just prior to the war had become engrossed in Zen meditation, and his claims for it Chou viewed with great skepticism and some disappointment.[14] With the onset of war, Feng retired into the countryside. Late in the war he published two theoretical articles on Zen and poetry in *Wen-hsüeh chi-k'an* (Literary Collections), produced a volume of his prewar poems, *Shui pien* (Water's Edge), and a collection of his prewar lectures on New Poetry, for which Chou wrote a warm personal introduction.[15] But the two had little mutually supportive contact. Shen Ch'i-wu (Shen Yang) remained in Peking with Chou, but their relationship grew increasingly strained, and in 1944 Chou "excommunicated" Shen for reasons that are discussed below. There were other acquaintances in Peking, to be sure, who were sympathetic to Chou personally and professionally, such as Ch'ien Tao-sun, Ch'ü Tui-chih, Hsieh Kang-chu, and Hsieh Hsing-yao.[16] Chou was also visited by writers from the south. At the same time, however, he was visited by a stream of Japanese scholars and officials, which he no doubt often felt a strain. This surfaced, in one instance, after a series of newspaper and magazine articles attempted to portray him in close collaboration with the Japanese White Birch Society writer Musakōji Saneatsu, who had at long last announced his support for the Greater East Asia War.[17] In an essay of his own, Chou listed his meetings with Musakōji, which were few and public, and stated that any exchanges with him had been on the basis of longtime personal acquaintance, and not as national cultural representations.[18] There is apparently little material available on Chou's actual conduct in office as minister of education. That he found it stifling is virtually certain. In April 1943 his mother died, and aside from his personal grief at this loss, it became a plausible reason to resign, which he promptly did. The remaining years of the war he spent teaching and writing essays, until following the war he was sentenced to imprisonment by the Nationalist government for holding office in the puppet regime.

Chou has stated that he originally intended to remain silent under the enemy occupation.[19] However, this outline of his life at that time suggests several motives for the numerous essays he published during the war years. His closest associates had turned to what he must have considered escapist practices (Feng Wen-ping's uncritical interest in Zen), become silent (Yü P'ing-po), or proved undependable (Shen Ch'i-wu). Meanwhile, other friends and self-styled followers or protégés were involved in teaching in a Japanese-dominated education system, or occupying posts in puppet-government bureaucracies, looking to Chou for some signs of leadership as a cultural figure. Chou was in an even more conspicuous position than these men, one required by the positions he had taken to endorse statements that were treasonous. Finally, there was the added income from writing that could always be put to use in support of his dependents. Thus, although he entered the war period still skeptical of the ability of literature to provide lessons or influence people, he must have felt impelled to reassert his position as an individual with a responsibility to society, since he had allowed his public position to coopt his patriotism insofar as that involved resisting the Japanese by force.

His writing began in fits and starts. During the first two years of the occupation he jotted down notes in private on various readings, later collected in *Shu-fang i-chüeh* (A Corner of the Study, 1944), and wrote three or four occasional pieces for publication.[20] He did not, in fact, begin sustained writing until late in 1939 with the essay "Yü chi ssu" (Temple of Yü's Footprint, October 1939).[21] Chou begins the essay with legends on the sage Yü's greatness as an engineer and political leader, his ten years' absence from home, and his consequent emaciation, which led to an impairment of his legs that resulted in a distinctive, crippled gait imitated in Confucian rituals into modern times. Exactly what Yü's trouble was, Chou notes, is uncertain; but, he reflects, he had also seen it among peasants with complications to foot injuries. Chou then turns to the memorial temple to Yü, still in existence, and discusses the local village and customs of the peasant descendants of Yü, who compel his respect. He quotes from gazetteers to discuss the temple itself, as well as other local sights, many now vanished. He closes with an apology that his style is awkward after having not written for two years (apparently he did not keep his few earlier pieces in mind).

"Temple of Yü's Footprint" is exemplary of Chou's early essays during the war, especially as an expression of continuity with a personal and cultural past. Chou had visited the temple in the past, was familiar with the region, and had written essays on the topic before the war as well.[22] The style shows the same appreciation of *wen-yen* and extensive use of quotations that he had developed in the previous decade. The themes are a continuation of earlier ones: the Confucian as an exemplar of humane service, the bond of suffering that joins the present world to the past as a shared experience, attention to the customs of a local region and to the relationships of the "natural world and human feelings." These and other themes he would expand on continually during the war.

Having thus reoriented himself in his early pieces, Chou began continuous writing and in 1942 published the first volume of his wartime essays, *Yao-wei chi. Yao-wei* is a term that suggests two meanings, both relevant to Chou's life and work: one is "bitter taste," and another is "prescriptive ingredients" for a medical compound. Many of these essays deal with Ming and Ch'ing prose writers, and what may be abstracted from them that is of value to the present. One term that recurs is *p'ing-ch'ang* (the ordinary). It is, Chou argues, in the ordinary aspects of life that one must find significance to sustain oneself. Hence, in a discussion of the merits of a miscellany by a Ch'ing writer, Ts'ao T'ing-tung, titled *Lao-lao heng-yen* (Venerable Words for Posterity), Chou quotes and comments:

> "It is the disposition of the elderly to enjoy chatting about old things and to love listening to the new. But it cannot be to the point of tiresomeness, nor for too long. When one feels a bit weary, then one just calls it a night, while the others remain in their seats without going through social formalities. It's just as Chang Ch'ao said: 'When I've drunk to my capacity and want to sleep, I can just go along. Raised voices and loud laughter waste energy. When one socializes, one must use restraint.'"

One look at passages like this and they seem very commonplace. But actually they are rather rare, and what is rare about them is their very ordinariness. Chinese teachings are for the most part too lofty, in other words, one can also say, immoderate. To accomplish this ordinariness is rare and valuable.[23]

Chou goes on to recommend *Venerable Words for Posterity* as a book suitable for the elderly at a time when there were few such works. Books for the elderly, Chou says, should not be devoted to creeds and doctrines, although they should offer some tranquillity and faith, "compatible with the science of human nature, capable of augmenting wisdom and nourishing our personalities."[24] This same approach is evident in his recommendation of Yü Yüeh's introduction essays, also dating back to the Ch'ing dynasty:

> Certainly for the most part these introductory essays have a routine superficiality about them, and yet it has been my experience that if there are several introductory essays in a given book, and one of them is by Mister Ch'ü-yuan [Yü Yüeh], then the most readable one will inevitably be the one by Mister Ch'ü-yuan. . . . Why should this be so? These introductions, even if they have something in common with routine superficialities, being more or less occasional pieces, still have differences with routine superficiality. For example, in chatting about the weather, one way is to say such-and-such about the weather today being the same as always; another way is to say that today the weather is pleasant or cold, but then, concerning this cold, develop it in some way. Say that this morning one saw frost, or it is so cold and damp that it is gloomy. Given some foundation in human feeling and the natural order, then there is a little meaning. Mister Ch'ü-yuan's introductions generally have some opinion to express about this physical aspect, and he does it with sincerity and charm. As one reads, one feels one has gotten something out of it. Yet what he writes is not, for the most part, some all-embracing principle. It is just this which is its rareness and value—a point to which most writers in recent times have had the utmost difficulty in approaching.[25]

Hence, in the first essay quoted above, Chou's value of moderation, the Confucian "mean," is expressed; in this last quotation, he repeats his view that literature should pay close attention to the relationship of man and nature as a sound approach to life. Both themes are linked by reference to their place in ordinary life.

Another aspect of ordinary life is humor, which Chou discusses in several essays. Humor he regarded not as an end in itself, but a balance to serious discussion and writing, and he cites the late Ming writer Chang Tai (Tsung-tzu) as exemplary of a man who maintained a wry humor while engaged in a serious discussion of the destruction of his nation and his home.[26] It is notable that these discussions of the value of humor were ensconced in essays whose subject was Japanese culture, including "Sa tou" (Scattering Beans), "T'an p'ai-wen" (On *Haibun*), "Tsai t'an p'ai-wen" (More Talk on *Haibun*). These, in turn, are made to serve his cosmopolitan views by discussing humorous anecdotes as an international and cross-cultural phenomenon: "No matter whether they are native or foreign, there is no difference in their meaning."[27] This cosmopolitanism is further stressed as he expands his discussion of *haibun* to include all essays and lumps together the works of Bashō, Montaigne, Milne, and Lamb as examples "fundamentally of one genre, regardless of their age, or whether or not they are Chinese or foreign. The distinguishing feature of this genre is that it is a personal statement, not a prescription written on behalf of a political or religious entity. And if such works hold this in common, then they naturally fall into a single genre, embracing what the English term *essai* [spelling as in the original], the Japanese call *zuihitsu,* and the Chinese know as *hsiao-p'in wen*."[28] Such statements may be taken not only as literary criticism, but also as refutations of notions on cultural purity, then in vogue in Japanese propaganda. Chou repeats this theme in various ways throughout his wartime essays, such as in "Wen-hsüeh yü hsüan-ch'uan" (Literature and Propaganda), in which he stated flatly his distaste for propaganda, as opposed to didactic literature, and quoted one of his favorite Western scholars, Havelock Ellis.[29]

While espousing cosmopolitan views, at the same time Chou voiced doubts about his understanding of Japan in "Jih-pen chih tsai-jen-shih" (Reacquaintance with Japan). In this essay, Chou noted that his earlier impressions of Japanese culture had been based too much on the art and literature produced prior to the contemporary period. These works, as the finest expressions of a culture, had led him to an imbalanced overall assessment. There was, he noted, much about Japanese culture he did not understand, including its approach to Confucianism, which exhibited characteristics different from those found in Chinese Confucianism. Chou originally submitted this essay in response to a request for works commemorating the anniversary of the birth of Japan. Chou called attention to the essay more than once in later works. In his memoirs he noted it as a trial expression of his renunciation of the role of cultural interpreter and mediator on behalf of Japanese militarists. To his surprise, there were not strong repercussions, though some Japanese considered him rude, and he continued to express his unorthodox views on Confucianism and literature.[30] But even before the war had ended, he was discussing the import of this essay in 1945:

> I've written quite a few essays. The contents have been as varied as I could make them, and thus I can only take "*tsa-wen* (random notes)" as my domain. But, to reflect for a moment, one can draw out two conclusions from the past few years, and from these see the road my writing and thought have taken. First, in the winter of 1940 I wrote "Reacquaintance with Japan," formally announcing that I was closing the shop on Japanese studies, and thereafter would not presume to say much more on foreign matters which I didn't understand. I would carry out the Confucian principle of admitting ignorance about what I did not know.[31]

In fact, Chou continued to write about Japanese literature and cultures, but confined himself to earlier periods. Chou generally was much more concerned with other issues, and this is reflected in the second of the "two conclusions" to be reached concerning his wartime writing: "Second, in the winter of 1942 I wrote 'Chung-kuo ti ssu-hsiang wen-t'i'' (The Issue of Chinese Thought), leaving the confines of the garden of literature, and concerning myself with the sources of national tranquillity."[32]

What Chou meant was that his attitude toward his own work underwent a change during the war. First, even as late as "More Talk on *Haibun*" he was discussing the requirements of the familiar essay, such as the need to balance seriousness with humor, but thereafter he did not consciously attempt to write according to such prescriptions. Second, he switched the order of his priorities when writing, contrasting his attitude with that of the thirties, expressed in his work "Tzu-chi ti yuan-ti" (One's Own Garden):

> At that time I said, "Our own garden is literature," and added, "writing is like planting a rose garden. The blossoms are sure to be beautiful, and it cannot be said that they are without benefit to others." My present wishes lie in being of benefit to others, and it cannot be said that the blossoms are not beautiful.[33]

The principal expression of this new attitude, Chou wrote, was "The Issue of Chinese Thought." Later, in his memoirs, he expanded the examples to include three more essays: "Han wen-hsüeh ti ch'uan-t'ung" (1940) (The Tradition of Han Literature), "(Chung-kuo wen-hsüeh-shang ti liang chung ssu-hsiang" (1943) (Two Modes of Thought in Chinese Literature), and "Han wen-hsüeh ti ch'ien-t'u" (1943) (The Future of Han Literature). These are the four model essays in the style he termed "penetrating and forceful (*shen-k'o p'o-la*)," as opposed to those which strove more for linguistic and artistic effect, "mild and natural (*p'ing-tan tzu-jan*)."[34] In these four essays Chou consolidated his main ideas on Chinese literature and Confucianism. The fundamental themes in all four are that Confucianism is humanitarian service, and that Han literature (Han being an ethnic reference, not an historical one) is a reflection of this notion.

The first of these essays, "The Tradition of Han Literature," offers Chou's definition of Han literature: It is the expression of the Chinese people themselves, apart from that body of literature in Chinese whose thought and style stems from foreign literature, all of which may be included in the scope of Chinese literature. The central thought in Han literature is Confucianism, but Chou is careful in introducing it: "I often hear people discussing this or that about Asian culture or the national character of China, and I find it on the whole ridiculous."[35] Chou emphasizes that what humanity has in common is far more profound than its differences: "Humanity is alike, regardless of particular details, and I find it difficult to believe that there is a race which enjoys dying and finds life distasteful."[36] Confucianism, Chou then asserts, is that uniquely Chinese expression of the humaneness and common sense on which all cultures are founded. Turning to style, he notes that formal aspects of the Chinese language, such as characters and tones, are elements that influence its literary style and set it apart from even Korean and Japanese. This holds true for the colloquial language as well as the classical. Nevertheless, Chou comments that what was fresh and original in the colloquial works of the early twentieth century had degenerated into a flat, stale prose style, and he recommends reviving certain elements of the old styles. For example, "if we can infuse *pai-hua* with some of the aesthetic of *p'ien-wen*, we could surely create a style superior to the present one.''[37] Reading this essay, it is apparent that, while his exposition of Confucianism and his advocacy of *wen-yen* parallel prose were nothing new in themselves, Chou had taken a more extreme position in discussing these notions. In using the word "Han," he was careful to avoid sounding chauvinistic, but was intent on delimiting the scope he advocated, and concerning himself only with native expression. The discussion of language is equally drastic. Language changes naturally, and should change, but Chou advocates that such conscious change be based on a Chinese tradition which had been seriously attacked by generations of writers who felt *p'ien wen* was far too artificial a style. Both concerns seem designed to shut out Japanese cultural domination.

"The Issue of Chinese Thought" allowed aspects of his first essay to flow in a new form. Chou announced that one of the few topics he regarded with optimism was the continued health of Chinese thought, as a resilient, deeply rooted aspect of the people. Confucianism originated with the people, and was simply codified by the sages. Its principles are humaneness, service to the people, and courtesy in relationships. As a thought without divine miracles or lofty proposals, it is concerned with basic questions of survival. Hence, although there is no belief in martyrdom to enter heaven and no urge for self-sacrifice, Confucian moderation may give way to rash actions and social chaos when the survival of the people is threatened. It is the duty of governments, then, to see to the welfare of the people and thus nourish the roots of their beliefs. Literature provides a mirror of the times, and one can see, even in the discussions of a Taoist recluse in the *Lao-hsüeh-an pi-chi* (Sung dynasty), the concern with the order and welfare of society as a responsibility of the rulers. Foreign literatures may expound other notions of human relationships, but it is, after all, the Chinese who know best how to manage their own society. This is reflected not in heroics and propaganda, but in the words and deeds of ordinary life.

In this essay the challenge to Japanese propagandists is clear and forcefully expressed. Japanese theorists had long before decided to use Confucianism as an ideology, but insisted that the Chinese themselves no longer understood Confucianism, and hence needed guidance. To this end, quite a number of articles and treatises were written to advocate "the kingly way" (*ōdō*) and the warrior code (*bushidō*), and prominent figures were made to give testimonials such as the following, which appeared in newspapers:

> K'ung Hsien-chang, seventy-second descendent of Confucius, who is here [in Tokyo] to undergo medical treatment for an eye disease, declared that in China, "the people must be made to realize that they have been blinded by Western trends of thought." He pointed out that Confucius has been the mental stimulus of the Nipponese people. He added that in China, however, owing to oppression by Chiang Kai-shek, Confucianism is no longer remembered by its people.[38]

This statement, pathetic in itself, was multiplied by the hundreds in political tracts, and at the time Chou wrote "The Issue of Chinese Thought," Kataoka Teppei, as a Japanese army advisor in North China, was calling for recognition of this theme in Chinese literature as well.[39] Hence, Chou's essay was very much a pointed rebuttal of this propaganda and its incursion into literature. Chou repeated his denial that Confucianism was a political theory; it was, rather, a set of principles for human relationships that political activities could nourish. It is the failure of governments to provide for the welfare of the people that results in social chaos, and

> . . . the responsibility for this rests with the government and not on "indoctrination." . . . With a sigh I have said that the period from the Northern and Southern Sung down to the end of the Ming was almost by design entirely given over to disorders and calamities. This is indeed an extraordinary state of affairs, and yet, turning it over in my mind, how does the present state of affairs differ from that of the past? Surely it is as with Louis XIV, who saw clearly that the deluge would come after him but made no plans to provide for the future so that the people could live— was he not the stupidest man on earth? . . . But also because Chinese thought is fundamentally concerned with the people's livelihood, if their livelihood is at stake, then their thoughts will begin to waver, and that in turn will lead to the danger of disorder. This danger does not arise from questions of ideology, and therefore it is not decrees and speeches which will preserve us against the threat. . . . But concerning anything touching China, especially her thought and way of life, I feel it is still our own people who are best informed, or whose knowledge is most accurate.[40]

Chou followed up this attack with two more essays a few months later, turning his focus more toward literature again, but also using literature for broader social themes. In "The Future of Han Literature," he again stressed the value of Confucianism, this time in relation to other traditions in China and to natural science:

> Taoism and Buddhism, legalism and Christianity all tend to extremes and to ideals which demand all or nothing. The Confucian does not resolve things in this manner. However much of a trial life is, he feels there is no need to fast to death, nor does he harbor the hope of longevity by abstaining from cereals. The only path left is earnestly to seek a livelihood, with Yü and Chi as models. One lives until death comes, and one dies content. In my personal view, is this not a way of life which coincides exactly with the principles of biology?
>
> This view of life among the Chinese may be said to constitute the ethical tradition of Han literature, which, as I see it, has always remained potent and has never changed. It is the root of a very sturdy tree or an abundant wellspring. From it wholesome art as well as wholesome life can arise. It is the course along which the literature of the future must move forward.[41]

He dug at the notion that China had been poisoned with an overdose of Western culture first by alluding only to "foreign culture," thus including Japan, they by noting that Japan had absorbed far more "foreign" influence than China, and then suggesting that China, indeed, had not absorbed enough:

> For many years now China seems to have had an excessive influx of foreign thought, and this seems to have caused the spread of corruption. However, on careful examination, this influx has not amounted to a third of what Japan had earlier received, nor has it been fully digested and absorbed, and the so-called abuses stem for this, because indigestion can also be toxic.[42]

Chou then restates his desire for a cosmopolitanism the war and Japanese propaganda have retarded:

> In contemporary China I look forward to the introduction and dissemination of all the advanced, scholarly thought on biology and anthropology, on children and women, though this appears to be an unlikely event. Even so, at least in the realm of culture, there should at least be a climate of opinion favoring this, and at least all those intent on a literary career should possess a modicum of this knowledge. To put it simply, this means that literary creation should no longer take place in the ivory tower, but seek its inspiration at the crossroads of human life.[43]

In his final essay of this series, Chou returned to the broader notion of "Chinese literature," as opposed to the ethnic confines of "Han literature," but only to stress points he had made before. Hence, in "Two Modes of Thought in Chinese Literature," Chou argues that beginning with the *Shih ching* (Book of Odes) and continuing up to its highest expression in the poems of Tu Fu, Chinese poetry has been overwhelmingly concerned with the welfare of the people, as opposed to the minor stream of court literature beginning with *Li sao,* which is primarily concerned with the elite. He stressed that his conclusions applied only to China and might not apply to other nations and cultures, just as the conclusions about other countries do not apply to China. Scientifically there is only one world, but culturally there is more than one. That Chou should go to such extremes to make such a dubious point as that Chinese poetry is primarily concerned with the welfare of the people suggests he was intent on impressing the social message delivered so pointedly in "The Issue of Chinese Thought," and on snubbing Japanese-sponsored propaganda. Indeed, Yoshikawa Kōjirō, on reading the essay, took its theme to be that there were aspects of Chinese literature "with which we foreigners ought not to concern ourselves."[44]

Judged as literature, the essays show the characteristic looseness of style and emotional restraint, the unsystematic discussion of a topic from various approaches. They are filled with quotations from Chinese literature and spiced with allusions to foreign literatures, Japan being conspicuously absent. The imagery is simple, even rustic. There is nothing exceptional in his metaphor for Confucianism as the roots of Chinese culture, yet it is a happy conjoining of tradition and modernity. On the one hand, it is associated with Liu Tsung-yuan's phrase: "What I can do is comply with the nature of the tree, so that it takes the way of its own kind."[45] On the other hand, the use of roots corresponds with Chou's advocacy of human values being based on a scientific understanding of the natural world. Of the four essays, "The Issue of Chinese Thought" and "The Future of Han Literature" are the most valuable, for they express Chou's most important arguments in trenchant fashion. Of these two, "The Issue of Chinese Thought" is the more unified piece, expressing forcefully his views and dissent from Japanese propaganda, while avoiding many of his more dubious or debatable arguments on literary history, style, and theory. These arguments tend to confuse the important and valid points he has to make regarding what the role of literature *should* be.

How little the Chinese and Japanese wanted to listen to each other, how empty the ideological debate, and how considerable was Chou's prestige are all revealed in the confrontation to which these essays in part led. In fact, it was less a confrontation than an incident that took a serpentine course through a mire of sad comedy and trivial nastiness and sputtered out in a series of swipes rather than a genuine debate. The affair was placed in the following context by Chou in a series of articles published in 1944.[46] According to Chou, his protégé Shen Ch'i-wu was dissatisfied with his own lack of success even in the ailing literary scene of North China. In the spring of 1943, when Chou was preparing the last two of these four essays, the literary scene in Peking was dominated by the periodicals *Chung-kuo wen-i* (Chinese Arts and Letters), edited by Chang Shen-ch'ieh, and the new monthly *I-wen tsa-chih* (Arts and Letters Review), edited chiefly by Yu Ping-ch'i. In a bid to assert preeminence, Shen sought the backing of Kataoka Teppei, then the Japanese army cultural advisor in North China, to begin to rival publication, *Wen-hsüeh chi-k'an* (Literary Collections). (In his wartime account, Chou noted that Kataoka was not respected by literary circles informed on modern Japanese literature, and since Kataoka had been so ignored, Chou had not been personally introduced to him. Only Shen Ch'i-wu had sought his company.)[47] Shen quarreled with the other editors, and his own magazine failed. While Chang Shen-ch'ieh was eventually removed from editorship of *Chinese Arts and Letters*,[48] which also thereafter ceased publication, *Arts and Letters Review* was under the patronage of Chou Tso-jen himself, and Shen and Kataoka could not arrange to cut off its paper ration. Shen urged Chou to withdraw his patronage, and when Chou refused, Shen warned him his reputation might suffer.

Veiled attacks on Chou began shortly. The first was at a meeting of Peking writers during which Kataoka Teppei denounced the "old writers" of China. Chou ignored the address and, apparently, so did everyone else. In August Kataoka gave a scathing speech in Tokyo at the Greater East Asia Writers Congress. He announced that in the "pacified zone" (occupied China) there was still an enemy writer publishing "reactionary" works. There was no need to name him; the numerous "negative" essays of this "old writer" were an obstacle to the literary movement to found the ideals of Greater East Asia, and he should be "swept out."[49] Since Kataoka delivered his speech in Japanese, most of the Chinese delegates present did not understand, and those who did were quite unsure as to whom Kataoka was referring. It remained for Hu Lan-ch'eng to publish an article identifying Chou Tso-jen as the target of Kataoka's attack. Chou was inclined to ignore it, but when the attack was published in the official organ of the Japanese Literature Patriotic Association, *Bungaku hōkoku,* Chou was moved to action. He wrote to the president of the association, Kume Masao, for confirmation of whether he was under attack, and whether the association supported Kataoka's views. Kume, however, had just been removed from his position, and replied to Chou that the matter did not concern him personally. A reply from Kataoka would be forthcoming. In his letter, Kataoka informed Chou of the subversiveness of his views, and condemned his pose as a bystander: "Even if the Chinese endorse the liberation of Greater East Asia, but do not wish their hopes for survival to be threatened, that is, if they do not share any of the hardships nor consider joining in the Greater East Asia War, and if this kind of thinking becomes the general consensus, then what is China's stand in this war?"[50] This was the last that Kataoka, then back in Japan, had to say. By November 1944 he had died of tuberculosis.

What bothered Chou particularly, he claimed, was how a Japanese like Kataoka, who neither spoke nor read Chinese, knew what Chou was writing. There were, Chou noted, only a handful of Japanese specialists who had any understanding of what was being written in China, and he was certain Kataoka was not among them.[51] Chou found the answer in an article by Shen Ch'i-wu, under a pen name, denouncing the "old writer" who contributed to *Arts and Letters Review.*[52] It was then apparent to Chou that this protégé had supplied Kataoka with the contents of his essays, on which Kataoka had based his attack. In a public notice Chou "excommunicated" Shen, and then in later articles derided him as an imitator and plagiarist of Chou's own work. He recalled that when gunmen had attacked them on New Year's Day 1939, the Japanese press had reported Shen as being wounded trying to shield Chou from his attackers. Chou had informed them then that Shen was seated away from Chou when he was hit. At that time, the newspaper had explained that they assumed Shen was performing according to the ideal that a student defends his professor. Now, Chou noted, he could reveal how ideals had sunk recently, and professors "only hope their students won't eat their mentors."[53]

While Shen was driven into obscurity, protesting his innocence, Kataoka's attack backfired, with no one clearly supporting him. The Japanese-language Shanghai newspaper *Tairiku shimpō* (Mainland News) urged both parties to heed the words of Wang Ching-wei, for each (Chou and Kataoka) to look to his own faults.[54] The editors of the supposedly pro-Japanese newspaper *Hsin chung-kuo pao* (New China Herald, Shanghai) seemed to throw up their hands in despair at the thought that Chou might retire altogether and leave the movement for international cultural understanding. They reminded readers that international cooperation "must be based on the spirit of mutual respect."[55] Kataoka was openly ridiculed by T'ao Ching-sun in the *Hsin shen pao*, the Shanghai newspaper controlled by the Japanese army. T'ao Ching-sun, the Japanese-educated writer formerly with the Creation Society, wrote that Kataoka's attack in Tokyo had at first left many writers in Shanghai wondering if they were the "old writers" under attack. Had not T'ao declined the requests of Kataoka and Hayashi Fusao to organize a literary movement in Shanghai? Had not Chang Tzu-p'ing offended someone by a characterization in one of his novels? Kataoka's attack had become a standing joke among the "old writers" of Shanghai, and they were incredulous to learn that Kataoka was referring to Chou Tso-jen. T'ao concluded by suggesting that for his rudeness to the venerable Chou, Kataoka should consider *seppuku,* ritual disembowelment.[56]

Propagandists for the Peking puppet regime also made no attempt to attack Chou. In an effort to elucidate a "central ideology," one propagandist explicitly agreed with Chou that *jen* (humaneness) was indeed at the core of China's inherent thought and embedded among the people. Further, he continued, it was also at the core of Sun Yat-sen's Great Asianism:

> That Greater Asian-ism advocates the union and alliance of all East Asian peoples is really an expression of *jen*. We are alike the people of one race, we share a single wellspring of culture, and we should with our collective strength and wisdom attain our ideals. *Besides* the spirit of the word *jen* contained in Confucian thought, as regards the topic of China's inherent thought, we should mention in particular the spirit of moral relationships. It is this which is the vitality of the Chinese people. For this we must first understand the development of racial characteristics. . . .[57]

Thus the writer neatly spliced Chou's dissent together with racist propaganda, and buried it in fascist rhetoric rather than confront it.

While Chou did not cease to write remarks that were clearly in dissent against propaganda activities, he discreetly did not push the issue of Kataoka's attack. The Japanese, for their part, allowed the affair to disappear and did not attempt reprisals.

In essence, Chou was less interested in defending Confucianism as such than in looking to it for some constructive sense of continuity with the past and using it to challenge the abuses and follies of the present.[58] In 1944, Chou wrote, typically, "I myself admit that I belong to the Confucian school of thought, but this designation of Confucianism is all mine, and I am afraid my interpretation of it may differ greatly from the general opinion."[59] In fact, Chou's interpretation differed even from the liberal revisionist views in the twentieth century. For example, in 1940 he wrote:

> Truthfully, while I am often fond of Confucianism, I am at the same time not fond of Confucianism. When I used to chat with old friends, and the topic would turn to ancient philosophers, they were generally tolerant of the pre-Han, but not of the Han, or they also tolerated the Han, but not the Sung. Rather than take a stab at turning the clock back to return to antiquity and look into whatever contradictions there might be in Confucianism, they considered that on the whole it was distorted by later generations. We generally hold to the convention that Confucius and Mencius were the "pure" Confucians, first to be misinterpreted in the Han, giving rise to a school of absurdities, and again misinterpreted in the Sung, turning increasingly harsh. However, this is not quite correct, for these contradictions are not absent from the works of Mencius and Confucius.[60]

Chou then quotes a passage from Mencius on Yü, Chi, and Yen Hui, and debates the interpretations given in Mencius itself. He concludes, returning to his favorite theme:

> One only needs to read through the whole passage to see that it fails to explain itself. Seen in this light, it cannot but appear somewhat unjust when we put the blame entirely on neo-Confucianism. I believe that this flaw really rests in Confucianism itself, and that it is quite natural that when we compare the earlier and later schools, they are not in agreement. In labeling the earlier and later schools, two stock phrases best illustrate their different viewpoints: "to take hunger and cold as one's own responsibility," and "the people serve the lord." In other words, though the positions of the earlier and later schools were not the same, they both maintained the distinction between lord and servant. Looked at in this fashion, the reason we are ambivalent toward Confucianism can be understood.[61]

Chou also repeatedly remarks that his own research has not been systematic. He stresses the qualities of humaneness and skepticism in the exemplary writers of the past whom he has recommended. For example, he says of Li Chih: "Although there are some today who place importance on Li Chih, yet what I abstracted from his work was not an iconoclasm on which to build; its value is in its reason and feeling. The wild attacks and the lack of restraint are but the outside appearance."[62] More than once Chou places value on such men as Wang Ch'ung, Li Chih, and Yü Cheng-hsieh for their skepticism.[63] In writing about his own time, Chou attempted to practice some of what he preached. Several essays were devoted all or in part to the status of women in Chinese society. On this topic Chou could be alternately theoretical and very practical. The oppression of women, he theorized, was largely based on Neo-Confucianism, and since the hold of that thought on the people was less severe than in cultures where religions dominated life, the situation for women's liberation in China was comparatively hopeful.[64] He rejected all traditional standards for judging women as wives and mothers, and felt that strict standards no longer existed. Women in higher education should turn their attention to needed work in cultural history, where they might not be in such severe competition with men for jobs.[65]

Chou's own attitudes on literature were ambivalent and skeptical. That he rejected forecasts of a literary renaissance in China has already been noted.[66] He denigrated much of traditional Chinese literature and explained that he had read so much of it recently because of the shortage of books from the West.[67] He cautioned young people against taking up careers in literature,[68] and when asked to discuss Japanese women writers, he singled out for praise the late Meiji writer Yosano Akiko, who had advocated the study of philosophy and science over literature.[69] As for the essay itself, he felt that in form and in style it had reached a critical impasse. The forms and styles of tradition were either irrelevant or impractical for the present, and there were no critical standards left. He thought that the possibilities for the development of drama and fiction were more promising. He himself wrote simply as a substitute for smoking.[70] Probably in response to the efforts of propagandists to organize writers, Chou declared he was no longer a writer, and wanted neither to be the leader of the pack nor a member of the pack.[71] The essay had attracted him, just as it had attracted Feng Wen-ping, precisely for its freedom from artistic rules. His favorite recent book was on the art of making paper.[72]

But Chou could not be so utterly negative. He did, he stated, have a purpose in writing, after all.[73] That purpose he codified as the "naturalization of ethics" (*lun-li ti tzu-jan-hua*), and "the rationalizing of moral relationships" (*tao-i chih shih-kung-hua*), concepts which permeate his essays, as discussed above, and which he described as the task left to writers of fiction in the wake of the failure of the social revolution in the twentieth century.[74] Still, he had longstanding and continuing doubts about whether literature was of any use in affecting social change and human behavior.[75]

Added to this seeming welter of contradictions and repetitiveness is the fact that, even as he expressed so many doubts concerning literature, as he had prior to the war, his writing reached its full maturity during those years. This is testified to, in part, by the number of citations and quotations of his wartime work in David Pollard's survey of his literary values, *A Chinese Look at Literature: The Literary Values of Chou Tso-jen in Relation to the Tradition*. As we examine these values, we find that they are also qualities of character and per-

sonality: *ch'ü-wei*, the projection of personality, together with mildness, naturalness, temperateness, sincerity, and lack of affectation. If
anything flagged in his literature during the war, it was his sense of
humor. Thus we see essay writing, in Chou's work, as a mode of self-
cultivation, much in the tradition of Chinese essayists of the late
Ming and Ch'ing.

Self-cultivation was usually expressed in terms of an avocation,
rather than a vocation, and hence it is not surprising to find Chou
denying that he is a writer and disparaging his kind of literature as a
vocation. Nevertheless, he was serious about the idea of writing not
just as self-cultivation, but as his subject matter during the war indicates, in serving the needs of society. Chou had early on, with some
digressions, termed his view of literature as "art for life's sake," and
during the war he defined his kind of Confucianism as "the art of
life."[76] The connection between the two is represented in Chou's
literary values and his choice of subject matter. Pollard has noted that
Chou preferred Chinese literary terms, inherited from tradition,
rather than perfectly viable alternatives imported from Western
literatures.[77] When we see how closely his view of Chinese literature
was connected with his views on Confucianism, the reason for his
choice seems more apparent. So also is his disparagement of his own
abilities to achieve these goals. On the eve of the war he had modestly
declined Hu Shih's assertion that he had achieved "blandness" or
mildness, saying that he had merely achieved irascibility.[78] In his
memoirs he was to write that the penetrating and forceful expression
he sought in some essays was but an ideal, basically unattainable.[79]
This coincides with his other discussions of literature and values,
both literary and human, and is in keeping with his vision of the
Confucian as one who "knows a thing cannot be done, and yet does
it."[80]

Shanghai Essayists

Chou Tso-jen was very much an individualist, and yet in the pattern of his life and work, in the traditionalism with which he viewed
literature, he provided a model for other writers and their work dur-

ing the war. This model has strong affinities with the traditional notion of the *ch'ao-yin*, or "court recluse," known especially in modern times as the *kuan-yin*, or "official recluse," connoting a man who renders bureaucratic service by day, but in leisure seeks detachment from that role.[81] This is expressive not simply of relaxation and rest, but of the fundamental disenchantment of the official-recluse with society and his role in it. Hence, we find the leaders of the Nanking government, Wang Ching-wei, Chou Fo-hai, and Ch'en Kung-po, as well as officials in the education system such as Li Sheng-wu and Fan Chung-yün, together with dozens of lesser functionaries, all writing nonfiction prose in considerable quantities during the war. Much of it was autobiographical and none of it was oriented politically as propaganda for the Nanking regime, although as essayists describing themselves, these writer-officials sought a personable, ingenuous style. As familiar, relaxed, and unaffected prose, it was supposedly intended as relief from politics and the grimness of current affairs.[82]

In addition to Chou's model as an official-recluse, his style and literary values had considerable influence, especially on a number of writers whose concern was more properly literature than official life. Among the familiar essayists of the thirties, Chou's influence was dominant. Yü Ta-fu was held in esteem by several essayists of the occupation, but primarily for his sensitivity, his careful studies of nature and affected rusticism, not his earlier romanticism. Very little of his bohemian style and scandalous affairs, none of his expressions of passionate love, carrier over into the forties. Lu Hsün's imitators were forced by fashion and politics to turn for the most part to other modes of expression than the *tsa-kan*, although his works continued to be quoted and studied. Lin Yü-t'ang as a champion of humorous literature went into a decline with the coming of war. A brief discussion of this occurred in the first literary periodical in occupied Peking, when some readers found the contents not humorous enough for their tastes. The editor, Fang Chi-sheng, rejected a policy emphasizing humor over other modes of expression, and responded that just as Lin Yü-t'ang had championed humor as something that is *not* forced, so one cannot force humor or make it a policy. Moreover, while Lin had said that the achievement of recent literature had been the success of the familiar essay (*hsiao-p'in-wen*), it should not be regarded solely as a vehicle for humor.[83] This is not to say that Lin was not influential, for he was, but that the popularity of some of his chief contributions was reduced, while other aspects of his work blend indistinguishably with those of Chou Tso-jen.

In fact, a number of essayists in occupied Shanghai and Peking were protégés of Lin Yü-t'ang. Before the foreign concessions fell to the Japanese, their chief vehicle had been *Yü-chou feng i-k'an* (Cosmic Wind II), a subsidiary publication of the Lin Yü-t'ang publishing ventures devoted to the familiar essay, edited by Chou Li-an and T'ao K'ang-te. This magazine included contributions from virtually all Shanghai writers given to essay composition, but folded with the fall of the International Settlement. In early 1942 Chu Hsing-chai, better known as Chu P'u, a vice-minister for communications in the Nanking regime, began *Ku chin* (Past and Present) as a literary periodical, ostensibly to divert himself from the gloom of the times.[84] In addition to attracting contributions from the leaders of the Nanking regime, he persuaded Chou Li-an and T'ao K'ang-te to assume editorial positions, and through their contacts with writers for earlier magazines effected a merger of the official and unofficial worlds. The writers and officials not only appeared together in print, but at social gatherings in Chu P'u's home as well, and several writers made occasional complimentary remarks about Wang Ching-wei, Chou Fo-hai, or Ch'en Kung-po in their essays.

No particular style or theme was developed by these writers as a whole. There were writers who were almost exclusively bibliophiles and antiquarians, such as Chou Yüeh-jan, whose articles were collected under the apt title *Shu, shu, shu* (1944) (Books, Books, Books), and Hsieh Hsing-yao (Wu Chih, Yao Kung), who had edited the prewar magazine *I ching* (Unorthodox Classics), devoted to nonfiction prose. Chou Pan-hou (Pan Kung) specialized in commentary on modern English literature, which he had studied at Tsinghua University, and worked at National Southwest United University in Kunming early in the war. Su Ch'ing's style had little in common with these writers, and she enjoyed taking issue on topical questions. P'an Hsü-tsu (Yü Ch'ieh), also discussed above, imitated Lin Yü-t'ang in his skeptical, humorous jottings and personal enthusiasms, which, however, went in the direction of Chinese fortunetelling rather than the British hobbies of Lin. Much of Yü Ch'ieh's writing became nearly pointless and tedious toying with subjects. For example, he reflects on the notion of shouldering responsibilities as tougher than being irresponsible and concludes that this is not so. It is, rather, difficult to be irresponsible among responsible people, in letters as well as in life:

> Announcements and articles with statistical references are the most responsible. Diverting articles and humorous discussions are the most irresponsible, and difficult to do. Take lectures and booklength, substantial critical writings: as long as you think each and every phrase is responsible, you can blurt out whatever comes to mind, and just pick up the pen and write. If you think of each word as irresponsible, you have to think for a long time. A day will go by without anything being accomplished, and without considerable talent one could not get started. This is not just difficult, it's extremely difficult.[85]

T'ao K'ang-te and Chou Li-an were themselves distinctly different writers, but were never very important figures, at least as writers. During the war T'ao wrote very little. One of the few pieces that ran beyond a few hundred characters was his account of his stay in Japan. Written in diary form, it is studied trivia, occasionally poking mild fun at his Japanese hosts and avoiding substantive remarks.[86] T'ao's main work was as an editor and publisher. With Liu Yü-sheng he began *Teng-yü t'an* (Wind and Rain Chats), the title deliberately taken from one of Chou Tso-jen's essay collections. T'ao and Liu also together operated the Pacific Bookstore (T'ai-p'ing shu-chü), one of the most prolific publishing houses under the occupation.

Chou Li-an, prior to the war, had been a strong advocate of Lin Yü-t'ang's views. In one essay he argued that humor was that amount of irreverence for habits and unreasoned traditions that allowed the individual to think for himself:

> As for *Lun-yü* magazine advocating humor and the Kung-an School advertising "self-cultivation" [*hsing-ling*], I can say on top of that: self-cultivation *is* humor. People without self-cultivation who merely recite set formulas are utterly humorless, and therefore, self-cultivation is the mother of humor.[87]

He cites the private letters of Yuan Mei and Cheng Hsieh as exemplary of this view in late imperial times, when they felt freer to express their true feelings in private letters than in works destined for publication. He concludes his discussion with the following exhortation:

> Pan-ch'iao's [Cheng Hsieh] poems and prose are both familiar pieces. He was not mouthing insincere phrases, but willing to talk honestly, to discuss how to conduct oneself along the path of life, to offer a few words on domestic trivia unrelated to urgent topics. I say, you who have been clutching Marx's *Das Kapital* or Gorky, and your stomachs are still just as empty as ever, hurry up and toss them aside. It's more important to spend a few bits on Pan-ch'iao's collected works.[88]

Once the war began, however, Chou Li-an went through a period of writing *tsa-wen*, supposedly in the Lu Hsün style. What concerned him most in these essays were the issues of Chou Tso-jen and the "patriotic eight-legged essay" (*k'ang-chan pa-ku*). He fretted over Chou's situation, wrote him, and urged him to come south as the only resolution to the dilemma of avoiding serving the Japanese while remaining under the occupation.[89] His defense of the patriotic eight-legged essay was as enthusiastic as his defense of Lin Yü-t'ang had been. In "Yin Liang Shih-ch'iu ti yao-ch'iu erh hsiang-ch'i" (Reflecting on Liang Shih-ch'iu's Appeal), Chou Li-an regarded Liang's call for a literature unrelated to the war activities as identical with the distaste of some for the patriotic eight-legged essay:

> These two kinds of people must be dealt harsh attacks, because even if writings on the war have all turned into cliché-ridden eight-legged essays, as long as the writer's standpoint is grounded in the resistance, his work is meritorious and unsullied. One absolutely cannot, because a work is "about the same" as others or because it lacks the "timelessness of literature," refuse to acknowledge its worth, and instead advocate the need for writings that relinquish their bond with their time.[90]

By the middle of 1941, Chou Li-an had long since abandoned patriotic literature, and virtually all writing. At that time, he wrote in his introduction to a collection of his essays:

> The transformations in the world and human events during the last few years have indeed been overpowering. When I recall things from four or five years ago, I feel as though it might as well have been a different world. I have lost any sense of happiness and well-being, I have lost all sense of pleasure, and when I am depressed, I have even lost a sense of hope. I don't mean that we've been sent here to play a fixed role in a

predetermined tragedy. That is wrong, and I absolutely oppose it as being wrong. But who can decide right from wrong?

The daily wrongs in the environment have day by day crushed my enthusiasm. I have not only gagged myself and stopped writing, but what's more, aware that it's wrong, I've sunk into escapism. Although I often wish for an opportunity to flee this suffocating atmosphere, still, once one has settled here for two or three years, a false sense of security and inertia, after all, bring a loss of self-awareness. Late every night my thoughts usually brighten, and I have overwhelming, soaring feelings.

The suffocation of this environment and the confusion I experience have kept me from writing a word, and so each day I only do some work in a mechanical way. I really mean that I've set my pen aside, since over the last two years I've no longer had the old exhilaration I used to feel when I took up the pen. Even so, I still haven't found a way to break off writing. . . . This book is the last batch of goods.[91]

Judging from this passage, it is not surprising that Chou Li-an was an admirer of Yü Ta-fu, whom he ranked at the top of the profession.[92] Nor is it really surprising that Chou continued to write. However, his work petered out in occasional antiquarian articles and editorial notes of unexceptional quality. The devotee of Lin Yü-t'ang, the successor of Lu Hsün, and the admirer of Yü Ta-fu became in the forties a promoter of Wang Ching-wei's memoirs[93] and a history buff of unrestrained nostalgia. In particular he followed the faddish interest in Tseng P'u's late Ch'ing novel, *Nieh-hai hua* (Flower on an Ocean of Sin). This vogue, which attracted several writers, was sparked both by the early wartime revival of interest in Sai Chin-hua as a patriot as well as a prostitute and by the appearance of the authorized sequel by Chang Hung (Chang Yin-nan), *Hsü nich-hai hua* (Sequel to Flower on an Ocean of Sin), in the Peking journal *Chung-ho* (Equilibrium and Harmony). Chou Li-an, as editor of *Cosmic Wind II,* had passed up the first offer to publish it, a choice he later regretted. Some people were interested in the two works because of Sai Chin-hua herself, but others, like Chou Li-an, enjoyed the novels as portrayals of Ch'ing officialdom:[94]

To look back from our time on the T'ung-chih and Kuang-hsü periods, just as the people of the T'ung-chih and Kuang-hsü looked back on the courtiers of the Chia-ch'ing and Ch'ien-lung, is enough to make one throw away one's pen and sigh over and over for a culture and refinement now irretrievably lost.[94]

Chou Li-an's employer, Chu P'u, was also a self-made antiquarian and bibliophile by avocation who filled his library with Ch'ing *pi-chi* jottings and presided over antiquarian chats at the social gatherings he held for his contributors. In his own essays, autobiographical for the most part, he introduced himself with affected rusticism. "I'm every inch a countryman," he wrote, and in a series of articles he leads the reader through his life and hobbies, indicating that he is anything but a countryman. Rather, at age sixteen he arrived in Shanghai for schooling and had not since been back to his "rural roots," a period of twenty years. Now he longed "to let my hair down and go into the hills."[95] Chu P'u played the court recluse par excellence as one "alienated from this world," without talent, yet a connoisseur and enthusiast of Chinese culture as well as mountain climbing (another pastime steeped in tradition) and travel, including a grand tour of Europe and India. His writing is filled with the conventions of the rustic essayist, with no lack of insistence that he is speaking with utter frankness (*"lao-shih shuo"*), apologies for the awkwardness of his *wen-yen* style, humorous "confessions," protests of his simplicity, and pages of bland trivia.

Others took their own work more seriously than those, like Chou Li-an and Chu P'u, who represent the historical and personal nostalgia prevalent among some writers of the period. In March 1943 *Past and Present* published a special anniversary issue that attempted a self-analysis of itself as representative of literature under the occupation. Ch'ü Tui-chih, the Peking historian and editor of *Chung-ho*, compared *Cosmic Wind* in the thirties with *Past and Present* in the forties. He found that, although many of the writers were the same, interests and styles had changed:[96]

> What has enabled *Past and Present* recently to arouse the enthusiasm of readers is its willingness to say something in a straightforward manner. Previous publications needed a bit of the offbeat and unique, since the things of ordinary life were deemed not sufficiently stimulating. But the events of these part few years have stimulated us all too much. . . . No matter where or under what circumstances, people feel that there is no need for a biting style, but a need for composure; that it is better to discuss matters of fact rather than to prattle emptily, to speak slowly in a low key rather than in a high voice, to sketch lightly in pale tones, rather than daub on heavy colors.[96]

Ch'ü's carefully balanced prose, filled with *wen-yen*, is then directed to the signifiance of the interest in antiquarian studies:

> Retrospection is not nostalgic infatuation with the past, but [the principle that if we] do not forget the events of the past [then they will be our] guide to what follows them. If we do not understand the past, then we cannot understand the present. If we cannot understand the present, then we cannot conceive of hope for the future. . . . No matter what our images of the future may be, we must assume some sense of responsibility. We must not remain aloof. The greater the distress, the more we must have confidence in our ability to ease and offset the bitterness of this time.[97]

Thus, Ch'ü Tui-chih raised the themes of style as bland and content as being of service to the present age, views close to those of Chou Tso-jen. Whether they offered valuable historical insights or not, Chou Tso-jen expressed little favorable criticism of writers during the war, probably in large part because of his desire not to be read as an oracle or a "leader of the pack."

One writer who might have come close to following through on Chou Tso-jen's notions of literature was Liu Ts'un-jen. Liu had graduated from Peking University on the eve of the war and spent the early years of the war in Hong Kong, contributing to *Cosmic Wind* and *Cosmic Wind II,* as well as other magazines, which led to a collection of his pieces called *Hsi hsing chi* (Western Star) in 1941. This volume included his studies of traditional Chinese fiction, a detective story, and the series of articles, "Pei-ta yü pei-ta jen" (Peking University and Peking University Personages), on which his reputation as a writer was chiefly founded. In fact, there is little in these essays on Peking University that is exceptionally perceptive, but it was an unusual attempt to view the university against the ideals set for it. In 1942, with the fall of Hong Kong, Liu moved to Shanghai, changed his name to Liu Yü-sheng (a fact he made no attempt to conceal), and changed his topic to food.[98] Unfortunately, Liu also took employment as a propagandist for the Nanking regime, and even his blandest essays are permeated with tension. For instance, he concludes a two-thousand-word description of Cantonese food with the following statements:

> People who write essays usually avoid talking very much about what they eat and drink, as though they were immortals who had achieved the

way. I'm ashamed that I can't be a Po-i or a Shu-ch'i, but instead talk to
excess about food and drink. Probably in the eyes of gentlemen of the
way, the crime is not just one of bohemian affection.[99]

Here Liu is arguing that, at this point, what concerns him and
what concerns all people under the occupation are the basics of survival and not becoming dissident recluses who starve themselves to
death, like Po-i and Shu-ch'i. The implication is that if those who
would criticize him as a traitor were truly loyal to their convictions,
they would take the improbable course of fasting to death. Liu had a
point, at least to some extent, but he was never comfortable emotionally with his own actions, and it colored his work of that period.
Liu's most studied essays are those written in 1943 concerning his
visit to Japan as a cultural representative of the Wang Ching-wei
government. While he stresses the personal nature of these articles,
they were expected of him by Japanese propagandists for both
Chinese and Japanese audiences, the latter presumably in some need
of reassuring words from Chinese writers. Hence, these essays are
never free from an obvious political role. Like the essays of T'ao
K'ang-te and Yü Ch'ieh on their trips to Japan, Liu's are cluttered
with polite trivia about what Liu saw and heard here. Unlike his
colleagues, Liu goes on to serious praise of Kikuchi Kan's fiction (in
Chinese translation), to admiration of Japanese habits of courtesy
and discipline, to dismay that so few Chinese have any understanding
of Japanese culture. Yet, within these scattered remarks that,
whether personally felt or not, were the kind of sentiments expected
to him, Liu returns at various times to stress the paramount need of
the Chinese people for material, economic well-being and to
challenge the theme in Japanese propaganda that East Asian civilization rests on spirituality alone, not as in the West on materialism.[100]
Such statements seem rooted in Hu Shih's thought in the May
Fourth era, and they are probably influenced more immediately by
Chou Tso-jen's dissenting essays.

On the subject of Chou Tso-jen, Liu could express his appreciation
in a style that reflected Chou's own: meandering and digressive, filled
with long quotations, the style moving from wen-yen to vernacular as
the focus seemed to dictate, with attention to the values Chou discussed.[101] Liu's fiction shows further the influence of his nonfiction

prose style. The narrative is restrained and meandering, with an eye for detail that is often not linked to the work as a whole. Characters may be carefully described, only to disappear. There is a pronounced concern with ethics, but the artistic achievement is limited.

Wen Tsai-tao and Chi Kuo-an

In 1944, Chou Tso-jen recommended two essayists who had appeared during the war, Wen Tsai-tao and Chi Kuo-an, as writers suited to his tastes. Since Chou's recommendation was rare, if not unique, and since both writers published a considerable number of essays and are representative of traditionalism in the essays of the time, their work is worth some examination.

Wen Tsai-tao, the pen name of Chin Hsing-yao, began his career as part of Shanghai's "Lu Hsün current." He contracted to write *tsa-wen* essays on patriotic themes for a Shanghai newspaper. In 1939 he was editor of *Lu Hsün feng* (The Lu Hsün Current), voicing sentiments left of center and praising the appearance of new translations of Marx and Lenin,[102] as well as the *Complete Works on Lu Hsün*. Joining in the fashionable research into late Ming patriots, he declared that recluse types such as Hou Fang-yü, Ch'en Chen-hui, and others, while they refused to act as collaborators with the Ch'ing regime as did henchmen like Juan Ta-ch'eng, were still too willing to "bend with the breeze" and do not deserve to be remembered as much as martyrs like Shih K'o-fa.[103] But the suppression of the *tsa-kan* essays following 1939 was then succeeded by the fall of the International Settlement, and these events worked their changes on Wen Tsai-tao, as they had on Chou Li-an. In 1943, in an occasional piece, he wrote of Chou Fo-hai's memoirs that they are "written frankly and honestly, not like the two-faced, empty acerbity of those hypocritical scholars of the *tao*." Moreover, Chou Fo-hai was *sa-t'uo*, "casual and graceful," in the sense that Chou Tso-jen had defined the term as "without the pretense of propriety which arises from dissipation."[104] The pen name Wen Tsai-tao, taken from the classical doctrine *wen i tsai tao* ("literature as a vehicle of the way"), perhaps first represented the writer's patriotic, progressive standpoint. But in 1943 he explained himself thus:

Frankly, I approve of literature as a vehicle of *tao*. In other words, there is indeed no literature which does not convey a *tao*. It is only that my *tao* and my reasons for using *yeh* as punctuation [an indication of Wen's use of *wen-yen* style] are one thing, and not at all that kind of *tao* wherein there must be "one road and the same tastes," and only in what I say is there a center of gravity. Nor is it the *tao* which resides in the bosom of the old-fashioned orthodox school which does not allow mention of the existence of anyone else (whether ancient or modern, foreign or Chinese). What I term my *tao* is simply ordinary life, though life is many-faceted. "Tread in the path of the blood of national martyrs; advance along the road to revolution" is one aspect of *tao*. But the cuckoo's call on a rainy night, the cry of the wild geese in the rush pond, and the murmuring creek, forever flowing ceaselessly—do these not also comprise an aspect of *tao*?[105]

Clearly Wen Tsai-tao, in his style and emphasis on the ordinary and natural, had shifted his esthetic from Lu Hsün to Chou Tso-jen. If this introduction thus far has put him in an unpromising light as a person and a writer, there are some aspects of his work worthy of attention. Indeed, his shift from activist to rustic was not without some bridges. Before the war he had been engrossed in the literature of the Wei-Chin period, which had attracted the attention of both Lu Hsün and Chou Tso-jen, and even at the height of his limited gifts as a *tsa-kan* polemicist in 1938 he showed some indication of his proclivities later in the war:

With what style and what state of mind should we extol the bitter, aggressive steadfastness of China's cultural circles during this war of resistance? Rather, with what kind of hatred and sorrow should we frame our indignation for the martyrdom of so many cultural fighters whose blood has been shed by the enemy's weapons?

Every time I look at a newly published book or magazine—no matter whether it is concerned with the present state of resistance or not, just as it is related to our freedom, righteousness, and humanity—then I receive it with unbounded joy and unbounded enthusiasm. Just so, we must as always preserve, as ever it has been, the life of our normal spirit.[106]

Hence, despite his apparent reversal politically, Wen Tsai-tao really did not have so far to travel artistically from his standpoint as a *tsa-kan* writer to that of his familiar essays of the forties, when his proclivities for exploring the cultural past were again fashionable. Other continuities between his work before and after 1942 will be noted further on.

Chou Tso-jen's appreciation of him is impressionistic and historical. Chou remarked that reading Wen's essays was like "meeting an old friend away from home," and that they carry "a ruefulness I seem to be able to appreciate."[107] Historically, Chou notes, Wen Tsai-tao's essays recall the "leisure moods" (*hsien shih*) that have traditionally appeared in or following times of national calamity which discuss the native regions of the authors, now living at a remove, such as Meng Yuan-lao's *Meng hua lu* (Record of Dream Flowers) and Chang Tai's *T'ao-an meng i* (T'ao-an's Dream Recollections). What attracted Chou in part was the description of the natural and cultural life of regions with which he was familiar, as he had stressed the need for literature to be relevant to daily life before the war:

> The customs of any place, whether they are the same or different from one's own locality, are all of interest to us; if different, they supply a comparison; if the same, then there is a sense of intimacy.[108]

During the war, Chou had gone beyond this to urge the social value of such records. In "Feng-t'u chih" (Records of Local Customs) Chou remarked on the neglected value of local gazetteers:

> Some thirty or forty years ago, China advocated converting the records of local customs into textbooks for lectures in primary and middle schools. The idea was that cultivating a love of one's native region was a foundation for patriotism. The idea was a good one; only, as with so many other good ideas, before long it disappeared without leaving behind any trace of success.[109]

Whether Chou knew of Wen Tsai-tao's earlier satire of him or of his apparent shift in political alignment, Chou now found something of patriotic value in his work, commenting that while it "could not save the nation," it would not "wrong the nation" either.[110]

Wen Tsai-tao did seem to do his best to fulfill what Chou saw in his work. In his discussion of Chou's work at that time (1944), he paraphrased Chou's quotation from Andreyev on the value of literature: "On account of what literature has offered and disseminated, the distance between people is narrowed. In developing such understanding is the greatest contribution of literature and the most solid testimonial to its value."[111] That Chou's essays had, in fact, turned off many young readers instead of bringing them closer to anything Wen Tsai-tao discussed as a problem, but he noted that, after all, Chou had shown considerable concern for youth, unlike many writers. Chou had likened his reading books "to those who smoke cigarettes. When their hands and mouths are empty they don't know what to do with themselves. It's just that in my case I mean only to cover my eyes." Wen Tsai-tao, in quoting the bitterness of these lines, argued that Chou's pessimism still gave rise to valuable work. Most pressing on the literary scene was the overall failure of the literary revolution, which, despite its achievements, was still not taken seriously by most readers. In the wake of this failure it was important to curb the excessive Westernization of literature and reinfuse it with traditional resources, as Chou advocated. This last point figures repeatedly in Wen Tsai-tao's essays.

Wen Tsai-tao could sound the call of the May Fourth movement at times, as in his accounts of Chinese customs:

> [As to] the investigation of folkways sufficient to survey the growth and decay of a nation: If there are those who, with purposefulness, can add to research and study on the people's interests, customs, common knowledge, practices, and habits, and from these find means to elevate, liberate, and strengthen them, then it seems not without some geniune, if small, assistance to the "masses" of which we talk day and night. However, to do this work requires care and selectivity, lest one be drawn into Return to Antiquity cliques or the cliques of the National Essence lunatics, with the results being as irrelevant to the welfare of the people as ever.[112]

On the other hand, Wen Tsai-tao did not himself attempt any systematic investigations, and much of his writing is nostalgic or escapist, as in this passage, constructed around the time-tested image of taste to evoke the fashionable quality of literary blandness:

> I cannot drink wine. Even if I drink several cups, I don't appreciate the qualities of wine. Before what is termed "the Incident," for several years I occasionally took my leisure in my old home region, to which I had once been so close and had long ago taken leave of. When I put myself in the scenes I have narrated above, I really feel as though I were intoxicated with wine. After all, we are from the countryside, and the strong breath of the soil always remains secreted in a corner of our souls and overcomes the burdens of life. . . . To bring about the unification of the beauty of human life and nature is my lifelong ideal. I certainly don't consider my

native region a utopia among mankind, but I have long been tired of the shifty, turbid ugliness of this ten-*li* foreign mall [Shanghai]. I wish for a plot of land restful to the spirit, and among those *li* for the sincerity, simplicity, and tranquillity of life with nature. Even if it amounts to drinking mild tea and smoking the ordinary pipe tobacco from the fields, I would have my love and pleasure.[113]

Wen's escapism was abetted by his interest in Wei-Chin "pure talk" (*ch'ing-t'an*), and that in itself gave him support for the validity of his work, for the bohemian poets and writers of that period were so disdainful of authority that "even emperors had no means of controlling their wills."[114] Wen Tsai-tao summed up their Neo-Taoist cult with the following statement on their views and motives:

> In other words, all external forms are false, empty, and contrived. Only sorrows and joys stored up and cherished internally are substantial and simple, pure and true. The philistines chose to value forms. Moreover, they enlisted all sorts of alluring fronts from the sages and philosophers. Therefore, it was necessary to break down the fetters of tradition. Then they could drain the pool of selfish desires, relatives and enemies were equalized, the world and the self both forgotten. Men could then pass a pacific and unbounded life.[115]

That this had personal relevance to Wen Tasi-tao is evident from earlier essays, such as "Tsun K'ung tsa-kan" (Random Thoughts on Honoring Confucius), written in 1940. In that essay he noted, not originally by any means, that the teachings of the sages had become the puppets of politicians to manipulate as they wished. Men like Sun Che-yuan and Wu P'ei-fu had made Confucianism an "opiate of the masses," and under the circumstances it was best not to bother any more with honoring Confucius, whatever he had to offer.[116] Wen was later to find more constructive things to say about Confucius, but the point is the exploitation of tradition by tyrants, including modern warlords like Sun and Wu.

Wen's literary answer was not to advocate actually returning to the countryside, especially under contemporary conditions, but to urge the experience of recalling one's rural roots. In this sense, his emphasis on the value of the emotions of this daydreaming over the actual action is inherited from his interpretation of Wei-Chin literature. Repeatedly he practices this form of mental levitation, emphasizing that the dream and the anticipation are more gratifying than actual fulfillment. Sometimes this recurs in the phrase "the sorrow of triumph,"[117] or an explicit comment that attainment is not always fulfilling (see p. 30). At other times, the notion appears as part of the five-elements tradition, blended with European romanticist phrases:

> If winter comes, can spring be far behind? In the south, no matter how cold the winter, it seems there is always some sense of a thread of warmth secreted within that will again become that ray of genial sunshine, spreading over the veranda eaves and into the corners of the rooms. Indeed, winter is really pregnant with spring. And we are favored with the winter sun no less than the seeds of the great earth. (pp. 142–143)

On other occasions, Wen's vision takes the form of a late Ming literati's prescription for self-cultivation. For example, although a friend proposed buying a cottage and living on the shore of West Lake, Wen declined:

> But I couldn't agree to living for an extended period of time by West Lake. For we should maintain a touch of psychological distance in our appreciation of all beauty. If we were to be confronted day and night with the sparkle of the lake and the color of the hills, then the landscape would no longer necessarily be able to arouse our continued love and deep pensiveness. Rather, it would become tiresome. (p. 102)

To Wen, the ideal would be living ten *li* from the lake and visiting it occasionally: "When we snatch leisure in the midst of pressing affairs, then it is truly something which cultivates our appreciation of leisure" (p. 102).

The mechanisms of Wen's essays are constantly those of association and contrast. Despite his occasional references to modern literary works, such as Chu Kuang-ch'ien's *I-ch'ing tso-yung* ("Empathy"), he does little to develop such allusions. They remain superficial ornaments on essays firmly embedded in tradition. Unlike Chou Tso-jen, with his restraint and even fear of seeming sentimental, Wen Tsai-tao unfurls sentimentality. The essay "Feng-t'u jen-ch'ing" (On Local Customs and Practices) reflects Chou's belief that sorrow is what binds people together, while developing the theme in Wen's sentimental and associational manner:

> Sometimes, sitting before a lamp or dreaming at midnight, one silently ponders the swift passing of time and the ubiquity of misfortune, raising

ever more emotional turmoil until it seems that one lacks any settled spot. I still recall the verse of Yü-ling kuan-chu [?Kung Tzu-chen] with the lines:

Vase flowers arranged; silk, stand and incense set.
I discover the child's heart of twenty years ago.

Suddenly it sends my thoughts racing back to a moment in my own childhood. This sort of sentimentality and nostalgia is universal, throughout all times and places. Yet, at this time and place, it is especially easy for such feelings to arise. I would add that this experience seems to have points quite distinct from such symptoms of the scholar's ailment as weeping at the sight of flowers, moping at the moon, or imagining a prostitute to be a *chia-jen*. This difference is rooted in the vapidness and substance, the truth and falseness of an individual's emotions. Thus, Tu Shao-ling's sorrows over "a city given over to the grass and trees of spring" and Li Hou-chu's anguish at the "east wind in the small tower" have become two of the supremely beautiful poems of the ages. In forlorn circumstances, people often have an unspoken grief which they can't express, and they feel there is nothing which will raise a tear or a laugh. Those among humanity who are worthy of the term "higher order of animal" are for the most part in this situation. Hence, a sad and fatal disease of this world, whether it be within an individual or a people, is just this paralyzed numbness. (pp. 1–2)

Introducing himself as a "vagabond of Chekiang," Wen then launches into casual talk on the flora and fauna, the food and atmosphere of his home region, filled with allusions to Lu Hsün, Chou Tso-jen, Chu Kuang-ch'ien, Liu Ling, Liu Tsung-yuan, and assorted Ming and Ch'ing writers in vogue during the thirties and forties.

Wen Tsai-tao's contrasts are of four interrelated kinds. There is the social and cultural past versus the present, as in the essay "Tung-hsin ts'ao" (Winterheart Herb) which, following the theme of lamb dishes, explores the decline of traditional small pleasures before the advance of Westernization. There is the contrast of the elite versus the common people, as in "Teng-shih" (The Lantern Festival). Here Wen portrays the peasants' love of tradition against the modernizing trends of the elite and their traditional control of every facet of the peasants' recreational life. In essays such as "Shui-sheng ch'in-yü" ("Water Sounds and and Bird Calls"), he portrays the simplicity and sincerity of the people in the countryside, and the beauty of the harmonious blending of man and nature against the dreariness of Shanghai urban life. Finally, he recalls his childhood and upbringing as something altogether distinct from his present life, especially in the essays "I san-chia ts'un" (Recollections of Three-Family Village) and "Sheng-ming ti tiao-yen" (Elegy for a Life).[118]

Such disparities are also reflected in the work of Chi Kuo-an, the other essayist recommended by Chou Tso-jen for his descriptions of regional customs. Chi Kuo-an was the pen name of Chi Kuo-hsüan, a graduate of Peking Normal University, who had gone to live in the countryside outside Peking until 1940, when he joined the Nanking regime's educational ministry and was appointed principal of the secondary school attached to Nanking Central University. As with most members of the Nanking regime educational establishment, Chi was not prosecuted following the war, but continued to teach and assisted the noted historian Ku Chi-kang in his research. Like other essayists of the official-recluse group, he portrayed himself as a refined but humble rustic. His style varies from classical to colloquial, but does not attempt ornateness or a fusion of the classical and colloquial, as Wen Tsai-tao's does.

Chi's expressions of sadness and pessimism are second to none of his colleagues. As he stated in 1943:

> Several years ago, out of despair with human events, I gradually took up history, feeling that all scholarship was in vain, but that history could tell us something authentic and reliable. It was as if I had happened to discover a place to which I could commit my feelings, or which could explain them.[119]

Chi invariably presents himself as a simple, timid man, at home in bland accounts of rural life, seeking the comfort of literary circles in urban jungles, or patiently laboring at antiquarian pursuits. Uneasiness and discomfort dog him as he confronts the awesomeness of Shanghai or the decay of Peking, and the rude and dangerous life of the masses everywhere. He approaches an essay on how men have faced death with his own fear of death readily admitted. Inadequacies haunt him: "I write few essays of the type that record impressions. Since most ordinary things drift by my eyes like so much vapor and smoke, I cannot gather enough to form any impression. I have seen few special events, and even then, before long they become so muddled that it has been best not to write about them."[120] So he appears sitting shyly and appreciatively among the circle of writers for *Past and Present* gathered at Chu P'u's home, taking note of his company: Yü Ch'ieh, bald and provocatively humorous, plays fortuneteller, while Wen Tasi-tao talks animatedly; Chou Yüeh-jan is old, but healthy and spry; Liu Yü-sheng is elegant and graceful; and Su Ch'ing, Chi's favorite writer, sits quietly fanning herself. Outside is the chaos of society.[121] There are a few mild sallies against the cynicism he sees in modern life, but the historical past is also by no means a golden age, merely an escape from the present. The result is a series of essays on rural customs and arcane bits of history that tend to be bland in the extreme. A typical passage reads as follows:

> In my region the women like to take the newly harvested wheat before it is sun-dried and while it is still rather green, husk and fry it, grinding it while it's still moist, and making it into coarse threads called "rolled meal." It seems the Kuang-hsü Gazetteer of the Shun-t'ien Prefecture records this method. But, unfortunately, I don't have the book and cannot cite the text.[122]

Such ruminations, Chi notes, are his wine and his dreams, for he is merely an old man living in a "filthy room" in Nanking. In fact, Chi was apparently still in his thirties, but deliberately chose a literary convention from tradition that suited his mood. Chou Tso-jen before the war had quoted a Ch'ing writer's view of age and literary taste: "In youth one loves the beautiful, in full manhood the heroic, in middle age the brief and condensed, in old age the mild and distant [*tan-yuan*]."[123]

This contrast between the heroic taste of full manhood and the esthetic of mild detachment in old age becomes the basis, ironically, for Chi's most emotional essay, "Chih-chi p'ien" (Knowing Oneself). Here Chi's frustration bursts out of his careful blandness, and he flails out with despair over society and self-abasement. "Knowing Oneself" opens with an explanation of his inability to write fiction, despite the encouragement of friends. In a thoroughly quaint manner, Chi categorizes all fiction under the heading *ch'uan-ch'i*, and contrasts it with nonfiction prose, *san-wen*:

Ch'uan-ch'i are poetic, imaginative and bold; and they are structured and organized, a crystallized form that has been completely worked out. . . . The world's structures and organizations are all based on imagination, and imaginative people definitely have genius, passion, and boldness.[124]

Chi's concept of fiction becomes rather incoherently bound up with poetry and drama as romantic in essence and oriented toward achievement. The examples he cites are Byron and Schiller. With them, Chi has nothing in common as a man or as a writer of *san-wen*:

As to *san-wen*, that's not the same: casual, open and poised, with no place to conceal the psyche, and with no organization. If fiction is gorgeous silk, then this is but a swath of plain cloth. If *ch'uan-ch'i* is fully prepared clothing, *san-wen* is just a handkerchief, a walking stick, or a pair of glasses for the nearsighted. (p. 16)

Chi goes on to argue that while *ch'uan-ch'i* arouses tension, *san-wen* tranquilizes readers. He denies the charge that he writes "pure talk" (*ch'ing-t'an*), for the "pure talk" writers of the Wei-Chin period had both philosophical principles and a romantic temperament evident in their work, which his lacks. This leads again to the question of character:

Those with determination and courage should bravely face what comes and examine reality. I lack courage. To view the vast ocean dizzies me. Even if I am on a bridge watching the flow of a river, I soon feel that the bridge, no less than I myself, is growing dizzy, and it seems that both it and I will be carried away by the current. I quickly avert my gaze and get off to walk on level ground and go along a road with the breath of the soil. (*Ibid.*)

Chi goes on to conclude that he is fit only to be a farmer and is a superfluous man in a society that calls on men to perform the heroic tasks of revolution, nation building, and cultural creativity. Yet this is but a prelude to an outburst the like of which is hardly to be found in his other work:

Now I am peddling this immature knowledge, working in the so-called penurious profession of education, with what benefit to mankind? The education people need today is how to push and shove to get a train ticket, how to find a loophole in the carefully thought-out laws to make some illegal profits, how to locate a lead to make a contact and win over an influential person who may be useful someday, how to extort money, intimidate, revile, and all the knowledge that people outwardly regard as mean but inwardly admire! Chinese composition courses do not offer this, and the civics courses even less. Every time I see the boys I teach dutifully figuring out their algebra problems under a fifteen-watt lightbulb, or looking up new English words, so very earnest and well-mannered, their clean-shaven heads quite endearing with a bluish hue that emanates the splendor of youth, I cannot keep from thinking: Stupid dolts—you waste so much of your foolish energy and what will it get you? When you go outside the gates of this school, of what use is it? When you buy a train ticket, do you need good manners? When you vie with others for a girl, do you need a clean-shaven scalp? Then I feel my own efforts at improving myself and my law-abiding ways amount to a great travesty, and I am filled with discontent. Indeed, we have hoodlums for emperors, and the bullies and hoodlums have their fiefdoms. The students can only study etiquette and the rites. The most they can accomplish is to codify court ritual to enhance the pomp of the hoodlum turned emperor, so that all intellectuals everywhere may kowtow according to form beneath his palace courtyard. (*Ibid.*)

These last sentences deliberately recall the founding of the Han dynasty, when Shu-sun T'ung introduced court etiquette among the undisciplined retainers of Liu Pang.[125] But Chi denies that he has any ambitions in society. He continues to describe himself as a "pool of stagnant water" and a person of so little consequence that he "would no more dare to call on a doctor of philosophy than walk into a restaurant and defecate."[126] The essay is written in part to answer criticisms of his essays as superficial, untalented, and bland, and he responds that he is well aware of all these flaws, but as an "old man over thirty" he can only pursue his interests with his limited gifts.

The essay may be imitative of Chou Tso-jen's series of "fierce" essays, and it certainly shows the influence of Chou in Chi's statements of his interests: biology, history, and folk customs. It is also a defense as well as a confessional, since Chi's sustained self-abasement also reflects his qualities of humility, simplicity, and honesty, just the qualities he denounces society for lacking. For all that, and for his idiosyncratic theory of literature, it remains a compelling piece, filled with imagery, stripped of pedantry, and more revealing than any of his other pieces. Even if saturated with self-pity, it is eloquent.

One of the things essays such as this reveal is the profound discontent beneath the surface of blandness and detachment, a discontent in no way opposed to the romantic spirit, though the author contrasts himself with that spirit. Indeed, the return of tradition exhibited in many of the plays and essays of the period shows a continuation of the intrinsic romanticism of earlier decades. These "traditionalists" were very much concerned with the present. In the case of both drama and essay, the major motivation was supposed to be service to the nation, however much the heroics of the theater differed from the restrained ordinariness of the essayist of "blandness." Both playwrights and essayists sought to appeal to the Chinese as Chinese in a time of foreign invasion. That each genre gave rise to decadent works has been discussed. The achievement of *Malice in the Ch'ing Court* was followed by *Ch'iu Hai-t'ang,* and the sentiments of Chou Tso-jen were followed by the sentimentality of Wen Tsai-tao. But all these works, in their return to tradition, opposed not the romanticism of an earlier period, but what seemed to be regarded as the excessively Western form in which it had promulgated itself. The promoting of Byron and Shelley, Goethe and Schiller was replaced by whatever writers could find to show that the spirit of endeavor, progress, and optimism were inherent in the Chinese people. True, the image of the irresponsible Bohemian was replaced with a more somber, reclusive style. But this hypothetical individual was no less at odds with the status quo, and he portrayed himself as building on the foundations of the May Fourth period. The commitment to risk, adventure, and heroism waned, but the spirit of defiance remained.

To claim that writers in a return to tradition maintained affinities with romanticism is not to say that they were romantics. This would only further becloud the meaning of term "romantic" and ignore the positive contributions they made: the experiment in merging indigenous forms with progressive values and modern styles. But their position in the continuities of artistic development in modern China may be contrasted with that of certain artists who had apparently turned to other sources of influence, chiefly the antiromantic literature of the West in the twentieth century.

CHAPTER FIVE

Antiromanticism

Wu Hsing-hua

In 1955 the critic and poet Stephen C. Soong (Sung Ch'i) commented on his changing attitudes toward literature at the time of the war:

> My attitude toward the literature of the nineteenth century changed from unreserved support to doubt, and then to criticism and rejection. I gradually came to feel that the greatest and most harmful of all influences on the new literature since May Fourth had been romanticism: it carried affected sentimentality, emotionalism, and exposé to the point of ruinous indulgence, and delighted in slogans, big words, and impulsiveness at the expense of self-restraint, individualism, and so forth.[1]

It is not my purpose here to question the attributes Soong gave the term romanticism, for it is the perception of the writers of the period that is of concern in this discussion. Soong found this strong reaction against this view of romanticism among many writers of the war period. While he himself did not join in the belief that romanticism was historically responsible for the social debacles of the twentieth century, as many Western writers did, he nevertheless felt that in literature romanticism had so narrowed the scope of verse, either to lyricism or "high seriousness," that it threatened the very existence of poetry itself. To break away from the perceived binds and flaws of romanticism, Soong and others looked to the most recent poets in England, such as W. E. Auden and Stephen Spender, and to more varied types of classical poetry and classical concern with form.

Soong himself spent the war in Shanghai and made little progress with his own verse; he turned instead to writing essays and plays. He was nevertheless impressed with the poetry of his friend Wu Hsing-hua, another young, multilingual academic who remained in Peking. Wu's poetry embodies some of the aspects of an antiromantic verse that concerned Soong, and Soong was to praise his work highly after the war.[2] Ironically, Wu had given up writing poetry by the end of the war, discouraged with his own efforts and perhaps with poetry itself.[3] Yet Wu remains the most interesting poet of the occupation period. To be sure, many under the occupation tried their hand at new poetry, but none achieved even a fleeting reputation as a major new poet.[4] Tai Wang-shu in Hong Kong wrote a number of pieces deserving attention, but there is nowhere the straining after technical superiority that characterizes Wu's verse.

That Wu was unimpressed by his elders in the new poetry movements is clearly stated in a caustic verse titled "Pei Yuan shih ch'u, huo kei i-ko nien-ch'ing shih-jen ti ch'üan-kao" (North to Ch'u, or Advice to a Young Poet).[5] Wu begins by crediting only Pien Chih-lin and Ho Ch'i-fang with respectable verse, alluding otherwise to "scholars or fools who don't understand Chinese." The poem then takes up the tale in the *Chan kuo ts'e* (Warring Kingdoms Chronicle) of Chi Liang's advice first to a fellow countryman, and then to the king of Wei. In the first instance old Chi Liang tries to convince a foolish brave that Ch'u lies to the south, while the warrier, boasting of the superiority of his equipment and retinue, insists on attempting to get to Ch'u by the road north. Chi Liang uses this anecdote to persuade the king of Wei that, despite his apparent strength, his campaign to take the city of Hantan is also foolishly conceived. The king withdraws his force on Chi Liang's advice, but without realizing how he has been mocked by Chi Liang. The sardonic tone Wu employs to satirize modern poetry is unusual both for Wu and for modern poetry in China. Otherwise the verse has representative features: a classical allusion set to a tight form, in this case quatrains for a kind of doggerel effect, and a narrative technique inherited from the West, in this instance the use of tough, colloquial speech in a historical setting reminiscent of Browning or perhaps Ezra Pound.

Wu's poetry developed into a neoclassical style, but not before considerable experience in Western poetry and experimentation in

Chinese. His early poetry, from the eve of the war to the Pacific War period, was heavily Westernized and showed considerable romantic influence, perhaps particularly that of Conrad Aiken. As a translator, Wu showed distinction in his skillful and accurate handling of a wide range of foreign writers, and it seems not unlikely that his very return to classicism was stimulated by the various concerns of Western writers with their own traditional resources: the symbolist folklore of Maurice Maeterlinck, passed on to the national conscious-ness of W. B. Yeats and the Irish Renaissance, and the new tradi-tionalism of T. S. Eliot. Wu was familiar with all these writers and more.

The classical world to which Wu turned was in many instances obscure to all but the most highly educated Chinese. One such poem, "Shu Fan Ch'uan chi 'Tu Ch'iu-niang shih' hou" (On Reading Fan Ch'uan's Poem on Tu Ch'iu-niang) Wu introduces one of Tu Mu's five-word old-style verses. Tu Mu's poem on vicissitude centers on the fate of Tu Ch'iu-niang, a beautiful T'ang courtesan eventually exiled from the imperial palace. Tu Mu's poem becomes a collage of brief images and allusions, first outlining Tu Ch'iu-niang's biography, and then spanning the range of pre-T'ang history to consider the lesson to be drawn from her misfortunes. Wu's poem opens with a misty, lonely setting and a reverie on Tu Ch'iu-niang's appearance, followed by the same kind of pell-mell images linking both Tu Ch'iu and Tu Mu to their time. Then, again following Tu Mu's example, Wu poses a series of rhetorical questions, identifying himself in his own time with classical times, adapting lines by Tu Mu, who took them from Confucius: "I perceived that all phenomena can be traced on a single thread to one principle./Then I realized how my own gains and losses were insignificant and not worth reckoning."[6] Having found this orientation, Wu concludes, "Songs of lament, past and present, follow the same score." Hence, by repeating Tu Mu's poetic experience, Wu finds order and solace in disordered times.

Wu's classical world is a vapid one, filled with clouds, mist, and fog, with flowing water and shifting light. It is vast, unbounded, limitless, empty, and illusory (*maya*). Past and present are constantly being linked into a timeless state, a chasm of existence, filled with perhaps more terms for sorrow and sadness than any other modern poet has collected. There is constantly a tension between the weight of the mood and the insubstantiality of the phenomenal world, between the limitations of the individual and the vastness of creation. Into this Wu injects the notion of love, sometimes as a commitment to an individual, but often as love for humanity or for the nation, and this, too, touches base with the casuistry of classical literature. It is love that motivates many of the numerous words for "suddenness," lifting the mood to some sudden awareness of the mystery of human action and commitment in a mysterious universe. Yet Wu's verse seems guided by the solace of detachment in its studied use of the past and its literary offerings.

His use of the techniques of modern poetry was actually extensive and complex. An evident example is the poem "T'ing mei-hua tiao Pao-yü t'an ping" (Hearing 'Pao-yü Pays a Sick Call' to the Tune of Plum Blossoms).[7] The poem gives a description of a tawdry girl entertainer which has close affinities with traditional descriptions of women entertainers, such as Tu Fu's poem on the dancer Kung-sun and her disciple, Po Chü-i's "P'i-p'a hsing," or Tu Mu's "Chang Hao-hao." Similarly, he suggests old age and the loss of the woman's health and beauty. But this is further complicated by identifying her with the song she is giving to a drumbeat on Lin Tai-yü and Chia Pao-yü. Her frail appearance is contrasted with her vigorous performance, the impassiveness of the lute player with the emotional audience, and the song of refined sentiment she sings with the sleazy world to which she has prostituted herself. These ironies turn through the poet's mind, leaving him "unable to distinguish the boundary between the story and her," the singer, and carry him into some private world of illusion and reality, vanity and loss. The constant shifts of vision, tension, and irony mark the poem as unmistakably modern.

Stephen Soong has credited Wu Hsing-hua with making a major contribution to the development of forms for modern colloquial verse, and to bringing back technical standards by which to judge poetry as a distinct and challenging form. In this classical consideration, there is no doubt that Wu exercised ingenuity, adapting blank verse and five-line old-style verse (*wu ku*) to colloquial language. His concern with restraint and form is impressive. On the other hand, it is not surprising that Wu's achievement has not been readily recognized, for although he was able to apportion five beats to a line and impose a regularity on the genre, the beats do not fall with the rhythm of blank verse or old-style verse. In blank verse, the iambic foot, and in old-style verse, the caesura between the second and third characters of a five-word line, both provide a steady rhythm, an underlying musical regularity, to each line. In Wu's verse, what is essentially prose is divided into lines each containing five stressed syllables (or any number of stressed syllables), but without any further fixed rhythmic element, such as an iambic foot or recurring caesura, or even end-stopped lines. Hence, while there is regularity on paper, the poems can only be read aloud as prose without any rhythm.

This technique offered certain freedoms with a kind of regularity, but it is not a musical one, and it lacks the appeal of actual classic rhythm. Wu did on occasion employ rhyme, but it does not seem to have been a final consideration in his work, nor were tonal arrangements. Wu's attention in part seems to have been focused on developing a verse form for sustained pieces beyond the experiments with sonnet-length works and *chüeh-chü* adaptations that he and others engaged in. This may have been prompted by his interest in epic poetry. On the eve of the war, poets in Peking were discussing the possibilities of epic verse, and Sun Yü-t'ang produced a historical poem of considerable length titled *Pao ma* (The Precious Steed).[8] This poem, while it has no absolute regularity in its verse, is sensitive to a euphonic arrangement of tones and reads quite smoothly. Wu Hsing-hua may have been influenced by such local experiments, as well as by foreign works, and his several poems involving the heroics of men like the prince of Hsin-ling, taken from the *Chan kuo ts'e* and the *Shih chi,* suggest a deep interest in the possibilities of this material for a long work.

Wu's poems reached a point of frustration when they so nearly approached the classical idiom that the colloquial language seemed to be as much in the way of the classical vein he was mining as it was a viable medium to revive a great tradition. The poems quoted by Stephen Soong in his *Lin I-liang shih-hua* (Poetry Talks of Lin I-liang) show all the order and none of the rhythmic grace of classical verse. And, whatever sentiments Wu had as a modern man to counterpoint the heavy use of classical diction and mood, they did not need the use of colloquial language or modern terminology. Whether or not Wu's verse might have provoked a classically oriented reaction to romanticism, it proved in fact a dead end, at least during the war. Yet Wu's experiments marked a level of sophistication in poetry few other contemporaries could claim, and he was joined, though not personally, by other writers who were also concerned with their work as part of a tradition and unimpressed with the romanticism of a previous generation.

Modern British Literature and the Concept of a Chinese Antiromanticism

The work of three other writers during the occupation may be cited within the context of modern Chinese literature as antiromantic. The essays and stories of Chang Ai-ling, the plays of Yang Chiang, and the essays and fiction of Ch'ien Chung-shu each in their own ways contributed to a rejection of the pose and values of romantic writers. They did not identify themselves with Western romantic writers, or any writers of any movement. They did not attempt to embody in their lives any notion of romantic values. No idealized conceptions appear in their works, not of heroic characters, revolution, or love. Instead there are disillusionment, the exposure of fraud, and compromise with reality. The climactic gives way to the anticlimactic. Emotionalism gives way to restraint, irony, skepticism. Slogans are replaced with wit. Unlike other writers before them who stayed well outside the bounds of romanticism, they propounded no social goals or panaceas.

The important link these writers had with modern literature was less within their own country than with British literature following World War I, when the sardonic Somerset Maugham was joined by another set of writers who shocked their elders with their "disillusioned, unreforming literature" and "absolute rejection of romantic hopes and romantic diction."[9] Edwin Muir suggested the profound doubts that shaped a generation of emerging writers in *The Present Age:*

In Aldous Huxley's early stories the only real things about the characters are their desires and their sensations; their emotions, on the other hand, are exposed as hypocritical, for emotion is associated with ideas of human hope, and at the time all ideas connected with human hope seemed presumptuous and false. There was accordingly a radical distrust and dislike of general ideas, and this was not confined to the few; it was popular, as can be seen from the early plays of Noel Coward and the early stories of Beverly Nichols and Evelyn Waugh. This skepticism was probably inevitable; but it was also a sort of indulgence which could be had only at a time when there was no call and no energy for immediate action, a time when, after the immense effort of the war, people felt there was nothing to be done. Europe was in confusion; society was dislocated; private hopes of a kind were still possible; but there was no common hope.[10]

Muir continues that the international threats of the thirties roused writers from their "indulgence." Yet, for many the thirties were a time of disenchantment, as Ch'ien Chung-shu wrote in his story "Mao" (Cat):

In these two years, Japan occupied the three provinces of Manchuria, the structure of government in Peiping was reconstituted once, Africa lost a nation and gained an imperialist state, and the League of Nations revealed its true appearance, amounting simply to a League of Dreams or a League of Delusion. But Mrs. Li did not change husbands, and Darkie [her cat] kept his mistress's doting attention and his own naughty disposition. In this world of repeated misfortunes how many persons could maintain the same patience and perserverance toward ideas and creeds?[11]

The zeugma Ch'ien employs to satirize Mrs. Li is but part of his sardonic portrait of Peking society before the war. When it came, the war provided not a few heroes, but it did little to shore up confidence in society as a whole, and the influence of this aspect of the times figures no less in the visions of Chang Ai-ling and Yang Chiang than it does in Ch'ien Chung-shu.

None of these writers was imitative; their skepticism had its own individual roots, and the experiences of China were not identical with those of Europe in World War I. But for individuals of skeptical disposition, the times were ripe to allow the influence of an earlier generation of foreign writers to take its place in their work. To these Chinese writers, there was no point in imagining that the fulfillment of ideals was a relevant theme. Personal hopes might be attained by a stroke of fortune, but it was fate that was in control, and not the individual. Three decades later, another writer, not of this group, was to make a cogent remark on the attitudes and fate of many other writers of the time: "We thought we were setting a new course and pulling a good oar; in reality, we were merely being swept along by the overwhelming torrent of the Chinese Revolution."[12] Ch'ien Chung-shu, Yang Chiang, and Chang Ai-ling nowhere voiced any sentiments on the inevitability of the Chinese Revolution as it developed following the war, but neither did they share in any illusion that it was they who were setting the course.

Chang Ai-ling

Chang Ai-ling grew up in the Shanghai International Settlement and was attending Hong Kong University as an undergraduate when the colony was attacked and occupied by the Japanese in early 1942. Returning to Shanghai, Chang began contributing essays to English-language publications, some of which she also published in Chinese to be included in her volume of essays titled *Liu-yen* (Gossip).[13] In 1943 she submitted manuscripts of two long stories in Chinese to Chou Shou-ou, editor of *Tzu lo-lan* (Violet), a monthly literary magazine generally regarded as part of the Mandarin Duck and Butterfly school. Chou commented that her two "Aloeswood Ashes" tales were reminiscent both of Somerset Maugham's stories and *The Dream of the Red Chamber.*[14]

There is much that is apt in this comment. The reader of Ch'en hsiang hsieh—ti-erh lu-hsiang" (Aloeswood Ashes—The Second Burning) is reminded of Maugham's tales of the British expatriate community in the Far East. The story is framed in a gossipy session between the author and a British classmate, much as many of Maugham's stories are introduced. The vision of hysteria and pathological claustrophobia underlying this community is an element of Maugham's fiction that caused much discomfort and indignation among the British in the Far East, and it reappears within Chang's story in force. Susie's dream, fraught with Freudian imagery, is a prelude to disastrous behavior in Chang's story that also has its counterpart in Maugham's works, notably "Rain," one of his best-known short stories prior to the war. The disgrace of Roger for being involved in a breach of the rigid appearance of manners and his suicide are both actions familiar to Maugham readers, and Chang has employed them with the same cynicism. "Aloeswood Ashes—The Second Burning" is a harsh look at refinement going to seed, and its harshness was hardly surpassed by Maugham. For all these similarities, Chang Ai-ling's theme is not altogether that of Maugham's, as is revealed by a reading of her other stories. Indeed, the companion story, "Aloeswood Ashes—The First Burning," continues the theme of social entrapment and psychological retardation, but by exploring the Chinese and Eurasian community in Hong Kong, leaving behind immediate comparisons to Maugham.

In both stories Chang's interest in and employment of imagery surpasses Maugham's. Especially in "Aloeswood Ashes—The First Burning," in its deliberate attempt to portray the decaying façade of old-fashioned Chinese culture against elements of Westernization, there begins to emerge what C. T. Hsia has noted as an "intimate boudoir realism" unmatched since *The Dream of the Red Chamber*.[15] This story, too, deliberately harks back to old tales in which a young girl is set out by an older woman as bait to entice young men. Of course, in the old stories the protagonist is the young scholar or shopkeeper, whereas Chang uses the motif to explore the experience of the young girl herself. Moreover, the degree of cynicism present, while less harshly expressed, is still more comparable to that of a writer like Maugham rather than an old tale in the Chinese tradition. One would agree with Shui Ching in recommending her fiction over Maugham's, both for its technical virtuosity and the more serious concern with human anguish. Nor was Chang Ai-ling, any more than Maugham, an utter disbeliever in human goodness and a total cynic. However, when Shui Ching compares "Aloeswood Ashes—The First Burning" to Henry James's *Portrait of a Lady,* he seems to have failed to keep in mind that the Chinese girl Wei-lung is motivated by a desire for economic security and social advancement and is thus trapped in her self-contempt, unlike Isabel Archer, who is trapped through her affection for the child Pansy. Chang evinces sympathy for her protagonist, but is equally absorbed with the theme that the girl has paid a heavy price for a vain ambition.

Despite traditional influences and an innate skepticism born of her own experience, it is difficult to see these elements of Chang's artistry transformed into her early short stories, *Ch'uan-ch'i* (Romances), without the mediating influence of post-World War I British literature. Indeed, when asked in 1944 what foreign authors she enjoyed reading, she gave the names of Somerset Maugham and Aldous Huxley.[16] Although her work nowhere shows the intellectual breadth of an Aldous Huxley, nor does she experiment with form in his manner, he was the leading writer of a wave of artists given to general skepticism in their early works, and there are distinct echoes of this in Chang Ai-ling's work. In the essay "Chin-yü lu" (Embers), Chang wrote:

> This thing reality is unsystematic, like seven or eight phonographs playing at the same time, each its own tune, forming a chaotic whole. . . . Painters, writers, and composers bring what they have found as random and fragmented into a harmonious association, creating an artistic whole. If a work of history strives too much for artistic completeness, it becomes fiction. . . . Neatly formulated visions of creation, whether political or philosophical, cannot avoid arousing dislike.[17]

That Chang wrote this following the experience of the protracted battle for Hong Kong is not fortuitous, for she explictly compares the atmosphere and behavior of the population of Honk Kong following the battle to the "roaring twenties" after World War I.[18] Her distrust of idealizations and general skepticism found expression in numerous essays, from her disbelief in such panaceas of modern man as the return to primitive society to restore humanity (p. 168), to her dislike of the romantic tradition in art as artificial (p. 184). There is, in contrast, an intense interest in the sensual world, a delight in what can be immediately sensed, and a striving to put intelligent consideration before emotional affirmation, which could result in skeptical witticisms:

> Although it can be a little difficult, I like my profession. Heretofore "learn proficiency in civil and martial arts, and sell it to the nobility" was the way for artists reliant on the ruling classes for their livelihood. Present circumstances are rather different. I'm quite happy that my patrons are not the nobility but the magazine-buying masses. That's not to pat the masses' rear end—the masses really are the dearest of employers, not so mercurial, their tempers not so unpredictable. They do not assume

affectations and do treat one sincerely. For your slight touch of quality they will remember you for five or ten years. Moreover, the masses are an abstraction. If there must be a master, naturally I'd prefer that it be an abstract one. (pp. 10–11)

To find the quality of *ch'i*, or "strangeness," in her modern *ch'uan-ch'i* stories, Chang replaced the superstitions of the past with the forces of the subconscious mind as outlined by Freud. Freud's influence on postwar British literature needs no elaboration here. In one of her frankest passages in "Szu-yü" (Whispered Words), Chang alluded to the work of Beverly Nichols, another British writer of brief but considerable popularity among the young and disillusioned following World War I whose work was readily available in Shanghai and Peking even during the war in secondhand bookstores:

> In Beverly Nichols' work there is a poem on the twilight world of the insane: "There is moonlight sleeping in your mind." When I read it I think of the blue light on the floorboards of our house, shining there with quiet, murderous intent. I knew my father couldn't really kill me. However, during those years of crisis, until I escaped and fled, I had not been myself. In several weeks I aged many years. I kneaded the wood porch railing in my hands as if I could squeeze water out of the wood. The blue sky shone brightly above. At that time the sky was thunderous, filled with aircraft. I longed for a bomb to fall on our house; and that we should all die together I also wished for. (p. 152).

The power of the irrational as a force in human life is affirmed here. The moonlight is present as that longing for an unattainable bond with a powerful physical existence, while the engines of war fly overhead as embodiments of the mind's fantastic desires. Usually the desires do not appear so fantastic, but they are strong and equally vain, as in a passage from "T'ung-yen wu chi" (The Guileless Words of a Child). In this passage, Chang witnesses the mental destruction and physical abuse of her younger brother at the hands of her father. Chang recalls that she hid in her room, contemplating her brother's misfortune:

> Sobbing, I stood before the mirror and looked at my own drawn face, watching the tears trickling down like a closeup in a movie. I ground my teeth and said, "I'll get revenge. Someday, I'll get revenge." (p. 18)

Again, the mirror represents an illusion of reality on which Chang imposed herself, just as she is absorbed in imposing her fantasy of revenge upon her father. Turning to the real situation, she noted that in fact her brother quickly forgot the episode and accepted his mal-treatment weakly. Chang forgot revenge and nourished a "cold sor-row" instead. Characteristically, Chang refuses to idealize or even to trust emotions, and seeing how many of the refinements of civiliza-tion are built on such quicksand, she finds much to distrust in it as well. The horrors of wars engineered by modern civilization are not inveighed against. Rather, as in the essay "Embers," Chang renders a random account of ordinary people destroyed, terrified, or even raised in their fortunes or character by the senseless folly and vain ruthlessness of the battle for Hong Kong. Done with characteristic irony and restraint, "Embers" concludes with a searing pronounce-ment:

> Time's chariot rumbles on forward. What we pass by as we ride along are probably no more than a few familiar streets. Yet, while the sky is ablaze, we are rocked with fear and horror. Then, alas, we only look hurriedly in the window of a shop as it flashes by, searching for our own image—we see only our own faces, pale and dim: our selfishness and vanity, our shameless blindness and stupidity—everyone is like us, but each of us is alone. (p. 54)

This dissociation from what offers itself as great or uplifting together with the cultivation of a sense of the sadness and ruthlessness that attend ordinary life are reflected in the opening of *Lien huan t'ao* (The Interlocking Rings), an uncompleted novelette. In this story, the narrator stands listening to a symphony concert, describing the sad and disturbing associations the music produces in her mind. As she turns to leave the lobby the music reaches its climax, and from behind the curtain at the entrance to the audience emerges an old woman, the maltreated and castoff product of civilization's backside.

Despite the heavy use of archaic phrases and the deliberate harking back to novels such as *Hung lou meng* and *Chin p'ing mei*, *The Interlocking Rings* owes much to the traditions of Western picaresque literature and the visions of life found therein. Had Chang created a stronger central character and more robust satire, it might have proved a memorable piece. But Chang is more characteristically concerned with those who have little control over their environment and the sadness of their pathetic struggles to escape or remake their world. Moreover, Chang's art is a more delicate achievement, always poised on the surface tensions between the submerged world of her characters' desires, which in their ruthlessness and amorality are part of but opposed to the ruthlessness of existence. It is no surprise that Chang took little interest in the topic of revolution, for there the individual is subordinated to the discipline of collective action, and revolution implies modifications of human behavior that run counter to Chang's vision of humanity. In love the individual is left unrestrained, in subconscious sensations and overt behavior. "Unadorned" *(su-p'u)* and "unlicensed" *(fang-tzu)* are the words Chang used (p. 22). While the word "ruthless" may be excessive for some of her comic pieces, it is apt enough as an adjective for most of her short stories, in which concern for good and evil, spiritual and physical, is secondary to the image of the vanity of the subconscious against the powerful though common substance of physical existence, of which the subconscious is a part. Moreover, the occasional positive characters who appear to mediate in the lives of the protagonists are characterized by their sense of compassion: the medical student in "Nien-ch'ing ti shih-hou" (Time of Youth) and the mother in "Hsin ching" (Heart Sutra).

Chang Ai-ling's stories may be primarily grouped into those in which an impersonal force in the environment acts out an individual's fantasies, and those in which an active protagonist attempts directly to impose his or her will. Those discussed in the first group (the fantasy externalized) are "Aloeswood Ashes—The Second Burning," "Hung mei-kuei yü pai mei-kuei" (Red Rose and White Rose), "Feng-o" (Blockade), and "Ch'ing ch'eng chih lien" (Love in a Fallen City). Those of the second group (the fantasy acted out) include: "Chin-so chi" (The Golden Cangue); "Heart Sutra"; "Aloeswood Ashes—The First Burning," and "Mo-li hsiang-p'ien" (Jasmine Tea).

The protagonist of "Aloeswood Ashes—The Second Burning" is introduced as "a fool," Roger by name, a forty-year-old science professor at Nanhua University, the name Chang usually uses for the University of Hong Kong. Over the course of his fifteen-year career, Roger has slipped into a comfortable place in Hong Kong society as a quiet, respectable bachelor living in a campus house, giving unrevised lectures and telling stale classroom jokes. He has successfully courted a British girl half his age, Susie Mitchell, and the story opens on the day of their marriage, continuing for a few days thereafter, during which time Roger is brought to ruin through Susie's hysteria. In his childlike delight, Roger has neglected to question Susie's maturity until too late. In the last hours before the wedding, the widow Mrs. Mitchell and two of her three daughters, Millicent and Susie, weep at the recollection of Millicent's earlier marriage in Tientsin to a man rumored to have treated her "like an animal." When Roger questions Susie, however, she maintains her vapid, infatuated pose. Roger is still to her the attractive older man, above the run of her young companions.

But the wedding night proves that Roger's pursuit of a chaste bride has only won him a hysterically frigid child. The moon shines down on the folly of his hopes and the erotic, insect-filled nightmares of his bride. She runs in blind panic from the house. Roger, unable to find her, finally locates her at Mrs. Mitchell's house the next day and brings her home, everyone apparently filled with conciliatory plans and good intentions. Only later does he learn, and not from Susie, that she in fact had sought refuge in the men's dormitory, where she reviled him as an animal, and that the students, faculty, and soon local society in general are all too ready to believe that sexual aberrations lie beneath his respectable manner. His friend, Dean Bach, asks him to stay through the term, but unhesitatingly accepts Roger's resignation, even though he does not question Roger's integrity.

Roger, to his disgust, soon becomes an attraction to repressed women. One such character urges him to sleep with her, spouting popularized jargon on the unhealthiness of repressed desires. As an example, she discusses the suicide of Millicent's former husband, who was the object of scandal in Tientsin for his supposed animalistic treatment of Millicent. Only then does Roger draw the link between Millicent and Susie and realize that Mrs. Mitchell, behind her pleasant and encouraging façade, has all along contrived to bind her daughters to her in a cloistered life. In the insular and stagnant world of overseas British society have arisen both Mrs. Mitchell's need and the chances for the success of her plan. Nor does Roger, having committed himself to this society, have much chance of righting the scandal or of escaping to reestablish himself among his countrymen elsewhere in East Asia.

As always, there is skillfully employed imagery to enhance the quality of the work and especially its central theme. Millicent and Susie are given similar treatment as objects of their mother. Millicent is described thus: "When she mentioned her former husband's name, Frank, her thin lips curled upward, revealing a row of tiny teeth which under the light were so white they seemed blue, small, blue teeth . . . Roger shuddered."[19] Shortly he comes to see the same in Susie, but not to recognize it: "Laughing, she showed a row of small teeth, so white they were blue . . . small, white teeth, but how beautiful" (p. 336). In the final contemplation of his ruin, Roger glances at his lamp:

> The gas flame seemed a large, dark-centered, blue chrysanthemum, with fine long petals curving in a bunch toward the center. He slowly turned the gas flame down. The petals slowly grew shorter and shorter, and suddenly vanished. All that remained was a tidy ring of small, blue teeth, the teeth gradually fading. But, just before they vanished completely, they suddenly shot outwards, reaching out as two-inched sharp fangs. Only for a moment, and then this lash of flame went dark. He turned off the gas, closed the door and bolted it. Then he turned up the gas again, but this time he did not strike a match. (p. 382)

Suicide, as an overt act, is not common in Chang's work, although she noted that as a child she wrote of a woman drowning herself, and the urge was certainly present in her personal life as an adolescent. Here, it is used as an extension of Mrs. Mitchell's pathological desire through an environment that reinforces Roger's weaknesses and then strips him of his life with discreet brutality. Just as Mrs. Mitchell has bred her daughters to destroy their own chances for happiness for her benefit, so Roger is bred to dispose of himself with mechanical neatness. No one need call for his resignation. He will offer it. No one need openly ostracize him. He will put himself out of the way. The absurd advances of a bored, frustrated woman do not rouse Roger's defenses against hypocrisy, but simply confront him with how far he has blundered away from the fold and that his real offense lies in having ruffled the dignity of the establishment. He will always pose an embarrassment or a threat to their order, and order is the overriding concern of the British establishment. Tragedy is precluded by Roger's inability to conceive of himself apart from that order. Thus, in his inability to escape or even attempt to escape, Roger becomes a pathetic victim of his own blindness and the desires of Mrs. Mitchell.

Another version of blindness is operating in "Red Rose and White Rose" as well, and so too is the imposition of the subconscious, though not in the logical pattern that appears in "Aloeswood Ashes—The Second Burning." The protagonist, T'ung Chen-pao, is introduced as a man who judges himself on his mastery of social conventions and social order. As a self-made man he has aspired successfully to a respectable position in the order, as he sees it, including his profession as an engineer and his impeccable attitude toward his mother, relatives, and friends. His hypocritical flaw is his attempt to define women and his relationships with them by such neat formulas. The title "Red Rose and White Rose" alludes to the contrasting categories he designates for the women he courts or uses, the one group defined as illicit and the other as socially recognizable. But such an order, based on his will, is no match for his desires or those of the women he meets.

One of T'ung Chen-pao's characteristics is to attempt to reduce the significance of the woman to a fetish object. Hence, he defines a Parisian prostitute, his first sexual partner, by her foxy smell and cheap perfume. But he is distressed at the involuntary associations that arise as he looks at her in a mirror, and in that illusory world sees a disordered, surrealistic threat to his sense of order:

> There was yet one detail he had been unable to put out of his mind. It was as she was again putting on her clothes, slipping them on over her head. As they were pulled part way on, her dress heaped in a disorderly pile on her shoulders, it seemed she thought of something, and paused slightly. In that moment he saw her in the mirror. Her abundant, disheveled blond hair, stretched taut in the dress, revealed a thin face. Her eyes were blue, yes, but for a moment these spots of blue sank into the green make-up under her eyes, and the eyeballs themselves turned into transparent glass balls. It was a severe, cold, and masculine face, the face of a warrior from distant ages. Chen-pao's nerves were jolted. (p. 60).

The connection between what the prostitute thinks and Chen-pao sees is not given, but stated paratactically: "It seemed she thought," and "he saw in the mirror." The fundamental point of the passage is Chen-pao's sensation of losing control, of being threatened and dominated. And yet it is based on an action by the prostitute, not one logically connected with Chen-pao's sensation, but nevertheless suggested by coincidence. The intent of this passage is to foreshadow the more evident assertions of a woman that she has transcended Chen-pao's order. Here the unstated and unstatable suggestion is that the prostitute imposed a momentary fantasy of freedom onto the illusory world of the mirror, and that fantasy, being a common one, registered unpleasantly on Chen-pao's mind as he unwittingly lowered his defensive sense of order and gazed into the mirror also.

A similar experience occurs to Chen-pao in England as he courts a Eurasian girl, but it is less severe, as Chen-pao is intent on maintaining self-control and "being his own master." This girl is seen looking into a birdcage: "With big eyes she looked at the bird in the cage. As her eyes opened wide, the whites shown blue as though she were gazing into the deepest of blue skies" (p. 62). The passage reinforces Chen-pao's conclusion that she is too outgoing, active, and nonchalant to be transplanted to his household in China.

When Chen-pao returns to China from studies overseas and moves into a flat with his friend Wang Shih-hung, he is surprised to see that Shih-hung's wife is Wang Chiao-jui, formerly an overseas student in England with a reputation for loose morals. Chen-pao is stimulated by the touch of soap bubbles falling from her hand to his as they shake hands, and by the strands of hair left on the bathroom floor after she washed. Yet he comforts himself that she is married and so poses no danger. However, when Shih-hung leaves on a business trip, Chiao-jui packs off the servants as well, and begins to attempt to entice Chen-pao. He is attracted but still cautious. He soothes himself that she is the kind of woman for whom he need have no sense of responsibility. Having determined this, he feels free to decide, and desire overtakes him:

> He stood at the glass door, watching her for some time. Tears welled in his eyes, for he and she were finally in the same spot—two people each with flesh and heart. He hoped just a little that she would see his tears. But she only concentrated on playing the piano. Chen-pao grew exasperated. He moved in closer to help her handle the musical score sheet and deliberately distract her. But she didn't respond. She really wasn't looking at the sheet music. The tune had been memorized thoroughly, and from the keys, from her hands, it gently flowed out.

Chen-pao was suddenly both upset and afraid, as though he and she were
utterly unrelated. He squeezed next to her on the piano bench and,
reaching out, embraced her, pulling her around. The sound of the piano
broke off with a discordant note. She deftly inclined his head—more than
deftly. They kissed. Chen-pao wildly pressed her against the keyboard,
which banged out a deafening cacophony. Had anyone else, at least, ever
given her such a kiss? (p. 79)

In this well-wrought anticlimactic passage is contained the suggestion
that, although Chen-pao has given her the kiss, it is Chiao-jui who is
in control. As the affair develops, Chen-pao is confidently contemptuous of her, while she begins to fall for him in earnest and suggests
that she divorce Shih-hung to marry him. Chiao-jui is thrilled to see
Chen-pao's look of genuine pain at this proposal, for "to cause a man
to suffer genuine hardship for her was really something hard to come
by" (p. 82). Chen-pao actually falls sick over this impending threat
to his respectable position and is finally able to get rid of Chiao-jui.

Chen-pao then attempts to restore his sense of order by marrying a
bland, frigid girl just finishing college. Yet even this apparently
proper and obedient nonentity has an early, sublimated sensation of
rebellion from the sterile order prepared for her. On her wedding
night, "facing the mirror, she had a sensation of a strange endeavor,
as though having been loaded into a glass test tube, trying to get to
the top" (p. 93). Chen-pao's order, as fragile and confining as the
test tube, cannot hold, although for some time his wife remains
passive and unresponsive, and he entertains prostitutes in hotel
rooms. The breakdown of his system comes in two consecutive
incidents in which Chiao-jui and then his wife confound his
categories and thus his sense of identity. In the first of the scenes, with
Chiao-jui now Mrs. Chu, as in the scene with the prostitute, an
unexpressed thought imposes itself on a physical object, again a
mirror, representing Chen-pao's illusory vision of himself. The
encounter between Chen-pao and Chiao-jui takes place on a tram:

Chen-pao said, "Do you love that man named Chu?" Chiao-jui
nodded. When she answered him, though, she paused every couple of
words: "It was from you that I learned how to love, earnestly . . . Love
after all is good. Even though we may suffer, afterwards we still want to
love, so. . . ."

Chen-pao rolled up the square collar flap that hung down the back of her son's sailor suit and said softly, "You're very happy." Chiao-jui chuckled and said, "I'm just moving on forward. Whatever I run into I take as it comes." Chen-pao smiled coldly, "All you've run into are men."

Chiao-jui didn't become angry. She tipped her head to one side thoughtfully and said, "Yes, when I was young, when I was good looking, no matter what I got into socially, it was always men I ran into. But since then, there have been other things besides men, after all—finally something else. . . ."

Chen-pao was looking at her, unaware at the moment that the sensation he felt was unbearable envy. Chiao-jui said, "And you? How are you?"

Chen-pao wanted to wrap up his fulsome, successful life into a couple of simple sentences. Just as he was framing these words, he raised his head and saw his face in the small mirror that protruded to the right of the operator's seat. It was quite calm. But since the bus jolted, the face in the mirror trembled unsteadily with it. It was a very odd sort of calm tremor, as though someone had massaged his face lightly. Suddenly his face actually began to tremble. In the mirror he saw his tears streaming down. Why, he didn't know himself. In such an encounter as this, if someone had to cry it should be she. This was all wrong, and yet astonishingly he could not restrain himself. She should be the one to cry. It was up to him to comfort her. She did not comfort him, but remained silent. In a half whisper she said, "Are you getting off here?" (pp. 96–97)

Just as the Parisian prostitute's sex appeared reversed in the mirror in the hotel, Chiao-jui's reversal of roles threatens Chen-pao's order. This is reinforced shortly when Chen-pao discovers his wife in an affair with a tailor. Husband and wife immediately try to pretend nothing has actually happened:

She relaxed and gradually forgot that she herself had anything to hide. Even Chen-pao grew doubtful, and it seemed she essentially had no secrets of any kind. It was like a white double door shut tight on a wild prairie land, its two sides faintly lit by lamplight. One could bang on the door with all one's might, certain that behind the door a murder plot was being hatched. Yet when one finally broke open the door and entered, there was no murder plot. There wasn't even a room, only a stretch of wasteland overgrown with grass and enveloped in mist under a few stars—that was truly frightful. (p. 105)

Chen-pao's behavior breaks down in this emptiness. He deserts his

wife and child. After she matures considerably to support herself and
her daughter in his absence, he returns sullenly, heaving furnishings
at her when she tries to enter their bedroom. Having reimposed
himself, he drifts off to sleep, waking to see his wife's slippers by the
bed, "one a little to the front, one a little to the rear, like a ghost not
daring to materialize, timidly approaching, entreating" (p. 108). The
image of his wife having been subdued under his new order, his
repose interrupted by concerns and responsibilities like so many mosquitoes, "the next day, Chen-pao got out of bed and turned over a
new leaf. Once again he became a good man." This ending recalls
the beginning of the story, in which Chen-pao has been described as
an "ideal" man, whose compartmentalized psyche values "all things
in their place." In bringing the story to such a conclusion, Chang Ai-
ling with characteristic irony notes the inability of her protagonist to
transcend his flawed vision. His wife is reduced to a pair of slippers
in a ghostlike presence before he is ready to face her again as part of
his ordered world. At the same time, however, the slippers complete
the function of the imagery in the story by externalizing the desires of
women and allowing them to encroach upon Chen-pao's consciousness without actual confrontation of the characters. Chen-pao's desire
to turn a blind eye is itself a hopeless trap of unfulfillment. Through
the imagery, the fantasies of various characters are allowed action
while the characters themselves remain passive.

The coincidence of personal fantasy and physical phenomenon, to
the extent that the latter appears as the projection of the individual's fantasy, is the mechanism underlying two complete stories,
"Blockade" and "Love in a Fallen City." In these, the unlicensed
desires of the protagonists are but suggested, while the environment
plays out the theme in unrestrained terms as though it were releasing
the individual's desire. This mechanism, introduced in such essay
passages as Chang's watching bombers fly overhead while she longs
for the destruction of herself and her family, and in critical moments
in the stories above, is brought to its full development in the two
stories discussed below.

Set in Shanghai, the title of the story "Blockade" refers to the
Japanese military police practice of cordoning off a block of the city
and searching randomly those persons detained within the cordon. In
the story, ironically, the blockade symbolizes the security of the indi-

vidual mind, within which one dares act out fantasies of longing and escape, but outside which one shrinks from acting for fear of consequences. At the same time, the blockade symbolizes the fantasy of a new social order or human condition within which longings may be realized.

In the story, as police suddenly cordon off a block, fearful shopkeepers shutter and lock their premises in the faces of those attempting to escape through their stores. The cries of numerous beggars are cut short in the growing stillness. A streetcar halts, and a number of passengers descend to mill in the street. Among the few remaining on the streetcar is a teacher in her mid-twenties, Wu Ts'ui-yuan, in the English department of a local university. Despite her outstanding academic achievements, she is now lonely, feeling despised in the family and at school, with no relief in sight:

> She had been a good woman in the family and a good student in school. After her college graduation, Ts'ui-yuan had assumed a position at her alma mater as an assistant in the English Department. At the moment she decided to use the spare time the blockade imposed to correct some papers. She opened the first composition, one done by a male student, decrying vehemently the evils of the city, filled with righteous indignation, in awkward grammar, stammering sentences that cursed "lipstick whores . . . the world . . . depraved dance halls and bars." Ts'ui-yuan skimmed it for a while, then fished out a red pencil to mark it with an "A." As always, she went on correcting. Yet today she had too much time for her cares and involuntarily asked herself why she had given him such a good grade. Had she not asked that, there would have been an end to it. But once she had asked that question, a blush rose to her face. She suddenly realized it was because that student was the only man who dared to speak unhesitatingly to her about such things. He looked up to her as an intelligent, knowledgeable person; he treated her as a man, as a confidant. He respected her. Ts'ui-yuan constantly felt that no one in the school had any respect for her. (p. 489)

When she is thus stimulated, into her train of thought is introduced a businessman in his mid-thirties, attempting a furtive, awkward approach. Only after some delay does allow some rapport to develop, in which she defensively tries to keep the upper hand:

> Ts'ui-yuan replied, "Who isn't a bit tired of his family?" Tsung-chen said, "But you don't understand—in my family—oh, don't even bring it up!"

Ts'ui-yuan thought, "It's coming. His wife hasn't an ounce of sympathy for him! It seems every married man in the world is anxiously craving another woman's sympathy."

Tsung-chen hesitated for a moment, then hemmed and hawed, and with great difficulty said, "My wife—doesn't have an ounce of sympathy for me." (p. 494).

Yet, even as Ts'ui-yuan in her cool condescension draws an ounce of vanity from the conversation, her own longing and loneliness emerge, defying her rational contempt for the situation and propelling her to make the deepest emotional commitment to the encounter. Having surrendered herself to this fantasy of relationship, she then witnesses him begin to withdraw his confidence and is reduced to tears of mortification, only sharpened by his feeble, transparent gesture of taking her telephone number without writing it down. As the police cordon is lifted and the tram starts up, he abandons his advances and, fearful of any commitment, moves away from her: "She knew what he intended by this. It was to be as though during the whole span of the blockade nothing had happened. The whole city of Shanghai had dozed away into an irrational dream" (p. 499). The story, then, portrays the vain fantasy of the young woman through the blockade, illuminating her irrational longings even as she parries the businessman's complaints with reasoned statements that he should willingly submit to his condition. She, in turn, is crushed when, the "irrational dream" ended, she realizes the vanity of having hoped for escape for herself. The episode is punctuated by the final cry of a distressed beggar: "Pigs!" This rude deflation is present even in one of Chang's stories that ends successfully for the protagonists, "Love in a Fallen City."

The settings for "Love in a Fallen City" include the two types Chang's stories are most noted for: a formerly prominent, extended family in decay, and the abnormal, decadent society of Hong Kong on the eve of World War II. Pai Liu-su is a Chinese woman of twenty-eight *sui* who has divorced, and with no skills to support herself, returned to the family household. With the family in financial straits, Liu-su is held in contempt as a parasite, a situation she finds increasingly intolerable. A wealthy overseas Chinese in his early thirties, Fan Liu-yuan, is introduced to one of Liu-su's younger sisters during a visit to Shanghai. But he is instead attracted to Liu-su herself. Subsequently, he discreetly arranges to have Liu-su's aunt accompany her to Hong Kong, where he ensconces her in a Repulse Bay hotel in an attempt to make her his mistress. While Liu-yuan is witty, gentlemanly, and patient, he is uncommitted, and Liu-su's primary consideration is the economic and social security marriage provides. Realizing that in the eyes of society Fan Liu-yuan has already compromised her, Liu-su feels trapped and flees back to Shanghai and the resentful contempt of her relatives. Liu-yuan, however, after allowing her to pass the autumn in Shanghai, invites her back to Hong Kong. There they at last fall into each others' arms, and having consummated their affair, Liu-yuan provides her with a flat and servant and leaves for a year-long business trip in Europe. His steamer, however, sails on the eve of the Battle for Hong Kong and is forced back into port when the fighting breaks out. Liu-yuan rejoins Liu-su, at first trying to sit out the battle at the Repulse Bay hotel, then forced to to return to Liu-su's ravaged flat. Even after the weeks of fighting are over, they are made to eke out a humble existence in the ruins of the city until Liu-yuan can secure passage on a boat to Shanghai, where he has funds. Against the background of this experience, Liu-yuan's genuine concern for Liu-su is aroused, and he finally agrees to marry her.

The title of the story, "Love in a Fallen City," may also be read "Love That Topples Cities," the Chinese characters being a deliberate reference to a number of femme-fatales in the Chinese tradition. The deliberate play on a traditional motif is repeated at the conclusion of the story:

> The fall of Hong Kong fulfilled her. But in this world past reason, who knows what is cause and what is effect? Who knows? Perhaps it was just to fulfill her that a great metropolis was levelled. It brought death to thousands, brought suffering to tens of thousands in its earth-shaking reform. Liu-su indeed did not feel she had any even slightly extraordinary place in history. (p. 251)

Insofar as the story concerns the fulfillment or completion (ch'eng-ch'üan) of Liu-su, much of it is devoted to portraying the sense of incompleteness and unfulfillment. As Shui Ching has pointed out, Liu-su is introduced in the story as a character who does not

altogether fit her surroundings.[20] She is first described against the
sounds of a *hu-ch'in* violin in the background, associating her with a
character in a Peking opera as a model Chinese woman, yet leaving
her image too vague for her role to be defined. At the same time, as a
divorcée she is hardly model, and in the description she is not playing
her role, since the lute is playing alone. Still, she moves almost
unconsciously to the musical rhythm, at the same time smiling coldly
at the tune, which tells a story of filial piety and constancy, a theme
no longer related to her. Her smile is given a ghostly quality, *yin-yin
ti.* Ironically, it is because Liu-su learned how to dance Western-style
that she becomes acquainted with Liu-yuan, who sees in her the
quintessential Chinese woman he is looking for, jaded with Western-
style living. In sum, Liu-su is tense and uncertain, and Liu-yuan is
inconsistent and not fully committed.

Their interior lives are represented in a number of passages that
emphasize vagueness and elusiveness. Eyeing the flowers at Repulse
Bay in the sunset, Liu-su must guess that they are red. Her features
have "an indistinct beauty."[21] When Liu-yuan apologizes for his
unsavory acquaintances, Liu-su questions whether he can really distinguish himself from the company he keeps (p. 227). Liu-yuan, gazing idly into a glass filled with leaves swimming in the tea, invites
Liu-su to go away with him to the "rain forests of primitive man"
(pp. 229–30). They lie on the beach under the dizzying force of the
sun, and when Liu-yuan is tired of Liu-su's evasiveness, he entertains
the exotic Princess Saheiyini to stimulate Liu-su's jealousy and bring
her to submission. She replies with evasive sarcasms. Liu-yuan passes
an evening making repeated telephone calls to Liu-su, who is so tense
that she can no longer believe these words of love on the telephone
are not part of a dream. Once she is back in Shanghai, time is distorted by her emotion, as she "ages two years" in two months (p.
238). Returning to Hong Kong, Liu-su is made to realize that Liu-
yuan's telephone calls were a reality, but at that moment, she accepts
his embrace and the line between reality and fantasy is again blurred:

> This was the first time he'd kissed her. And yet both of them felt it
> was not the first time, for in their fantasies it had occurred countless
> times. . . . He pressed her towards the mirror. It seemed they were
> slipping into the mirror, into another, dizzying world. (pp. 239–40)

It is only against the absolute reality of destruction and death that the
characters emerge distinctly, set apart from a background of deepen-
ing chaos and gloom: "All that she could rely on was this breath in
her chest and this man who slept at her side" (p. 248). Chang is
deliberate in underplaying her characters' development and in keeping it from the realm of the ideal: "He is only a selfish man and she
is only a selfish woman. In time of war and trouble the egoist has no
place in the sun, but there is always a place for a commonplace married couple" (p. 249).

The fall of Hong Kong and the resolution of the story are
foreshadowed chiefly in a speech by Liu-yuan as he is courting Liu-
su in Repulse Bay: "Someday our civilization will be utterly
destroyed, everything ended—burned out, seared out, crushed out.
Perhaps this wall will remain. Liu-su, if at that time we were to meet
at this base of this wall . . . Liu-su, perhaps you would be sincere
toward me, and maybe I would be sincere with you" (p. 226). The
story is based on the proposition of what it would take to reduce such
a man as Liu-yuan to submit to the will of a woman like Liu-su. Liu-
su's role as a femme-fatale is jokingly referred to early in the story in
a casual remark by Liu-yuan. When Liu-su insists that she is but a
useless woman, Liu-yuan responds that they are the most dangerous
kind (p. 221). Liu-su in physical reality may not be a femme-fatale,
but in her fantasies she might well be. The story places in conjunc-
tion the intense longing of the lonely, desperate woman with the
ruthless fury of the battle that destroys the world she sees as separat-
ing her from her desire, be it the commonplace satisfaction of marriage. Hence, the submerged desire of the protagonist is projected
onto physical reality. And while it is a sophisticated joke, the story
also suggests the amoral ruthlessness at the heart of human desire,
and in the world in which that desire exists. It may be argued whether
Chang is always complete in her depictions of psychological realism.
But the details which comprise that realism are ordered to embody a
particular view of psychological reality, and to this end her achievement is considerable.

"Love in a Fallen City" plays out to the limit the representation of
a passive character's desire on a scale that can only be portrayed as
an ironic joke of fate. In turning to the stories in which Chang

presents more active characters as protagonists, it is not surprising to find several studies in abnormal psychology. Although such stories do not offer the range of spectacle and subtlety sometimes found in the stories discussed above, they offer powerfully concentrated visions of ruthlessness with the same eye for imagery and detail.

"The Golden Cangue" is starkly but deliberately divided into three major sections that chronicle the deterioration of Ts'ao Ch'i-ch'iao from frustrated young wife to luckless, suspicious, and cynical widow to vengeful, pathologically dependent mother. But while this chronicle consistently follows the pathetic and terrible manipulations of Ch'i-ch'iao, the focus of the narrative is allowed to shift in order to admit the full implications of the plot.

Ch'i-ch'iao's life as the wife of a cripple dying of tuberculosis is portrayed through the events of a single day in the household of the extended family by which she is enveloped, held in contempt for her humble origins and frustrated by her lack of sexual satisfaction. The inflexible brittleness of this world is constantly underlined by women's duties of shelling walnuts, scraping walnut shells against felt. A minor episode is climaxed when one of the sisters-in-law splits her fingernail while cracking a walnut. There are the tinkling of chopsticks and ornamental chains and toilet articles, the rustling of dried camphor leaves and clothing. The atmosphere is claustrophobic and short on privacy. The family, like families in traditional fiction, is bound together by an endless series of inflexible formalities and rituals: the women's wedding ceremonies, the matriarch's breakfasts, prayers, audiences, and the visits of relatives. These are seen against Ch'i-ch'iao's seething discontent and frustration. She is late to pay her morning call on the matriarch on account of her opium habit. She is heard attempting to manipulate the matriarch into setting an early date for her daughter's wedding, an act the implications of which would humiliate the matriarch's daughter just as Ch'i-ch'iao lives in humiliation. Ch'i-ch'iao's temper flares out of control when her relatives visit her, though she still forces herself to present them with the gifts they are looking for. Alone, Ch'i-ch'iao drifts into a reverie of her girlhood, freely walking the streets to the admiration of local men. This, too, descends into an unpleasant association:

Ch'ao-lu was always after her, calling her Miss Ts'ao, and on rare occasions Little Miss Ch'iao, and she would give the rack of hooks a slap that sent all the empty hooks swinging across to poke him in the eye. Ch'ao-lu plucked a piece of raw fat a foot wide off the hook and threw it down hard on the block, a warm odor rushing to her face, the smell of sticky dead flesh . . . she frowned. On the bed lay her husband, that lifeless body.[22]

The passage not only serves to reinforce the imagery discussed above and her revulsion towards her husband, but also implicitly suggests the impasse she is in. Earlier she has been describing her husband's flesh to the object of her sexual desire, her brother-in-law Chiang Chi-tse. He has put her off by pinching her foot. Now, even in her reveries, she cannot find escape from her sense of disgust. She is trapped, fixed in this household of fixed etiquette and responsibility: "She stared straight ahead, the small, solid gold pendants of her earrings like two brass nails nailing her to the door, a butterfly specimen in a glass box, bright colored and desolate."[23]

The transition from this section of the story to her widowhood ten years later has been aptly described as the use of the fadeout technique:

Ch'i-ch'iao pressed the mirror down with both hands. The green bamboo curtain and a green and gold landscape scroll reflected in the mirror went on swinging back and forth in the wind—one could get dizzy watching it for long. When she looked again the green bamboo curtain had faded, the green and gold landscape was replaced by a photograph of her deceased husband, and the woman in the mirror was also ten years older.[24]

Yet, in this context, the passage is not simply technique to shift from one point in the narrative to another. It serves as a statement of the rigidness of Ch'i-ch'iao's own mind. Although if she had turned her ambitions outside the household events might have intervened in her development or lack of it, she has waited with fixed purpose for her husband's death to win financial independence and take Chi-tse as a lover, thus tying her own interior life to the fixed world of the household. She is to find that in her widowhood her desires are to remain in large part unfulfilled. This section of the story portrays

Ch'i-ch'iao losing control, venomously disrupting the etiquette of the household, but to no effect. Her attempts during the *fen-chia* proceedings to enhance her independence and bring Chi-tse to a form of submission leave her with adequate resources to reflect the respectability of the family, but as the author laconically notes, "The widow and orphans were still taken advantage of."[25] When Chi-tse visits her to swindle her by pandering to her fantasy of desire, the theme of loss of control is given its most brilliant touch:

> Ch'i-ch'iao continued to smile but her mouth felt dry, her upper lip stuck on her gum and would not come down. She raised the lidded teacup to suck a mouthful of tea, licked her lips, and suddenly jumped up with a set face and threw her fan at his head. The round fan went wheeling through the air, knocked his shoulder as he ducked slightly to the left, and upset his glass. The sour plum juice spilled all over him.[26]

Here, at the moment that her own lip has refused to obey her will and betrays in its dryness the tension behind her smile, she pauses to control herself, and then, in an act of self-dramatization, hurls the fan at Chi-tse. But as with her hysterical performance at the *fen-chia* ceremony, she cannot control her act and it falls wide of the mark, to futile and self-destructive effect. The expulsion of Chi-tse is not simply the routing of a common rake, but the rejection of even the fantasy of love itself. That her own mind is now cut off from reality, disjointed in its own interior world, and enclosed by the soured ambition for material independence is portrayed neatly as she gazes out the window of her house, looking after the departing Chi-tse through the distorted glass:

> The tiny shrunken image of a policeman reflected faintly in the top corner of the window glass ambled by swinging his arms. A rickshaw quietly ran over the policeman. A little boy with his long gown tucked up into his trouser waist ran kicking a ball out of the edge of the glass. The postman in green riding a bicycle superimposed his image on the policeman as he streaked by. All ghosts, ghosts of many years ago or the unborn many years hence. . . . What is real and what is false?[27]

The story then turns to its final extended struggle, for if Ch'i-ch'iao is unable to manipulate the world beyond her household to any sense of gratification, she is even more ruthless in her dependence on her children to share in her rejection of the world. In such a situation, she is largely reduced to a razor-sharp voice or a prisoner battering others with her shackles, the golden cangue. While her identity is given a last sympathetic look as she recalls her girlhood, even this is seen against the image of her shriveled arm, and there might have been little material to develop in recording her final descent into madness alone. But the situation is given its full share of horror by turning largely to the destruction of her daughter Ch'ang-an, whose genuine hopes, as opposed to the fantasies of the young Ch'i-ch'iao, are crushed all the more cruelly. There is little need to recite the succession of cruelties that bring the story to its conclusion, nor the evident sexuality of Ch'i-ch'iao's dessicated mind. The chief device Chang employs to heighten the tragic progression is to suggest in Ch'ang-an's actions a reprise of similar scenes from Ch'i-ch'iao's life, and in the context of Ch'ang-an's genuine hope against the background of Ch'i-ch'iao's futile fantasies. Thus, Ch'ang-an is allowed to pose fancifully before a mirror:

> As a young maid squatted on the floor buttoning her up, Ch'ang-an scrutinized herself in the wardrobe mirror and could not help stretching out both arms and kicking out the skirt in a posture from "The Grape Fairy." Twisting her head around, she started to laugh, saying, "Really dolled up to look like the celestial maiden scattering flowers."[28]

When Ch'ang-an is victimized by Ch'i-ch'iao's calumnies and her admirer retreats, she follows him silently to the front gate of the house, but another scene, Ch'i-ch'iao's parting look at Chi-tse, is recalled:

> Ch'ang-an felt as though she were viewing this sunlit courtyard from some distance away, looking down from a tall building. The scene was clear, she herself was involved but powerless to intervene. The court, the tree, two people trailing bleak shadows, wordless—not much of a memory, but still something to be put in a crystal bottle and held in both hands to be looked at some day, her first and last love.[29]

C. T. Hsia's judgment of "The Golden Cangue" as "a perfect fable to serve as the dramatic correlative to her emotion" may be supplemented by the appraisal of the story as a key work in the various motifs and elements employed. The trademark imagery of moon, mirror, and glass is present, together with those images that give the story its individuality. The use of a setting of monolithic abnormality and its distorting effects on characters and their perceptions is another feature strongly in evidence. While the setting is thoroughly Chinese, the insights are Freudian in their concern with sublimation and sexuality. As elsewhere, the projection of fantasies—unattainable, unworthy of attainment, or both—is seen against moments of desolation and de-idealization.

Ch'i-ch'iao is the most powerful and fully developed of Chang's assertive characters. In her emotional dependence on her children, she carries to a ruthless extreme similar traits in other of Chang's mother figures, such as the protagonist of *The Interlocking Rings* and the amah in "A-hsiao's Autumnal Lament." As a widow of voracious habits, she is presaged by the sane but cruel Mrs. Liang in "Aloeswood Ashes—The First Burning." As the widowed concubine of a wealthy Cantonese merchant, Mrs. Liang is never very well developed as a character, but remains the catalyst of the tale, manipulating the schoolgirl Ko Wei-lung into the clutches of a decadent Hong Kong society. Wei-lung is actually Mrs. Liang's niece, cautioned by her family to stay away from her after Mrs. Liang has been disowned for her opportunistic behavior. Wei-lung, left alone in Hong Kong to finish middle school, finds she is short of funds. When she turns to Mrs. Liang for help to complete her studies, she finds herself being used to lure young men into affairs with her aunt. Wei-lung rebels by attaching herself to one of her aunt's former lovers, George Ch'iao, who is now in bad repute with Mrs. Liang as well as Hong Kong society, including his own father, who has cut off funds to him. Wei-lung finally allows George to make love to her, only to discover him shortly with one of the maids in Mrs. Liang's house. Wei-lung hysterically attacks the maid, rousing Mrs. Liang from her sleep and opening up scandal. Mrs. Liang decides to make the best of the situation by cajoling and threatening Wei-lung into marrying George. A comfortable life is proffered, George's father prepares to restore his funds, and Wei-lung submits. The story is, then, focused on the degradation of Wei-lung's dreams, of her journey from naive ambition to stagnant surrender to security, and the price is self-contempt. The final scene is set during a winter festival in the Wanchai section of Hong Kong. As the couple browse through its curios, they are confronted with the spectacle of a fragile-

looking teenage prostitute flanked by husky European sailors who
momentarily eye Wei-lung as well. As the couple drive out of
Wanchai, they converse:

> George laughed, "What did those mudfish take you for?"
> Wei-lung replied, "After all, what's the difference between those girls
> and me?"
> George steered their car with one hand and covered her mouth with the
> other: "More nonsense from you and I'll . . ."
> Wei-lung, smiling, apologized, "Okay! Okay! I admit I said something
> wrong. Of course there's a difference, right? They have no choice. I've
> done it of my own free will."
> The car passed out of Wanchai. The explosive sound of firecrackers
> bursting and popping gradually subsided. Red and green traffic lights
> followed one after another in quick succession, fading into dimness once
> they flowed over the glass of the car windshield. The car entered a dark
> stretch of road. George had not yet turned to look at her. When he did, he
> still couldn't see, yet he knew she was surely crying. With his free hand
> he groped for his cigarettes and lighter. A cigarette in his mouth, he
> struck a light. As the flame glowed in the chilly winter night his lips
> seemed an orange blossom. The fire faded quickly, into coldness and
> darkness.[30]

In this final imagery of flame, blossom, and darkness is a symbol of
the death of Wei-lung's hopes and her integrity. The image also
recalls an earlier episode when Mrs. Liang crushes the love life of a
serving girl who has interfered in Mrs. Liang's plans. The girl states
she intends to leave Hong Kong, just as Wei-lung is later to threaten,
but Mrs. Liang assures the maid, "You can't run away," reminding
the maid that her poor family relies on her, Mrs. Liang. Her victory
complete, "Mrs. Liang stepped into her shoes and, dropping her
cigarette into an azalea plant, stood up and walked out. The azalea
plant was covered with blossoms. The cigarette butt disappeared into
the petals, and they quickly burst into a ball of flame" (p. 300).

The decor of Mrs. Liang's house underlines her opportunism:

> Above the fireplace were arrayed kingfisher snuff jars and ivory Kuan Yin
> statuettes, while behind the sofa was a folding screen of speckled bamboo.
> But the presence of this slight touch of Oriental color was obviously for
> the benefit of foreign friends. Englishmen constantly come from far away
> to see China; how could one not give them a bit of China to view? But the

China in here was the China in the mind's eye of a Westerner:
preposterous, delicate and ridiculous. (p. 290)

Mrs. Liang, in turn, embodies a culture in Hong Kong which is
stagnant and materialistic. George Ch'iao and his sister, both
Eurasians, represent the plight of those doomed to entrapment in this
culture, rejected by both Chinese and Europeans, save in a purely
commercial setting. Thus, Wei-lung's marriage to George is the final
burial within such a culture. Ultimately, such a society is portrayed
not for itself, but as a representation of the failure of the human condition in which the protagonist must either destroy herself or submit
her vain longings to the destruction that life inevitably carries out. To
think otherwise is naiveté or madness, two extremes found in Wei-
lung and in characters in other stories.

The moon imagery is present to underscore the unreality of Wei-
lung's vision. As she walks away from her first successful interview
with Mrs. Liang, "the further she walked the more she felt the moon
was just ahead among the tree thickets, but when she arrived, there
was no moon" (p. 292). Later, as she awaits her lover, floral imagery
is used to foreshadow the doom of her fantasies, described in overa-
bundance and ripeness, "so that all had a dizzying, murderous
atmosphere, and on the breeze that wafted across there was the faint
odor of meat" (p. 317). Again the moon is used to represent her fantasy and its vanity: "Although the moon had already sunk, she had
been soaked in its light, her whole body embued with its mantle" (p.
324). Finally, once the affair is blighted, she sets her mind on dreams
of a new life in Shanghai, but she is described thus: "Her face bore a
smile; her eyes, however, were dead" (p. 331).

Perhaps the shortcoming of "Aloeswood Ashes—The First Burning" is that it has, like its companion piece, despite the assertiveness
of protagonist and antagonist, created a memorable atmosphere
without creating memorable characters. The "strange" (ch'i) in this
ch'uan-ch'i remains focused on the environment in its varied elements, albeit they reflect aspects of character. In stories such as
"Heart Sutra" and "Jasmine Tea," Chang has more deliberately
worked on character by making the protagonists examples of
abnormal psychology, as well as assertive, while allowing their sur-

roundings an appearance of health not to be found in such stories as "The Golden Cangue" and "Aloeswood Ashes." However, the aberrations of the protagonists are made to be an oblique comment on their apparently healthy surroundings, implying that their defiance of time, circumstance, and convention is an extreme manifestation of desires common to their fellow beings.

"Heart Sutra" does not aim at tragedy. Nevertheless, it presents an ironic and moving portrait of an inevitably vain obsession. Beautiful, aggressive, and clever, Hsiao-han, at twenty *sui,* maintains an attachment to her father that has become a passionate and sensual devotion. Her Electra complex is complete with her contempt for her homely, retiring mother, who passively submits to being ignored by her husband and slighted by Hsiao-han. Chang remarks in another story, sardonically, "The beauty of a mature woman with the mind of an infant is the most seductive combination."[31] As this may also be taken to apply to Hsü Hsiao-han, she is accorded a striking introduction, partially reflected in the following passage:

> Hsiao-han sat high on the railing around the rooftop garden of the apartment building, five girls arrayed below her, one couched slightly against her legs, the others leaning against the rail. It was a midsummer evening, pure and clear, starless and moonless. Hsiao-han was wearing a peacock-blue blouse and white slacks. The peacock-blue blouse vanished into the peacock evening sky, and in the twilight could be seen only her pale, delicate face. Below this there was nothing until the stretch of two long white legs. Although she was not really tall, yet her legs were proportionately long, and hanging down from the railing, they appeared unusually long. She was leaning back, hands propped up behind her. Her face was that of a child in a myth, rounded cheeks, delicate chin, long sweeping dark eyes that curved upward at the corners. Her nose was short and straight, her thin red lips fell slightly. A strange and disturbing beauty. . . . There was nothing it seemed but the sky, Shanghai, and Hsiao-han. No, it was the sky, Hsiao-han, and Shanghai, since where she sat was between the sky and the city.[32]

This ethereal unreality is very much to the point of the story. As a child from a myth, Electra, her appearance is one of transcending mortality. But it is a precarious position, one she cannot long maintain, at an impasse between the dreamy sky and the reality of the city. The moon itself is not present, but her own pale face, seemingly suspended in the sky, is itself a suggestion of the moon symbol. The pose she takes offers an illusion of a stature she does not really have.

Shortly a scene is presented in which Hsiao-han's striking resemblance to one of her girlfriends is revealed, as Hsiao-han stares into a mirror, gazing at her friend Ling-ch'ing's features with envious identification. The passage is also an ironic foreshadowing of events. Behind Mr. Hsü's control and reserve, he is attracted to Hsiao-han sexually as well, and she is skeptical of his resolve to break the impasse in their relationship by sending her to her aunt's home in Peking. While she reasons aggressively, her basic assumptions are wrong. While she connives to match her admirer, a medical student, with Ling-ch'ing, she discovers that just as she does not accept him, the student rejects Ling-ch'ing, who has sought the security of a father figure by engaging in an affair with Hsiao-han's father. He, of course, is attracted to Ling-ch'ing for her resemblance to Hsiao-han.

There is in this story more than ample irony, but its pace, carried by the machinations of the characters, is swift and agile, a technical feat that also transforms the story into an interesting one. Hsiao-han's reasoning and lying are both evidence of the same self-deception, that she is above the human lot, that she is different and superior, that she can put something over on the world. In essence, it is to preserve the time in her life that was "the golden age" of seven or eight years past, the time of security and unquestioned love. Her father knows as much and explains to her that her devotion arises from her insecurity in facing adulthood. He counters her not with arguments of incest and moralizing, but with considerations of the disparity of age and the pointless sacrifice it would mean for her. When Hsiao-han learns of the manifest hypocrisy of his reasoning, she acts with frantic, and equally ironic, swiftness. She attempts to use the medical student to break the affair between her father and Ling-ch'ing by lecturing him on the social ruin such an affair will mean for Ling-ch'ing. The young man merely responds that he has no right to interfere, that there are plenty of young girls who prefer the security of an older man to someone like himself, and if their relationship is within legal bounds, then nothing can hinder them. Next Hsiao-han turns to her mother, holding out proof of her father's infidelity. But this is no revelation to her mother, who has long accepted it with resignation. Yet, as Hsiao-han searches out the house of Ling-ch'ing's guardian, Hsiao-han's mother takes the initiative and heads her off, forcing her to return home. Hsiao-han's frenzy collapses into exhaustion, and the arrogant adolescent is reduced to the emotional child, clinging to her mother and weeping while her mother pets and reassures her.

In addition to the Freudian basis of the story, the title "Heart Sutra" suggests the theme of *maya,* the illusions and self-deceptions of desire on the part of characters who are literally pursuing illusions of each other. Moreover, the theme of compassion is also present as both a traditional allusion and a modern response. Hsiao-han's failure and submission effectively portray the delusion of challenging the arbitrariness of time and circumstance. Chang does not slight this vanity, but contrasts it with one of the few characters who rise to embody a positive force, Mrs. Hsü. For although Mrs. Hsü's actions are to preserve order without justifying it, she does so with consummate sense and genuine compassion. And that is the best humanity can offer in the world of "Heart Sutra."

The Hong Kong world of the story "Jasmine Tea" cannot offer this much. As C. T. Hsia has pointed out in some detail, "Jasmine Tea" is one of Chang's severest portraits, certainly far more so than "Heart Sutra."[33] But as in "Heart Sutra," "Jasmine Tea" attempts to suggest the protagonist's sickness not in terms of his own rarefied vision alone, but as an aberration of normal experience. The central figure is Nieh Ch'uan-ch'ing, a college student drowning in self-hatred and pity, whose contact with his opposite, the wholesome, naive girl Yen Tan-chu, serves only to sound the depths of his sickness. Nieh is in search of a father figure in Tan-chu's father, a professor at the university. Just as Nieh's search is futile, so too Professor Yen, in chastising Ch'uan-ch'ing for his lack of masculinity and identifying it with Chinese youth in general, reveals his own frustration in finding his image of a son.

Aside from the violent ending of the story, another aspect of "Jasmine Tea" is particularly notable. This is the concentrated thoroughness with which the sensual world about this psychologically trapped youth is constructed. The social observations present in other stories are in large part beyond the range of Ch'uan-ch'ing's confined perceptions. The narrator sets the atmosphere by offering the reader a cup of bitter jasmine tea, cautioning him that it is burning hot as well as bitter. Yet its aroma is attractive. So too the scent of opium that permeates Ch'uan-ch'ing's home and the musty smell of the attic in which he ponders the relics of his dead mother are images of the attractiveness of his bitterness, the obsession with the past that avoids confrontation with the present and the reveries and fantasies that stave off reality. He has been wronged by the world; his vanity lies in his desperate insistence that the world owes him his fantasies.

In a pointed pun, he is described as consuming "ifs" (*ju-kuo*), the character for *kuo* being the same as that for fruit (*shui-kuo*). The more of the ifs he ponders, the less clearly he can see:

> But he had an uncanny sensation, as though the sky had quickly darkened—was already dark—and alone before the window, the sky in his mind had darkened with it. Silent, dark misery . . . as though in a dream, the person watching by the window at first was he, and in the next moment, he saw clearly that it was his mother. Her bangs hung low. Her head was bowed. There was but a pale, vague image of the sharp lower portion of her face. Those ghostly eyes and eyebrows were like dark shadows in moonlight. Yet he knew for a certainty that it was his dead mother Feng Pi-lo.
>
> He had lost his mother at four *sui,* but he recognized her from her photograph. There was only one photograph from before her marriage. She was wearing an old-fashioned short jacket of embroidered satin with tiny bat designs. Now the person before the window seemed gradually to become more distinct. He could see the bats on her satin jacket. She was waiting there for some person, some news. She knew well this news would never come. The sky within her mind had slowly gone black . . . Ch'uan-ch'ing's body involuntarily convulsed with grief. He did not know whether after all he was his mother or himself.[34]

Ch'uan-ch'ing also ponders himself as the girl Tan-chu, as well, but inescapably and bitterly he sees himself as his father, Nieh Chieh-chen: "He discovered how closely he resembled his father, not only physically, in the outline and form of his features, but even in his mannerisms and small gestures. How deeply he detested the Nieh Chieh-chen existing in his body" (p. 268).

His tactile world is limited to what is hard and cold. At his encounter with Yen Tan-chu on the streetcar, his head rests against a windowpane. When she descends, a man who has been carrying azaleas gets off with her, and Ch'uan-ch'ing is left alone, his head against the glass. Later he is described as he contemplates the encounter: "He sat atop a desk with redwood side panels and reclined against the marble surface. The desk surface was ice-cold, like the streetcar window. The azaleas outside the window; Ten Tan-chu inside. . . ." (pp. 259–60). The azaleas suggest life and fulfillment. But even though Yen Tan-chu is beside him, she too is rendered in hard, cold images—for example, "dressed in a white woolen, tight-fitting sweater that molded her ripe breasts and small waistline into a plaster statue" (p. 254). Again, her appearance becomes that of a rigid object as Ch'uan-ch'ing gazes at her in the classroom: "The lines of her face curved with great beauty, especially her childlike, small nose. With a small bead of perspiration on her nose, she seemed like a glistening wet bronze statue" (p. 267). Ch'uan-ch'ing's own face is twice described as creased with the twisted surface of a rattan chest against which he lays his head (pp. 261, 268).

All these images support the principal frustration, that he cannot hear what he wants to hear. Partially deaf from a beating his father inflicted on him, he resents automatically Tan-chu's chatter on the tram. This suggests early in the story the dominance of his self-pity. He also does not like his own voice. When Professor Yen calls the roll in class, "Ch'uan-ch'ing answered, but he himself thought the sound of his own voice somewhat strange, and he blushed with embarrassment" (p. 265). He is scolded by his stepmother and father for his failures. Later he cannot find his voice at all when Professor Yen gives an oral quiz in class, and he is ordered out of the classroom in tears. As Professor Yen was to be his father image, the professor's shouts add despair. In Ch'uan-ch'ing's malevolent envy of Tan-chu, everything she says to him he regards as a hidden slight. As he beats her, he screams back her casual remarks in accusation and in defense of his revenge.

This review of some of the total use of the senses in "Jasmine Tea" is to illustrate that, however unpredictable, the final beating is well motivated artistically as well as psychologically. For the story has carefully built up the sensory onslaught on Ch'uan-ch'ing's mind, imaging a more abstract psychological pattern. Slowly the story increases the intensity of this imagery until it fairly demands a physical reaction from Ch'uan-ch'ing.

In Chang Ai-ling's fiction of the war period there is frequently a turn of phrase, an allusion, a setting, that deliberately recalls traditional Chinese fiction and its love of the supernatural. sometimes these allusions are overt, sometimes suggestive. When the Parisian prostitute in "Red Rose and White Rose" lifts her skirt above her head she seems to undergo a transformation, like the demon of "Hua-p'i" (The Painted Skin) in *Liao-chai chih-i*. There are moments when the widow Liang in laying her snares recalls Madame White Snake, and Wei-lung her slave girl. Chinese fiction and drama had for centuries amassed a chaotic, vast world of supernatural creatures, and whether the authors took their work seriously or not, it testifies to the persistent interest in the irrational experience outside the Confucian heritage and a collective imagination that refused a systematic explanation of its vision. One of Chang's achievements lay in gathering this rich heritage into a thoroughly modern portrayal of human desire and vanity.

Twentieth-century writers, on the whole, looked at this tradition as merely the social phenomenon of an ignorant fascination with superstition rather than the uninformed expression of a fundamental aspect of the human psyche. Although some writers themselves remained superstitious, the majority dismissed this part of their cultural heritage in favor of a fascination with the new (or the advent of the new) society. As regards this oft-noted preoccupation with the new society, it is worth recalling T. A. Hsia's brief but trenchant comment on two major currents of modern Chinese literature: the romantic May Fourth literature of "New Youth" and the tradition-bound Saturday School of "Mandarin Duck and Butterfly literature."[35] The writers of the former group were concerned only with affirming their ideals and passions, while the latter could only find an eye for the manners and concrete details of the new. Each group lacked and disregarded the better qualities of the other. If we look at Chang Ai-ling's work in the light of this statement, we find that she represents a strong departure from their work. Her concern is neither to gather comforting visions of an old society nor to extol visions of a new one. Her settings are sometimes antiquated, sometimes quite modern, but they are always peopled with characters within whose interior lives lies a world that has not outstripped the old society. Nor will it be liberated in the new. The characterization of both manners and passions, then, is disengaged and ironic.

While Chang Ai-ling resorted to Freudian psychology and elements of traditional fiction to underscore her departure from the more well-traveled paths of modern literature, her sense of disengagement and irony was shared by another woman writer, the dramatist Yang Chiang, whose theme became predominantly the disparity of what an act is intended to mean and what it reveals itself to mean. And in taking up this theme, Yang also explores in both comedy and tragedy aspects of human nature that will not be schooled by social debate.

Yang Chiang

During the Pacific War years, Yang Chiang's name emerged as the creator of dramas that were both popular with audiences and respected by fellow playwrights and critics. A student of foreign languages at Tung-wu and Tsinghua universities in the early 1930s, Yang Chiang had married the scholar-writer Ch'ien Chung-shu, traveled with him to study at Oxford, and returned to China with Ch'ien in 1937 upon the outbreak of the war. While her husband was noted for his loquacious gregariousness on social occasions as well as his wit and erudition in print, Yang Chiang was socially modest and retiring, an obscure name until, as she noted, acquaintances in Shanghai urged her to try her hand as a dramatist in 1942.[36] Her first two works took the form of comedies of manners with a sizable number of characters, speaking lively, individualized dialogue in a conventional, workmanlike structure, concluding with a denouement gathering up all threads in the plot and bringing all the characters on stage. The central characters are young people on the fringe of the bourgeois society of Shanghai, looking for a place in it.

In Yang Chiang's first play, *Ch'en-hsin ju-i* (As You Desire), the heroine is an orphan Li Chün-yü: not the stereotypical dour, humorless, destructive orphan, but a charming, undemanding one, bright, considerate, and willing. This delightful paragon has been led to believe that she can find a home and some work among aunts and uncles on her mother's side of the family in Shanghai. The play begins with her arrival from Peking, bearing as gifts paintings of nudes done by her late father in his futile determination to make a living as a Western-style artist. Respectable nude paintings and the hopelessness of making a living painting them are both jokes of the era which can be immediately appreciated. As innocently proffered by the heroine, they also suggest the qualities of frankness, vulnerability, and an unsullied appreciation of beauty, none of which sit well with Chün-yü's aunts. One of these, Chao Tsu-i, affects a smart European pose, while another, Chao Tsu-mao, maintains a severe, Neo-Confucian attitude. Regardless of their styles, whether they regard her as abetting threats to one's marriage or as a passive obstacle to the ideal marriage of another's daughter, the aunts are only determined to get rid of her.

Through three acts Chün-yü is ejected from three households with an awkward show of propriety and hypocritical concern until she is delivered to the home of her great-uncle. This thoroughly eccentric creature has a great appreciation for Western art, including nude paintings. He has lost both his wife and his daughter, and the heroine lacks a home. Given this symmetry, the relationship of Chün-yü and her great-uncle, Hsü Lang-chai, develops so well that the aunts fear that the old man will devote all of his considerable wealth to Chün-yü and ignore them and their children. The aunts know the old man to be as strict and priggish in his views of courtship as he is liberal in his views on art. To discredit Chün-yü, the aunts locate her boyfriend, who has trailed her from Peking, and direct him to Lang-chai's home, hoping he will be discovered making advances to her. Indeed, the reunited couple are discovered by Lang-chai, but his fury suddenly changes to joy as he recognizes the boy to be the son of an old friend. Guided by ties of friendship, Lang-chai insists on arranging a wedding for the couple and putting them through the rest of their university education.

Yang Chiang's artful concern with symmetry, in the structure of the play and in the matching of characters such as the paragon Chün-

yü and the eccentric Lang-chai, her unobtrusive use of imagery, be it
the obtrusive prop of the paintings, her satiric sketches of affluent
Shanghainese, and her portraits of characters who offer as much or
more to the reader than they demand from him, are all technical
achievements that make for a well-proportioned and entertaining
play. But beyond that, the business of comedy is reconciliation, and it
is in this theme that Yang Chiang employs her mastery of a classic
form of drama to make her critique as a contemporary artist. The
play concludes on a full note of reconciliation: Chün-yü has found
her home, her place in society, and her future. Nor would one want it
any other way, for Chün-yü's character is altogether one which
deserves an opportunity for fulfilment. But it is not the heroine's
character which brings her such a kind fate. She is good so that it is
revealed how little society can tolerate its own image of a paragon.
And she is good so that her good fortune is accepted, instead of ques-
tioned.

Yet in the end that good fortune is also not the result of any voice
of reason, nor the impact of revolution, nor the deeds of heroism.
There is no attempt to offer such an optimistic, gratifying resolution.
In Li Chien-wu's *Youth,* for example, the fortune of two anguished
young lovers is resolved happily when the Widow T'ien's heart of
gold comes to the fore, trouncing inhuman traditions that threaten
the happiness of youth. To the contrary, in Yang Chiang's *As You
Desire,* as cheerful as the ending is, the reconciliation is brought
about by means of money, traditional values, and chance. The aunts'
greed for money reunited Chün-yü with her admirer, and the power
of money insures their opportunities for the future. It is a traditional
syndrome of feminine jealousy and suspicion which drives Chün-yü
from her aunts' homes, and it is the arbitrary decision of an old man,
Lang-chai, committed to a traditional code of friendship which
"arranges" the love match. Finally, it is accidents of birth and death
in the fullest sense throughout the play which turn the outrageous use
of chance into a pointed social comment. *As You Desire* is an
entertaining comedy, but it is also an intriguing one, and the elements that form the vision of its world and mechanism of its plot are
those that also underlie the most explicit social criticism.

As You Desire was staged in 1943 under the direction of the accomplished Huang Tso-lin. The character of Hsü Lang-chai was played by Li Chien-wu, who had the previous year encouraged Yang Chiang to write plays. In October 1943, Yang Chiang's second comedy, *Nung chen ch'eng chia* (Swindle), was staged by the T'ung-mao company. The degree of ironic disengagement evident in *As You Desire,* the teasing play with conventional expectations, is also evident in *Swindle.* The Chinese title more literally reads "turning truth into jest," a reversal of a phrase "turning jest into truth," which more amply suggests the fruitfully ambiguous play with sincerity and truth in the comic action.

The opening of this comedy presents a classic conflict: a well-to-do Shanghai businessman, Chang Hsiang-fu, with no confidence in the judgment of his daughter, insists on arranging a marriage for her, while the daughter, Wan-ju, holds out for her own choice, the handsome, polished young Chou Ta-chang, who claims to be a well-connected, rising young executive. Of course, there seems little room for a romantic theme in such a mercantile setting and, moreover, Chou Ta-chang is an imposter, a picaro looking to marry into a wealthy family. Once this is established for the audience, the play takes on the flavor of a number of previous modern farces about hoaxes and swindles. But the play moves on from that to scenes of emotional intensity, revealing the situations and motives of the characters. The defiant daughter Wan-ju has a stepsister, Yen-hua, who is bitter at the unfair treatment she feels she has received since her father remarried. Yen-hua is determined to win the smart young executive Chou Ta-chang away from her sister. But Ta-chang is not really altogether his own master, and is struggling to meet his lower-class widowed mother's expectations of him as her future source of security and the family salvation. Pushed by his mother to make good and fearful his suspicious prospective father-in-law may expose him, Ta-chang runs away with Yen-hua. (This does not overwhelm Wan-ju, who finds suddenly that she admires her father's choice for her, an amusingly pedantic and awkward young professor.) Now the play again takes a new turn as Ta-chang's mother, unaware of her son's maneuvers, storms into Chang Hsiang-fu's home and in a vulgar, superstitious tirade of outraged widowhood, accuses the Chang family of stealing her son from her. This deliberately overloads the intensity of the play and returns it to the point of farce. In this same vein, the climax of the play is delivered in a scene of unalloyed mirth as Ta-chang and Yen-hua are located by the family and forced through a wedding ceremony. Yet this moment of hilarity fades into a philosophic tone as Ta-chang now warmly and sincerely attempts to soothe and reconcile Yen-hua's dismay and indignation with him and her family.

The play teases conventional presentations of the free love theme. Chou Ta-chang is wrong in principle, but correct in point of fact, and he stands entirely unopposed, in fact gleefully aided by everyone save the bride herself, in staging a shotgun wedding at the end. In going from the defiant espousal of free love to an acceptable scene of forced marriage as something amusing, the play is ultimately concerned with the theme that any principle, free love in this case, is based on the underlying assumptions and perceptions of the characters and their situations. Any shift in these tenuous assumptions may completely alter the application of principle in practice, as demonstrated by the characters in *Swindle*.

The dynamics of this play apply not only to its plot and theme, but also to its characterization, chiefly Chou Ta-chang himself. He is first introduced as a slick blowhard, but is then given a more sympathetic scene at the cramped, shabby flat of his relatives. This scene shows that his obnoxious image is one that he believes he must convey as a con-man, and that it is an image in imitation of world that both charms and repels him. He emerges now as a bitter outsider of the elite world he studies, and almost frantic to live up to his mother's insatiable craving for his success in a world she and her relatives are utterly ignorant of. Beleaguered by their expectations, Ta-chang responds:

> Ancestors! Ancestors! What ready-made good fortune have I enjoyed from our ancestors? Others lord it over everyone from the time they're born. I've climbed step by step and gotten nowhere. I know perfectly well they hold me in contempt. They don't like me and they don't trust me. I have to put on a thick face and keep on climbing! Talk about ready-made good fortune: their ancestors were big officials, and what were ours? All we had was a government clerk, a real bigshot! And then their estates, and what about ours? There's not a tile over our heads or a piece of land under our feet—good fortune! Since I was a kid, what good fortune have I enjoyed? I just keep my head raised and climb on. Let them spit and let

them stamp. When I succeed I'll watch them snort with anger; when I fail I watch them laugh.[37]

Hence the image of Ta-chang as a picaro is softened by his bitter dissatisfaction with himself and his lot, and by tones of an unsentimental but genuine filial concern. However, this portrait of him is not introduced in order to prepare for his victory. He is, after all, still a morally ambiguous figure in a morally ambiguous setting, and he goes down to his defeat, for Yen-hua, whom he finally seduces, has not a penny to her own name, and they are both cheated of their expectations.

It is time then for a reconciliation, to accept moral consequences and settle with society. Now Ta-chang steps to a new plane of dignity as he gently persuades and encourages his distraught bride at the flat his mother lives in:

> YEN-HUA (*looking around with a cold smile*):   Oh, what a fine, cultured family of renown. Yes, a fine family renowned for its culture. So *this* is your clean, well-lighted little apartment! This is your large desk and swivel chair (*smiles coldly*), and the bed you daydream on. And that thing is your educated, your refined and talented, your upright and esteemed mother. Downstairs, why that's your Hua Yang Department Store. And that cheerful matron is your wealthy mother's gracious sister. *You swindler.* You've cheated me to a fare-thee-well!
>
> TA-CHANG: Oh, Yen-hua, don't be so hard on me. After all, we're even, aren't we? I knew the dowry you said you had was no match for Wan-ju's. Still, there should have been something. Who would have thought you don't have a cent—just your two empty hands. But do I blame you?
>
> YEN-HUA (*gives a long sigh*):   Heaven's treated me just the way my stepmother did. You put all you've got into something and get nothing back.
>
> TA-CHANG: Who isn't that way—when you want something, you never get it. When you get something, you don't want it!
>
> YEN-HUA: I suppose fate hasn't treated me badly. It was I who planned it and wished for it. In the end, I brought it on myself.
>
> TA-CHANG: Ai! Yen-hua, don't take it so hard. How can the world be all just the way people want it to be. If you want something a certain way, then there's only one thing to do: these are the facts—okay, I don't accept these facts! I say they're wrong. I change them, recreate them! Just as I wish, as I want something made over, I make it over that way. You say this was all hot air, this was a cheat. Say what you

will. It is the art of living, the only way you're inner life can triumph
over the outer world. It is the only way the spirit conquers material
life. Doesn't this world then become our world? Doesn't it all become
as we would wish it?

YEN-HUA (*sighs*):   From now on, I'll accept it. I'll be content with it.

TA-CHANG: Right, content. Heaven sent you to me. There's no one else
for me. Match the art of living I have with that determination in you—
how can we not come out on top. Come on, come on, have a drink.
This world is ours. (pp. 118–19)

In the end, a reconciliation is made, but in this fragile world the
question is posed how convincing it is. The reader can only pause to
ask just what in the world is theirs, after all. There is the uneasy
sense that this speech of Ta-chang's is the touching wisdom of a fool
or the self-delusion of a wise con-artist. In allowing her characters
this moment of satisfaction in defeat, Yang Chiang seems ultimately
to point to the artist as con-man, to a sense of the sublime and the
ridiculous balanced in one graceful moment, probably unprecedented
on the modern Chinese stage.

Li Chien-wu, resuming his role as an impressionistic critic, was
thoroughly impressed with Yang Chiang's work from the start. He
publicly eulogized her artistic vision in verse and declared that
Swindle was the second milestone in modern Chinese comedy, the
first being the plays of Ting Hsi-lin.[38] Other critics emphasized that
while Yang Chiang enjoyed playing jokes on her characters in a
gentle and sincere fashion, her view of life was essentially serious and
sad. She was really a writer of *pei-chu*, serious or tragic drama.[39]

Yang Chiang's third play, *Yu-hsi jen-chien* (Sport with the
World), was produced in the summer of 1944 by the K'u-kan Players
under the direction of Yao K'o. While it was billed as a *nao-chü*, or
melodrama, it confirmed the critics in their view of Yang Chiang as a
serious playwright.[40] Unfortunately, the script does not seem to have
been published and is apparently unavailable today.

Indeed, for her fourth and final play of the war period, Yang
Chiang turned to tragedy. The play *Feng-hsü* (Windswept Blossoms)
develops in tragic terms the vision introduced in the earlier comedies.
At the end of *Swindle* the bride is reconciled while the reader is left
both to enjoy and to question the wisdom that has swayed the bride.
Such an attitude of disengagement may easily embrace tragedy as

well as comedy, and when Yang Chiang's tragedy appeared, it brought forth similar questions about characters who will not be reconciled with society. *Windswept Blossoms* was apparently not produced, unlike the popular comedies. But this does not reflect a decline in her creative abilities. Rather, it was probably owing to a decline in the theater at the end of the war, when her manuscript was ready for staging. At that point the remaining theater companies were probably unwilling to risk mounting a production. While Yang Chiang's comedies offered a smooth and contented surface that could please any audience, *Windswept Blossoms* is charged with a portrait of fury and despair that could not guarantee a successful response from Shanghai audiences. The play was published in 1946.

In Yang Chiang's tragedy of social iconoclasts there is no question of exposing the corruption of society. It is corrupt. There is no revealing clash of generations and ideals. They have clashed. And there is no question that the hero will be vindicated in the social context, for the play begins with his triumphal release from prison. But the play is concerned with the psychological defeat of the victors. As in Yang Chiang's earlier plays, what might have been a romanticized theme is, on the contrary, turned into one that questions the romantic vision of earlier conventions, and social ideals are set apart from realities of human psychology.

The title *Windswept Blossoms* of course connotes something insubstantial, transient, an entity subject to forces rather than a moving force itself. The setting for the opening of the play uses this image as part of a scene designed ironically to reflect the pastoral beauty of the rural village: a tumbledown temple renovated as a schoolhouse and residence, drenched in a flurry of windblown poplar blossoms, framed by a peach tree with its blossoms reaching out halfway along the length of its branches. In the background are green rice fields and a blue sky with a puff of smoke from a passing train. Fang Ching-shan is being given a hero's welcome by the villagers on his return from a year in prison on false charges. As a young college graduate he had originally come from the city with his educated lover, Shen Hui-lien, and her amah Wang Nai-ma, who followed her in her rejection of her wealthy family. Ching-shan and Hui-lien set up a program of education, medical care, and rural agrarian reform that ran afoul of the interests of a powerful landlord who framed Ching-shan in an arson case and brought about his imprisonment as a radical.

As the play opens, the landlord has been prosecuted and Ching-shan released, but it soon becomes evident that his return to the village is a hollow triumph. An old gentry figure, Yeh San, who has supported Hui-lien during Ching-shan's imprisonment, has not been motivated by sympathy for Ching-shan. When he returns, Yeh San refuses to pay attention to Ching-shan's revised plans for agrarian reform and orders him and Hui-lien to vacate the property he has provided them in order to make way for paying tenants. Hired hands arrive to evict the couple, shrugging off any appreciation for the education Ching-shan and Hui-lien have offered their children. It simply makes them too lazy and unfit for farm work. Other peasants have lost employment and income on account of Ching-shan's legal war with the landlord, and they blindly resent his presence. Ching-shan's bourgeois relatives pay a visit only to argue that he is on a manifestly ruinous course and should prudently take up conventional employment in the city. T'ang Shu-yuan, a young lawyer who has done more than anyone else to secure Ching-shan's release, has done so clearly out of unexpressed love for Hui-lien. While Shu-yuan prepares to back off before permitting an adulterous affair to develop, Hui-lien is drawn to him as an escape, on the one hand, from her absolute disillusionment and contempt for society, and on the other, from the burden of supporting Ching-shan in his preoccupation with his image of himself. The resulting triangle ends in Hui-lien's suicide. For all that, her suicide is not portrayed as a noble act, but a sad and meaningless one. It is an extension of the faults of the hero and heroine, which lie in their excesses. The suicide is abrupt, and the question is how well it is motivated.

The pistol that is used in the suicide is introduced in the first act. But then Hui-lien brandishes it aggressively. She should have, she says, used it on the police instead of letting them take Ching-shan off to prison in the first place; for now, having waited for this day of his liberation, she doesn't want him back. She refuses to join in the short-lived hypocrisy of welcoming Ching-shan back, bitterly observing, "Is there anything less interesting than success?"[41] As she is fired with contempt for the guilt and weakness in the society about her, so she is estranged from her lover. His imprisonment has separated him from the reality she has faced and stimulated his dreams. But for Hui-lien it has meant being separated from him and plunged into an ugly reality to save the hapless dreamer. For her, though the struggle to vindicate him has been gratifying, his actual return can only be disillusioning. His dependence on her to shore up his futile dreams she speaks of as "my cross" and "my burden," and concludes, "It's then that I know I hate him" (p. 19).

On his return he is still ready to use her for himself, and attempts to embrace her physically as part of his vision. She refuses. Eyeing the mementos of his mother who died while he was in prison, he emotes, "Hui-lien, I didn't have the right to sacrifice her!" Hui-lien unleashes her attack: "You didn't have the right to sacrifice anyone else. . . . Long ago you swallowed me, digested me, all of me, all became you, you, you! Poor you, poor, poor you—you don't have the right to sacrifice anyone. But you want to swallow me, because you say you love me!" (p. 37). When Ching-shan turns to planning a dinner for Yeh San and T'ang Shu-yuan, Hui-lien responds with triumph that they have gone off. With this psychological triumph over Ching-shan's vision, Hui-lien asserts that she will monopolize him. Ching-shan refuses her advances.

To reassert himself, Ching-shan attempts to lecture Yeh San on new plans for agrarian reforms. Yeh San leaves unimpressed. At dinner with Shu-yuan, Ching-shan's efforts to cast himself in a heroic mold also fall short at each attempt, though Shu-yuan willingly plays the role of an admiring friend: "Ching-shan, I envy you your self-confidence." To this Ching-shan replies in cavalier fashion, "I don't have anything in this world except some self-confidence" (p. 53). While he wants to boast, "I'm a man who relies on himself to break through," he admits he's had to temper his belief with gratitude for Shu-yuan's help (p. 54). Shu-yuan is suitably self-effacing. When Ching-shan remarks, "But we had nothing more than an ordinary friendship—you haven't respected my ideals, and I haven't respected your success," Shu-yuan replies, "My success! My load is too heavy. Family burdens are too much trouble. I can't have ideals" (p. 54). Ching-shan recounts that he loved Hui-lien so passionately he was ready to commit suicide if he failed to win her. Shu-yuan replies, "You've done all the romantic things" (p. 55). Finally, Ching-shan breaks down and confesses with great emotion that he has no self-confidence, no self-respect, and stands alone, deserted by everyone. Shu-yuan withdraws, and Ching-shan now turns on his wife, accusing her of having an affair with Shu-yuan, urging her to follow him in a comfortable life. Hui-lien stalks out to find Shu-yuan.

Ching-shan is then left alone to self-pitying contemplation, reflecting that if he were a hero he would have the sympathy of the ages, instead of being deserted by everyone to suffer alone in vain. He writes a suicide note and leaves with the pistol to shoot himself. Hui-lien then returns, escorted by Shu-yuan, after her unsuccessful advances toward him. Reading Ching-shan's suicide note, she is deeply moved and leaves to find him and reassure him of her love. Ching-shan clearly has an overweening need to see himself as a hero, all the more so against the threats he has suffered to his self-esteem. Ultimately, his own suicide would be too pathetic, meaningless, and forgotten, if he were not to destroy Hui-lien as well, who has done so much to reveal his weaknesses. His hatred for Hui-lien, then, causes him to return to the house and wait in hiding for her return, to shoot her also. It is, in sum, a pathetic gesture of a man desperate for some sense of self-importance, the inversion of the heroic ideal.

Hui-lien returns filled with guilt and remorse, believing Ching-shan is dead. Shu-yuan at first attempts to comfort her. He is, no doubt, aroused by Hui-lien's weakness, and loves her for that. Hui-lien in her surrender to his embrace betrays a subtle touch of contempt that he has not had the courage to take her before, that it is her plights, not her strengths, that attract Shu-yuan. It is then, when Hui-lien is confronted with her sense of weakness, that Ching-shan steps out and in his pathetic, jealous attempts to act out a grand revenge confronts Hui-lien with her guilt. Raising the pistol to shoot her, Ching-shan is grabbed by Shu-yuan. A scuffle ensues in which Hui-lien grabs the pistol. "Fight! Quarrel! Wretched things born in the morning to die in the evening. I am so tired of it," she says and dispatches herself (p. 126). Yang Chiang's irony is completed. In her last moments, Hui-lien has suffered all the contempt she has had for the guilt and weakness of others turned inward on herself.

Windswept Blossoms seems to bear the impress of certain of Ibsen's plays. Ching-shan is like many of Ibsen's heroes, a demon idealist returning from isolation to disrupt the surface order of life, ready to sacrifice others to his ideals. The play most closely resembles *The Wild Duck,* an unusual play for Ibsen in that, though it reveals the flaws of society, it focuses on a revelation of the flaws of the idealistic protagonist in no less harsh terms. Hui-lien too bears a resemblance to Hedda Gabler in her theatrical gestures of strength and emancipation that only culminate in self-destruction out of weakness. But Ibsen provides no more than a starting point for Yang Chiang's creation. Not only is the characterization thoroughly adapted to a Chinese society, but the characters are also modern in a way that Ibsen's do not seem to be, inwardly tortured by their awareness of their illusions as well as a torture to each other. Their anguished self-awareness, even as they are unable to rise above their weaknesses, it might be said, sets them apart from Ibsen's characters in a significant way.

It may be argued that a reading of the final act gives an impression of its being technically flawed; that, however well motivated, the action is too contrived and the suicide is too abrupt. (There is in this view an echo George Bernard Shaw's admission that there is something forced yet intelligently conceived in the suicidal ending to *The Wild Duck.*) In Yang Chiang's play the disengagement caused by irony is so strong that the reader, though ultimately aware of the writer's sympathy for her characters, is immediately overwhelmed by the folly of their excesses. Yet it is certain that Yang Chiang has provided not only a powerful motive for the heroine's suicide, but also a play that from beginning to end achieves superior psychological tension and insight. It is, as well, an intelligent and incisive critique of the romantic cult of emotion and devotion to impossible ideals of passion and heroism. A flaw that is less reconcilable with the overall superiority of the play occurs in the penultimate scene of love between Hui-lien and Shu-yuan. Here the irony and tension between the lovers must slacken (though not entirely abate) and shift to the fact that the vengeful Ching-shan lurks listening in the shadows, leaving the dialogue of Shu-yuan and Hui-lien to glide from conscience to comfort to love. The scene is not without its share of banalities and threatens to make the characters less interesting, their conflict as a love triangle a well-worn convention. This does little justice to the rest of a play that superseded so many conventions of modern Chinese drama. This shortcoming threatens but does not dismiss the work as a distinguished and unusual achievement.

Ch'ien Chung-shu

The critical impressions of Yang Chiang's work during the war might be, and in fact were, applied by critics to Ch'ien Chung-shu's fiction when it appeared following the war. To play jokes on characters, to sport with the world, to write in a manner suggesting self-satisfaction, and to suggest a sad and serious vision beneath a comic surface are all impressions of Yang Chiang that apply to Ch'ien Chung-shu. The words of Yang Chiang's picaroon in *Swindle* anticipate a major theme in Ch'ien Chung-shu's novel *The Besieged City:* "Who isn't that way—when you want something you never get it. When you get something, you don't want it!" Moreover, the theme suggested in *Swindle*—that, as the ideal must forever mock the reality, human activity must continually attempt to imagine other worlds and enter them—is also an important aspect of Ch'ien's work and his discussions of literature.

This theme is implied in some of the essays Ch'ien wrote during the thirties, through which he built his reputation for wit, erudition, and skepticism. Literature, Ch'ien implied, was an activity much the same as many other forms of human activity, and no more futile in the long run. In the essay "Lun jen-wen" (On Writers), Ch'ien discussed attitudes toward literature, and particularly focused his satire on writers of the time who expressed their own disappointment with being writers, implying that they were meant for better and more valuable activity:

> Literature must perish, but there is no harm in encouraging writers—
> encouraging them not to be writers. An [Alexander] Pope may produce
> elegant literature every time he opens his mouth (lisp in numbers), and a
> Po Chü-i appeal alike to the illiterate and the erudite. Yet such
> untreatable, congenital writers are, in the end, a small minority. As for
> most writers, to speak frankly, there is little love for literature and little
> excellence. They get into the literary profession the way girls from good

families in the old novels got into prostitution: it was said that it was against their will, and there was just nothing to be done about it. Had they but the opportunity that would permit them to leap from the fiery pit, there is not one of these potential geniuses who would not throw out his books and abandon his pen, reform and cleave to virtue. Literature is a thankless, luckless profession, the least remunerative, verging on penury, bringing disease in its wake. . . . All men of learning are filled with a sense of their importance and prestige. They are self-satisfied, heaping praise on the special discipline they study with 120 percent conviction. Only writers are filled with self-doubts, make placating smiles, and feel endless shame. Even if they happen to run off at the mouth about patriotic literature, the weapon of propaganda, and so on, it's like beating on a water-logged drum; there's just no resonance to it.[42]

Much too skeptical to embrace a conventional belief in God or a benevolent controlling force in nature, Ch'ien nevertheless took considerable interest in the comparisons made by others between mysticism and poetry. In his study *T'an i lu* (On the Art of Poetry), Ch'ien discusses at great length the compatibility of views on poetry by the twentieth-century Roman Catholic critic Abbé Bremond and the Sung critic Yen Yü, the former arguing the notion of the annihilation of the self as common to both the poetic and mystical experience as a Roman Catholic, and the latter arguing the same as a Zen Buddhist.[43] Ch'ien expands the discussion to include related concepts of self and mystic self-annihilation in various cultures at various times to show that there is nothing exclusive about these notions, nor are they necessarily mystical in reality. In fact, he has stated earlier in the book that Yen Yü was wrong to equate Ch'an thought with poetry and that his *Ts'ang-lang shih-hua* (Poetry Talks of T'sang-lang) is superficial.[44] Nor does Ch'ien concede that Bremond's views on the actual existence of mystical experience are realistic. He does, however, agree that many forms of human activity, including poetry, provide the sense of a transcendent experience.[45]

Ch'ien's own views on notions of a God are rendered in a parody of Genesis titled "Shang-ti ti meng" (God's Dream), which, as C. T. Hsia has noted, has the appearance of a "flippant" piece,[46] a clever and amusing satire of vanity, and is perhaps questionable as a serious contribution to literature. Oddly Western in its parody of God as the ultimate product of the twentieth-century obsession with progress, the fable does offer one statement of particular relevance to Ch'ien's more important works. Although Adam and Eve are originally created by God to flatter his vanity by bowing at his feet and chanting, "True Lord, omniscient and omnipotent, we shall praise you ceaselessly," God soon grows annoyed at their attempts to play on his vanity to serve their own ends. He creates wild animals to frighten them back into cringing, submissive respect, but finds that the humans are able to subdue or vanquish these animals and turn them to their own uses. The fable implies, then, that even ideals are a product of vanity, and that even God cannot control his creation. Ch'ien's vision of nature is thus far from an optimistic belief in a benevolent and rational order. It is a dream submitted to a process of chaos and dissolution.

That the world created by a writer's fancy is equally subject to these forces is granted in the phrase "literature must perish," and becomes the basis for another fantasy tale, "Ling-kan" (Inspiration). In this story a renowned Chinese author who has "killed" so many of his characters by his lifeless, hackneyed representations of them in his work dies when he turns to writing his own autobiography. Both the author and his characters represent a composite portrait of much modern Chinese literature, and Ch'ien showed frequently that he was more than willing to side with his vision of nature and participate in the process of tearing down the literary scene of the previous decade. Ch'ien's satire of modern Chinese literature could be broad in scope. In "Inspiration" he observes:

> In foreign countries the market is determined according to the tastes of the middle class. But we Chinese, as befits a nation with an ancient literary heritage, do not speak about the material side so much, rather taking the mental level and erudition of middle-school students as the standard for a work.[47]

Ch'ien could also be specific. In "Cat" Ch'ien creates a social gathering of Peking's cultural elite in the 1930s, and one by one introduces well-known writers and scholars through his irreverent gaze, including Lin Yü-t'ang (Yuan Yu-ch'un), Chou Tso-jen (Lu Po-lin), Shen Ts'ung-wen (Ts'ao Shih-ch'ang), and Chu Kuang-ch'ien (Fu Chü-ch'ing).[48] But Ch'ien's lampoons were not supplemented by serious literary criticism of modern Chinese literature, and his real contribution, in a positive sense, lay in his own fiction when it turned to psychological realism.

Ch'ien's fictional world is as de-idealized as his essays are irreverent. The story "Cat," with its lampoon of the 1930s literary scene combined with a realistic depiction of a feuding couple futilely jockeying for recognition in Peking society, represents both these modes. But the ironies within the tale, discussed by C. T. Hsia in his *A History of Modern Chinese Fiction,* are supplemented by the implicit view that the society in "Cat" was, in any case, on the verge of being destroyed by the war, and the poses and pretensions of its characters overwhelmed by time and fate. At the end of the story the socialite Li Ai-mo is ready to give up her tiresome occupation: "She only wanted to escape to a place where she could forget her pride, avoid her present friends, and afford to neglect her appearance and social style. A place where she wouldn't have to look beautiful and young for anybody."[49] As if to pick up the thread of that wish in counterpoint, Ch'ien turned away from fantasy and the cultured scene to write his most substantial piece of realism in short form, "Chi-nien" (Souvenir).

"Souvenir" is primarily the portrait of a young woman, Man-ch'ien, who married a plain, unaffected young man, Ts'ai-shu, against her parents' will:

> The mother blamed the father; the father scolded the daughter and then blamed the mother. Then both father and mother railed against Ts'ai-shu. Then, together, they admonished the girl. Ts'ai-shu's family was poor, they said. There was no hope for his future. Man-ch'ien shed a few tears, but her tears only made her more determined—if the rope gets wet, it tightens.[50]

Once married, Man-ch'ien's sense of victory is short-lived. Ts'ai-shu, a civil servant, is posted to a crude town in the interior periodically attacked by Japanese planes. Not only are refinement and luxury eliminated for the moment, but hopes for social status and its vanities are also dimmed. Ts'ai-shu's easygoing nature, in which Man-ch'ien had found so much comfort and from which she had drawn vanity, now appears as a lack of ambition: "He could only spend the rest of his life peacefully grinding away at his desk" (p. 127).

At this point it might be noted that Ts'ai-shu, dull and unheroic as he is, still is one of Ch'ien's more positive characters. His love for Man-ch'ien is an outgrowth of a long and steady affection, not a whirlwind of passion. Ts'ai-shu pretends to himself that he is content with the dreariness of the town while others have fretted over renovating its dilapidated villas. The walls that surround these villas formerly were a particular object of vanity, each household covering them with a coat of whitewash. Yet, though Ts'ai-shu's contentment is only a pretense, the other residents do discover to their horror that Japanese planes have taken to using their bright walls as markers for bombing targets and hastily set about stripping the walls. Later, when a mass meeting is held to honor Ts'ai-shu's close friend T'ien-chien, an air force pilot killed defending the town, Ts'ai-shu refuses the requests of officials to make a speech: "Ts'ai-shu was unwilling to use the dead man to expose his own feelings, or to put on an emotional display to publicize his grief. And this dignity of spirit greatly increased Man-ch'ien's respect for him." (p. 153). Finally, despite the irony that his wife has cuckolded him and, unknown to him, is carrying his dead friend's baby, he is portrayed gazing on his "wife's back which had not yet lost its slim outline, his eyes filled with boundless tenderness and concern" (p. 155). And this image seems stronger than the irony implicit within it. But, precisely because Man-ch'ien has difficulty in accepting these qualities, the story is hers, for Ch'ien is a writer fascinated by the blindness and complexity of human vanity, by its unceasing attempts to weave a haven for its fantasies in a physical reality that can only be the destroyer of those fantasies.

The shabby clay wall surrounding their house becomes a focus of Man-ch'ien's dislike of the physical world to which she has committed her dreams. The wall has now become a prison shutting her off from them. "I'm old and ugly and nothing more than your housekeeper," she cries when Ts'ai-shu announces that his cousin T'ien-chien has arrived in town with the air force detachment and is eager to admire the proof of Man-ch'ien's reputation as a beauty. But Man-ch'ien's self-degrading statement is an act of concealment, followed by many others. As the house must be drearily camouflaged to protect it from destruction, so she camouflages her dreariness with makeup and her best clothes to attract T'ien-chien.

Although Man-ch'ien desires to attract T'ien-chien rather than to sleep with him, the basis for her hopes is in arousing his physical desire. As their secret relationship develops, they slight each other to arouse a taste for intimacy, even bringing each other to the point of despair so that they may pose as the fulfillment of each other's hopes. This is portrayed in all its artificiality, as both lovers in their own ways seek to master this small arena of the physical world and make it seem to hold out hope for them. Their assumptions are sadly leveled. The child T'ien-chien carelessly and unknowingly gives her crushes her fantasies of mastery and hope as surely as T'ien-chien is shot down in his fighter plane: "He who had played out his life in the sky now rested beneath the ground" (p. 154). That the child is a symbol of Man-ch'ien's mortality is pointed enough. When Ts'ai-shu, with no idea that an affair has occurred, suggests that they name the baby after T'ien-chien, Man-ch'ien struggles to suppress the truth as well as hide it in a symbolic gesture of escape:

> Man-ch'ien didn't know what she was looking for. She walked to the window and opened a desk drawer. As she bent her head to rummage, she replied at the same time, "I couldn't. Did you see 'the mother ship of the air force' at the memorial ceremony? Greeting everyone with that teary-eyed, 'oh, so dignified' look, dressed up to look just like T'ien-chien's widow! T'ien-chien was a man, you know what I mean. Those two weren't just casual friends. Who knows if she hasn't preserved T'ien-chien's seed for him? Let her give birth to a son to commemorate T'ien-chien. I don't want mine to. And what's more, I can't love my child. I didn't want him." (p. 154)

The knowledge that she is caught irrevocably in the destructive force of the physical world is something she cannot acknowledge. Earlier in the story, this is portrayed in an air raid scene:

> Like many people, Man-ch'ien was oddly convinced that, while others could be killed by bombs, she herself couldn't die in that fashion. Often Ts'ai-shu quoted his wife's witty epigram to his friends: "As for getting hit by a bomb in an air raid, it's about as difficult as winning first prize in an air force lottery contest."
> After a while the second alarm sounded. The distant, listless sound of the siren was like a great, metallic voice, sighing into the vast sky.

Listening to the surrounding silence, the two of them became afraid. What had been an indifference to making a move now was fear of making a move. Man-ch'ien alone in the courtyard held her breath, watching the enemy planes penetrate the sky above the town. As though with an attitude of contempt, they made passes at the anti-aircraft guns, which seemed to stammer back in ineffectual response, as though unable to get their meaning across to the heavens. Then, too, it seemed a hacking cough that could force up no phlegm. Weakness suddenly permeated her body, and, no longer daring to stand and watch, she ran back into the bedroom. . . . The entire sky was dumped into her brain, the sounds of anti-aircraft fire and bombs tumbling from the wombs of planes, their bursting reverberating through her head. There was no way to shake them off. (p. 153)

The scene repeats the theme that there is no sanctuary from the destructiveness of existence except in the vain imagination of one. Ch'ien's characters are always in need of such sustaining myths, and they are inevitably confronted with destruction:

The spring before the enemy planes had bombed this place for the first time, destroying a few homes, and, as usual, killing a few peasants who were hardly worth the bombs. But this greatly unnerved residents, the high and the lowly. And even aborigines innocent of modern education also realized that bombs falling from aircraft were indeed not eggs dropped by a great chicken in the sky. After this, they didn't dare, upon hearing the siren, mill about in the streets, looking up and clapping their hands. (p. 129)

It is a very different sort of person from aborigines who, in *Wei ch'eng* (The Besieged City) ponders his latest exposure to life: "Now he *knew* that that great expanse of sky was not the residence of god in heaven; it merely offered bombs and convenience for smugglers."[51]

In *The Besieged City,* as in Ch'ien's short stories, nature and society are exclusive forces in the literal sense that they function inexorably to reject characters, to cut them off from their ambitions, to erode the tenuous positions they have established, to isolate them from their fellows. The essential ingredient in the satire is that the characters act as willing dupes. As C. T. Hsia has pointed out, the scurrilous professor Li Mei-t'ing is an obvious type, a purely satirical creation, but one that will be discussed here as offering obvious examples of the ways in which the characters of the novel as a whole behave. Nearly midway through the novel, the hero, Fang Hung-chien, together with four other college teachers, including Li Mei-t'ing and Hung-chien's future wife, the teaching assistant Sun Jou-chia, are making their journey from Shanghai to a wartime university in the interior:

> The journey that day was from Ningpo to Ch'i-k'ou, first by boat, afterward switching to rickshaws. When they had boarded the boat, the sky let fall a light rain, every so often one or two drops, as if they did not fall from the sky above their heads. You looked intently at the mist and it was not there. Shortly, a fine, misty rain fell, yet it still did not seem to be raining, but rather, as though many small droplets were playing mischievously in midair, tiring themselves out with their rapid darting about until, as circumstance would have it, they fell to the ground. Hung-chien and the others crowded and pushed to the front of the boat to guard the baggage, rummaging about to pull out and put on rain gear. The exception was Mr. Li. He held that the rain was slight, and it wasn't worth opening the suitcases to take out the rain gear. The rain continued, increasing, the drops strung like silk threads. It looked as if the surface of the water had been stricken with smallpox, as raindrops imprinted it with innumerable pockmarks. Now swelling, now fading, without pause, the streaming shower grew denser, looking as though the smooth surface of the water were growing a coat of fur.
>
> Mr. Li had cherished his newly bought raincoat and had been reluctant to wear it on the trip. Now he grumbled about his lack of foresight since, after all, it shouldn't have been put away in the bottom of the trunk. If he opened the trunk at this point, all the clothes would get soaked. Miss Sun tactfully mentioned that she had a rainhood, and so could loan him the small green silk umbrella she was holding. The umbrella was originally intended for overcast days, but Miss Sun had used it as a parasol, and fearing that its struts would be broken if it were packed with the luggage, she normally carried it about. After the boat docked Mr. Li entered a teahouse and closed the umbrella. Everyone stepped back in astonishment, then burst out laughing. The rain had caused the green dye to run. Mr. Li's yellow face had turned green. Then too, the green dye had spread down the front of his white shirt, like an unfinished draft of a watercolor. Miss Sun blushed and stammered apologies. (pp. 142–43)

As one of several delightful, self-contained episodes in the novel, this scene is not vital to plot or characterization. However, its construction follows the pace and theme of the work. The lightly humorous vision of nature and man gives way to a hint of powerful forces that yet seem innocuous. But the steady, grinding build of the rain grows ever deeper, more confusing and alarming, like the experiences of Fang Hung-chien in the course of the novel. Suddenly the image of disease appears in one of Ch'ien's many similes, carrying the theme of destructiveness. Then the borrowed, flimsy umbrella makes its appearance, seemingly a shield against the elements, as Hung-chien's diploma and then Sun Jou-chia herself seem like guarantees to Hung-chien. But, like the inadequate pretenses in the lives of the characters, it dyes the bearer in a grotesque mockery of his pretensions.

In this passage Li Mei-t'ing's behavior is that of one who disbelieves the intent of his environment and its inexorable force. This attitude has its analogues in Hung-chien's life, as mentioned above, and is pointedly described when, during his courtship of T'ang Hsiao-fu, Hung-chien takes an empty delight in imagining himself part of a benevolent scheme as he listens to the seemingly carefree calls of birds in spring (see p. 43). This attitude has its analogue as well in Hung-chien's family and their neighbors, who are at first unconcerned that war may break out and later incredulous that it might ever come to their doorsteps (see pp. 32, 36). Hung-chien draws a false sense of encouragement from their contented vision of the future.

The desire to capitalize on the exclusive forces of society and nature is also exemplified by Li Mei-t'ing in his attempts to smuggle drugs into the interior to sell later at inflated prices. When Sun Jou-chia falls ill, rather than break the seal on a container of effective medicine, Li simply offers cod-liver pills from a packet he has already opened for himself to supplement the poor diet from which the group has suffered (see p. 180). Hung-chien is by no means such a callous figure, but in a subtler way he too has capitalized on suffering and death by writing a rather hypocritical letter of condolence to the Chou family on the death of their daughter, to whom Hung-chien was most unwillingly engaged. In return, Hung-chien has been provided with funds to study overseas and uses the money to enjoy himself and purchase a diploma. Hung-chien has never intended, like Li, to capitalize on others, but as a moral coward he accepts opportunities to do so without fulfilling obligations or satisfying his conscience. There are other analogues as well. On his return to China from his studies in Europe, Hung-chien is pursued by the refined Su Wen-wan, a beauty who has obtained a genuine degree in France and is surrounded by a coterie of intellectuals on her return. But with the coming of war she takes to smuggling luxury items from Hong Kong to the interior. It is this display of profiteering that moves Hung-chien to the realization that the heavens offer only bombs and conveniences for smugglers. Hung-chien's friend Chao Hsin-mei tells him that he can be most useful as a teacher by flunking out pretty girls, the sooner to make them available for courtship. And, as always, Ch'ien finds a place for writers in this theme:

> Writers are happiest when others die: It gives them a topic for an elegiac essay. Coffin shops and funeral parlors can only make a living off those newly deceased. The man of letters lives off those dead for a year, several years, several decades, or even several centuries. A commemoration of the first anniversary and an elegy on the three hundredth are both equally good topics. (p. 223)

Li Mei-t'ing arrives at the university only to find that the chairmanship he expected has been seized by another professor. Li then attempts to regain power and prestige by acting as the official moral watchdog of the university to ensure that all behavior and activities conform to the demands of patriotism in a time of national emergency. In this way Li plays his third and final role, exemplifying the desire to imitate the exclusive forces of nature and society in the guise of morality. Among those he threatens with his ethical knife are Hung-chien and Jou-chia. As Hung-chien is feeling increasingly isolated in faculty politics, he allows himself to be drawn into the net Jou-chia is spreading for him. Li Mei-t'ing forces the issue in his role of safeguarding ethics when Jou-chia is making one of her periodic visits to Hung-chien. She is talking to Hung-chien about one of Li's allies:

> "I don't know what creep did it—I suspect Lu Tzu-hsiao—sent an anonymous note to my father—to spread a rumor about you and me. Father wrote back to ask—"
> Hung-chien listened. It seemed as though heaven and earth were caving in. Simultaneously he heard people calling out behind his back, "Mr. Fang! Mr. Fang!" Turning, he saw that it was Li Mei-t'ing and Lu Tzu-hsiao briskly walking over to join them. Miss Sun gave a peep, like the sound of an ambulance siren reduced a thousandfold, and reached out, grabbing Hung-chien's right arm as though pleading for protection.

Hung-chien was aware that Li and Lu were gazing at him. Finished, done for, he thought. In any case, the rumor has gotton around even to the Sun family. Let it.

Lu Tzu-hsiao looked fixedly at Miss Sun, though still trying to get his wind back. Li Mei-t'ing chuckled craftily, "You must be having a very cozy conversation. I called several times but you didn't hear. I want to ask you, when did Hsin-mei leave—Oh, Miss Sun, my apologies for interrupting your lovers' chat."

Hung-chien, reckless of all consequences, said, "Since you knew it was a lovers' chat, you shouldn't have interrupted."

Li said, "Ah, you really are setting a precedent. Walk in broad daylight, holding hands. Give the students a good example."

Hung-chien replied, "We haven't managed to follow the dean's example of dallying among flowers and willows [hanging out with prostitutes]."

Li Mei-t'ing's face went white. Feeling the sting of the sarcasm, he turned the direction of the conversation, saying, "You enjoy jokes so much. Let's not change the topic—seriously, when do you plan to invite us to the wedding?"

Miss Sun hesitantly added, "When the time comes we"ll not forget to invite you, Mr. Li—"

Li Mei-t'ing cried out; Lu Tzu-hsiao rasped, "Tell us what? Engagement? Yes or no?"

Miss Sun held on to Hung-chien's arm harder, not answering. The two inquisitors cried, "Congratulations! Miss Sun, has he proposed today? Time to treat us!" They forced handshakes and teased them with many pleasantries.

Hung-chien, as though in a cloud, lost his self-control, giving them total freedom to shake hands and pat shoulders and promising to treat them. It was only then that the two made a move to leave. When they were far enough away Miss Sun apologized: "When I saw those two I panicked. I didn't know how to get out of it. Please, Mr. Fang, forgive me—what we said just now, I know it isn't true."

Hung-chien, mind and body, suddenly felt exhausted. He didn't have the spirit left to cope with the situation. Taking her hand, he said, "You can believe everything I said. Probably, it's what I wanted."

Miss Sun didn't make a sound. After a while she said, "I hope you don't regret it," and raised her head as though waiting for a kiss. But he forgot to kiss her. He only said, "I hope you don't regret it." (pp. 264–65)

Here Hung-chien, feeling a sense of isolation, has allowed Li Mei-t'ing and his friend to force him into a compromise with the threat of moral sanctions and ostracism, and the theme of exclusion is again implied. Yet Hung-chien's employment at the university in the first place stemmed from an analogous situation. For Hung-chien was hired based on the glowing recommendation of Chao Hsin-mei, who is really looking for a way to get Hung-chien out of Shanghai and eliminate him as a rival for the hand of Su Wen-wan. Once at the university, Hung-chien also practices this game. While he himself holds a fraudulent diploma, his contribution to faculty politics is to inform on a fellow "alumnus" from the same nonexistent school, Professor Han Hsüeh-yü. Later, Hung-chien quits a job as a journalist for a Shanghai newspaper to protest its being taken over by Japanese collaborators. Hung-chien's act is a moral one in itself, but one that serves egotistical face-saving at the expense of reality, as will be noted below. In all these episodes, ethical values are invoked by the various characters for morally ambiguous acts of exclusion.

In Hung-chien's gray existence there are characters who embody positive values, and Hung-chien is attracted to them. But even they have their vanity and do not escape satire. Most notable is T'ang Hsiao-fu, the "genuine" young woman whom Hung-chien courts behind Su Wen-wan's back. When Su vengefully gossips to Hsiao-fu, she delivers an acid scolding to Hung-chien, who retires in great contrition. Attempting to repair the damage to their relationship, Hsiao-fu calls Hung-chien's home, but the servant who answers assumes it is Su Wen-wan calling. When Hung-chien picks up the phone he rashly lashes out with curses intended for Su Wen-wan, and Hsiao-fu faints under the withering blast. Later, however, she realizes that Hung-chien thought he was speaking to Su, but at this point vanity triumphs. She prefers the pose of the wronged lover to another effort to restore their relationship. Another positive character is Mr. Wang, the editor in chief of the newspaper Hung-chien works for in the Shanghai International Settlement after his return from the interior. When the paper is taken over by Japanese collaborators, Wang at first cautions Hung-chien and others not to follow his example and rashly quit their jobs with him. But Wang really derives too much satisfaction from Hung-chien's following his example to protest too much:

Mr. Wang was a man of integrity, forced to leave for the sake of a just cause. He enjoyed going out in a way that stirred up things a little, to lessen the dismalness of resigning. He was unwilling to go down alone as though eloping. He had been around many years and understood that in any organization a person could always be replaced, that there were always others to fill the places. To quit in a huff just meant hardship for the person who quit. (p. 133)

In quitting the newspaper with Wang, Hung-chien is guided by a desire for "face," and in reviewing Hung-chien's actions during the course of the novel, one sees how dominant is his concern with face, and how much of the novel is devoted to a satire of this form of vanity. It is, after all, the most manifest form of the desire to be accepted, to be included, on terms that answer to the individual's vanity. The passages quoted above all reveal the concern with face, and could be supplemented by many others. In the beginning of the novel, Hung-chien is concerned lest he be rejected by other students on board the steamer for taking a second-class cabin over their third-class ones. He is mortified to see how ungainly Miss Pao's fiancé is after she lured him into an affair by comparing his looks to her fiancé's. He belittles the worth of an overseas academic degree to T'ang Hsiao-fu, implying that he has aspired to greater things. His thoughts as he vomits at a party designed to humiliate him in front of Su Wen-wan are that he is glad Hsiao-fu is not there for his "great loss of face." He is indifferent to teaching itself, seeing it rather as a hopeful step to a more prestigious official position. When, at a dangerous bridge in the interior, Jou-chia leads the way across for him, he saves face by pretending he was guarding her from behind. It is but one of many episodes the author creates at his expense, and the journey concludes with Hsin-mei cheerfully telling him he is "useless." No sooner has he arrived at the university than he discovers he has been demoted in rank and given only one course—in ethics. Later he temporarily gains ground as an English instructor, only to learn how faulty his English is. He is too proud to court Miss Liu, the daughter of a superior, and this paves the way for his dismissal, an event rendered easier to bear when a few students unexpectedly call on him to say goodbye. Returning to Hong Kong with Jou-chia, he decides on a quick marriage for fear that she is already pregnant, and envies the success of his old friends. His various acts to save face once back in Shanghai culminate with his resigning his job on the newspaper, while refusing to accept the humiliation of being employed by one of Jou-chia's relations.

His fear of isolation and his sensitivity to it begin early in the novel, and the scenes expressing his isolation build slowly until, upon his departure from the university, they fill the final chapters. As he prepares to leave the university, he feels how unendurable the trip would be without Jou-chia's company. The narrative observes:

> To leave a place is like suffering death; you know you have to die but you still hope to see people express the desire that you live on. You are very much concerned about the good or bad name you leave behind in a place, just as about your posthumous reputation, but you have no means of knowing and you are deeply afraid that after your departure, as after your death, you leave behind only a bad odor, such as the candle gives after its flame is snuffed out.[52]

In Hong Kong, Hung-chien has a reunion with Chao Hsin-mei that begins as a revelation of Jou-chia's cunning, but turns to point to the theme of isolation. Chao Hsin-mei observes:

> "Didn't I tell you that Miss Sun thinks ahead? As for your getting together this time, the way I see it as a third party, she must have planned hard."
>
> Way down in Hung-chien's consciousness a hazy thought that had been sound asleep was rudely awakened by Hsin-mei's words.
>
> "That's not right. That's not right. I'm already drunk and was talking nonsense. Hung-chien, don't tell your wife what I said. I'm really thoughtless, forgetting that who you are now isn't who you were in the past. Afterward, there must be a boundary drawn in talks between old friends." And as he said this he took the knife in his hand and sliced the air an inch or so above the table.
>
> Hung-chien said, "The way you talk about marriage is really frightening, as though people all turn their backs on each other because of it."[53]

Indeed, Hung-chien's marriage is seen as a threat by the sisters-in-law in his family household, and they, together with his conservative parents, make life unpleasant for Jou-chia. Jou-chia, far from meek and admiring, puts the pressure back on Hung-chien, only increasing his sense of isolation. The final scenes of his arguments with Jou-chia include images of broken objects to underscore separation and the destruction of their bond. As Hung-chien walks in the street, he sees an old peddler and compares himself with the primitive toys in the peddler's basket: "Hung-chien thought that nowadays children in the cities wouldn't care for these primitive toys, since they could have their pick of nice foreign-made ones; this old man didn't know how to do business. Suddenly in his mind he linked himself with the toys in the basket; he was not wanted in a time like this; that's why he had difficulty in getting jobs."[54] Jou-chia dislikes Hung-chien's more conservative attitudes and teases him by comparing his face to that of an old, broken-down clock given them by his father. Later, when she has walked out on him and Hung-chien has drifted into sleep, the clock reappears: "This timepiece, which lagged behind in time, contained an unintended irony toward, and disappointment with, humanity which was more profound than any language, than any tears or laughter."[55] The clock, itself overtaken by time, presides over Hung-chien as he is lost to sleep, with its implication of the ultimate isolation of death: "His sleep became so sound that it could no longer be nipped, without dreams and without sensations, humanity's primordial sleep, and also a sample of death."[56]

Hung-chien, in fact, does not lack for rescuers, or would-be rescuers. As the novel closes, he looks forward to Chao Hsin-mei to give him a new start in the interior. Chao is but the last of a series of characters who restore the hero. Following his affair with Hsiao-fu, Hung-chien is in despair:

> His own individual world was suddenly cut off from the world of others, as though he were a solitary ghost in the land of the living. There was no way to slip into the joyous life he saw about him. The sun of this bright land was still visible, but he no longer basked in its warmth. The world of others he could not enter, and into his world, anyone could. The first who would not be hindered was Mrs. Chou. All relatives of the older generation are unwilling to let the young conceal their secrets from them. To coax their secrets out of them, to force them to admit them, is an obligatory responsibility of elder relatives.[57]

Hung-chien is thus restored, and is so repeatedly, but it is to a world intent on his ultimate destruction, and therefore to be included in any part of it can be no more satisfying than to feel excluded. This is the intent of the motif, stated in the passage quoted above, and also at a party during a discussion of a French saying about the *forteresse assiegé*: "People outside the fortress want to rush in and people inside want to get out."[58] Throughout the novel, Hung-chien is attempting to enter a situation, only to discover upon entering that he has not found sanctuary from isolation. As Ch'ien observes, in the manner of a donkey led on forever by the sight of a carrot forever dangling beyond his nose, so Hung-chien is led on by promises, promises that others cannot keep or have no intention of keeping.

Given Ch'ien Chung-shu's pessimistic theme, *The Besieged City* ultimately has more affinity with British fiction than Chinese literature. Ch'ien once remarked: "The Chinese satirists glide off the surface and never probe into the essential rottenness of human nature. They accept the traditional values, social and moral, believe in the innate goodness of man, and poke gentle fun at what they regard as unfortunate backsliding from probity and decorum."[59] So Ch'ien believed, and even in the context of the caustic literature of modern China, no writer approached Ch'ien's determination to attack inflated or optimistic notions of human nature.

This is not to say that no elements in Ch'ien's fiction draw on Chinese motifs.[60] Nor did Ch'ien incorporate wholesale standard motifs in Western satire. For example, Ch'ien's imagery is notably free, at least in *The Besieged City,* from violent, nightmarish settings, the "demonic imagery" outlined by Northrop Frye and used in modern British satire.[61] Yet Ch'ien employs images in a manner characteristic of twentieth-century Western literature in its skepticism of civilization. In *The Besieged City* there are boats, trains, planes, and cities, but these emblems of civilization and progress do not betoken salvation for the human condition. The protagonist falls prey to predatory women on boats, is crushed in trains, gets sick on a plane, and despises the cold impersonality of the city. Moreover, no matter what mode of transport is used to what city, the destination, in psychological terms, remains the same. The intensity of his condition only increases.

The Besieged City also opens with picaresque potential, but soon turns darker. Hung-chien may at first appear the picaroon who, by fraud, has abandoned his modest, Neo-Confucian home for the academic citadels of Europe and begun his climb up the social ladder, weaving his way through the snares of love and marriage through one decadent episode after another. But that Hung-chien bears some resemblance to a picaroon is less important than the modern treatment of the dilemma of his fraud. Hung-chien, while again and again restored to hope with the luck of the traditional picaroon, is yet an isolated and tortured outsider, a product of the twentieth century. As he recalls T'ang Hsiao-fu toward the end of the novel, Hung-chien ponders the transience of his feelings, the marker of the self, and the disappearance of even the deepest ones.

> The reason was that the self that had loved her a year before was long dead. The several selves that had loved her, feared Su Wen-wan, and succumbed to Miss Pao's wiles had all died one by one. There were several dead selves buried in his memory, the tombstones erected and inscribed to serve once in a while to evoke the past, such as his feelings toward T'ang Hsiao-fu. There were several selves which, as though they had died on the road, he would not bother with, but let rot and decay to be eaten by birds and beasts—but never to be eliminated, such as the self who bought the diploma from an Irishman.[62]

Unlike the picaroon who thrives on his fraud, Hung-chien is haunted by the meaning of his. Nor is he a rake, in whose progress and decline the reader may take delight from a comfortable moral distance.

Although Ch'ien Chung-shu was only occasionally given to quoting modern British authors, there is no doubt that he read them, Waugh and Aldous Huxley, as well as D. H. Lawrence, T. S. Eliot, and other major and minor literary figures. As early as 1932 he cited Huxley's *Brave New World* in a book review.[63] In the mid-thirties he studied at Oxford where, "unwilling to devote himself to mundane academic pursuits, he spent an inordinate amount of time on popular fiction and drama, feasting omnivorously on D. H. Lawrence, Aldous Huxley, Francis Brett Young, and even Agatha Christie's detective stories."[64] During the war a friend recalled Ch'ien's enthusiasm for Huxley's *Point Counterpoint*.[65] Ch'ien's work, as distinctive and individual as it is, appears to have absorbed in particular the art of Waugh and Huxley. Like them, he created an isolated antihero in the framework of traditional satire. The plot is used only to intensify the hero's condition, not to liberate him, and his character is not allowed to develop to a higher plane of awareness. The protagonist is essentially a dupe of uncontrollable forces, yet his suffering is as much self-inflicted as socially inflicted. And, like Waugh and Huxley, Ch'ien focused on the faults of the educated elite in a disintegrating society. Brief comparisons of works by Waugh and Huxley with Ch'ien's *The Besieged City* suggests their influence.

Readers of *The Besieged City,* as C. T. Hsia has suggested, may be reminded in many ways of the adventures of Paul Pennyfeather in Waugh's *Decline and Fall.* Pennyfeather is, like Ch'ien's character Hung-chien, a man who "doesn't know how to do business"; who is ill-suited to deal with the fast, deceitful world around him. Pennyfeather and Hung-chien are both driven early from their aspirations on charges of "indecent behavior." In Pennyfeather's case, it is Oxford's sheltering setting, and in Hung-chien's it is his courtship of T'ang Hsiao-fu. Each protagonist then takes a journey to the uncouth interior of their respective lands and takes a post at an unsavory teaching institution. Pennyfeather teaches at the infamous Llannabba Academy in Wales, controlling his class of rowdies by offering a crown to the student who can complete the longest in-class essay, regardless of quality. Hung-chien's destination is San-lü University, the name being an allusion to Ch'ü Yuan, who went to a watery grave after losing in court politics. Hung-chien cultivates the art of stretching his scanty lecture material to a full class period. Each protagonist avoids one woman to be snared by another and suffer unpleasant consequences. In Pennyfeather's case, it is the owner of a chain of South American brothels. Pennyfeather is unjustly imprisoned for his fiancée's activities, but she later secures his release. He returns to Oxford and a mild, shadowy existence, having been certified legally dead, an action that deliberately suggests his survival in the world is at the expense of his identity. Hung-chien moves from one psychological prison to another, always seemingly to be rescued, but slowly vanishing as a person-death before him, death behind him, and only the fraudulent diploma as a marker of who he is.

Both Waugh and Ch'ien also delight in depicting the outrageous and absurd poses of a full gallery of minor characters. However, Ch'ien does not follow Waugh in creating situations that are patently fantastic. Ch'ien is much more concerned with the absurdities of situations that more closely resemble everyday realities. Moreover, while a Paul Pennyfeather is totally uncalculating, Hung-chien is a calculating type, albeit an inept one devoid of malice. The fact that Penneyfeather is quite innocent and Hung-chien is not so innocent is an important difference. Finally, Waugh never allows his characters dimensions that might lead them to a genuine sense of anguish, or any psychological depth. Ch'ien is very concerned with the psychology of his protagonist; so was Huxley.

True, the structure of Ch'ien's novel is not imitative of Huxley's earlier experiments. And although Ch'ien's novel is sustained in great part by the intrusive wit of the narrator, Huxley's is sustained as much by the intrusive play of a plethora of ideas. In *Antic Hay*, even the gentleman's tailor who appears in a single scene is memorable for his cynical ideas: all advertisements for freedom, all avenues of escape, are but paths to new slavery. But thereby hangs not only the theme of *Antic Hay*, but in very real part much of the connection between the work of Huxley and Ch'ien. In *Antic Hay*, British society is floundering in the wake of World War I; the destruction of old ideas and romantic ideals leaves people unable to face thought, emotion, or reality, unable to assert dreams or dignity. It is "Nil" that hangs over the lives of the characters: a logical positivist who flees from emotion only by embracing fatigue; an artist moved to suicide over his impotence to express outmoded ideals; an architect who dreams of putting London under a dome but builds houses advertised as "retreats" from society; a writer who can define himself only by a decadent defiance of good; and so forth. The plight of this cross section of British intelligensia is primarily seen in Gumbril Junior, a young teacher filled with a sense of the futility of his role as a teacher for a British public school. He turns to marketing his invention of cushioned trousers, an inflatable pocket of air that symbolizes the characters' padding themselves from reality. His listlessness he conceals behind a padded coat and beard that transform him into an image of the "complete man." To this he adds a claim that he is an artist and writer, and thereby attracts several women. But the sincere, frigid woman whom he endeavors gently to win over is lost in his inability to displease the emotionally frigid Myra Viveash, who sustains herself with an endless round of titillations. Vowing to escape from the loss of one woman and the clutches of another, and from the great Nil, Gumbril at the close of the novel plans to go to Europe.

Antic Hay and *The Besieged City* share much the same views of the human condition, whether expressed by a London tailor who believes that all liberation movements end in new forms of slavery or by a Chinese Anglophile intellectual recalling the theme of the *forteresse assiegée*. And these views are worked out in similar motifs. The inevitable differences between the characters of Hung-chien and Gumbril Junior are outweighed by their similarities. Each is compelled by his nature to inflate himself through fraud, and the pursuit of fulfillment through love based on their fraudulent images leads only to further compromise and entrapment in the emptiness they sought to escape. Their lives become a series of escape attempts, and they are each last seen planning another attempt, as the Nil threatens to overcome them both, like a "taste of death." The wars and societies that each novel takes for its background are different, but each novel frames its portrait of human nature in settings of decay and destruction. And in each the authors have selected a mediocre man to parade his pathetic pretenses and suffer estrangement and isolation. Ch'ien propels the reader through much of *The Besieged City* on his wit. Yet, when he drops this mode of irony, as when Huxley's characters can no longer sustain the babble of their ideas, the deflation is a long sigh of empathy and dismay, profound and abiding.

In comparing the antiromantic Chinese writers of the occupation period to post-World War I British writers, the former could be distinguished from the latter as *un*illusioned rather than *dis*illusioned. For both, war had intervened, and from their experiences they each rejected rather than affirmed or continued the work of preceding decades. The Chinese antiromantics had no monopoly on pessimism, but they did not focus that pessimism on specific sociopolitical issues, and they drew from a number of British writers who were equally intent on capturing an image of existence beyond immediate social and political phenomena. No one would want each of these Chinese writers individually to be labeled simply for what he or she rejected. But in the context of their time, as a group their work was a form of antiromanticism: unreforming and de-idealized; the emotions of characters viewed ironically rather than exploited for themselves; transcendence either a dream or a work of art, but not a reality.

CHAPTER SIX

Conclusions

Unlike Mao Tse-tung in his land-
mark directives to writers in Yenan during 1942, the Japanese
authorities and the Chinese regimes under their sponsorship worked
no radical changes on the whole of Chinese literature in the areas
they occupied. Their varied but limited attempts to experiment with
literature as a medium for political propaganda coexisted with rather
than ruled literary expression as a private or individual enterprise. If
they suppressed, in the main, a literature of resistance, the literature
that developed under their censorship was largely one of variation on
and response to Chinese literature of previous decades. Hence, the
importance of the literature of the occupation lies in the development of
trends by and large evident since before the outbreak of the war in
1937.

The Sino-Japanese War of 1937–1945 and the occupation under
Japanese authority were extensions of the conditions of a divided
nation threatened by foreign aggression and domination that had
been developing for decades, rather than sudden, absolute shifts in
social conditions. The savagery of armies, authoritarianism, and economic hardships may have been brought to extremes by the Japanese,
but were certainly not introduced by them. It is significant that the
major Chinese literary works that depicted life under the Japanese
occupation as encapsulated experiences were by writers who spent
the war in the interior of China, rather than under the occupation:
the novels *Ssu-shih t'ung-t'ang* (Four Generations Under One Roof)
by Lao She, *Yin-li* (Gravitation) by Li Kuang-t'ien, and the plays

of Hsia Yen, for example. True, a comparable patriotic resistance play was written by the Communist playwright Yü Ling in 1939 and produced in the Shanghai International Settlement that year, when it was engulfed by the Japanese military. But that play, *Yeh Shanghai* (Shanghai Night), is little different in theme from Mao Tun's *Tzu-yeh* (Midnight), portraying Shanghai in 1930; indeed, the image of "night" refers to the same phenomenon in both works. That is, in *Midnight,* foreign economic aggression has reached its zenith and Chinese society its nadir, while in *Shanghai Night* it is specifically Japanese economic and military aggression that have reached their extreme. In each case, the Chinese villains are those who act as compradores or collaborators with foreign powers, and the heroes are those who trust and support the Communists for their inevitable future deliverance, primarily by means of the Red Armies.

Other portrayals of patriotism and resistance most often took the form of historical drama. Although they may be seen to some extent as veiled criticism during a time of harsh censorship, the costume dramas also had greater popular appeal among a wider audience. They predated the war, and during war they had widespread success throughout China, not just in the occupied zone. Moreover, being historical, these works implied that the present situations to which they alluded had important features in common with past events and were not unique. There was, by contrast, a lack of the broad and systematic analysis of society in the realist tradition. But this too is not simply a reflection on the conditions of occupation literature alone. The occasional remarks of critics under the occupation that writers had too little grounding in the wisdom of the social sciences found its echo in China after 1949 in the frequent denunciations of writers for their "vulgar sociology."

Just as the occupation was not an absolute break with earlier circumstances of Chinese society, the interest in traditional Chinese values and literary forms was hardly a development unique to the occupation period. But in the ultimate disruption of war and occupation, in the absence of legitimate authority or an open intellectual forum, and in the presence of censorship, the concern with the past and what might be salvaged from it became of greater value as a viable outlet for expression. In fact, the uses to which tradition was put (as indirect censure of contemporary authority, as bases for social reform, and as a guide for esthetic creation) were the same as the functions it served at other times in the history of modern Chinese literature.

In the conscious traditions of the familiar essay, the most practiced hands and considered views were those of Chou Tso-jen. For Chou, the essay was a medium for putting cosmopolitan views and interests into a specifically Chinese context and for maintaining literature as the voice of individual experience. His immediate contribution was his dissent with the authoritarian traditions of Confucianism being advocated by the Japanese, and his counterclaim that the value of Confucianism lay in its espousal of humaneness, moderation, and skepticism. But in the broader scope of his work and its place in modern Chinese letters, Chou provided an important critique of a Naturalist view of ethics, against authority mundane and spiritual, and in its relationship to persistent Confucian traditions, both good and bad. Other essayists responded to Chou's espousal of a Naturalist ethic, based on the inquiries of the social, behavioral, and biological sciences, but at their best they are seen less as cultural anthropologists than as regional writers. Essayists such as Chi Kuo-an and Wen Tsai-tao were men with strong emotional ties to their home regions in rural China. They reacted to the turmoil of social events, to the destructiveness and sense of alienation they fostered, as against the vision of belonging to a place and a culture with all its faults and comforts. In these essays are the personal testimonies of men attempting to rescue themselves from a vision of social superfluousness and cultural disinheritance.

The influence of tradition in form and content was no less apparent in the modern spoken drama than in the familiar essay, and it was to costume drama that the modern stage owed the greater part of its popular success in competition with classical opera. The modern costume drama could also appeal more to the concerns of the times and introduce greater psychological refinement in character portrayals. Certainly the foremost accomplishment in historical drama was Yao K'o's *Ch'ing kung yuan* (Malice in the Ch'ing Court). Yao's concern for the psychological development of his leading characters, the Kuang-hsü emperor and the Pearl Concubine, and the attention to technique which he employs to that end, justify the place of the work as one of the major dramas of modern Chinese literature. Modern as it is, it has not only borrowed elements of classical form, but appealed to a classical vision. While bent on modernizing reforms, the emperor is righteous by any traditional measure, and it is through his righteousness and virtue that the Pearl Concubine's love for him takes on significance. The potentials for oppression and liberation within the Chinese are seen through inherently Chinese ideals. But, just as thoughtful reflection in many a familiar essay was replaced with cultural trivia, in the theater the modern re-creation of past sentiment often gave way to a thoroughly traditional sentimentality, embodied in the unprecedented success of *Ch'iu Hai-t'ang* (Begonia). This play, though set in modern China, employed many scenes of Peking Opera, and though it opens with the scene of a female impersonator whose chief concern is to demonstrate his progressive patriotism, it concludes by emphasizing the destruction of his love life and his career as an opera singer. *Begonia* is of primary importance as the most successful play in modern Chinese commercial theater and as a major representative work of what is called Mandarin Duck and Butterfly literature. The novel *Begonia* was revised and circulated in the People's Republic of China years after *Malice in the Ch'ing Court* was condemned by Mao Tse-tung personally.

The trend to traditionalism in the literature of the occupation primarily signified two things. Traditionalist writers took the role of upholding certain inherent Chinese ideals and values in the light of more modern concepts of what might make for salvation or survival in contemporary challenges, and in repudiation of previous reactionary defenders of Chinese traditions. Second, they demonstrated their appreciation of older Chinese literary forms and identified their modern works as being a continuation of traditional art forms, rather than a purposeful departure from them.

That family relationships formed the central arena of action in so many plays and stories is also a continuation of earlier trends in modern Chinese literature. Family conflicts inform the action of an overwhelming number of works. Interestingly enough, resistance writers such as Yü Ling in *Shanghai Night* and A Ying in *Ming-mo i-hen* (Sorrow for the Fall of the Ming) took up the theme of family solidarity, centered on the father, but based on the guiding patriotism of youth. Japanese-sponsored works still argued the case for family solidarity based on a conservative, Confucian father as the proper source of authority. But the majority of works were concerned with love and courtship, and in these the family is also forever a source of conflict. The failures of the traditional extended household are delineated in Chang Ai-ling's fiction, the failures of family-arranged marriage are depicted in Su Ch'ing's *Chieh-hun shih-nien* (Ten Years of Marriage), and disillusionment with marriage based on free love is seen in Ch'ien Chung-shu's fiction and Yang Chiang's dramas. Little sense of satisfaction or comfort from family relations is evinced in these and other works. Conversely, however, the reader's sympathies are frequently enlisted by introducing orphans and widows, as in Li Chien-wu's *Ch'ing-ch'un* (Youth), Shih T'o's *Ma Lan* and *Ta ma-hsi-t'uan* (*The Big Circus*), and Yang Chiang's *Ch'en-hsin ju-i* (As You Desire). Given that the arena of action was typically the family, it is in turning to the themes of love and concepts of the self that the concerns and methods of the literature emerge more clearly, as represented by three main trends: the traditional, the romantic, and the antiromantic.

Essayists such as Chou Tso-jen and his followers did little to explore sexual love but generally referred the reader to Havelock Ellis or an incident of antiquarian interest and left the matter at that. In Yao K'o's historical drama *Malice in the Ch'ing Court,* the love between the Pearl Concubine and the emperor is ultimately that of virtuous people engaged in a righteous cause, a conscious and rational loyalty. By contrast, the works growing out of the romantic heritage of the May Fourth literature give a more central place to the sexual and nonrational aspects of love, emphasizing the individual's worth in emotional terms and shucking the values that define the significance of love in traditionalist literature.

In Shih T'o's novel *Ma Lan,* the heroine renders her ultimate critical judgment of her admirer, Li Po-t'ang, by saying that his intolerance of evil, his humaneness, is based on a sense of righteousness rather than love. And the novel shows that such a sense of righteousness is inadequate, or even worse than useless, in dealing with the fundamental needs of the characters. Similarly, Su Ch'ing's heroine in *Ten Years of Marriage* is torn between the righteous fulfillment of her role as a wife and the realization that, as she puts it, she doesn't really love her husband but simply doesn't want to lose him to another woman. Clinging to her role of virtuous wife, however, proves useless when her husband fails to provide for the support of their children. The heroine then feels justified in obtaining a legal divorce, an act that proves an emotional triumph over a constricting, debilitating sense of virtue. Shih T'o and Su Ch'ing, in their very different ways, affirm their protagonists in heroic roles, ready to break conventions as part of a valid search for emotional fulfillment. These affirmations of their protagonists also convey messages of the unworthiness of society for the potentials of their heroines. It is the vision of the iconoclastic hero pitting himself against a decadent society that is also at the heart of the polemical essays of the leftist writer T'ang T'ao in his praise and imitation of Lu Hsün as a hero of Promethean proportions. By contrast, it is the very lack of heroic proportions and idealizations that immediately distinguishes the work of the so-called antiromantic writers. In their place, even in the work of a writer as concerned with the portrayal of love and the faults of society as Chang Ai-ling, there are skeptical attitudes toward the ideal of individual love and more cynical appraisals of lovers' behavior. In Chang Ai-ling's stories love is the setting for her characters to throw off conventional restraints, but what she finds beneath these restraints is more a Freudian vision of irrational drives, of psychopathology, rather than ideals, conformist or iconoclastic.

This characterization of Chang Ai-ling's stories serves to introduce the contrasts between antiromantic writers and the traditionalists and romantics, but the fundamental concerns of the antiromantic writers go to the concept of the self. What defines the self in the works of traditionally oriented writers is the individual's social role in championing certain ethical values, and there is little to be said of the self beyond this rational, conscious role in society. There is no lack of emotion, but it is always focused on how an act, whether of survival or martyrdom, reflects a conscious wish to fulfill a value or an ideal of social significance. The romantic writers, however, put their priority on an affirmation of the self, championing the individual's energies and emotional needs. It was only in fulfilling the individual that society could thereafter accomplish its renewal, reform, and salvation. While traditionalists examined how to redefine the bases of the roles to be played in society by the individual, the romantics plunged into a celebration of the self; its unleashed energies were to be the guiding principle for a new society. The fundamental optimism underlying the romantic vision of the self liberated from conventional roles was not something the traditionalists were prepared to deal with, though they too were determined to reshape society in a modern vein. It was the antiromantic writer, however, who emerged as the chief doubter of the individualism so radically championed by romantics. What the antiromantic writers shared were their doubts that individual needs could be attained and their concern with the theme of self-delusion, upon which both individual ambitions and social institutions were based. For traditionalists and romantics alike, nothing was more detestable than the hypocrisies of Neo-Confucianism, and its vestiges and influences in modern China. But the muse of the antiromantic writer was turned toward self-delusion under whatever social setting or cultural myth. The championing and idealizing of the individual and his energies is then de-idealized by the antiromantic writers.

The failure of individuals' pretensions and their ill-conceived, unreflective ambitions are everywhere evident in the work of the antiromantics. The god in Ch'ien Chung'shu's story "Shang-ti ti meng" (God's Dream) cannot control his own creation, born out of vanity, his Adam and Eve meant to reflect his glory, but inheriting only his vanity. Chang Ai-ling's widow, Ch'i-ch'iao, in "Chin so chi" (The Golden Cangue) has a malicious habit of controlled theatrics that gives way to uncontrolled madness. Yang Chiang's young, activist couple with worthy ideals for social reform in the play *Feng hsü* (Windswept Blossoms) fall into a neurotic love triangle and destroy themselves through their own feelings of contempt, which their ideals had implied. In Wu Hsing-hua's poem "Lan ku" (On Viewing Ancient Sites), the poet attempts an attitude of quietude, only to be overwhelmed by sensations of irresistible turmoil: "The universe rushes along an unchanging course,/The profound sorrows of the ages on one man's shoulders." The irony behind antiromanticism was perhaps as strong as the irony these writers expressed. In their individual ways, they took up the theme of the ultimate annihilation of the self, but their mistrust of the self was not that of Buddhism in its radical denial of the existence of self. Rather, it was reflective of modern disillusionment in the West with what were considered the excesses of romanticism and romantic ideals of the nineteenth century, and which reinforced interest in Buddhism, mysticism, and other forms that seemed avenues of escape from the self.

In the context of modern Chinese literature, the occupation period was one of considerable literary achievement. Yet the occupation opened up no new intellectual debates on such issues as determinism, pragmatism, or religion, that might have stimulated or altered the course of literature. There was also a considerable diversity in the writing of the period. Yet even with this variety, writers contributed relatively little of immediate use to the dominant political interests. Thus, literature took little part in developing the myths and themes that were to sweep across China following the war.

True, in the postwar years a number of dramas written during the war in Shanghai received considerable attention as films, and a number of playwrights active in wartime Shanghai, as well as actors, had prominent careers in the People's Republic. Moreover, the short stories of Chang Al-ling have received more critical attention and probably had more influence on fiction in Taiwan than any other single Chinese author since the May Fourth generation. Yet these are secondary considerations in reviewing the significance of Chinese literature in wartime Shanghai and Peking; the achievement of the period lies primarily in the accomplishments of the works themselves. In theater there were important developments in both historical and realistic trends that had been growing steadily prior to the war. Yao K'o's *Malice in the Ch'ing Court* achieved more classic proportions in the universality of its theme, without sacrificing in the least the sense of patriotism and social justice that had consumed earlier works of narrower vision. Most important, perhaps, were the plays of Yang Chiang, whose innovative and independent vision of character and situation brought comedy to a new level and tragedy to a confronta-

tion with stereotypes of social situations most ably portrayed by
Ts'ao Yü, but too successfully for playwrights thereafter to do more
than imitate or recall his motifs until Yang Chiang presented a bold
and intelligent alternative.

In essays, the trend was from polemic to familiar. Where death in
war had failed and life was to go on in defeat and spiritless compromise, the essayists took up the unglamorous task, that lacked
utterly the glory to which so much of modern literature had aspired,
of recalling what was familiar in an age increasingly at odds with and
estranged from the familiar. The return to blandness took on a new
significance, a rejection of the new rhetoric of global ambition in total
war imposed by an invader and a balm to those whose dreams were
the black ashes of anxiety in a society scorched with hatred. Finally,
the genre of fiction, which had dominated the literary achievements of
earlier decades and nearly disappeared in the late thirties and early
forties, made a startling comeback in the last years of the war. The
appearance of works by Chang Ai-ling during the war and by Ch'ien
Chung-shu immediately thereafter restored fiction to its place as an
important form. As in theater, it testified to the appearance of new
writers whose art could move interest in fiction beyond the controversy over its function as a vehicle of propaganda or sheer entertainment and reaffirm the autonomy a work of art could achieve. If
the historical record reaps anything but a harvest of bitterness from
the years of occupation, it will be this literary harvest of achievement.

Notes

INTRODUCTION

1. Some of these writers described their experiences in Shanghai and their departure from it for readers in the interior. For example, see Erh Pin (Hsü Hsü), "Ts'ung Shanghai kuei-lai" (Returning from Shanghai), *Wen-hsüeh ch'uang-tso* (Literary Creation) (15 January 1943), 1(4):55–62 and *ibid.* (15 February 1943), 1(5):66–72. Also, Ou-yang Yü-ch'ien, "Hou-t'ai jen-yü" (Backstage Talk), *Wen-hsüeh ch'uang-tso* (15 January 1943), 1(4):42–47 and (1 April 1943), 1(6):105–9.

1. LITERATURE AND POLITICAL INITIATIVES

1. Takeda Taijun, personal letter, 4 September 1976.
2. Huang Chih-kang, "Wo tui-yü chiu hsing-shih ti chi tien i-chien" (A Few of My Opinions on Old Forms), *K'ang-chan wen-i* (12 November 1938), 2(10):150.
3. Ishikawa Nobuo, "Sempu ban engeki tai," *Genchi hōkoku* (September 1941), no. 48, p. 106.
4. *Ibid.*, p. 111.
5. "Conduct of Japanese as Military Occupants," *The China Yearbook 1940–41*, pp. 357–58.
6. Sha Kua, "Hsin-hun chih ch'ien," *Hsin shen pao* (Shanghai), 2–9 September 1939.
7. Ching, "Fu tzu chih chien," *Hsin shen pao*, 22 April 1939.
8. For an account of theater in Peking in the late thirties, see Okuno Shintarō, *Zuihitsu Pekin* (Peking Essays) (Tokyo, 1940), pp. 116–24.
9. Ch'en Ta-pei's wartime activities are cited in Ishikawa, "Sempu ban engeki tai," p. 110.
10. Keng Hsiao Ti, "Ch'ing-nien tso-chia hsieh-hui" (Youth Writers Association), *Hsin min pao* (Peking), 5 March 1938, p. 8.
11. Keng, "Wo-men suo hsü-yao ti wen-i" (The Literature We Need), *Hsin min pao*, 11 March 1938, p. 8.
12. Keng, *Hsin min pao pan-yüeh k'an* (1 June 1939), 1(1):51–52.

13. Wei Shao-ch'ang [?Ch'ien Hsing-ts'un], *Yüan-yang hu-tieh p'ai yen-chiu tzu-liao* (Research Materials on the Mandarin Duck and Butterfly School), p. 272.

14. See Joseph Schyns et al., *1500 Modern Chinese Novels and Plays,* entry no. 460, p. 214.

15. "Wen-hsüeh ying fu ti shih-ming," *Hsin shen pao,* 29 December 1939, p. 4.

16. Man Chün, "Ho-p'ing wen-hsüeh," *Hsin shen pao,* 28 December 1939, p. 4.

17. Li Po-chün, "Hsien chieh-tuan chung-kuo wen-hsüeh chih lu-hsiang" (Trends in Chinese Literature at the Present Stage), *Hsin shen pao,* 14 and 28 September 1939.

18. Fang Chi-sheng, "*Shuo feng* shih cha-chi" (Record from the Office of *Shuo feng*), *Shuo feng* (October 1938), no. 1, p. 43.

19. Among the lesser-known writers cited here, Ch'ien Tao-sun was educated in Japan and since the 1920s had taught Japanese literature at several universities in Peking. His work includes translations of the *Manyōshū,* the *Genji monogatari,* and the *Ise monogatari.* Shen Ch'i-wu (b. 1902) was a graduate of Yenching University, a poet after the style of Feng Wen-ping, and an essayist in the style of Chou Tso-jen, Ch'en Mien (b. 1901) held a Ph.D. from the Université de Paris and was well known as a director, writer, and translator of modern drama in the 1930s. During the war, Ch'ien Tao-sun was president of Peking University.

20. Mi Sheng, "Kuan-yü *Chung-kuo wen-i* ti ch'u-hsien chi ch'i-t'a" (On the Appearance of *Chinese Arts and Letters*), *Chung-kuo wen-i* (September 1939), 1(1):17.

21. "Chien-she hsin wen-i ti ke-chieh hung-lun," *Chung-kuo wen-i* (January 1940), 1(5):10–15.

22. One factor which vitiated attempts to make *Chinese Arts and Letters* a pro-Japanese organ was the attitude of the staff. The chief editor, Chang Shen-ch'ieh, was a Taiwanese who arrived in Peking after its occupation. In Taiwan he had been associated with circles seeking cultural autonomy from the Japanese, and he continued these activities in Peking until he was removed from his position and subsequently sentenced to death for subversive activities. He was spared by the timely surrender of the Japanese. See articles commemorating him in *Hsia ch'ao* (The China Tide) (Taiwan) (September 1977), 3(3):68–69.

23. See "Hua-pei wen-i hsieh-hui hui-k'an" (Bulletin of the North China Literary Association), *Chung-kuo wen-i* (March 1941), vol. 4, no. 2.

24. Lin Po-sheng and Miki Kiyoshi, "Bunka undō no kichō" (The Keynote of the Cultural Movement), *Chūō kōron* (May 1940), pp. 86–92.

25. See Chang Tzu-p'ing, *Hsing-chien ti-i nien* (The First Year of Reconstruction) (Shanghai, 1940), for Chang's early career in the peace movement. Chang also contributed fiction to the *Hua-wen ta-pan mei-jih pan-yüeh k'an.*

26. *Chūgoku bungaku* (July 1942), No. 85, p. 142.

27. See T'ang T'ao, "Tien-ying ch'üan" (The Film Circle), in *T'ang T'ao tsa-wen hsüan,* pp. 172–73.

28. *The Chinese Yearbook 1938–39,* p. 700.

29. *South China Morning Post* (Hong Kong), 10 August 1939, p. 13.

30. Quoted in translation in *The Chinese Yearbook 1943,* p. 675.

31. K'o Ling, "Wo yao k'ung-su" (I Accuse), in *Yao yeh chi,* pp. 115–16.

32. See "Moku Shiei no koto" (The Mu Shih-ying Affair), *Genchi hōkoku* (August 1940), no. 48, pp. 196–201. Kao Ming and Mu Shih-ying were fellow contributors to *Hsien-tai* magazine (*Les Contemporains*) in the early 1930s. Like Kao Ming and Mu Shih-ying, many of the members of the Les Contemporains Society remained in occupied China, including Liu Na-ou, Wang Fu-ch'üan, and Lu I-shih in Shanghai, and Tai Wang-shu and Yeh Ling-feng in Hong Kong. Ironically, Mu Shih-ying's reputation has since been cleared in an article that reveals he joined the peace movement as an informant for a Nationalist agent in Hong Kong. When Mu moved to Shanghai, however, he was mistaken for a traitor by local underground workers, who killed him. See K'ang I [pen name], "Lin ti shan yang," *Chang-ku* [Antiquarian] (Hong Kong) (October 1972), no. 14, pp. 48–50.

33. Tseng Hsü-pai, *Chung-kuo hsin-wen shih* (A History of Chinese Journalism), 1:425, states that the newspapers *Wen-hui pao, I pao, Tao pao,* and *Kuo-chi jih-pao* were bought out in 1940.

34. Cheng Chen-to, *Chih-chü san-chi,* p. 97.

35. Wen Tsai-tao, "Ch'iang yü pi" (Gun and Pen), in K'ung Ling-ching et al., *Heng mei chi,* p. 139, mentions these works together with the *Collected Works of Lu Hsün* as published in Shanghai.

36. Cheng Chen-to, *Chih-chü san-chi,* p. 97.

37. *Ibid.,* p. 85.

38. See *Tsa-chih* (Review) (August 1942), 9(5):143.

39. For one account of Lu Li's work and his fate, see Liu Hsi-wei [Li Chien-wu], "Lu Li ti san-wen" (Lu Li's Essays), in *Chu-hua erh chi* (Ruminations II), 2:147–58.

40. Yao Hsin-nung, personal letter, 8 November 1975.

41. Jay Leyda, *Dianying,* p. 146.

42. M. [Klaus Mehnert], review, "On the Screen," *The Twentieth Century* (March 1942), 2(3):235.

43. Eileen Chang, review, "On the Screen," *The Twentieth Century* (October 1943), 5(4):278.

44. *Ibid.*

45. *Ibid.*

46. Chang, review, "On the Screen: Mothers and Daughters-in-Law," *The Twentieth Century* (August–September 1943), 5(2–3):202.

47. Chang, review, "On the Screen: Educating the Family," *The Twentieth Century* (November 1943), 5(5):358.

48. *Ibid.*

49. *Ibid.*

50. T'ang T'ao, "Tien-ying ch'üan" (The Film Circle), in *T'ang T'ao tsa-wen hsüan,* p. 173.

51. Leyda, *Dianying,* p. 147.

52. Ch'in Shou-ou, "Ch'iu Hai't'ang ti i-chih" (The Transplanting of Ch'iu Hai-t'ang), in *Ch'iu Hai-t'ang* [novel version] (reprint ed., Hong Kong, 1975), p. 2.

53. Yao Hsin-nung in a personal letter dated 14 August 1975 remarks that there were no significant differences between the original script and the film version. The reader may also refer to Leyda, *Dianying,* plate 18, following p. 418, which offers a still shot taken from the film showing Ch'iu scarred and posed as in an illustration for the novel, following p. 202.

54. M. [Klaus Mehnert], review, "On the Screen," *The Twentieth Century* (March 1942), 2(3):235.

55. *Ibid.*

56. Klaus Mehnert, interview held in Hong Kong, 30 April 1977.

57. Chang Si-ling, review, "On the Screen: Wife, Vamp, Child," *The Twentieth Century* (May 1943), 4(5):392.

58. *Ibid.*

59. Donald Keene, "Japanese Writers and the Greater East Asian War," *Journal of Asian Studies* (February 1964), 23(2):216ff.

60. "Hua-pei tso-chia hsieh-hui ch'eng-li tien-li ping ch'üan-t'i hui-yuan ta-hui" (Ceremonies Founding the North China Writers' Association Together with an All-Member Congress), *Chung-kuo wen-i* (October 1942), 7(2):27–28.

61. Ting Ting [Ting Chia-shu], interviewed in Hong Kong, 18 November 1973. Of the writers not mentioned previously, Ting Ting was well known in the Shanghai area as the author of several volumes of criticism, essays, and short stories during the 1930s and 1940s. Like Chang Tzu-p'ing, Chou Ch'üan-p'ing and Chou Yü-ying were members of the of the Creation Society (Ch'uang-tsao She) in the 1920s and later wrote proletarian fiction and Literature for the Masses in the 1930s. Kung Ch'ih-p'ing was in all likelihood Kung Ping-lu, educated at Waseda University and author of one of the earliest pieces of "revolutionary literature" during the May Fourth movement, "T'an k'uang fu" (Coal Miner).

62. Ozaki Hideki, "Daitōa bungakusha taikai ni tsuite" (On the Greater East Asia Writers Congress), *Bungei* (May 1961), 29(5):14.

63. *Ibid.,* p. 15. Yü P'ing-po was then a professor at Peking University and, inevitably, a member of the North China Writers Association. In fact, he contributed but a few short essays to *I-wen tsa-chih* and *Wen-hsüeh chi-k'an* during the war, and researched T'ang-Sung poetry. T'ao Ching-sun was formerly a member of the Creation Society and editor of *Ta-chung wen-i* (Literature for the Masses) in the 1930s.

64. Chang Wo-chün, a native of Taiwan, graduate of Waseda University and Peking Normal School, had translated a number of Japanese works on social issues during the 1920s and 30s and taught at Peking Normal School. His own essays were collected by his son, K. C. Chang, and published as *Chang Wo-chün wen-chi* (Collected Works of Chang Wo-chün) (Taipei, 1975). Yu Ping-ch'i was a graduate of Tsinghua and Imperial Universities and a professor of Chinese literature at Peking University.

65. *Hong Kong News,* 29 October 1942, p. 1.

66. *Asahi shimbun,* 2 November 1942, quoted in Ozaki Hideki, "Daitōa bungakusha taikai ni tsuite," p. 13.

67. Ozaki Hideki, "Daitōa bungakusha taikai tsuite," p. 15.

68. *Nam-wah yat-po* (South China Daily News), 6 November 1942, p. 3.

69. *Ibid.*

70. Ozaki Hideki, "Daitōa bungakusha taikai ni tsuite," p. 16.

71. *Hong Kong News,* 7 November 1942, p. 3.

72. See *Hsin-min pao pan-yüeh k'an* (15 August 1943), 5(18):29.

73. Feng Chieh-chung, "Hsün chih" (Killed in the Line of Duty), *Hsin-min pao pan-yüeh k'an* (15 August 1942), 4(18):26–31.

74. Yang Kuang-cheng, "I-chiu-szu-szu nien ti chung-kuo wen-i chieh" (The Chinese Literary World in 1944), *Wen-yu,* (1 January 1945), no. 40, p. 10.

75. Schyns, *1500 Modern Chinese Novels and Plays,* entry no. 997, p. 327.

76. Ping-kuen Yü, "Memorandum: Availability of the *Shih pao,*" 2 June 1969.

77. Chin Hsiung-pai, *Wang cheng-ch'uan shih-mo chi,* 2:44.

78. Wen Tsai-tao, "Kuan-yü *Wen-ch'ao* chi *Feng-t'u hsiao-chi*" (On *Quotations* and *Notes on Customs*), *Ku chin* (1 August 1944), no. 48, p. 23.

79. Iizuka Akira, "Kahoku bungaku tsūshin" (News on Literature in North China), *Shinchō* (September 1943), 40(9):40–41.

80. It appeared in *Bungakukai* (October 1943), 10(10):12–18.

81. New People's Press advertisement, *Chung-ho,* inside back cover, 1945 issues.

82. *Pei-k'o* (Peking, 1943), p. 68.

83. Schyns, *1500 Modern Chinese Novels and Plays,* p. 116.

84. Liu Hsin-huang, *Fan-kung* (Counterattack) (October 1974), no. 391, pp. 28–29.

85. New delegates included the playwright and director Ch'ien Mien, the director of the North China Writers Association Liu Lung-kuang, the Shanghai bibliophile Chou Yüeh-jan, and a Communist agent working as a pro-Japanese propagandist, Lu Feng. Also from Shanghai was Chang K'o-piao, who in 1943, together with the former Creation Society writers, edited a magazine for the Nanking regime that bore the same title as one he had edited in 1926, *I-pan* (In Common).

86. Ozaki Hideki, "Daitoa bungakusha taikai ni tsuite," p. 18.

87. Keene, "Japanese Writers," p. 218.

88. Iwamoto Yoshio, "The Relationship between Literature and Politics in Japan, 1931–45," p. 324.

89. *Chung-kuo wen-hsüeh* (Chinese Literature) (October 1944), no. 10, p. 6.

90. Liu Lung-kuang was an editor for *Wu-te pao* (Martial Virtue Herald) and was then an editor for the *Osaka mainichi shimbun.* After 1942, he edited *Chung-kuo wen-hsueh, Chung-hua chou-pao* (China Weekly), *Yen-ching yüeh-k'an* (Yenching Monthly), and *Tso-chia sheng-huo* (Writer's Life).

91. Mei Niang's *Crab* was published in the fortnightly *Hua-wen Mei-jih-hsin-wen pan-yüeh k'an,* in serial form, for the most part prior to the outbreak of the Pacific War and the start of a Greater East Asia literature program.

92. The actual process for selecting works for awards as Greater East Asian literature has never been fully explained. One final note that bears on the situation is that the awards were supposedly worth twenty thousand yen each, provided by *Mainichi shimbun.* See "Bungei ji-kan" (Current Survey of Literature), *Shinchō* (October 1943), 40(10):3.

93. The contents of *The Writer* (1941–44, Nanking and Soochow), edited by Ting Ting, cannot be verified. Its contributors, however, were those associated with officially sponsored programs: Chang Tzu-p'ing, Chang K'o-piao, Kung Ch'ih-p'ing, and Fu Yen-ch'ang. *In Common* (1943) was a short-lived effort at politicized literature with contributions from Chang K'o-piao, Fu Yen-ch'ang, Kung Ch'ih-p'ing, Lu I-shih, Liu Yü-sheng, and T'ao Ching-sun. Propaganda works by Ch'en Ta-pei and Chang Tzu-p'ing appeared in *Greater Asianism and the East Asia League* (1942). In 1944 *Chung-lun* (Mass Forum) appeared briefly, edited by Chang Tzu-p'ing and Yang Chih-hua, literary editor for *Chung-hua yüeh-pao,* the monthly

magazine published by the Nanking regime *Central China Daily News.* Even these magazines were by no means wholly given over to politicized works.

94. Chin Hsiung-pai, interviewed in Hong Kong, January 1974.

95. Chin, *Wang cheng-ch'uan shih-mo chi,* 3:30–34.

96. Chin, *Wang cheng-ch'uan ti k'ai-ch'ang yü shou-ch'ang* (The Wang Ching-wei Regime from Overture to Curtain), 6:168.

97. Su Ch'ing, "Wen-hua chih XX" (The XXing of Culture), *T'ien ti* (August 1944), no. 11, pp. 3–4.

98. *Chung-lun* (April 1944), 1(3):3.

99. Yang Kuang-cheng, "I-chiu-szu-szu nien," p. 10.

100. "The Magazines of China," *The Twentieth Century* (April 1943), 4(4):281.

101. Wei Shao-ch'ang, *Yüan-yang hu-tieh p'ai,"* p. 489.

102. Chin Hsiung-pai, *Wang cheng-ch'uan ti k'ai-ch'ang yu shou-ch'ang,* 6:170. Chin also mentions other writers with a reputation for satire during the war.

103. P'an Liu-tai, interviewed in Hong Kong, March 1974. The Library of Congress has a complete set of *Wen yu* (Literary Companion), save for the first issue.

104. "Edible Edition," *T'ien ti* (November 1944), no. 14, p. 12.

105. Chin Hsiung-pai, *Wang cheng-ch'uan ti k'ai-ch'ang yü shou-ch'ang,* 6:177.

106. Stephen Soong, interviewed in Hong Kong, 7 December 1976. It was in calling my attention to a copy of *Six Arts* in his possession that Professor Soong pointed out the role of the Soviet consulate.

107. For accounts of Tsou T'ao-fen's last years, see the appendix to *Huan-nan yü-sheng chi,* and Cheng Chen-to, *Chih-chü san-chi,* pp. 74–82.

108. See Ku Chung-i, *Shih-nien lai ti Shanghai hua-chü yun-tung* (The Modern Drama Movement in Shanghai During the Past Ten Years, 1937–47) pp. 21–24.

109. Yao K'o, personal letter, 18 May 1975.

110. Ku Chung-i, *Shih-nien lai,* pp. 27–28.

111. Yao K'o, personal letter, 18 May 1975.

112. See Sanetō Yoshihide, "Chūgoku sakka ni yōbō suru mono—shohimbun no fukkō" (What Is Expected of Chinese Writers—The Resurgence of the Familiar Essay), *Shinchō* (October 1943), 40(10):14–15; also Kung Ch'ih-p'ing, "Chung-kuo wen-hsüeh hsin-sheng chih lu" (The Road to Revival for Chinese Literature), *I-pan* (February 1943), no. 1, pp. 14–19.

113. Quoted in Ozaki Hideki, "Daitōa bungakusha taikai ni tsuite," pp. 20–21.

114. Chou Tso-jen, *K'u-k'ou kan-k'ou* (The Bitter and the Sweet), pp. 12–17.

115. See "Kuo-yü wen ti san lei" (Three Kinds of Standards in Style), in Chou, *Li-ch'un i-ch'ien (Before the Spring),* p. 121.

116. "Ming-shih ts'ai-ch'ing yü shang-yeh ching-mai" (Noted Wits and Commercial Auctioneers), in T'ang T'ao, *T'ang T'ao tsa-wen-hsüan,* pp. 250–51.

117. Hu Lan-ch'eng, in *T'ien ti* (August 1944), no. 11, pp. 20–21.

118. *Steppes of the Korchin Banner* was written by Tuan-Mu Hung-liang in Peking in 1932–33. It was not, however, published until 1939.

119. Chou Yang, in *Chieh-fang jih-pao* (Liberation Daily), 19 July 1941, p. 2, quoted in translation in T. A. Hsia, *The Gate of Darkness* (Seattle: University of Washington Press, 1968), p. 243.

120.   According to Liu Hsin-huang, Ma Li (Ma Ch'iu-ying) was editor of the Peking journal *Chung-kuo kung-lun* (China Forum), and his stories reflect the capitulationist sentiments of a collaborator. See *Fan-kung* (August 1974), no. 389, p. 34. Ma Li's employment notwithstanding, it seems to me that the stories, in avoiding the war issue and focusing concern on the unhappy plight of the peasants of his native region, was continuing a theme common to regional literature before the occupation and not serving as propaganda for a puppet regime.

121.   Yao Hsin-nung, interviewed in Hong Kong, 3 December 1976.

2.   The Decline of May Fourth Romanticism

1.   Yi-tsi Feuerwerker, "Women as Writers in the 1920's and 1930's," in Margery Wolf and Roxanne Witke, eds., *Women in Chinese Society* (Stanford, Calif.: Stanford University Press, 1975), p. 164.

2.   *Ibid.*, p. 165.

3.   See Leo O. Lee, *The Romantic Generation of Modern Chinese Writers*, pp. 275–96.

4.   See "Ch'ung chin Lo-ma ti ching-shen" (The Spirit of Returning to Rome), quoted in Olga Lang, *Pa Chin and His Writings*, p. 193. In July 1938 Pa Chin wrote this piece to a young man to argue the need and value of remaining in Japanese-dominated areas, alluding to the Apostle Peter's return to Rome to die on the cross.

5.   See Chou Li-an, *Hua fa chi*, pp. 1–6.

6.   Wang Jen-shu recounts his early experience writing *tsa-wen* in "Kuan-yü *Pien ku chi* (On *Border Drums*), in *Heng mei chi* (Shanghai, 1939), pp. 77–80.

7.   See Pa Jen, *Tsun-ming chi*, pp. 143–44.

8.   K'o Ling, "T'a" (Treading Down), in *Yao yeh chi*, pp. 153–53.

9.   *Tsa-wen ts'ung-k'an* (The Tsa-wen Anthology), a short-lived periodical, was the chief vehicle of this revival.

10.   Pa Jen, *Lun Lu Hsün ti tsa-wen*, p. 10.

11.   Chou Li-an, *Hua-fa chi*, p. 110.

12.   K'o-Ling, "Hai-shih hsü-yao feng-tz'u: wu, tso-ch'e ou-kan" (Still In Need of Satire: 5, Sudden Feelings Riding a Rickshaw), in *Yao yeh chi*, pp. 108–9.

13.   Ko Ling, *Yao yeh chi*, p. 89.

14.   T'ang T'ao, *T'ang T'ao tsa-wen hsüan*, pp. 145–46.

15.   *Ibid.*, pp. 228–30.

16.   *Ibid.*, pp. 186–87.

17.   "Ts'ung 'k'u-chu' tao 'ho-tao'" (From Bitter Recluse to Town Crier), in T'ang, *T'ang T'ao tsa-wen hsüan*, pp. 188–89.

18.   T'ang, *T'ang T'ao tsa-wen hüsan*, pp. 155–57.

19.   *Ibid.*, pp. 216–17.

20.   *Ibid.*, pp. 122–23.

21.   *Ibid.*, pp. 149–50.

22.   T'ang, *Yü-chou feng i-k'an* (March 1940), no. 22, pp. 176–84.

23.   T'ang, *Yeh chu chi* (Night Pearls), p. 147.

24.   "K'u i-ko wu-chih ti ling-hun" ("Weeping for an Unknown Soul"), in T'ang, *Yeh chu chi*, pp. 118–26.

25. *Ibid.,* pp. 165–69.

26. *Ibid.,* p. 144.

27. Su Ch'ing, "T'ao," in *T'ao,* p. 48.

28. For example, "Lun li-hun" (On Divorce), *Ku chin* (16 October 1942), no. 9, pp. 17–20.

29. Hsieh Ping-ying, *Girl Rebel: The Autobiography of Hsieh Ping-ying* (I-ko nü-ping ti tzu-chuan), Adet and Anor Lin, trans. (New York, 1940; reprint ed., New York; Da Capo Press, 1975), p. 160.

30. Su Ch'ing, *Chieh-hun shih-nien,* pp. 1–3. Page references hereafter given in text.

31. Su Ch'ing, See "Tzu-chi ti wen-chang" (My Essays), in Hsün Feng, ed., *Hsien-tai san-wen sui-pi hsüan,* pp. 272–73.

32. See Su Ch'ing, "T'an tso kuan," *Ku chin* (16 August 1943), no. 29, pp. 15–17.

33. *Wen-hui pao* (Shanghai), 6 August 1945, quoted in "Kuan-yü wo" (About Myself), in Su Ch'ing, *Hsü chieh-hun shih-nien,* p. 6.

34. *Ibid.,* pp. 1–6.

35. See Shih T'o, "Chih Lu Fen hien-sheng-men" (To the Mr. Lu Fens), in *Ma Lan,* p. 312.

36. Liu Hsi-wei [Li Chien-wu], "Li-men shih chi" (A Review of Collected Notes on Li-men), in *Chü-hua erh-chi,* pp. 13–22.

37. Shih T'o, *Kuo-yuan ch'eng chi,* p. 181.

38. *Ibid.,* p. 196.

39. *Ibid.,* p. 176.

40. C. T. Hsia, *A History of Modern Chinese Fiction,* p. 463.

41. Shih T'o, *Kuo-yuan ch'eng chi,* p. 204.

42. Slupski, "The World of Shih T'o," (1973), p. 11.

43. *Ibid.,* p. 16.

44. Shih T'o, *Ma Lan,* p. 207. Page references hereafter given in text.

45. Shih T'o, *Huang-yeh,* in *Wan-hsiang* (May 1944), 3(11):76.

46. *Ibid.* (August 1944), 4(2):97.

47. *Ibid.* (September 1944), 4(3):74.

48. Ku Erh-shun is actually described as *ta-fang pu-chü* ("open and generous to all, regardless of social status"), in chapter 5, *Wan-hsiang* (September 1943), 3(3):93.

49. Douwe W. Fokkema, "Lu Xun: The Impact of Russian Literature," in Merle Goldman, ed., *Modern Chinese Literature in the May Fourth Era* (Cambridge, Mass.: Harvard University Press, 1977), p. 97.

50. Shih T'o, *Ta-ma-hsi-t'uan.* p. 13.

51. *Ibid.,* pp. 14–15.

52. Leonid Andreyev, *He Who Gets Slapped,* p. 88.

53. *Times Week (Shanghai Times),* 10 May 1943, p. 30.

54. Gregory Zilboorg so states in his introduction to *He Who Gets Slapped,* p. x.

55. See "Chui yen" (Superfluous Words), in Shih T'o and K'o Ling, *Yeh tien,* pp. 1–6.

56. Gorky, *The Lower Depths,* p. 63.

57. See Richard Hare, *Maxim Gorky.*

58. *Ibid.*, p. 57.

59. Shih T'o and K'o Ling, *Yeh tien*, p. 116.

60. Gorky, *The Lower Depths*, p. 36.

61. Hung Shen, *The Palace of Eternal Youth*, Yang Hsien-i and Gladys Yang, trs. (Peking, 1955), p. 177.

62. Shih T'o and K'o Ling, *Yeh tien*, p. 53.

63. *Ibid.*, p. 208.

64. "Chui yen" in Shih T'o and K'o Ling, *Yeh-tien*, p. 5.

65. Pa Chin, "Yeh tien," in *Kuan-yü yeh-tien* (On *The Night Inn* [A Collection of Critical articles]) (Shanghai, 1945), p. 5.

66. Cheng Chen-to, *Kuan-yü yeh tien*, pp. 5–6.

67. Li Chien-wu, *Che pu-kuo shih ch'un-t'ien* (Shanghai, 1940), p. vi.

68. For Li's view of realism, see "Kuan-yü hsien-shih," in *Chü-hua erh-chi* (2d ed., Shanghai, 1947), pp. 103–13. For a contemporary note on Flaubert's attack on realism, see Chu Kuang-ch'ien, *Wen-i hsin-li hsüeh* (Shanghai, 1936; reprint ed., Taipei, 1971), p. 139. That Flaubert was "romanticized" in China is noted in Lee, *The Romantic Generation*, p. 277.

69. Li, *Chü-hua erh-chi*, p. 26.

70. *Ibid.*, p. 32.

71. *Ibid.*, p. 36.

72. Ku Chung-i, *Shih nien lai ti Shanghai hua-chü yun-tung (1937–47)*, p. 5.

73. Li's *Sa-huang shih-chi* (Family of Liars, 1939) was based on Shaw's *How She Lied to Her Husband*. *Yun Ts'ai-hsia* (1942) was based on Scribe's *Adrienne Lecouvreur* (1849). Adapations from Sardou include *Hua Hsin feng* (*Fernande*), *Feng-liu chai* (*Seraphine*), *Hsi hsiang-feng* (*Fedora*), and *Chin Hsiao-yü* (*La Tosca*). As a member of the Shanghai United Arts Company, he probably helped adapt Chang Hen-shui's *Man chiang hung* (*Fire Over the Yangtze*) in spring 1943. *A-shih-na*, an adaptation of Othello set in the T'ang dynasty, was published in *Wen-hsüeh tsa-chih* (June 1947). Both Su Hsüeh-lin (Schyns, p. xliii) and Ku Chung-i (p. 33) credit him with *Yuan Shih-k'ai* (a play by the same name was done by Hsiung Fo-hsi). The script of this historical play is unavailable, as is *Fire Over the Yangtze*.

74. Ku Chung-i, *Shih-nien lai ti Shanghai hua-chü yun-tung*, p. 4.

75. Li Chien-wu, "Hsü" (Introduction), in Fang Chün-i, *Li hen-t'ien*, pp. 1–5.

76. Li, "Pa" (Epilogue), in *Feng-liu chai* (Shanghai, 1944), p. 5.

77. Li, "Ch'ing-ch'un," *Wen-i fu-hsing* (Literary Renaissance) (March 1946), 1(2):235. Page references hereafter given in text.

78. Mai Yeh, "Ch'ing-ch'un," *Tsa-chih* (Miscellany) (August 1944), 13(5):165.

3. THE RESURGENCE OF TRADITION: MODERN DRAMA

1. Of particular note in this regard are propaganda themes (chapter 1), Shih T'o's novel *Wilderness* and Pa Jen's demonstration of Lu Hsün's use of traditional techniques in polemic (chapter 2), and Chang Ai-ling's short stories and Wu Hsing-hua's poetry (chapter 5).

2. See Schyns, entry no. 1459, p. 455.

3. Ku Chung-i, *Shih nien lai ti Shanghai hüa-chu yun-tung*, pp. 14–15.

4. See *Times Week* (*Shanghai Times*), 14 March 1943, p. 32; and 26 April 1943, p. 30. See also Chin Ni, "Pao-kao Shanghai chü-yun hsien-k'uang chien p'ing *Ch'iu Hai-t'ang,*" *Hsin-min pao pan-yueh-k'an* (15 April 1943), 5(8):20–21.

5. Ku Chung-i, *Shih nien lai ti Shanghai hua-chü yun-tung*, p. 22.

6. Stephen Soong, interviewed in Hong Kong, 8 November 1976. Huang Tsung-ying, who played the lead in *La Petite Chocolatiere,* went on to a very durable career in the People's Republic of China. Other members of the T'ung-mao company were Communists or fellow travelers who had earlier worked with Yü Ling.

7. Quoted in Ku Chung-i, *Shih nien lai ti Shanghai hua-chü yun-tung*, p. 13.

8. Little has been mentioned here of Yü Ling's entire background. For biographical notes, see Schyns, p. 112; and Leyda, *Dianying*, p. 389.

9. Ai Wu, "Kuan-yü chü-p'ing chieh ti o-lieh ch'ing-hsiang" (On Poor Trends in Theater Criticism Circles), *Shanghai chou-pao* (Shanghai guardian) (24 May 1941), 3(22):576.

10. The plays are *Ch'ün ying luan-fei* (Orioles Flight), *Pu yeh ch'eng* (City of No Night), *Wu chieh-mei* (Five Sisters), *Hung Hsüan-chiao, Ch'un feng ch'iu yü* (Spring Breeze, Autumn Rains), *T'ao-hua yuan,* (Peach Blossom spring), *Niu-lang chih-nü chuan* (Cowherd and Weaving Maid), *Ming-mo i-hen, Pi hsüeh hua* (Sorrow for the Fall of the Ming or Jade Blood Flower), *Hai-kuo ying-hsiung* (Hero of an Island Nation), *Yang O chuan* (The Story of Yang O), and *Hsüan-ao shen-yuan*.

11. Ku Chung-i, *Shih nien lai ti Shanghai hua-chü yun-tung*, p. 2.

12. Wen Tsai-tao, *Feng-t'u hsiao-chi*, pp. 209ff.

13. Quoted in Liu Hsi-wei [Li Chien-wu], *Chü-hua erh chi*, p. 82.

14. Hui T'ang, "Li-shih yü hsien-shih" (History and Actuality), *Shanghai chou-pao*, No. 2; reprinted in Wei Ju-hui, *Pi hsüeh hua*, pp. 182–87.

15. I-pai [Chou I-pai], in *Ta-mei wan-pao* (Shanghai), 12 November 1939; reprinted in Wei, *Pi hsüeh hua*, pp. 187–95.

16. Wei, *Pi hsüeh hua*, p. 62.

17. *Ibid.,* p. 83.

18. Liu Hsi-wei [Li Chien-wu], in *Chü-hua erh chi*, p. 105.

19. "Yang O chuan ku-shih hsing-ch'eng ti ching-kuo" (The Process of Creating *The Story of Yang O*), in A Ying, *Yang O chuan*, pp. 7–8.

20. Ku Chung-i, *Liang Hung-yü*, p. 157.

21. For a review of this character in fiction, as well as a note on her appearance in classical opera, see C. T. Hsia, "The Military Romance: A Genre of Chinese Fiction," in Cyril Birch, ed., *Studies in Chinese Literary Genres* (Berkeley: University of California Press, 1974), pp. 371ff. Professor Hsia also takes up other stock motifs related to this discussion of costume drama, such as the companion heroes, unworthy governments, and traitors.

22. "Tzu hsü" (Author's introduction), in Chou I-pai, *Pei-ti wang*, p. 1.

23. Yao k'o, "*Ch'ing kung yuan* hou-chi" (Postscript to *Malice in the Ch'ing Court*), *Hsiao-shuo yüeh-pao* (October 1941), no. 12, p. 115.

24. *Ibid.*

25. Yao, *Ch'ing kung yuan*, p. 14; Yao, *The Malice of Empire*, p. 42.

26. See Yao's introductory notes in the motion-picture script taken from the play, *Ch'ing kung yuan* (Hong Kong, 1957), pp. *i–ii*.

27. Yao, *Ch'ing kung yuan*, p. 162; Yao, *The Malice of Empire,* p. 155.

28. Yao, *The Malice of Empire,* p. 13.

29. Yao, *Ch'ing kung yuan*, p. 32; Yao, *The Malice of Empire*, p. 58.

30. Yao, *Ch'ing kung yuan*, p. 106; Yao, *The Malice of Empire*, p. 113.

31. Yao, *Ch'ing kung yuan*, p. 106; Yao, *The Malice of Empire*, p. 113.

32. Yao, *Ch'ing kung yuan*, p. 33; Yao, *The Malice of Empire*, p. 59.

33. Yao, *Ch'ing kung yuan*, p. 8; Yao, *The Malice of Empire, p. 38.*

34. *Yao, Ch'ing kung yuan*, p. 17; Yao, *The Malice of Empire*, p. 44.

35. Yao, *Ch'ing kung yuan*, p. 21; Yao, *The Malice of Empire*, p. 49.

36. Yao, *Ch'ing kung yuan*, p. 46; Yao, *The Malice of Empire*, p. 69.

37. Yao, *Ch'ing kung yuan*, p. 166; Yao, *The Malice of Empire*, p. 159.

38. Yao K'o, personal correspondence, 18 May 1975.

39. Yao, *Ch'u pa-wang*, p. 64.

40. *Ibid.,* p. 132.

41. "*Mei-jen chi* hou chi" (Postscript to *The Strategem of the Beautiful Woman*), in Yao, *Mei-jen chi*, pp. 141–42.

42. Yao, *Ch'i ch'ung t'ien, Ta-chung* (The Masses) (December 1943), p. 177.

43. Yao, *Yin-hai ts'ang-sang*, p. 127.

44. Yao K'o, personal letter, 8 November 1975. No further resemblance to Wu was intended or is evident.

45. Yao, *Yin-hai ts'ang-sang*, pp. 1–4.

46. Eileen Chang [Chang Ai-ling], "Still Alive," *The Twentieth Century* (Shanghai) (June 1943), 4(6):432.

47. Ch'in Shou-ou, "Wo p'ing *Ch'iu Hai-t'ang*" (I Evaluate *Ch'iu hai-t'ang*), *Tsa-chih* (February 1943), 10(5):166–68.

48. "*Ch'iu Hai-t'ang* ti i-chih" (The Transplanting of *Ch'iu Hai-t'ang*), in Ch'in, *Ch'iu Hai-t'ang*, p. 2.

49. Yao K'o, personal correspondence, 14 August 1975.

50. Detailed discussions of the play as performed in Shanghai in 1942–1943 also exist as further confirmation. For example, see Chin Ni, "Pao-kao Shanghai chü-yun hsien-k'uang p'ing *Ch'iu Hai-t'ang*" (Reporting the Current Scene in the Shanghai Drama Movement and Criticizing *Ch'iu Hai-t'ang*), *Hsin-min pao pan-yüeh-k'an* (15 April 1943), 5(8):20–21.

51. Ch'in Shou-ou, *Ch'iu Hai-t'ang chu-pen*, p. 220.

52. *Ibid.*, p. 220.

53. Ch'ih Ch'ing, "*Ch'iu Hai-t'ang* chi ch'i-ta," *Tsa-chih* (February 1943), 10(5):169.

54. Ch'in Shou-ou, *Ch'iu Hai-t'ang chu-pen*, pp. 63–64.

55. Chang Ai-ling, "Still Alive," p. 432.

56. For example, in Chou I-pai, *Yang kuan san tieh* (Three Variations on the Theme of Yang Pass), p. 100, a wife accused unfairly of infidelity by her unfaithful husband still seeks the company of an innocent college student and says to him: "The way you talk, that's just 'letting officials commit arson and forbidding the common people to light lamps!'" The student replies: "Confucius said, 'Is your conscience at ease eating rice and wearing embroidery?' [Tsai Wo] replied, 'It is at ease.' Confucius said, 'If your conscience is at ease, then do it!'"

57. Mai Yeh, "Shih-yüeh ying-chü tsung-ping" (Summary of Films and Theater for October), *Tsa-chih* (November 1943), 12(2):171–72.

58. Li Chien-wu, "Hsü" (Introduction) in Fang Chün-i, *Li-hen t'ien*, pp. 1–5.

59. Chou I-pai is primarily known as a theater historian. Yao K'o has filled in

the general lack of biographical information with the following notes: "He is a native of Hunan and a good friend of T'ien Han who, incidentally, also hailed from that amazing province, the hotbed of revolutionaries. He was not well known until after the outbreak of war in 1937. As a dramatist he belonged to the Nan-kuo school founded by T'ien Han which, since the rise of Ts'ao Yü and the new left-wing playwrights, such as Hsia Yen, had 'lagged behind' and was no longer considered as avant-garde. In the fall of 1940, Chou Chien-yün, then manager of the Star Motion Picture Company, asked me to organize a training school for young people who aspired to become film players. Chou I-pai was then in Shanghai, so I recruited him to be a member of the faculty to lecture on the history of Chinese drama. His three-volume *History of Chinese Drama,* published in the 1950s, was actually based on his lecture notes on the subject. At that time, the China Traveling Dramatic Troupe had returned to Shanghai after a prolonged stay in Hong Kong. As its founder-producer T'ang Huai-ch'iu was a Hunanese as well as a follower of T'ien Han and an original member of the Nan-kuo Dramatic Society, Chou I-pai became the principal playwright for Chung-lü." Yao K'o, personal letter, 8 November 1975.

60.   Chou's plays tended to have substantial runs. In 1943 *Canary* had 122 performances in Shanghai and 30 in Peking. *Three Variations on the Theme of Yang Pass* went for 90 performances from January into March 1944. Yao K'o has noted that the company's productions tended to the slipshod, however. Personal letter, 8 November 1975.

61.   Mai Yeh, "Shih-yüeh ying-chü tsung-p'ing" (Summary of Films and Theater for October), *Tsa-chih* (November 1943), 12(2):172.

4. THE RESURGENCE OF TRADITION: THE FAMILIAR ESSAY

1.   T'ang T'ao dealt with Chou in several essays during the war: "Ts'ung K'u-chu tao ho-tao," in *T'ang T'ao tsa-wen hsüan,* pp. 188–89; "Ma Shih-ying yü Juan Ta-ch'eng," *ibid.,* p. 206; "P'o-men chieh," *ibid.,* pp. 254–55; "Mo-lo hsiao-p'in," *Yü-chou feng i-k'an* (1 September 1940), no. 28, pp. 5–8. Ai Ch'ing composed a poem titled "Ch'an-hui pa, Chou Tso-jen!" *K'ang-chan wen-i,* vol. 1, no. 9, reprinted in *Ming pao yüeh-k'an* (Hong Kong) (July 1976), no. 127, p. 36. This same article also notes that Professor Niu in Lao She's *Ssu-shih t'ung t'ang* (Four Generations under One Roof) was a portrait of Chou Tso-jen. Hsü Kuang-p'ing's "Wo-men ti t'an-chü shih t'a-men ti pao-pei" (Our Paralysis and Ulcers Are Their Treasures) appeared in *Wen-hsüeh chan-hsien* (Harbin) (September 1948), vol. 1, no. 3), accusing Chou of being "a heap of dog droppings, a traitor, the slave of foreigners and corruptor of the people." Her charges reappeared during the Cultural Revolution as part of a denunciation of Liu Shao-ch'i and Chou Yang, who had patronized Chou up to that time. See "Our Scabs Are Their Treasures," *Chinese Literature* (March 1968), no. 3, pp. 124–31. Ch'ien Chung-shu included a satiric sketch of Chou along with other major cultural figures in Peking during the thirties in his short story "Mao" (Cat), in *Jen, shou, kuei,* p. 39. Outside China, Chou's reputation has been rehabilitated in recent years by a variety of scholars. See, for example, Chou I-fu, "Chou Tso-jen chu-tso k'ao," *Chu-hai hsüeh-pan* (Hong Kong) (January 1973), no. 6; Hsia Chih-ts'ing, "Hsien-tai chung-kuo wen hsüeh shih ssu-

chung ho-p'ing," *Hsien-tai wen-hsüeh* (Taipei) (August 1977); and "Jen ti wen-hsüeh" in *Jen ti wen-hsüeh,* pp. 223–44.

2. See *Pi-tuan* (Hong Kong) (1 January 1968), no. 1, quoted in translation in Ernst Wolff, *Chou Tso-jen,* pp. 11–12.

3. Chao Ts'ung, *Sa nien-tai wen-t'an-chiang lu* (Generals of the Literary Scene in the Thirties) (Hong Kong, 1970), p. 78.

4. Ernst Wolff has suggested this in *Chou Tso-jen,* p. 11.

5. See Chou Tso-jen, *Chih T'ang hui-hsiang lu,* 2:576–77.

6. See T'ang T'ao, "Ts'ung k'u-chu tao ho-tao" (From Bitter Recluse Town Crier), in *T'ang T'ao tsa-wen hsüan,* pp. 88–89.

7. The letter, to Chou Li-an in Shanghai, was published in Chou Li-an, *Hua fa chi,* p. 38.

8. See Wen Tsai-tao, "Chou an yü-i" (Further Remarks on the Chou Case), in *Pien ku chi,* p. 7.

9. The poems appear in translation in Ernst Wolff, *Chou Tso-jen,* pp. 13–14.

10. Chou Tso-jen, *Chih T'ang hui-hsiang lu,* 2:571–76.

11. Notably the congresses of the East Asia Cultural Association (Tung-ya wen-hua hsieh-hui, Tokyo, 1941) and the Sino-Japanese Cultural Association (Chung-jih wen-hua hsieh-hui, Nanking, 1943).

12. See pp. 18–19 and 36–37.

13. Chou Tso-jen "Ta-tung-ya chan-cheng chung hua-pei wen-hua jen chih shih-ming ju-he?" (What Is the Mission of the North China Literati During the Greater East Asia War?), *Chung-kuo wen-i* (June 1942), 6(4):5.

14. According to Hu Lan-ch'eng, "Sui-pi liu tse" (Essay on Six Topics), *T'ien ti* (July 1944), no. 10, pp. 15–16.

15. "T'an hsin-shih hsü," reprinted in Chou Tso-jen, *Li-ch'un i-ch'ien* (Before Spring), pp. 186–88.

16. Ch'ien Tao-sun was then president of Peking University. Ch'ü Tui-chih (Ch'ü Hsüan-ying, b. 1892) was a graduate of Fu-tan University and had taught at several universities in Peking and published works on Chinese history. During the war he held government office and edited the *Chung-ho yüeh-k'an* (Sino-Japanese Monthly). Hsieh Hsing-yao and Hsieh Kang-chu were both historians and anti-quarians.

17. See I Chai, "Wu-che-hsiao-lu Shih-tu yin-hsiang chi" (Impressions of Musakōji Saneatsu), *I-wen tsa-chih* (August 1943), 1(2):15ff.

18. Chou Tso-jen, *K'u-k'ou kan-k'ou,* pp. 99–103.

19. See Chou, *Chih T'ang hui-hsiang lu,* 2:576–77.

20. Chou discusses these in *Chih T'ang hui-hsiang lu,* 2:579ff.

21. Chou, *Yao-wei chi,* pp. 115–24.

22. See "Ku-o shih-hua," in Chou, *Yeh tu ch'ao* (From Night Readings, 1934).

23. Chou, *Yao-wei chi,* pp. 91–92.

24. *Ibid.,* p. 93. Perhaps Chou's most explicit statement on this topic during the war occurs in "Meng hsiang chih i" (One Wishful Thought), in *K'u-k'ou kan-k'ou,* pp. 6–11. He deplores the neglect and lack of interest in natural sciences and the behavior of animals, which is both interesting in itself and fundamental to human behavior. The ultimate fate of ignoring the natural world is an intolerant, immoral slave society. He urges the study of biology, anthropology, and cultural history for an

understanding of realistic moral standards, those that conform to nature and do not go against it. As for the present, the youth of China are drowning, and their first priority is to save themselves. Once a person has saved himself he can go on to save others. Again the topic comes up in "Wo ti tsa-hsüeh" (My Miscellaneous Studies), in *K'u-k'ou kan-k'ou*, p. 71.

25. *Yao-wei chi*, pp. 107–08.

26. "Tsai t'an p'ai-wen," in Chou, *Yao-wei chi*, pp. 222–26. For a discussion of Chou's view of the role of humor, see David Pollard, *A Chinese Look at Literature*, pp. 110–11.

27. "Sa tou," in Chou, *Yao-wei chi*, p. 133.

28. "Tsai t'an p'ai-wen," in Chou, *Yao-wei chi*, p. 228.

29. See *Chung-kuo wen-i* (October 1940), 3(2):2–3; reprinted as "Hsüan-ch'uan" (Propaganda), in Chou, *Yao T'ang tsa-wen*, pp. 89–92.

30. Chou, *Chih T'ang hui-hsiang lu*, 2:586–87.

31. Chou, "Hou chi" (Epilogue), in *Li-ch'un i-ch'ien*, p. 195.

32. *Ibid.*, p. 195.

33. *Ibid.*

34. See Chou, *Chih T'ang hui-hsiang lu*, 2:580.

35. Chou, *Yao T'ang tsa-wen*, p. 1.

36. *Ibid.*

37. *Ibid.*, p. 7.

38. *Hong Kong News*, 24 September 1942, p. 4.

39. *Ibid.*, 7 November 1942, p. 3.

40. Chou, *Yao T'ang tsa-wen*, pp. 14–16.

41. *Ibid.*, p. 26.

42. *Ibid.*, p. 27.

43. *Ibid.*, p. 28.

44. Yoshikawa Kōjirō, "Ni-ka no bungakusha ni," *Bungakukai* (October 1943), 10(10):13.

45. Chou Tso-jen, "Chung-shu Kuo t'o-t'o chuan" (Camel Kuo the Gardener), Cyril Birch, tr, in *Anthology of Chinese Literature*, 2 vols. (New York: Grore, 1965), 1:258.

46. The articles are "I feng hsin" (A Letter); "Kuan-yü lao tso-chia" (Concerning Old Writers); and "Wen-t'an chih fen-hua" (The Division of the Literary Scene), all reprinted, together with related articles by others, in "Kuan-yü lao tso-chia wen-t'i" (Concerning the Issue of Old Writers), *Tsa-chih* (May 1944), 13(2):177–86.

47. Chou, "Wen-t'an chih fen-hua," in "Kuan-yü lao tso-chia wen-t'i," *Tsa-chih*, p. 180.

48. See chapter 1, note 22.

49. Kataoka's speech, officially titled "Chung-kuo wen-hsüeh chih ch'üeh-li" (The Establishment of Chinese Literature), is reprinted in translation in "Kuan-yü lao tso-chia wen-t'i," *Tsa-chih*, pp. 177–78.

50. Chou Tso-jen, *Chih T'ang hui-hsiang lu*, 2:591.

51. Chou, "Kuan-yü lao tso-chia," in "Kuan-yü lao tso-chia wen-t'i," *Tsa-chih*, p. 179.

52. According to Chou, Shen used the pen name T'ung T'o. The article

appeared in *Wen-pi chou-k'an* (February 1944), no. 1. See "Kuan-yü lao tso-chia wen-t'i," *Tsa-chih*, p. 181.

53. *Ibid.*, p. 180.

54. *Ibid.*, p. 186.

55. Editorial reprinted in "Kuan-yü lao tso-chia wen-t'i," p. 185.

56. T'ao Ching-sun, "Kuan-yü ta-tung-ya wen-hsüeh-che," in "Kuan-yü lao tso-chia wen-t'i," *Tsa-chih*, pp. 182–85.

57. Chin Hsi-min, "Wen-hua yun-tung yü chung-hsin ssu-hsiang" (The Cultural Movement and the Central Ideology), *Hsin-min pao pan-yüeh-k'an* (15 November 1943), 5(22):8–9.

58. For discussions of Chou Tso-jen's Confucianism in this light, see C. T. Hsia, review of *Chou Tso-jen*, by Ernst Wolff, in *Journal of the American Oriental Society* (1974), 96(4):527–28.

59. Chou Tso-jen, *K'u-k'ou kan-k'ou*, p. 60. Also quoted in Wolff, p. 56.

60. "Tao-te man-t'an" (Casual Talk on Ethics), Chou, *Yao T'ang tsa-wen*, pp. 50–51.

61. *Ibid.* The passage in *Mencius* cited by Chou may be found in James Legge, *The Four Books* (Shanghai, 1923), pp. 760–61. It has been omitted here since it has no crucial bearing on the points being discussed above. The important point is Chou's ambivalence toward pre-Han Confucianism as well as Neo-Confucianism.

62. Chou, *Yao T'ang tsa-wen*, pp. 35–36.

63. *Ibid.*, pp. 39–44.

64. Chou, *Li-ch'un i-ch'ien*, pp. 44–50.

65. Chou, *K'u-k'ou kan-k'ou*, pp. 55–59.

66. See pp. 52–53.

67. Chou, *Li-ch'un i-ch'ien*, p. 58.

68. Chou, *K'u-k'ou kan-k'ou*, pp. 1–5.

69. *Ibid.*, pp. 24–28.

70. Chou, *Li-ch'un i-ch'ien*, p.111.

71. *Ibid.*, p. 163. How early Chou "announced" this is uncertain, but the statement appears also in "Kuan-yü lao tso-chia wen-t'i," *Tsa-chih* (May 1944), 13(2):178.

72. Chou, *Li-ch'un i-ch'ien*, pp. 190–91.

73. *Ibid.*, p. 169.

74. Chou, *K'u-k'ou kan-k'ou*, pp. 18–23.

75. *Ibid.*, p. 31.

76. Chou, *Yao T'ang tsa-wen*, p. 26.

77. Pollard, *A Chinese Look at Literature*, p. 84.

78. Cited in Pollard, p. 86.

79. Chou Tso-jen, *Chih T'ang hui-hsiang lu*, 2:580.

80. Chou, *Yao T'ang tsa-wen*, p. 26.

81. For an account of the "court recluse" prior to the twentieth century, see Li Chi, "The Changing Concept of the Recluse in Chinese Literature," *Harvard Journal of Asian Studies* (1962–63), 24:241–47.

82. I do not intend to discuss in detail these political figures as writers. For a discussion of their writing, see Liu Hsin-huang, "K'ang-chan shih-tai luo-shui tso-chia shu-lun," *Fan-kung* (Counterattack) (Taipei) (January 1974), no. 382, pp. 11–14; (February 1974), no. 383, pp. 11–14.

83.　Lin Yü-t'ang, *Shuo-feng* (Northern Wind) (10 December 1938), no. 2, pp. 86–87.

84.　See Chu Hsing-chai, "Fa-k'an tz'u" (Initial Publication Statement), *Ku chin* (March 1942), 1(1):2.

85.　"Yü Ch'ieh sui-pi" (Yü Ch'ieh's Jottings), in Hsün Feng, ed., *Hsien-tai san-wen sui-pi hsüan,* p. 164.

86.　See T'ao Kang-te, "Tung-hsing jih-chi" (Diary of Eastern Travel), *Ku chin* (1 October 1943), no. 34, pp. 10–17.

87.　"Yuan Tzu-ts'ai yü Cheng Pan-ch'iao chih yu-mo" (The Humor of Yuan Tzu-ts'ai and Cheng Pan-ch'iao), in Chou Li-an, *Feng-men chi,* p. 21.

88.　*Ibid.,* p. 29.

89.　Four of Chou Li-an's articles on Chou Tso-jen are included in the collection *Hua fa chi* (White-haired) (Shanghai, 1940).

90.　*Hua fa chi,* p. 110. For other remarks on the eight-legged essay issue, see essays beginning on pp. 59, 63, 65, and 127.

91.　"Hsü" (Introduction), in Chou Li-an, *Feng men chi,* pp. 1–4.

92.　Chou Li-an, "I Yü Ta-fu," *Ku chin* (16 January 1943), no. 15.

93.　Chou, "Pien-chi hou-chi" (Editor's Afterword), *Ku chin* (March 1943), anniversary issue.

94.　Chou *"Nieh-hai hua* jen-wu shih-chia" (Characters and Hereditary Families in *Nieh-hai hua), Ku chin* (16 August 1943), no. 29, pp. 1–4.

95.　Chu Hsing-chai (Chu P'u), "P'u yuan sui-pi" (Jottings from P'u garden), *Ku chin* (16 August 1943), no. 29, pp. 1–4.

96.　Ch'ü Tui-chih, *"Yü-chou feng* yü *ku chin," Ku chin* (16 March 1943), special anniversary issue, pp. 26–27.

97.　*Ibid.,* p. 27.

98.　Liu Ts'un-jen gives a biography of himself to 1942 in "T'an tzu-chuan, fu: tso-che lüeh" (An Autobiography with Appendix: A Sketch of the Author), *Ku chin* (1 November 1942), no. 10, pp. 14–16.

99.　Liu, "Fu-te Kuang-chou ti ch'ih" (On the Theme of Cantonese Food), *Ku chin* (September 1942), no. 7, p. 27.

100.　See Liu Yü-sheng, "Hai-k'o t'an-ying lu" (Ocean Voyager Talks of Overseas), *Feng-yü t'an* (October 1943), no. 6, pp. 133 and 138. This and other related essays were published together in this issue of *Feng-yü t'an* and later published as a book *Huai hsiang chi,* which also included the essay "I-kuo hsin-ying lu" (Mental Images of a Foreign Land), *Ku chin* (16 March 1943), anniversary issue, pp. 81–90.

101.　See Liu, "Kuan-yü Yao T'ang [Chou Tso-jen]" in Yang I-ming, ed., *Wen-t'an shih-liao,* pp. 95–99.

102.　Wen Tsai-tao, "Ch'iang yü pi" (Gun and Pen), in Wen Tsai-tao et al., *Heng-mei chi* (Angry Eyebrows) (Shanghai, 1939), pp. 137–39.

103.　"Sao-ch'u i-min ch'i" (Purge the Recluse Temperament), in Wen, *Heng-mei chi,* pp. 107–14.

104.　Chou Tso-jen, "P'u yuan ya-chi chi" (A Refined Gathering in P'u Garden), *Ku chin* (16 June 1943), no. 25, p. 9.

105.　"Shui-sheng ch'in-yü" (Water Sounds and Bird Calls), in Wen Tsai-tao, *Feng-t'u hsiao-chi,* p. 115.

106.　"Ch'iang yü pi," in Wen Tsai-tas et al., *Heng-mei chi,* p. 138.

107. *"Wen Tsai-tao wen-ch'ao* hsü" (Introduction to *Wen Tsai-tao's Copied Notes),* in Chou Tso-jen, *Li-ch'un i-ch'ien,* p. 182.

108. "Ch'ing chia lu," in Chou, *Yeh tu ch'ao,* quoted in translation in Pollard, *A Chinese Look at Literature,* p. 133.

109. Chou Tso-jen, *Li-ch'un i-ch'ien,* pp. 148–49.

110. *Ibid.,* p. 183.

111. Wen Tsai-tao, "Tu *Yao T'ang tsa-wen,"* *Ku chin* (1 July 1944), no. 50, p. 5.

112. Wen, *Feng-t'u hsiao-chi,* p. 35.

113. *Ibid.,* pp. 90–91.

114. Wen, "Wei-chin jen-wu chih" (An Account of Personages of the Wei-Chin period), *Ku chin* (1 January 1944), no. 39, p. 17.

115. *Ibid.,* p. 17.

116. Wen, *Yü-chou feng i-k'an* (November 1940), no. 32, pp. 34–36.

117. See Wen, *Feng-t'u hsiao-chi,* pp. 99, 254. Page references hereafter given in text.

118. Wen, "Sheng-ming ti tiao-yen" appeared in *Yü-chou feng i-k'an* (May 1940), no. 24, pp. 364–67. The other essays cited are included in the volume *Feng-t'u hsiao-chi.*

119. Chi Kuo-an, *"Ku chin* yü wo" *(Past and Present* and I), *Ku chin* (16 March 1943), special anniversary issue, p. 33.

120. Chi, "Chih T'ang hsien-sheng nan-lai yin-hsiang chui-chi" (An Impressionistic Reminiscence of Mr. Chih T'ang's Southern Visit), *Ku chin* (16 April 1943), nos. 20–21, p. 5.

121. See Chi, "Hai-shang chi-hsing" (Shanghai Travel Notes), *Ku chin* (1 August 1943), no. 30, pp. 23–27.

122. Chi, "Yü chia" (A Talk on Grain Farming), in Hsün Feng, ed., *Hsien-tai san-wen sui-pi hsüan,* p. 53.

123. Yeh Sung-shih, cited in Chou Tso-jen, "T'an wen," in *K'u-chu tsa-chi* (Peking, 1936), p. 289, quoted in translation in Pollard, *A Look at Chinese Literature,* p. 86.

124. Chi, *T'ien ti* (October 1944), no. 13, p. 15. Page references hereafter given in text.

125. See Ssu-ma Ch'ien, *Shih chi* (Records of the historian), ch. 99.

126. Chi Kuo-an, "Chih-chi p'ien," *T'ien ti,* p. 17.

5. Antiromanticism

1. Lin I-liang [Sung Ch'i], *Lin I-liang shih-hua,* p. 56.

2. See *Lin I-liang shih-hua,* pp. 1–31.

3. Stephen Soong, interviewed in Hong Kong, 15 March 1977.

4. Among writers of poetry, Tu Nan-hsing produced a small number of verses that have attracted no recognition. Lu I-shih (Lu Yü), on the other hand, wrote a large quantity of bad verse and received much unfavorable attention. Feng Wen-ping attracted attention with two essays on Zen and poetry: "Hsin shih ying-kai shih tzu-yu shih" (New Poetry Should be Free Poetry), *Wen-hsüeh chi-k'an* (September 1943), no. 1, pp. 2–11; and "I-wang ti shih wen-hsüeh yü hsin shih" (Past Poetic Literature and New Poetry), *Wen-hsüeh chi-k'an* (April 1944), no. 2, pp. 2–13.

5. In "Yen ku-shih ssu-p'ien" (Reenacting Four Old Tales), Wu, *Wen-i shih-tai* (June 1946), 1(1):20–22.

6. In "Shih ssu-shou" (Four Poems), Wu, *Wen-i shih-tai* (July 1946), 1(2):32.

7. *Ibid.*, pp. 31–32.

8. Prior to the war, Sun taught at Tsinghua University. Early in the war his lover, the writer-actress Feng Chi-jen (Feng Ho-tzu, Feng-tzu), left for the interior and he moved to Shanghai, where in 1939 his poems were published. He apparently did little creative work thereafter.

9. Edwin Muir, *The Present Age from 1914,* p. 24.

10. *Ibid.*

11. Ch'ien Chung-shu, *Jen, shou, kuei,* p. 23.

12. Yao Hsin-nung, personal letter, 18 May 1975.

13. For a biographical as well as critical introduction to Chang Ai-ling, see C. T. Hsia, *A History of Modern Chinese Fiction,* pp. 389–431. Hu Lan-ch'eng, with whom she lived during the last year of the war, discusses his life with her in *Chin sheng chin shih,* 2:299–332.

14. Quoted in Shui Ching [Yang I], *Chang Ai-ling ti hsiao-shuo i-shu.*

15. Hsia, *A History of Modern Chinese Fiction,* p. 396.

16. See "Nü tso-chia chü-t'an-hui" (Women Writers' Group Discussion), *Tsa-chih* (April 1944), 13(3):55. In the same article, Chang cautioned that among Chinese writers she was not solely interested in the work of Ts'ao Hsüeh-ch'in and cited a number of works from *Lao Ts'an yu chi* and *Hai-shang hua lieh-chuan* to *Li-hun* (Lao She) and *Jih-ch'u* (Ts'ao Yü) which she had enjoyed. Similarly, when asked recently to comment on the relationship of her early work to modern British literature, she wrote the following: "I came across the writers you mentioned—aside from Evelyn Waugh whom I have never read—in the HKU library when I was a student; read most of Beverly Nichols until he took up gardening, found him refreshing but had forgotten the entire contents almost rightaway, and tended to confuse him with Noël Coward; liked Maugham's short stories, admired Aldous Huxley, but lost interest in him after college. I daresay there is a lot of truth in your theory, although I believe skepticism is inborn. My formative years came earlier, at twelve, thirteen when I read *Hung lou meng* and *Chin p'ing mei;* fourteen, Maupassant, Chekhov, and W. W. Jacobs' "The Monkey's Paw" in *The World's Best Short Stories;* fifteen, sixteen, Shaw's prefaces and H. G. Wells' *The History of Mr. Polly, Kipps, Love and Mr. Lewisham,* and science fiction—and from then on through college, steadily rejecting Arnold Bennet, Hugh Walpole, and Compton MacKenzie when there was no other reading matter." (Personal letter, 6 June 1977). Chang's rejection of the last three writers named is not without significance, for they were usually labeled "romantic" and rejected by contemporaries.

17. Chang, *Liu-yen,* pp. 41–42. Cf. Aldous Huxley, *Point Counter Point* (Harmondsworth: Penguin Books, 1976), p. 29, describing an artist's response to a concert: "You seem to have found the truth; clear, definite, unmistakable, it is announced by the violins; you have it, you triumphantly hold it. But it slips out of your grasp to present itself in a new aspect among the cellos and yet again in terms of Pongileoni's vibrating air column. The parts live their separate lives; they touch, their paths cross, they combine for a moment to create a seemingly final and perfected harmony, only to break apart again. Each is always alone and separate and individual. 'I am I,' asserts the violin; 'the world revolves around me.' 'Round me,'

calls the cello. 'Round me,' the flute insists. And all are equally right and equally wrong; and none of them will listen to the others. In the human fugue there are eighteen hundred million parts. The resultant noise means something perhaps to the statistician, nothing to the artist. It is only by considering one or two parts at a time that the artist can understand anything." Page references hereafter given in text.

18. Chang, *Liu-yen*, p. 47.

19. Chang, *Chang Ai-ling tuan-p'ien hsiao-shuo chi* p. 366. Page references hereafter given in text.

20. Shui Ching, *Chang Ai-ling*, p. 44.

21. Chang, *Chang Ai-ling tuan-p'ien hsiao-shuo chi,* p. 225. Page references hereafter given in text.

22. *Ibid.*, p. 168; "The Golden Cangue," Eileen Chang, tr. in C. T. Hsia, ed., *Twentieth-Century Chinese Stories* (New York: Columbia University Press, 1971), p. 157.

23. *Chang Ai-ling tuan-p'ien hsiao-shuo chi,* p. 162; *Chinese Stories,* p. 151.

24. *Chang Ai-ling tuan-p'ien hsiao-shuo chi,* p. 168; *Chinese Stories,* p. 157.

25. *Chang Ai-ling tuan-p'ien hsiao-shuo chi,* p. 171; *Chinese Stories,* p. 161.

26. *Chang Ai-ling tuan-p'ien hsiao-shuo chi,* p. 176; *Chinese Stories,* p. 165.

27. *Chang Ai-ling tuan-p'ien hsiao-shuo chi,* pp. 177–78; *Chinese Stories,* p. 166.

28. *Chang Ai-ling tuan p'ien hsiao-shuo chi,* p. 189; *Chinese Stories,* p. 178.

29. *Chang Ai-ling tuan p'ien hsiao-shuo chi,* p. 201; *Chinese Stories,* pp. 189–90.

30. *Chang Ai-ling tuan p'ien hsiao-shuo chi,* p. 339. Page references hereafter given in text.

31. "Red Rose and White Rose," *ibid.*, p. 78.

32. *Chang Ai-ling tuan-p'ien hsiao-shuo chi,* pp. 400–01. Page references hereafter given in text.

33. See Hsia, *A History of Modern Chinese Fiction,* pp. 407–13.

34. Chang, *Chang Ai-ling tuan-p'ien hsiao-shuo chi,* pp. 260–61. Page references hereafter given in text.

35. Quoted in Hsia Chih-ts'ing, "Hsia Tsi-an tui chung-kuo su-wen-hsüeh ti k'an-fa," *Hsien-tai wen-hsüeh* (Contemporary Literature) (Taipei) (1964), no. 25, pp. 25–26.

36. Yang Chiang, *Ch'en-hsin ju-i,* p. 1.

37. Yang, *Lung-chen ch'eng-chia,* p. 54.

38. He is quoted in Meng Tu, "Kuan-yü Yang Chiang ti hua," *Tsa-chih* (May 1945), 15(2):110–12.

39. *Ibid.*, p. 111. See also Mai Yeh, "Ch'i-yüeh ying-chü tsung-p'ing" (Summary of films and theater for July), *Tsa-chih,* (August 1943), 12(2):172–73.

40. Mai Yeh, "Ch'i-hsi t'an chü" (Drama talk for the week), *Tsa-chih* (September 1944), 13(6):164–65.

41. Yang, *Feng-hsü,* p. 20. Page references hereafter given in text.

42. Ch'ien, *Hsieh tsai jen-sheng pien shang,* pp. 63–64.

43. Ch'ien, *T'an i lu* (Shanghai, 1942; rev. ed., 1948), pp. 332ff.

44. *Ibid.*, pp. 234–35.

45. It would seem that Ch'ien, given his skepticism and irreverence, was still seriously interested in mysticism, though a thoroughly worked out conception does

not appear in his works. It is interesting to note the fact of Aldous Huxley's contemporaneous interest in mysticism.

46. Hsia, *A History of Modern Chinese Fiction,* p. 441.

47. Ch'ien, *Jen, shou, kuei,* p. 89.

48. C. T. Hsia, *Jen ti wen-hsüeh,* p. 179, identifies caricatures of Chao Yuan-jen, Lin Tü-t'ang, and Shen Ts'ung-wen, also noting that the protagonists suggest Liang Ssu-ch'eng and Lin Hui-yin. The four identifications above were noted by Ssu-ma Ch'ang-feng in four articles in *Ming pao* (Hong Kong), 4, 9, 12, and 18 May 1977.

49. Quoted in translation in C. T. Hsia, *A History of Modern Chinese Fiction,* p. 439.

50. Ch'ien, *Jen, shou, kuei,* p. 126. Page references hereafter given in text.

51. Ch'ien, *Wei-ch'eng,* p. 289. Page references hereafter given in text.

52. Ch'ien, *Wei-ch'eng,* p. 272, cited in Hsia, *A History of Modern Chinese Fiction,* p. 448.

53. Ch'ien, *Wei-ch'eng,* p. 278.

54. Ch'ien, *Wei-ch'eng,* p. 336; Hsia, *A History of Modern Chinese Fiction,* p. 450.

55. Ch'ien, *Wei-ch'eng,* p. 342; Hsia, *A History of Modern Chinese Fiction,* p. 459.

56. Ch'ien, *Wei-ch'eng;* Hsia, *A History of Modern Chinese Fiction,* p. 458.

57. Ch'ien, *Wei-ch'eng,* p. 107.

58. Ch'ien, *Wei-ch'eng,* p. 91; Hsia, *A History of Modern Chinese Fiction,* p. 447.

59. Ch'ien in *The Chinese Yearbook, 1944–45,* p. 125.

60. Those sensitive to traditional imagery might point to Ch'ien's use of women and water as elements derived from traditional five-elements *yin-yang* theory. A dominant image in the novel is that of water, and the plot centers for the most part on Hung-chien's relations with women. Indeed, Ch'ien would be quite aware of the implications and enjoyed using the phrase "women's watery nature" (*nü-jen shui-hsing*), a reference to their fickleness, facetiously, in earlier works. For example, his essay "Shuo hsiao" (On smiling) contains the following passage: "Therefore, humor is at most a kind of temperament, and can't be offered as something to advocate, even less as a profession. We mustn't forget that the Latin source of the word "humor" means liquid. In other words, humor, like women, has a watery nature (i.e., attaches to anything)" (*Hsieh tsai jen-sheng pien-shang,* p. 26; see also *Jen, shou, kuei,* p. 9). That Ch'ien might seriously employ such a *yin-yang* motif in *The Besieged City* would be based on its consistent use for his theme of human vanity. In fact, the novel does begin with references to intense heat and strong sun as Hung-chien, still uninvolved with women, rides securely aboard the steamship above the ocean, in the confident image of the ideal returned overseas student. But this is a brief and unreal picture, and as the novel states shortly, ideals evaporate under the sun into mist, to fall again as rain (p. 29). Hung-chien is soon reduced to fear of being exposed as a fraud, and in his relations with women he has been manipulated and defeated. Hung-chien is soon plunged into the rain-soaked trip into the interior, where Jou-chia, a women's association, and a prostitute dominate the course of the group's progress, and Jou-chia begins to assert an influence on Hung-chien. Finally falling into Jou-chia's trap, Hung-chien returns with her to Shanghai to battle with her amah and

her aunt. In the end he is driven to wandering cold, dark streets through wind-driven snow.

61. See Northrop Frye, *Anatomy of Criticism,* (Princeton, N.J.: Princeton University Press, 1957), pp. 147ff. For the application of Frye's criticism to modern British literature, see Stephen Jay Greenblatt, *Three Modern Satirists: Waugh, Orwell, and Huxley,* pp. 112ff.

62. Ch'ien, *Wei ch'eng,* p. 326.

63. *Hsin-yüeh yüeh-k'an* (December 1932), 4(5):7.

64. Dennis Ting-pong Hu, "A Linguistic-Literary Study of Ch'ien Chung-shu's Three Creative Works," pp. 3–4.

65. Stephen Soong, interviewed in Hong Kong, 8 November 1976.

Glossary

A Ying *see* Ch'ien Hsing-ts'un
"Ai-kuo hu-chi 愛國護己
Ai Wu 艾蕪
  "Kuan-yü chü-p'ing chieh ti e-lieh ch'ing-hsiang" 關於劇評界的惡劣
    傾向
bushidō 武士道
Chang Ai-ling 張愛玲 [Liang Ching 梁京]
  "Ch'en hsiang hsieh—ti-erh lu-hsiang" 沉香屑—第二爐香
    Roger 羅傑
    Mrs. Mitchell 蜜秋太太
    Susie 愫細
    Millicent 靡麗笙
  "Ch'en hsiang hsieh—ti-i lu-hsiang" 沉香屑—第一爐香
    Ko Wei-lung 葛薇龍
    Liang T'ai-t'ai 梁太太
    George Ch'iao 喬琪喬
  "Chin So chi" 金鎖記
    Ts'ao Ch'i-ch'iao 曹七巧
    Chiang Chi-tse 姜季澤
    Chiang Ch'ang-an 姜長安
  "Chin-yü lu" 燼餘錄
  "Ch'ing ch'eng chih lien" 傾城之戀
    Pai Liu-su 白流蘇
    Fan Liu-yuan 范柳原
    Hsü T'ai-t'ai 徐太太
  "Feng-so" 封鎖
    Wu Ts'ui-yuan 吳翠遠
    Lü Tsung-chen 呂宗楨
  "Hsin ching" 心經
    Hsü Hsiao-han 許小寒
    Tuan Ling-ch'ing 段綾卿
  "Hung mei-kuei yü pai mei-kuei" 紅玫瑰與白玫瑰

Tung Chen-pao 佟振保
Wang Chiao-jui 王嬌蕊
Wang Shih-hung 王士洪
Meng Yen-li 孟烟鸝
Lien-huan t'ao 連環套
Liu-yen 流言
"Mo-li hsiang-p'ien" 茉莉香片
Nieh Ch'uan-ch'ing 聶傳慶
Yen Tan-chu 言丹朱
Yen Tzu-yeh 言子夜
Nieh Chieh-ch'en 聶介臣
"Nien-ch'ing ti shih-hou" 年輕的時候
"Nü tso-chia chü-t'an hui" 女作家聚談會
"Szu-yü" 私語
"Tao-ti shih Shanghai-jen" 到底是上海人
"T'ung-yen wu chi" 童言無忌
Chang Chieh 張杰
Chang Hen-shui 張恨水
Man chiang hung 滿江紅
Chang Hung, *see* Chang Yin-nan
Chang K'o-piao 章克標
"Chung-kuo wen-hsüeh hsin-sheng chih lu" 中國文學新生之路
Chang Shan-k'un 張善琨
Chang Shen-ch'ieh 張深切
Chang Ssu-hsü 張似旭 (Sammy Chang)
Chang T'ieh-sheng 張鐵笙
Chang Tzu-p'ing 張資平
Chang Wo-chün 張我軍
Chang Yin-nan 張隱南 (Chang Hung 張鴻)
Hsü nieh-hai hua 續孽海花
Ch'ang Feng 常風
K'uei t'ien chi 窺天集
Chao Ching-shen 趙景深
Ch'en Hsi-ho 陳西禾 (Lin K'o 林柯)
Ch'en-yuan 沉淵
Ch'en Kung-po 陳公博
Ch'en Mien 陳綿
Ch'en Ta-pei 陳大悲
Cheng Chen-to 鄭振鐸
Cheng Hsiao-hsü 鄭孝胥

Hai-tsang lou shih 海藏樓詩
Cheng-yen pao 正言報
　"Ts'ao yuan" 草原
Chi Kuo-an (Chi Kuo-hsüan)
Chi Kuo-hsüan 紀國宣 (Chi Kuo-an 紀果庵)
　"Chih chi p'ien" 知己篇
　"Chih-t'ang hsien-sheng nan-lai yin-hsiang chui-chi" 知堂先生南來印
　　象追記
　"Hai-shang chi-hsing" 海上記行
　"*Ku chin* yü wo" 古今與我
　Liang tu chi 兩都集
Chiang K'ang-hu 江亢虎
Ch'ien Chung-shu 錢鍾書
　"Chi-nien" 記念
　　Man-ch'ien 曼倩
　　T'ien-chien 天健
　　Ts'ai-shu 才叔
　"Shang-ti ti meng" 上帝的夢
　T'an i lu 談藝錄
　　Yen Yü 嚴羽 (I Ch'ing 儀卿)
　　Ts'ang-lang shih-hua 滄浪詩話
　Wei-ch'eng 圍城
　　Chao Hsin-mei 趙辛楣
　　Fang Hung-chien 方鴻漸
　　Han Hsüeh-yü 韓學愈
　　Li Mei-t'ing 李梅亭
　　Lu Tzu-hsiao 陸子瀟
　　Pao Hsiao-chieh 鮑小姐
　　Su Wen-wan 蘇文紈
　　Sun Jou-chia 孫柔嘉
　　Wang Hsien-sheng 王先生
Ch'ien Hsing-ts'un 錢杏邨 (A Ying 阿英, Jo Ying 若英, Wei Ju-hui
　魏如晦)
　Nan Ming shih-chü 南明史劇
　Hsüan-ao shen-yuan 懸嶴神猿
　Hai-kuo ying-hsiung 海國英雄
　Ming-mo i-hen 明末遺恨 (Pi hsüeh hua 碧血花)
　　Cheng Ch'eng-kung 鄭成功
　　Cheng Chih-lung 鄭芝龍
　　Feng Chin-tzu 馮金子

Ko Nen-niang 葛嫩娘
Mei Niang 美娘
Po Lo 博洛
Sun K'o-hsien 孫克咸
T'ang Wang 唐王
Ts'ai Ju-heng 蔡如蘅

Ch'un feng ch'iu yü 春風秋雨
Hung Hsüan-chiao 洪宣嬌
Niu-lang chih-nü chuan 牛郎織女傳
Pu yeh ch'eng 不夜城
T'ao-hua yuan 桃花源
Wu chieh-mei 五姊妹
Yang O chuan 楊娥傳

"*Yang O chuan* ku-shih hsing-ch'eng ti ching-kuo" 楊娥傳故事形成
的經過

Chien-she hsin wen-i ti ke-chieh hung-lun" 建設新文藝的各界宏論
Ch'ien Tao-sun 錢稻孫
Ch'ih Ch'ing 池清
"*Ch'iu Hai-t'ang* chi ch'i-t'a" 秋海棠及其它
Ch'ih Shu-jen 吃書人 "Edible Edition"
Chih T'ang (Chou Tso-jen)
Chin Hsing-yao 金性堯 (Wen Tsai-tao 文載道)

"Ch'a yen hsiao chi" 茶烟小記
"Ch'iang yü pi" 槍與筆
"Chou an yü-i" 周案餘議
"Fu shih ts'ao" 浮世草
"Hsi-hu chiu-chi lu" 西湖舊屐錄
"I Jo Ying" 憶若英
"I san-chia ts'un" 憶三家邨
"Kuan-yü feng-t'u jen-ch'ing" 關於風土人情
"Kuan-yü *Wen -ch'ao* yü *Feng-t'u hsiao chi*" 關於文抄與風土小記
"P'u yuan ya chi chi" 樸園雅集記
"Sao-ch'u i-min ch'i" 掃除逸民氣
"Sheng-ming ti tiao-yen" 生命的弔唁
"Shui-sheng ch'in yü" 水聲禽語
"Sui hsing chin i" 歲行盡矣
"Teng shih" 燈市
"Tsun K'ung tsa-kan" 尊孔雜感
"Tu *Yao T'ang tsa-wen*" 讀藥堂雜文
"Tung-hsin ts'ao" 冬心草

"Wei-Chin jen-wu chi" 魏晉人物記
Chin Hsi-min 金希民
    "Wen-hua yun-tung yü chung-hsin ssu-hsiang" 文化運動與中心思想
Chin Hsiung-pai 金雄白
    Hai pao 海報
Ch'in Shou-ou 秦瘦鷗
    Ch'iu Hai-t'ang 秋海棠
        Ch'iu Hai-t'ang 秋海棠 (Wu Yü-ch'in 吳玉琴, Wu Chün 吳鈞)
        Lo Hsiang-i 羅湘綺
        Mei Pao 梅寶
        Yuan Pao-fan 袁寶藩
    "Wo p'ing *Ch'iu Hai-t'ang*" 我評秋海棠
    "*Ch'iu Hai-t'ang* ti i-chih" 秋海棠的移植
    Ch'iu Hai-t'ang chü-pen 秋海棠劇本
        "Lo Ch'eng chiao kuan" 羅成叫關
        "Su San ch'i-chieh" 蘇三起解
Ching 靖 "Fu tzu chih chien" 父子之間
Chou Chien-yün 周劍雲
Chou Ch'üan-p'ing 周全平
Chou Hua-jen 周化人
Chou I-pai 周貽白
    Chin Ssu-ch'üeh 金絲雀
    Lien huan chi 連環計
        Lü Pu 呂布
        Tiao Ch'an 貂蟬
        Tung Cho 董卓
    Pei ti wang 北地王 (*Wang shu i-hen* 亡蜀遺恨)
        Li Shih 李氏
        Liu Ch'an 劉禪
        Liu Ch'en 劉諶
        Sun Ch'uan 孫權
        Teng Ai 鄧艾
    T'ien-wai t'ien 天外天
        Shun Chih 順治
        Tung Fei 董妃
    Yang kuan san-tieh 陽關三疊
    Hua Mu-lan 花木蘭
Chou Leng-ch'ieh 周楞伽
Chou Li-an 周黎庵 (Li K'an 笠堪)
    "I Yü Ta-fu" 憶郁達夫

"K'an jen lun shih" 看人論事

"*Nieh-hai hua* jen-wu shih-chia" 孽海花人物世家

"Wo yü tsa-wen" 我與雜文

"Yin Liang Shih-ch'iu ti yao-ch'iu erh hsiang-ch'i" 因梁實秋的
要求而想起

"Yuan Tzu-ts'ai yü Cheng Pan-ch'iao chih yu-mo" 袁子才與
鄭板橋之幽默

Chou Mu-chai 周木齋

Chou Pan-hou 周班侯 (Pan Kung 班公)

Chou Shou-chuan 周瘦鵑

Chou Tso-jen 周作人 (Chih T'ang 知堂, Yao T'ang 藥堂)

"Chung-kuo ti ssu-hsiang wen-t'i" 中國的思想問題

"Chung-kuo wen-hsüeh shang ti liang chung ssu-hsiang" 中國文
學上的兩種思想

"Han wen-hsüeh ti ch'ien-t'u" 漢文學的前途

"Han wen-hsüeh ti ch'uan-t'ung" 漢文學的傳統

"I feng hsin" 一封信

"Jih-pen chih tsai-jen-shih" 日本之再認識

"K'u-k'ou kan-k'ou" 苦口甘口

"Ku e shih-hua" 姑惡詩話

"Kuan-yü lao tso-chia" 關於老作家

"Kuo-yü wen ti san lei" 國語文的三類

"*Li-ch'un i-ch'ien* hou chi" 立春以前後記

"Lun hsiao-shuo chiao-yü" 論小說教育

"Sa tou" 撒豆

"Shih-tzu yü ju-chia" 釋子與儒家

"Ta tung-ya chan-cheng chung hua-pei wen-hua jen chih shih-ming
ju-ho?" 大東亞戰爭中華北文化人之使命如何

"Tao-te man-t'an" 道德漫談

"*T'an hsin shih* hsü" 談新詩序

"T'an p'ai-wen" 談俳文

"Tsa-wen ti lu" 雜文的路

"Tsai t'an p'ai-wen" 再談俳文

"Tzu-chi ti yüan-ti" 自己的園地

"Wen-hsüeh yü hsüan-ch'uan" 文學與宣傳

"Wen-i fu-hsing chih meng" 文藝復興之夢

"Wen-t'an chih fen-hua" 文壇之分化

"Wen-t'an chih wai" 文壇之外

"Wo ti tsa-hsüeh" 我的雜學

"Wu-che hsien-sheng ho wo" 武者先生和我

"Yü chi szu" 禹跡寺
Chou Yü-ying 周毓英
Chou Yüeh-jan 周越然
Chu Fan, *see* Kao Chi-lin
Chu Hsing-chai 朱省齋 (Chu P'u 朱樸)
  "P'u yuan sui-pi" 樸園隨筆
Chu Hsing-kung 朱興公
Chu P'u, *see* Chu Hsing-chai
Ch'ü I (Wang Jen-shu)
Ch'ü Hsüan-ying 瞿宣穎 (Ch'ü Tui-chih 瞿兌之)
  "*Yü-chou feng* yü *ku-chin*" 宇宙風與古今
ch'ü-wei 趣味
Chu Tuan-chiun 朱端鈞
ch'uan-ch'i 傳奇
Ch'üan-kuo wen-hua tai-piao ta-hui 全國文化代表大會
Chung-fa chü-she 中法劇社
Chung-fa lien-i hui 中法聯誼會
Chung-hua lien-ho tien-ying yu-hsien kung-szu　中國聯合電影有限公司
  (Hua ying 華影)
Chung-hua tien-ying kung-szu 中華電影公司
Chung-jih wen-hua hsieh-hui 中日文化協會
Chung-kuo lü-hsing chü-t'uan 中國旅行劇團
Chung-kuo wen-i hsieh-hui 中國文藝協會
Daitōa bungaku 大東亞文學
Fang Chi-sheng 方紀生
  "Shuo feng shih cha chi" 朔風室札記
Fang Chün-i 方君逸 (Wu T'ien 吳天)
   Chia 家
   Li hen t'ien 離恨天
    Liang Shan-po 梁山伯
    Chu Ying-t'ai 祝英台
   Man t'ing fang 滿庭芳
fang-tzu 放恣
Fei Ming, *see* Feng Wen-ping
Fei Mu 費穆
   Fu-sheng liu chi 浮生六記
    Shen San-pai 沈三白
   Mei-hua meng 梅花夢
   P'eng Yü-lin 彭玉麟
   Yang Kuei-fei 楊貴妃

Feng Chi-jen 封季壬 (Feng Ho-tzu 封禾子, Feng Tzu 鳳子)
Feng Chieh-chung 馮介中
  "Hsün chih" 殉職
Feng Ho-i 馮和儀 (Su Ch'ing 蘇青)
  Chieh-hun shih-nien 結婚十年
    Su Huai-ch'ing 蘇懷青
    Hsü Sung-hsien 徐崇賢
    Yü-pai 余白
  "*Ku chin* ti yin-hsiang" 古今的印象
  "Kuan-yü wo" 關於我
  "Lun li-hun" 論離婚
  "T'an tso-kuan" 談作官
  "T'ao" 濤
  "Tzu-chi ti wen-chang" 自己的文章
Feng Tzu, *see* T'ang T'ao
Feng Wen-ping 馮文炳 (Fei Ming 廢名)
  "Hsin shih ying-kai shih tzu-yu shih" 新詩應該是自由詩
  "I-wang ti shih wen-hsüeh yü hsin-shih" 已往的詩文學與新詩
  Shui pien 水邊
  T'an hsin-shih 談新詩
Fu Lei 傅雷 (Hsün Yü 迅雨)
  "Lun Chang Ai-ling ti hsiao-shuo" 論張愛玲的小說
hakkō ichiu 八紘一宇
Hayashi Fusao 林房雄
Hino Ashihei 火野葦平
  Tsuchi yo hei 土與兵
Hsia Mien-tsun 夏丏尊
Hsiao Ti, *see* Keng Yü-hsi
Hsieh Ping-ying 謝冰瑩
  I-ko nü-ping ti tzu-chuan 一個女兵的自傳
Hsieh Hsing-yao 謝興堯 (Yao Kung 堯公, Wu Chih 五知)
hsien-shih 閒適
Hsin-hua tien-ying kung-szu 新華電影公司
Hsin i chü-t'uan 新藝劇團
Hsin min hui 新民會
Hsing-chien ti-i nien 興建第一年
Hsing Shao-mei 邢少梅
Hsü Ch'ü 徐渠
Hsü Hsi-ch'ing 許錫慶
Hsü Hsin-chih 許幸之

Ah Q Cheng-chuan 阿 Q 正傳

Hsü Hsü 徐訏 (Erh Pin 貳鬢)

　　"Ts'ung Shanghai kuei-lai" 從上海歸來

Hsü Kuang-p'ing 許廣平

Hsüan-kung chü-yuan 璇宮劇院

Hsün Yü, *see* Fu Lei

Hu Lan-ch'eng 胡蘭成 (Liu Sha 流沙)

　　"Luan-shih wen t'an" 亂世文談

Hua-pei tso-chia hsieh-hui 華北作家協會

"Hua-pei tso-chia hsieh-hui ch'eng-li tien-li ping ch'uan-t'i hui-yuan ta-
　　hui chi" 華北作家協會成立典禮並全體會員大會記

Hua-pei wen-i hsieh-hui hui-k'an 華北文藝協會會刊

Huan-chu lou-chu 還珠樓主

　　Shu shan chien-hsia chuan 蜀山劍俠傳

Huang Chia-te 黃嘉德

Huang Chia-yin 黃嘉音

Huang Chih-kang 黃芝岡

　　"Wo tui-yü chiu hsing-shih ti chi tien i-chien" 我對於舊形式的
　　幾點意見

Huang I-chun 黃貽鈞

Huang Tao-ming 黃道明

Huang T'ien-shih 黃天始

Huang Tso-lin 黃佐臨

　　Huang tao ying-hsiung 荒島英雄

　　Liang shang chün-tzu 樑上君子

Huang Tsung-ying 黃宗英

Hui An, *see* T'ang T'ao

I Chai 以齋

　　"Wu-che-hsiao-lu shih-tu yin-hsiang chi" 武者小路實篤印象記

i-ch'ing tso-yung 移情作用

I-pao 譯報

I-wen yen-chiu she 藝文研究社

Iizuka Akira 飯塚朗

　　"Kahoku bungaku tsūshin" 華北文學通信

Jo Ssu, *see* T'ang T'ao

Jo Ying, *see* Ch'ien Hsing-ts'un

K'a-erh-teng hsi-yuan (Carlton Theater) 卡爾登戲院

Kai-liang ching-hsi 改良京戲

Kameya Riichi 龜谷利一

K'ang I 康裔

"Lien ti shan yang" 憐笛山陽

Kao Ch'en, *see* Wang Ch'ang-chien

Kao Chi-lin 高季琳 (Chu Fan 朱梵, K'o Ling 柯靈)

"Hai-shih hsü-yao feng-tz'u; wu, tso-ch'e o-kan" 還是需要諷刺：五，
坐車偶感

Min-tsu hu-sheng 民族呼聲

P'iao 飄

"T'a" 踏

Ta-ti hui-ch'un 大地回春

"Wo yao k'ung-su" 我要控訴

"Wu-sheng ti Shanghai" 無聲的上海

Yeh tien 夜店

Kao Ming 高明

"Moku shiei no koto" 穆時英のこと

Keng Yü-hsi 耿郁溪 (Keng Hsiao-ti 耿曉的, Hsiao Ti 小的)

"Ch'ing-nien tso-chia hsieh-hui" 青年作家協會

P'u-sa man 菩薩蠻

Ti? Yu? 敵？友？

"Wo-men so hsü-yao ti wen-i" 我們所需要的文藝

Kikuchi Kan 菊池寬

K'o Ling, *see* Kao Chi-lin

Ku-chuang hsi-chü 古裝戲劇

Ku Chung-i 顧仲彝

Jen chih ch'u 人之初

Liang Hung-yü 梁紅玉

San ch'ien-chin 三千金

K'o-chen 苛珍

Li Hsiang-tsun 黎襄僔

Mei-chen 梅珍

P'i Wang-t'eng 皮望騰

K'u-kan chü-t'uan 苦幹劇團

Ku Ming-tao 顧明道

Kuan I-hsien 管翼賢

Kuan Lu 關露

"Kuang-ming tsai wo-men ti mien-ch'ien" 光明在我們的面前

Kung Ch'ih-p'ing 龔持平 (?Kung Ping-lu 龔冰廬)

"T'an k'uang fu" 炭礦夫

K'ung Ling-ching 孔另境 (Ch'e Fang-i 車方儀)

Heng-mei chi 橫眉集

Chü-pen ts'ung-k'an 劇本叢刊

Kung Ming 共鳴
  "Wan ching" 晚景
Kuo-chi jih-pao 國際日報
Kusano Shimpei 草野心平
Lan-hsin ta hsi-yuan (Lyceum Theater) 蘭心大戲院
Li Chien-wu 李健吾 (Liu Hsi-wei 劉西渭)
  A-shih-na 阿史那
  Che pu-kuo shih ch'un-t'ien 這不過是春天
  Chin Hsiao-yü 金小玉
    Fan Yung-li 范永立
    Sun Shou-hsiang 孫壽祥
  Ch'ing-ch'un 青春
    Hsiang-ts'ao 香草
    Hung Pi-tzu 紅鼻子
    T'ien Hsi-erh 田喜兒
    T'ien Kua-fu 田寡夫
    Yang Ts'un-chang 楊村長
  Feng-liu chai 風流債
  Hua hsin feng 花信風
  Hsi hsiang-feng 喜相逢
  "Kuan-yü hsien-shih" 關於現實
  "*Li-men shih-chi*" 里門拾記
  "Lu Li ti san-wen" 陸離的散文
  "*Pa-yüeh ti hsiang-ts'un*" 八月的鄉村
  Sa-huang shih-chia 撒謊世家
  Yuan Shih-k'ai 袁世凱
  Yün Ts'ai-hsia 雲彩霞
Li Hsiang-lan 李香蘭
Li K'an, *see* Chou Li-an
Li Li-hua 李麗華
Li Po-lung 李伯龍
Li Chih-mo 李知默
Li Po-chün 李伯鈞
  "Hsien chieh-tuan chung-kuo wen-hsüeh chih lu-hsiang" 現階段中國
    文學之路向
Liang Ching, *see* Chang Ai-ling
Lin K'o (Ch'en Hsi-ho)
Lin Po-sheng 林柏生
Liu Hsi-wei, *see* Li Chien-wu
Liu Lung-kuang 柳龍光

Liu Mu-ch'ing 劉慕清 (Lu Feng 魯風)
Liu Na-o 劉吶鷗 (Liu Ts'an-p'o 劉燦波)
Liu Sha, *see* Hu Lan-ch'eng
Liu Ts'un-jen 柳存仁 (Liu Yü-sheng 柳雨生, Liu Ts'un-yan)
    "Fu-te kuang-chou ti ch'ih" 賦得廣州的吃
    "Hai-k'o t'an ying lu" 海客譚瀛錄
    Huai hsiang chi 懷鄉集
    "I kuo hsin-ying lu" 異國心影錄
    "Kuan-yü Yao T'ang" 關於藥堂
    "Pei-ta yü pei-ta jen" 北大與北大人
    T'a ch'i chi 撻妻集
    "T'an tzu-chuan, fu: tso-che lüeh" 譚自傳，附：作者略
Lo Chün-ch'iang 羅君強
Lou Lou 樓樓
    "*Ta kung pao* wen-i lan" 大公報文藝欄
Lu Fen, *see* Wang Ch'ang-chien
Lu Feng (see Liu Mu-ch'ing)
Lu Hsün feng 魯迅風
Lu I-shih, *see* Lu Yü
Lu Li 陸蠡
Lu Yü 路逾 (Lu I-shih 陸易士)
    Ch'u-fa 出發
Lu Yü-ping 陸語氷 (Lu Li 陸離)
lun-li ti tzu-jan-hua 倫理的自然化
Ma Ch'iu-ying 馬秋英 (Ma Li 馬驪)
    Chung-kuo kung-lun, ed. 中國公論
    T'ai-p'ing yuan 太平愿
Ma-hsü Wei-pang 馬徐維邦
Ma Li, *see* Ma Ch'iu-ying
Mai Yeh 麥耶
    "Ch'i-hsi t'an chü" 七夕談劇
    "*Ch'ing-ch'un*" 青春
    "Shih-yüeh ying-chü tsung-p'ing" 十月影劇綜評
Man Chün 曼君
    "Ho-p'ing wen-hsüeh" 和平文學
    "Wei shei hsi-sheng" 爲誰犧牲
Mei Niang (Sun Chia-jui)
Mi Sheng 迷生
    "Kuan-yü *Chung-kuo wen-i* ti ch'u-hsien chi ch'i-t'a" 關於中國文藝的
    出現及其他

Mu Shih-ying 穆時英
Mu Ya-p'ing 穆亞平
   "I-ko chien-tan ti hsin" 一個簡單的心
Nan Hsing, *see* Tu Nan-hsing
Nihon bungaku hōkokukai 日本文学報国会
Odake Fumio 小竹文夫
Okuno Shuntarō 奥野信太郎
   Zuihitsu Pekin 隨筆北京
Ou-yang Yü-ch'ien 歐陽予倩
   "Hou-t'ai jen-yü" 後台人語
Pa Chin 巴金
   Chia 家
   Ch'iu 秋
   Ch'un 春
   "Kuan-yü *Yeh tien*" 關於夜店
Pa Jen, *see* Wang Jen-shu
Pa-li ta hsi-yuan (Paris Theater) 巴黎大戲院
P'an Hsü-tsu 潘序祖 (Yü Ch'ieh 予且)
   Ch'i-nü shu 七女書
   "Yü Ch'ieh sui-pi" 予且隨筆
Pan Kung, *see* Chou Pan-hou
P'an Kung-chan 潘公展
P'an Liu-tai 潘柳黛
pen-wei wen-hua 本位文化
p'ing-ch'ang 平常
p'ing-tan tzu-jan 平淡自然
Sanetō Yoshihide 実勝恵秀
   "Chūgoku sakka ni yōbō suru mono—shōhimbun no fukkō" 中国作家
     に要望するもの―小品文の復興
Sao-tang jih-pao 掃蕩日報
Satō Toshiko 佐藤俊子
   ed. *Nü sheng* 女聲
sempu ban 宣撫班
Sha Kua 沙孤
   "Hsin-hun chih ch'ien" 新婚之前
Shanghai chou-pao 上海週報
Shanghai chü-i she 上海劇藝社
Shanghai i-shu chü-t'uan 上海藝術劇團
Shanghai lien-i chü-t'uan 上海聯藝劇團
Shen Ch'i-wu 沈啓无 (Shen Yang 沈楊, T'ung T'o 童陀)

shen-k'o p'o-la 深刻潑辣

Shih Hui 石揮

Shih pao 實報

Shih T'o, *see* Wang Ch'ang-chien

Su Ch'ing, *see* Feng Ho-i

su-p'u 素樸

Sun Chia-jui 孫嘉瑞 (Mei Niang 梅娘)

   Hsieh 蟹

   "Tung shou-shu chih ch'ien" 動手術之前

   Yü 魚

Sun Yü-t'ang 孫毓棠

   Pao ma 寶馬

Sung Ch'i 宋淇 (Stephen C. Soong, P'ang Kuan-ch'ing 龐觀清)

   Chieh ta huan-hsi 皆大歡喜

Sung-hua chiang 松花江

Ta-chung chü-i kung-szu 大中劇藝公司

"Ta fang yu" 大訪友

"Ta-yü sha chia" 打魚殺家

Takeda Taijun 武田泰淳

tan-yuan 淡遠

T'an Cheng-pi 譚正璧

   "K'u i-ko wu-chih ti ling-hun" 哭一個無知的靈魂

   "Ni *yeh-ts'ao*" 擬野草

   "i-ko yung-shih" 一個勇士

   "k'u yang" 枯楊

T'an Wei-han 譚維韓

T'ang Huai-ch'iu 唐槐秋

T'ang T'ao 唐弢 (Feng Tzu 風子, Hui An 晦庵, Jo Ssu 若思)

   "Chi-he-te sung" 吉訶德頌

   "Ch'ou" 丑

   "Fei" 飛

   "Hai-shih ch'ien-hsien" 還是前綫

   "Hsiao" 笑

   "Hsün-meng jen" 尋夢人

   "Liang chung lien-p'u" 兩種臉譜

   "Ming shih ts'ai-ch'ing yü Shang-yeh ching-mai" 名士才情與商業競賣

   "P'o-hsiao" 破曉

   "P'o-men chieh" 破門解

   "She" 拾

"Shu fen" 書憤
"Tien-ying ch'uan" 電影圈
"Ts'ung k'u-chu tao ho-tao" 從苦住到喝道
"Ts'ung tsa-wen te-tao i-chiao" 從雜文得到遺教
"Tzu ch'un ts'u ch'iu" 自春徂秋
"Wo yao t'ao-pi" 我要逃避
T'ao Ching-sun 陶晶孫
tao-i chih shih-kung-hua 道誼之事功化
T'ao K'ang-te 陶亢德
"Tung-hsing jih-chi" 東行日記
Tao pao 導報
T'ien-feng chü-t'uan 天風劇團
Ting Chia-shu 丁嘉樹 (Ting Miao 丁淼, Ting Ting 丁丁, Ting Yü-lin
丁雨林)
Ting Ti 丁諦
Jen-sheng pei-hsi chü 人生悲喜劇
Ting Ting (Ting Chia-shu)
Ting Yü-lin (Ting Chia-shu)
tsa-kan 雜感
tsa-wen 雜文
Tsa-wen ts'ung-k'an 雜文叢刊
Ts'ao T'ing-tung 曹庭棟
Lao lao heng-yen 老老恒言
Ts'ao Yü 曹禺
Shui pien 蛻變
Chia 家
Tu Nan-hsing 杜南星 (Nan Hsing 南星)
T'ung-mao chü-t'uan 同茂劇團
T'ung T'o, *see* Shen Ch'i-wu
Tung-ya wen-hua hsieh-hui 東亞文化協會
Wang Ch'ang-chien 王長簡 (Lu Fen 蘆焚, Shih T'o 師陀, Kao Ch'en
高岑)
"Chih Lu Fen hsien-sheng men" 致蘆焚先生們
Huang-yeh 荒野
Chiao Chieh 嬌姐
Ku Erh-shun 顧二順
Li Ssu-keng 李四庚
Kuo-yuan ch'eng chi 果園城記
"I wen" 一吻 (Hu-t'ou Yü 虎頭魚)
"Meng An-ch'ing ti t'ang hsiung-ti" 孟安卿的堂兄弟 (Meng Chi-

ch'ing 孟季卿)

"Shou-lieh" 狩獵 (Meng An-ch'ing 孟安卿)

"Shuo-shu jen" 說書人

"Yu-ch'ai hsien-sheng" 郵差先生

Ma Lan 馬蘭

Cheng Ta-t'ung 鄭大通

Ch'iao Shih-fu (Joseph) 喬式夫

Chu Ping-wu 朱秉午

Li Po-t'ang 李伯唐

Mo Pu-tu 莫步獨

Yang Ch'un 楊春

Shanghai shou-cha 上海手札

Ch'ien Ching-t'u 錢經圖

P Hsien-sheng P先生

Wei Hsien-sheng 魏先生

Ta-ma hsi-t'uan 大馬戲團

Hsiao Ch'ung 小銃

Hui Hui 回回

Kai San-hsing 蓋三省

Ma T'eng-chiao 馬騰蛟

Shui Mi-t'ao 水蜜桃

Ta Tzu 達子

Ts'ui-pao 翠寶

Yin Niu-erh 銀妞兒

Yeh tien 夜店

A-man 阿滿

Ch'üan Lao-t'ou 全老頭

Hsi-tzu 戲子

Lai 賴

Lin Tai-yü 林黛玉

Sai Kuan-yin 賽觀音

Shih Hsiao-mei 石小妹

Wen T'ai-shih 聞太師

Yang Ch'i-lang 楊七郎

Wang Jen-shu 王任叔 (Ch'ü I 屈軼, Pa Jen 巴人)

Wang Tan-feng 王丹鳳

Wang T'ung-chao 王統照

Wei Yü-ch'ien 魏于潛

T'ien chieh-erh 甜姐兒

"Wen-hsüeh ying fu ti shih-ming" 文學應負的使命

Wen-hui pao 文匯報

Wen Kuo-hsin 聞國新

  "Shui-chao ti jen" 睡着的人

Wu Hsing-hua 吳興華 (Liang Wen-hsing 梁文星)

  "Pei yuan shih ch'u, huo kei i-ko nien ch'ing shih-jen ti ch'üan-kao"
    北轅適楚，或給一個年靑詩人的勸告

  "Shu *Fan Ch'uan chi* "Tu Ch'iu-niang shih' hou" 書樊川集杜秋娘詩後

  "T'ing mei-hua tiao Pao-yü t'an ping" 聽梅花調寶玉探病

Wu Jen-chih 吳仞之

Wu T'ien, *see* Fang Chün-i

Wu Tsu-kuang 吳祖光

  Cheng-ch'i ko 正氣歌 (*Wen T'ien-hsiang* 文天祥)

Wu Yung-kang 吳永剛

Yang Han-sheng 陽翰笙

  Ch'ien yeh 前夜 (*Liang ko shih-chieh* 兩個世界)

Yang Chiang 楊絳 (Yang Chi-K'ang 楊季康)

  Ch'en-hsin ju-i 稱心如意

    Chao Ching-sun 趙景蓀

    Chao Tsu-i 趙祖貽

    Chao Tsu-mao 趙祖懋

    Chao Tsu-yin 趙祖蔭

    Ch'ien Ling-hsien 錢令嫻

    Ch'en Pin-ju 陳彬如

    Hsü Lang-chai 徐朗齋

    Li Chün-yü 李君玉

  Feng hsü 風絮

    Fang Ching-shan 方景山

    Shen Hui-lien 沈惠連

    T'ang Shu-yuan 唐叔遠

    Wang Nai-ma 王奶媽

    Yeh San 葉三

  Lung-chen ch'eng-chia 弄眞成假

    Chang Hsiang-fu 張祥甫

    Chang Wan-ju 張婉如

    Chang Yen-hua 張燕華

    Chou Ta-chang 周大璋

    Feng Kuang-tsu 馮光祖

  Yu-hsi jen-chien 遊戲人間

Yang Kuang-cheng 楊光政

  "I-chiu-ssu-ssu nien ti chung-kuo wen-i chieh" 一九四四年的中國文

藝界

Yao Hsin-nung 姚莘農（Yao K'o 姚克）

  Ch'i ch'ung t'ien 七重天

    Lo Ying 羅櫻

    Chin Ko-erh 金哥兒

  Ch'ing kung yuan 清宮怨

    Chen Fei 珍妃

    Kuang-hsü 光緒

    Tz'u-hsi 慈禧

    Yuan Shih-k'ai 袁世凱

  "*Ch'ing kung yuan* hou chi" 清宮怨後記

  Ch'u pa-wang 楚霸王

    Fan Tseng 范增

    Hsiang Yü 項羽

    Liu Pang 劉邦

    Yü Mei-jen 虞美人

    "Pa wang pieh chi" 霸王別姬

  Mei-jen chi 美人計

    Liu Pei 劉備

    Sun Ch'uan 孫權

    Sun Shang-hsiang 孫尚香

  Yin-hai ts'ang-sang 銀海滄桑

    Hsiao Han 蕭寒

    Lin Ying 林嬰

    Kao Shih-ch'i 高士奇

  Yuan-yang chien 鴛鴦劍

Yao K'o, *see* Yao Hsin-nung

Yao Kung, *see* Hsieh Hsing-yao

Yao T'ang, *see* Chou Tso-jen

Yoshitake Manabu 吉武学

Yü Ch'ieh, *see* P'an Hsü-tsu

Yü Ling 于伶（Yu Ching 尤兢, Jen Shang-chih 任尚之）

  Hsing-hua ch'un-yü chiang-nan 杏花春雨江南

  Hua chien lei 花濺淚

    Mi-mi 米米

  Nü-tzu kung-yü 女子公寓

  Yeh-kuang pei 夜光杯（P'u-t'ao mei-chiu 葡萄美酒）

  Yeh Shanghai 夜上海

    Ch'ien K'ai-chih 錢凱之

    Feng Feng 馮鳳

Mei O-hui 梅萼輝
Wu Chi 吳姬
Yun Ku 雲姑
Yu Ping-ch'i 尤炳圻
Yü P'ing-po 俞平伯
Yü Yüeh 俞樾 (Ch'ü-yuan 曲園)
　Ch'un-tsai-t'ang ch'uan shu 春在堂全書
Yuan Hsi 袁犀 (Hao Wei-lien 郝維廉 , Liang Tao 梁稻 , Wu Ming-shih
　吳明士)
　Pei-k'o 貝殼
　　Li Mei 李玫
　　Li Ying 李英
　　Pai Shu 白澍
　"Sen-lin ti chi-mo" 森林的寂默
Yuan Shu 袁殊 (Yuan Hsüeh-i 袁學易 , Yen Chün-kuang 嚴軍光)
Yuan-tung chü-t'uan 遠東劇團

Bibliography

CHINESE AND JAPANESE SOURCES: BOOKS AND ARTICLES

A Ying [Ch'ien Hsing-ts'un] 阿英 [錢杏邨] *Pu yeh ch'eng* 不夜城 (City of No Night). Shanghai, 1940.

—— *Yang O chuan* 楊娥傳 (The Story of Yang O). Shanghai, 1950.

Chang Ai-ling 張愛玲. *Chang Ai-ling tuan-p'ien hsiao-shuo chi* 張愛玲短篇小說集 (Collected Short Stories of Chang Ai-ling). Taipei, 1973.

—— *Chang k'an* 張看 (Chang's Outlook). Taipei, 1976.

—— Liu-yen 流言 (Gossip). Taipei, 1969.

Chang Hung [Chang Yin-nan] 張鴻 [張隱南]. *Hsü nieh-hai hua* 續孽海花 (Continuation to Flower on an Ocean of Sin). Peking, 1943; reprint ed., Hong Kong, 1971.

Chao Ching-shen 趙景深. *Wen-t'an i-chiu* 文壇憶舊 (Recollections of the Literary Scene). Shanghai, 1948.

Ch'en Kung-po 陳公博. *Pa nien lai ti hui-i* 八年來的回憶 (Memoirs of the Last Eight Years). Shanghai, n.d.

Cheng Chen-to 鄭振鐸. *Chih chü san-chi* 蟄居散記 (Memoirs of Life as a Recluse). Shanghai, 1951.

Ch'eng Ch'i-heng 程其恆. *Chan-shih Chung-kuo pao-yeh* 戰時中國報業 (Wartime Chinese Journalism). Kweilin, 1944.

Ch'ien Chung-shu 錢鍾書. *Hsieh tsai jen-sheng pien-shang* 寫在人生邊上 (Written on the Margin of Life). Shanghai, 1941.

—— *Jen, shou, kuei* 人獸鬼 (Men, Beasts, Ghosts). Shanghai, 1946.

—— *Wei ch'eng* 圍城 (The Besieged City). Shanghai, 1947; pirated edition, Hong Kong, n.d.

—— *T'an i lu* 談藝錄 (On the Art of Poetry). Shanghai, 1948.

Chin Hsiung-pai 金雄白. *Wang cheng-ch'üan shih-mo chi* 汪政權始末記 (The Wang Ching-wei Regime from Beginning to End). 5 vols. Hong Kong, 1965.

Chin Hsiung-pai [Chu Tzu-chia 朱子家]. *Wang cheng-ch'üan ti k'ai-ch'ang yü shou-ch'ang* 汪政權的開場與收場 (The Wang Ching-wei Regime from Overture to Curtain). Vol. 6. Hong Kong, 1971.

Ch'in Shou-ou 秦瘦鷗. *Ch'iu Hai-t'ang* 秋海棠 (Begonia). Shanghai, 1946; reprint ed., Hong Kong, 1975.

—— *Ch'iu Hai-t'ang chü-pen* 秋海棠劇本. Shanghai, 1946. This text is based on the unpublished script by Ku Chung-i, Fei Mu, and Huang Tso-lin, written in 1942.

Chou I-pai 周貽白. *Chin Ssu ch'üeh* 金絲雀 (Canary). Shanghai, 1944.

—— *Hua Mu-lan* 花木蘭. Shanghai, 1941.

—— *Pei ti wang* [*Wang shu i-hen*] 北地王 (King of the North) [亡蜀遺恨 (Sorrow for the Fall of Shu)]. Shanghai, 1946.

—— *Yang-kuan san-tieh* 陽關三疊 (Three Variations on the Theme of Yang Pass). Shanghai, 1944.

Chou Li-an 周黎庵. *Feng men chi* 葑門集 (Thatched Gate). Shanghai, 1941.

—— *Hua fa chi* 華髮集 (White-Haired). Shanghai, 1940.

Chou Tso-jen 周作人. *Chih T'ang hui-hsiang lu* 知堂回想錄 (Memoirs of Wisdom Studio). 2 vols. Hong Kong, 1971.

—— *K'u-k'ou kan-k'ou* 苦口甘口 (The Bitter and the Sweet). Shanghai, 1944.

—— *Li-ch'un i-ch'ien* 立春以前 (Before the Spring). Shanghai, 1945.

—— *Ping-chu t'an* 秉燭談 (Talks in Lamplight). Shanghai, 1936.

—— *Yao T'ang tsa-wen* 藥堂雜文 (Essays of Bitter Studio). Peking, 1944.

—— *Yao-wei chi* 藥味集 (With a Bitter Taste). Peking, 1942.

Chu Fan [Kao Chi-lin] 朱梵 [高季琳]. "P'iao" 飄 (Gone with the Wind). *Wan-hsiang* 萬象 (July 1943), vol. 3, no. 1.

Fang Chün-i [Wu T'ien] 方君逸 [吳天]. *Man t'ing fang* 滿庭芳 (Fragrance Fills the Courtyard). Shanghai, 1944.

—— *Li-hen t'ien* 離恨天 (Realm of Transcendence). Shanghai, 1944.

Hsia Chih-ts'ing 夏志清. *Jen ti wen-hsüeh* 人的文學 (A Human Literature). Taipei, 1977.

Hsü Kuang-p'ing 許廣平. *Tsao-nan ch'ien-hou* 遭難前後 (Before and After Misfortune). Shanghai, 1947.

Hsün Feng 迅風, ed. *Hsien-tai san-wen sui-pi hsüan* 現代散文隨筆選 (Selected Contemporary Essays). Shanghai, 1944.

Hu Lan-ch'eng 胡蘭成. *Chin sheng chin shih* 今生今世 (This Life, This World). 2 vols. Tokyo, 1958.

Huang Chun-tung [Wong Chun-tong] 黃俊東. *Hsien-tai chung-kuo tso-chia chien-ying* 現代中國作家剪影 (Profiles of Modern Chinese Writers). Hong Kong, 1972.

Iida Kichirō 飯田吉郎. *Gendai chūgoku bungaku kenkyū bunken mokuroku* 現代中国文学研究文献目録 (Catalogue of Research Documents on

Modern Chinese Literature). Tokyo, 1958.

Ishikawa Nobuo 石川信雄. "Sempu engeki tai" 宣撫演劇隊 (Pacification Theatre Troupes). *Genchi hōkoku* 現地報告 (September 1941), no. 48, pp. 109–17.

K'o Ling [Kao Chi-lin] 柯靈 [高季琳]. *Yao yeh chi* 遙夜集 (The Long Night). Peking, 1956.

Kondō Haruo 近藤春雄. *Gendai shina no bungaku* 現代支那の文学 (Modern Literature of China). Kyoto, 1945.

Ku Chung-i 顧仲彝. *Liang Hung-yü* 梁紅玉. Shanghai, 1941.

—— *San ch'ien-chin* 三千金 (Three Daughters). Shanghai, 1944.

—— *Shanghai nan-nü* 上海男女 (Men and Women of Shanghai). Shanghai, 1946.

—— *Shih nien lai ti Shanghai hua-chü yun-tung (1937–1947)* 十年來 上海話劇運動（一九三七－一九四七）(The Spoken Drama Movement in Shanghai during the Last Ten Years, 1937–1947). n.p., n.d., reprint ed., Hong Kong, 1976.

"Kuan-yü lao tso-chia wen-t'i" 關於老作家問題 (Concerning the 'Old Writer' Issue). *Tsa-chih* 雜誌 (May 1944), 13(2): 177–86.

K'ung Ling-ching et al. 孔另境. *Heng mei chi* 橫眉集 (Angry Eyebrows). Shanghai, 1939.

Lan Hai 藍海. *Chung-kuo k'ang-chan wen-i shih* 中國抗戰文藝史 (A History of Literature in the War of Resistance). Shanghai, 1947.

Li Chien-wu 李健吾. *Chin Hsiao-yü* 金小玉. Shanghai, n.d.

—— "Ch'ing-ch'un" 青春 (Youth). *Wen-i fu-hsing* 文藝復興 (February–March 1946), 1 (1–2).

—— *Hsi hsiang feng* 喜相逢 (So Glad to Have Met). Shanghai, 1944.

—— "Yun Ts'ai-hsia" 雲彩霞. *Wan hsiang* 萬象 (December 1942–April 1943), 2 (6–10).

Lin I-liang [Sung Ch'i] 林以亮 [宋淇]. *Lin I-liang shih-hua* 林以亮詩話 (Poetry Talks of Lin I-liang). Taipei, 1976.

Liu Hsi-wei [Li Chien-wu] 劉西渭 [李健吾]. *Chü-hua erh-chi* 咀華二集 (Ruminations II). 2d ed. Shanghai, 1947.

Liu Hsin-huang 劉心皇. "K'ang-chan shih-tai luo-shui tso-chia shu-lun" 抗戰時代落水作家述論 (Narrative on Writers Who Sold Out during the War of Resistance). *Fan-kung* 反攻 (January–October 1974), nos. 382–391 (Taipei).

Liu Ts'un-jen 柳存仁. *Jen-wu t'an* 人物譚 (On Persons). Hong Kong, 1952.

Lu Fen [Weng Ch'ang-chien] 蘆焚 [王長簡]. *Shanghai shou-cha* 上海手札 (Shanghai Correspondence). Shanghai, 1941.

Ma Li [Ma Ch'iu-ying] 馬驪 [馬秋英]. *T'ai-p'ing yuan* 太平愿 (A prayer for Peace). Peking, 1943.

Mei Niang [Sun Chia-jui] 梅娘 [孫嘉瑞]. "Hsieh" 蟹 (Crab). *Hua-wen ta-pan mei-jih pan-yüeh k'an* 華文大阪毎日半月刊 (1 August–15 October 1941, 15 November–15 December 1941), vol. 7, nos. 5–10, 12–14.

—— *Yü* 魚 (Fish). Peking, 1944.

Miki Kiyoshi and Lin Po-sheng 三木清與林柏生 "Bunkadō no kichō" 文化動の基調 (The Keynote of the Cultural Movement). *Chūō kōron* 中央公論 (May 1940), pp. 86–92.

Ozaki Hideki 尾崎秀樹. "Daitōa bungakusha taikai ni tsuite" 大東亜文学大会について (On the Congress for Greater East Asian Literature). *Bungei* 文芸 (May 1961), 29(5): 9–27.

Pa Jen [Wang Jen-shu] 巴人 [王任叔]. *Lun Lu Hsün ti tsa-wen* 論魯迅的雜文 (On Lu Hsün's Essays). Shanghai, 1940.

—— *Tsun-ming chi* 遵命集 (On Instructions). Peking, 1957.

Shih T'o [Wang Ch'ang-chien] 師陀 [王長簡]. *Huang-yeh* 荒野 (Wilderness). *Wan-hsiang* 萬象. (July 1943–June 1944), 3 (1–8, 10–12); (July 1944–June 1945), 4 (1–3, 5–7).

—— *Kuo-yuan ch'eng chi* 果園城記 (Orchard Town). Shanghai, 1946.

—— *Ma Lan* 馬蘭. Shanghai, 1948.

—— *Ta ma-hsi-t'uan* 大馬戲團 (The Big Circus). Shanghai, 1948.

Shih T'o and K'o Ling [Kao Chi-lin] 師陀與柯靈 [高季琳]. *Yeh tien* 夜店 (The Night Inn). *Wan-hsiang* 萬象 (September–October 1944), 4 (3–4); book edition, Shanghai, 1946.

Shui Ching 水晶. *Chang Ai-ling ti hsiao-shuo i-shu* 張愛玲的小說藝術 (The Art of Chang Ai-ling's Fiction). Taipei, 1973.

Su Ch'ing [Feng Ho-i] 蘇青 [馮和儀]. *Chieh-hun shih-nien* 結婚十年 (Ten Years of Marriage). Shanghai, 1944; reprint ed., Hong Kong, n.d.

—— *T'ao* 濤 (Swelling Wave). Shanghai, 1944; reprint ed., Hong Kong, 1954.

—— "Kuan-yü wo" 關於我 (About Myself). In *Hsü chieh-hun shih-nien* 續結婚十年 (Continuation to Ten Years of Marriage). Hong Kong, 1947.

T'an Cheng-pi 譚正璧, ed. *Tang-tai nü tso-chia hsiao-shuo hsüan* 當代女作家小說選 (Selected Fiction of Contemporary Women Writers). Shanghai, 1944.

—— *Yeh chu chi* 夜珠集 (Night Pearls). Shanghai, 1944.

T'ang T'ao 唐弢. *Lo fan chi* 落帆集 (Furled Sail). Shanghai, 1948; reprint ed., Hong Kong, 1962.

—— *T'ang T'ao tsa-wen hsüan* 唐弢雜文選 (Selected Essays of T'ang T'ao). Peking, 1955.

T'ang Wen-piao 唐文標. *Chang Ai-ling tsa-sui* 張愛玲雜碎 (Fragments on Chang Ai-ling). Taipei, 1976.

Tseng Hsü-pai 曾虛白. *Chung-kuo hsin-wen shih* 中國新聞史 (A History of Chinese Journalism). Taipei, 1966.

Tsou T'ao-fen 鄒韜奮. *Huan-nan yü-sheng chi* 患難餘生記 (Final Years of Adversity). Shanghai: San-lien shu-tien, 1949.

Wei Ju-hui [Ch'ien Hsing-ts'un] 魏如晦 [錢杏邨]. "Niu-lang chih-nü chuan" 牛郎織女傳 (The Story of the Cowherd and Weaving Maid). *Wan-hsiang* September 1941–January 1942, vol. 1, nos. 3–7.

—— *Pi hsüeh hua* 碧血花 (Jade Blood Flower), also known as *Ming-mo i-hen* 明末遺恨 (Sorrow for the Fall of the Ming). Shanghai, 1940.

—— *T'ao-hua yuan* 桃花源 (Peach Blossom Spring). Shanghai, 1947.

Wei Shao-ch'ang 魏紹昌. *Yuan-yang hu-tieh p'ai yen-chiu tz'u-liao* 鴛鴦蝴蝶派研究資料 (Research Materials on the Mandarin Duck and Butterfly School). Shanghai, 1962.

Wen Tsai-tao [Chin Hsing-yao] 文載道 [金性堯]. *Feng-t'u hsiao-chi* 風土小記 (Notes on Local Customs). Shanghai, 1944.

Wen Tsai-tao et al. *Pien ku chi* 邊鼓集 (Border Drums). Shanghai, 1938.

Wu Hsing-hua 吳興華. "Yen ku-shih ssu-p'ien" 演古事四篇 (Re-enacting Four Old Tales). *Wen-i shih-tai* 文藝時代 (Peking, June 1946), 1(1): 17–21.

—— "Shih ssu shou" 詩四首 (Four Poems). *Wen-i shih-tai* 文藝時代 (July 1946), 1(2): 26–33.

—— "Erh shou shih-ssu hang" 二首十四行 (Two Sonnets). *Fu-jen wen-yuan* 輔仁文苑 (15 April 1939), no. 2, p. 22.

Yang Chiang 楊絳. *Ch'en-hsin ju-i* 稱心如意 (As You Desire). Shanghai, 1944.

—— *Feng hsü* 風絮 (Windswept Blossoms). Shanghai, 1947.

—— *Lung-chen ch'eng-chia* 弄眞成假 (Swindle). Shanghai, 1945; reprint ed., Shanghai, 1947.

Yang I-ming [Yang Chih-hua], ed. 楊一鳴 [楊之華]. *Wen-t'an shih-liao* 文壇史料 (Historical Materials on the Literary Scene). Dairen, 1944.

Yao K'o [Yao Hsin-nung] 姚克 [姚莘農]. *Ch'i ch'ung t'ien* 七重天 (Seventh Heaven). *Ta-chung* 大衆 (July–November 1943).

—— *Ch'ing kung yuan* 清宮怨 (Malice in the Ch'ing Court). Shanghai, 1944.

—— *Ch'u pa-wang* 楚霸王 (Overlord of Ch'ü). Shanghai, 1944.

—— *Mei-jen chi* 美人計 (The Strategem of the Beautiful Woman).

Shanghai, 1945.

—— *Yin-hai ts'ang-sang* 銀海滄桑 (Vicissitudes in the Film World). Shanghai, 1945.

Yoshikawa Kōjirō 吉川幸次郎. "Ni-ka no bungakusha ni" 日華の文学者に (To the Writers of Japan and China) *Bungakukai* 文学界 (October 1943), 10(10): 12–18.

Yü Ch'ieh [P'an Hsü-tsu] 予且 [潘序祖]. "Jih-pen yin-hsiang chi" 日本印象記 (Impressions of Japan). *Chung-hua yüeh-pao* 中華月報. (January 1944), 7(1): 88–101.

—— *Yü Ch'ieh tuan-p'ien hsiao-shuo chi* 予且短篇小說集 (Collected Short Stories of Yü Ch'ieh). Shanghai, 1943.

Yü Ling 于伶. *Yeh Shanghai* 夜上海 (Shanghai Night). Shanghai, 1939.

—— *Nü-tzu kung-yü* 女子公寓 (Women's Hostel). Shanghai, 1939.

—— *Hua chien lei* 花濺淚 (Flowers Draw Tears). Shanghai, 1940.

Yuan Hsi 袁犀. *Pei-k'o* 貝殼 (Seashells). Peking, 1943.

CHINESE AND JAPANESE SOURCES: PERIODICALS

The most complete annotated guide to Chinese-language periodicals in occupied China is contained in *Chung-kuo hsien-tai wen-hsüeh ch'i-k'an mu-lu* 中國現代文學期刊目錄 (Shanghai, 1961; reprint ed., Washington, D.C., 1968). Chinese, Japanese, and English-language periodicals used in this study are cited below.

Asahi shimbun 朝日新聞 Morning Sun News.

Bungakukai (Bungakkai) 文学界 Literature World.

Bungei 文芸 Arts and Letters.

Bungei shunjū 文芸春秋 Arts and Letters Spring and Autumn.

Chūgoku bungaku 中国文学 Chinese Literature.

Ch'un-ch'iu 春秋 Spring and Autumn.

Chung-ho 中和 Equilibrium and Harmony: Sino-Japanese Mothly.

Chung-hua yüeh-pao 中華月報 Central China Monthly.

Chung-kuo wen-hsüeh 中國文學 Chinese Literature.

Chung-kuo wen-i 中國文藝 Chinese Arts and Letters.

Chung lun 衆論 Mass Forum.

Chūō kōron 中央公論 Central Forum.

Feng-yü t'an 風雨談 Wind and Rain Chats.

Fu-jen wen-yuan 輔仁文苑 Fu-jen University Garden of Literature.

Genchi hōkoku 現地報告 Spot Report.

Hong Kong News

Hsi feng fu k'an 西風副刊 West

Wind Supplement.

Hsi-yang wen-hsüeh 西洋文學 Western Literature.

Hsiao-shuo yüeh-pao 小說月報 Fiction Monthly.

Hsin chin 新進 Emergence.

Hsin min pao 新民報 New People's Herald.

Hsin min pao pan-yüeh-k'an 新民報 半月刊 New People's Herald Fortnightly.

Hsin shen pao 新申報 New Shanghai Report.

Hua-pei pien-i kuan kuan-k'an 華北 編譯館館刊 Gazette of North China Bureau of Translation.

Hua-wen ta-pan mei-jih pan-yüeh-k'an 華文大阪每日半月刊 Chinese language Osaka Daily (News) Fortnightly.

I-pan 一般 In Common.

I-wen tsa-chih 藝文雜誌 Arts and Letters Review.

K'ang-chan wen-i 抗戰文藝 Arts and Letters of the War of Resistance.

Ku-chin 古今 Past and Present.

Liu i 六藝 Six Arts.

Nam wah yat po (Nan-hua jih-pao) 南華日報 South China Daily Herald.

Nü sheng 女聲 Women's Voice.

Shanghai chou-pao 上海週報 Shanghai Weekly Herald.

Shanghai no bungaku 上海の文学 Shanghai Literature.

Shen pao 申報 Shanghai Report.

Shih pao 實報 Fact Herald.

Shinchō 新潮 New Tide.

Shuo feng 朔風 Northern Wind.

Ta-chung 大衆 Masses.

Ta-ya-chou chu-i yü tung-ya lien-meng 大亞洲主義與東亞聯盟 Greater East Asian-ism and the East Asia League.

T'ien ti 天地 Heaven and Earth.

Times Week (Shanghai Times)

Tsa-chih 雜誌 The Review.

T'ung-sheng 同聲 Accord.

The Twentieth Century

Tz'u-lo-lan 紫羅蘭 Violet.

Wan-hsiang 萬象 Phenomena.

Wen-hsüeh chi-lin 文學集林 Literature Grove.

Wen-i ch'un-ch'iu 文藝春秋 Arts and Letters Spring and Autumn.

Wen-i fu-hsing 文藝復興 Renaissance.

Wen-i shih-tai 文藝時代 Arts and Letters Epoch.

Wen-yu 文友 Literary Companion.

Yü-chou feng i-k'an 宇宙風乙刊 Cosmic Wind II.

WESTERN LANGUAGE SOURCES

Alter, Robert. *Rogue's Progress: Studies in the Picaresque Novel.* Cambridge, Mass.: Harvard University Press, 1965.

Andreyev, Leonid. *He Who Gets Slapped.* Gregory Zilboorg, trans. New York, 1922; reprint ed., New York: Samuel French, n.d.

Barzun, Jacques. *Classic, Romantic, and Modern.* Boston: Little, Brown, 1961.

Boorman, Howard L., ed. *Biographical Dictionary of Republican China.* New York: Columbia University Press, 1968.

Boyle, John Hunter. *China and Japan at War, 1937–45: The Politics of Collaboration.* Stanford: Stanford University Press, 1972.

Goodrich, L. Carrington. "Some Publications in Occupied China." *Pacific Affairs* (December 1947).

Gorky, Maxim. *The Lower Depths.* Alex Szogyi, trans. New York: Samuel French, n.d.

Greenblatt, Stephen Jay. *Three Modern Satirists: Waugh, Orwell, and Huxley.* New Haven: Yale University Press, 1965.

Hare, Richard. *Maxim Gorky: Romantic Realist and Conservative Revolutionary.* New York: Oxford University Press, 1962.

Hsia, C. T. Review of *Chou Tso-jen* by Ernst Wolff. *Journal of the American Oriental Society* (1974), 96(4): 527–28.

—— *A History of Modern Chinese Fiction.* 2d ed. New Haven: Yale University Press, 1971.

Hu, Dennis Ting-pong. "A Linguistic-Literary Study of Ch'ien Chung-shu's Three Creative Works." Ph.D. dissertation, University of Wisconsin, Madison, 1977.

Huters, Theodore David. "Traditional Innovation: Qian Zhong-shu and Modern Chinese Letters." Ph.D. dissertation, Stanford University, 1977.

Iwamoto Yoshio. "The Relationship between Literature and Politics in Japan, 1931–45." Ph.D. dissertation, University of Michigan, 1964.

Lang, Olga. *Pa Chin and His Writings.* Cambridge, Mass.: Harvard University Press, 1969.

Lee, Leo Ou-fan. *The Romantic Generation of Modern Chinese Writers.* Cambridge, Mass.: Harvard University Press, 1973.

Leyda, Jay. *Dianying: Electric Shadows, An Account of Films and the Film Audience in China.* Cambridge, Mass.: MIT Press, 1972.

Li Chi. "The Changing Concept of the Recluse in Chinese Literature." *Harvard Journal of Asian Studies* (1962–63), 24: 234–47.

Mote, Frederick W. *Japanese Sponsored Governments in China, 1937–45: An Annotated Bibliography Compiled from Materials in the Chinese Collection of the Hoover Library.* Stanford: Stanford University Press, 1954.

Muir, Edwin. *The Present Age from 1914.* London: Cresset Press, 1940.

Pollard, David. E. *A Chinese Look at Literature: The Literary Values of Chou Tso-jen in Relation to the Tradition.* Berkeley, University of California

Press, 1973.

Schyns, Joseph, Su Hsüeh-lin, and Chao Yen-sheng. *1500 Modern Chinese Novels and Plays*. Peiping, 1948; reprint ed., Hong Kong, 1966.

Scott, A. C. *Mei Lan-fang: The Life and Times of a Peking Actor*. Hong Kong: Hong Kong University Press, 1971.

Slupski, Zbigniew. "The World of Shih T'o." *Asian and African Studies* (Bratislava) (1973), 9: 11–28.

Whitbourn, Catherine J., ed. *Knaves and Swindlers: Essays on the Picaresque Novel in Europe*. London: Oxford University Press, 1974.

Wolff, Ernst. *Chou Tso-jen*. New York: Twayne Publishers, 1971.

Yao Hsin-nung. *The Malice of Empire*. Jeremy Ingalls, trans. London: Allen and Unwin, 1970.

Index

Studies of the East Asian Institute

The Ladder of Success in Imperial China, by Ping-ti Ho. New York: Columbia University Press, 1962.

The Chinese Inflation, 1937–1949, by Shun-hsin Chou, New York: Columbia University Press, 1963.

Reformer in Modern China: Chang Chien, 1853–1926, by Samuel Chu. New York: Columbia University Press, 1965.

Research in Japanese Sources: A Guide, by Herschel Webb with the assistance of Marleigh Ryan. New York: Columbia University Press, 1965.

Society and Education in Japan, by Herbert Passin, New York: Teachers College Press, Columbia University, 1965.

Agricultural Production and Economic Development in Japan, 1873–1922, by James I. Nakamura. Princeton: Princeton University Press, 1966.

Japan's First Modern Novel: Ukigumo of Futabatei Shimei, by Marleigh Ryan. New York: Columbia University Press, 1967.

The Korean Communist Movement, 1918–1948, by Dae-Sook Suh, Princeton: Princeton University Press, 1967.

The First Vietnam Crisis, by Melvin Gurtov. New York: Columbia University Press, 1967.

Cadres, Bureaucracy, and Political Power in Communist China, by A. Doak Barnett. New York: Columbia University Press, 1967.

The Japanese Imperial Institution in the Tokugawa Period, by Herschel Webb. New York: Columbia University Press, 1968.

Higher Education and Business Recruitment in Japan, by Koya Azumi. New York: Teachers College Press, Columbia University, 1969.

The Communists and Chinese Peasant Rebellions: A Study in the Rewriting of Chinese History, by James P. Harrison, Jr. New York: Atheneum, 1969.

How the Conservatives Rule Japan, by Nathaniel B. Thayer. Princeton: Princeton University Press, 1969.

Aspects of Chinese Education, by C. T. Hu. New York: Teachers College Press, Columbia University, 1969.

Documents of Korean Communism, 1918–1948, by Dae-Sook Suh. Princeton: Princeton University Press, 1970.

Japanese Education: A Bibliography of Materials in the English Language, by Herbert Passin. New York: Teachers College Press, Columbia University, 1970.

Economic Development and the Labor Market in Japan, by Koji Taira. New York: Columbia University Press, 1970.

The Japanese Oligarchy and the Russo-Japanese War, by Shumpei Okamoto. New York: Columbia University Press, 1970.

Imperial Restoration in Medieval Japan, by H. Paul Varley. New York: Columbia University Press, 1971.

Japan's Postwar Defense Policy, 1947–1968, by Martin E. Weinstein. New York: Columbia University Press, 1971.

Election Campaigning Japanese Style, by Gerald L. Curtis. New York: Columbia University Press, 1971.

China and Russia: The "Great Game," by O. Edmund Clubb. New York: Columbia University Press, 1971.

Money and Monetary Policy in Communist China, by Katherine Huang Hsiao. New York: Columbia University Press, 1971.

The District Magistrate in Late Imperial China, by John R. Watt. New York: Columbia University Press, 1972.

Law and Policy in China's Foreign Relations: A Study of Attitudes and Practice, by James C. Hsiung. New York: Columbia University Press, 1972.

Pearl Harbor as History: Japanese-American Relations, 1931–1941, edited by Dorothy Borg and Shumpei Okamoto, with the assistance of Dale K. A. Finlayson. New York: Columbia University Press, 1973.

Japanese Culture: A Short History, by H. Paul Varley. New York: Praeger, 1973.

Doctors in Politics: The Political Life of the Japan Medical Association, by William E. Steslicke. New York: Praeger, 1973.

Japan's Foreign Policy, 1868–1941: A Research Guide, edited by James William Morley. New York: Columbia University Press, 1973.

The Japan Teachers Union: A Radical Interest Group In Japanese Politics, by Donald Ray Thurston. Princeton: Princeton University Press, 1973.

Palace and Politics in Prewar Japan, by David Anson Titus. New York: Columbia University Press, 1974.

The Idea of China: Essays in Geographic Myth and Theory, by Andrew March. Devon, England: David and Charles, 1974.

Origins of the Cultural Revolution, by Roderick MacFarquhar. New York: Columbia University Press, 1974.

Shiba Kokan: Artist, Innovator, and Pioneer in the Westernization of Japan, by Calvin L. French, Tokyo: Weatherhill, 1974.

Embassy at War, by Harold Joyce Noble. Edited with an introduction by Frank Baldwin, Jr. Seattle: University of Washington Press, 1975.

Rebels and Bureaucrats: China's December 9ers, by John Israel and Donald W. Klein. Berkeley: University of California Press, 1975.

House United, House Divided: The Chinese Family in Taiwan, by Myron L. Cohen. New York: Columbia University Press, 1976.

Insei: Abdicated Sovereigns in the Politics of Late Heian Japan, by G. Cameron Hurst. New York: Columbia University Press, 1976.

Deterrent Diplomacy, edited by James W. Morley. New York: Columbia University Press, 1976.

Cadres, Commanders and Commissars: The Training of the Chinese Communist Leadership, 1920–45, by Jane L. Price. Boulder, Colo.: Westview Press, 1976.

Sun Yat-sen: Frustrated Patriot, by C. Martin Wilbur. New York: Columbia University Press, 1976.

Japanese International Negotiating Style, by Michael Blaker. New York: Columbia University Press, 1977.

Contemporary Japanese Budget Politics, by John Creighton Campbell. Berkeley: University of California Press, 1977.

The Medieval Chinese Oligarchy, by David Johnson. Boulder, Colo.: Westview Press, 1977.

Escape from Predicament: Neo-Confucianism and China's Evolving Political Culture, by Thomas A. Metzger. New York: Columbia University Press, 1977.

The Arms of Kiangnan: Modernization in the Chinese Ordnance Industry, 1860–1895, by Thomas L. Kennedy. Boulder, Colo.: Westview Press, 1978.

Patterns of Japanese Policymaking: Experiences from Higher Education, by T. J. Pempel. Boulder, Colo.: Westview Press, 1978.

The Chinese Connection, by Warren Cohen. New York: Columbia University Press, 1978.

Militarism in Modern China: The Career of Wu P'ei-fu, 1916–1939, by Odoric Y. K. Wou. Folkestone, England: Wm. Dawson & Sons, 1978.

A Chinese Pioneer Family: The Lins of Wu-feng, by Johanna Meskill. Princeton: Princeton University Press, 1979.

Perspectives on a Changing China: Essays in Honor of Professor C. Martin Wilbur, edited by Joshua A. Fogel and William T. Rowe. Boulder, Colo: Westview Press, 1979.

The Memoirs of Li Tsung-jen, by T. K. Tong and Li Tsung-jen. Boulder, Colo.: Westview Press, 1979.